The Mystic in Your Midst

Irene B. Manian

Trafford
PUBLISHING

Illustrated by: Irene B. Manian
Edited by: Pam Guerrieri
Cover Design by: Irene B. Manian
Photography by: Irene B. Manian

Note for Librarians: A cataloguing record for this book is available from Library
and Archives Canada at www.collectionscanada.ca/amicus/index-e.html

Printed in Victoria, BC, Canada.

ISBN: 978-1-4251-7845-1

Library of Congress Control Number: 2009931986

*We at Trafford believe that it is the responsibility of us all, as both individuals
and corporations, to make choices that are environmentally and socially sound.
You, in turn, are supporting this responsible conduct each time you purchase a
Trafford book, or make use of our publishing services. To find out how you are
helping, please visit www.trafford.com/responsiblepublishing.html*

*Our mission is to efficiently provide the world's finest, most comprehensive
book publishing service, enabling every author to experience success.
To find out how to publish your book, your way, and have it available
worldwide, visit us online at www.trafford.com/10510*

www.trafford.com

North America & international
toll-free: 1 888 232 4444 (USA & Canada)
phone: 250 383 6864 ♦ fax: 250 383 6804
email: info@trafford.com

The United Kingdom & Europe
phone: +44 (0)1865 487 395 ♦ local rate: 0845 230 9601
facsimile: +44 (0)1865 481 507 ♦ email: info.uk@trafford.com

10 9 8 7 6 5

CONTENTS

DEDICATION

For the Lord—As He Asked and As He Willed

My memoir of faith is dedicated to the Lord, to inspire faith, to bring joy, and to give hope. Deep in my heart resides a conviction that my source and wellspring come from Jesus, and that my faith experiences have surfaced from the Eternal Dimension. Born a Roman Catholic, I practice this ancient, beautiful faith and so can name my Lord with utter conviction.

Thomas Merton once wrote: "If you write for God you will reach many men and bring them joy." St. Peter mentioned that all Christians should be ready to give their hope to others. "Always be ready to give an explanation to anyone who asks you for a reason for your hope, but do it with gentleness and reverence." (See 1 Peter 3:15.) Joy overflows from my heart. I have so many reasons for my hope and my faith, woven, as they are, into the fabric of my life, that it just seemed such a shame not to share them. So my mission for this book is to share my joy, hope, and faith with all.

In his book, *Breaking Through God's Silence*, David Yount writes that God still gives exclusive revelations of Himself just as He did through the ancient prophets. He leaks a great story in vivid, dramatic detail to one avid listener. I am that listener. And just as if I was one of his star spiritual reporters whom He wished to tell a great story to so that it would hit people's "heart headlines," He hired me to write the story that He in His love sent. So exciting was the revelation that God gave me of Himself that I have spent countless hours writing down all the details in my journal, until God sent the message that it was time to assemble them into a unified whole—this book. Writing it has brought me the greatest joy, and it is my hope that reading my words will bring delight to your doorstep also.

Although this has probably not been a common human experience, it has certainly happened time and time again. Look at the prophets, the saints, and the mystics throughout all of recorded time. In fact, the prophets confirm that God taught them directly (John 6:44–45). I can confirm this statement for you absolutely. This is true! I still marvel at the awe, beauty, creativity, and the love poured into my soul. What a gift it has all been.

If you write for God, and share your faith experiences with the world, it is

3

possible that an additional dose of faith, joy, and hope will blossom into the world. It matters not a bit if the flower blossom produced is enormous, rainbow-hued, and lives for centuries, or if it is only the simplest pansy that opens its petals to the world for a mere moment. The Lord accepts all the roses, pansies, calla lilies, and cosmos laid at His feet as offerings of love.

And so, Dear Lord, here is my offering of flowers to lay at Your feet. May the seeds that this book contains root in the fertile spiritual soil of any soul that reads it, the beginnings of another reign of the Garden of Eden.

PREFACE

Someone once said that life begins after forty. For me, no truer words were ever spoken. Perhaps one reason for my awakening can be attributed to my age. The winds of rapid change and growth, which began at first as a gentle breeze when I was forty-one, eventually became hurricane gale gusts after my forty-second birthday. Once the winds died down again, I was just passing age forty-four. Then I was a new creation living on a different plane far above my old life, though still wedded to my physical body.

Christiane Northrup said that she "believed that menopause is a time when a woman's power, wisdom and creativity push to the surface, calling for her attention." Perhaps passing through this milestone of every woman's (and man's) life and all its various effects are really signs of a quantum shift from the physical to the spiritual—the realm where all wisdom and creativity live. So when the winds signaling the change of your life appear, embrace them and let them blow you where they will. Allow them to blow away all that is dirty, old, and dusty in your life—to sweep clean the surface and the depths of your being. I assure you, they will lead you on to transformation.

None of us will remain physical, but we will become something much better. All matter on earth is in a constant process of transformation. Someday all the atoms in your body will be clouds, a fish, a blade of green grass, a juicy apple. Allow yourself to wonder where all the physical matter that is your body came from and where it will all go. Perhaps you will embrace your transformation all the faster and consider it a beautiful gift. Imagine your current love for leather pants comes from those atoms, now a part of your body that were once a part of pterodactyl wings. Or your passion for riding the cresting surf of the ocean, from your molecules that were once an ancient porpoise. I believe that our consciousness will someday be allowed to experience all that is living, because we will all be children of the universe. As God's children we will be able to experience all that God experiences. We will know it all, experience it all, relive it all, be it all.

This change, this shift to the spiritual, is roughly equivalent to adding another dimension to life. If a person who lives only in the physical and mental worlds can be compared to a two-point line—lacking insight into any space not contained on the line or two-dimensional realm—then when the third dimension is added, the person changes from a single line to a triangle. That person gains much greater depth and insight into life, while at the same time remaining physically the same ... at least for now.

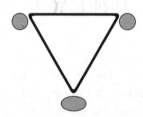

Think of it this way. In the above triangle, if you live only between the top two dots—just in the physical realm—then you will miss out on the great things happening in your "inner-self" or "inner-universe," which is your eternal side. Think of the bottom dot as a place deep in another realm inside yourself. For example, consider your inner self as a deep outer space or a galactic view full of unexplored planets that you can land on and discover; or if you prefer, as a vast ocean teaming with life while you enjoy the adventure of cataloging all the new life forms. Living at least sometimes in your deep inner place is a way for you to acquire "death insurance" because when you die, you will lose the line on the top totally and thus will sink automatically into your eternal self.

For most people, the thought of this transition is frightening. But if you have developed the ability to visit your inner place, you know that you will never die. Instead you will transform. Rather than fearing that transformation process, accept it. As we take this spiritual journey together, you'll step away with a new comprehension of life, and no longer will you have to fear the unknown. Walk with me into a new understanding ...

INTRODUCTION

This is a book about mysticism. Since it is one of the central themes of the entire work you are about to read, it might be fitting if I define my own personal understanding of this subject. Gained upon my awakening in early 2002, my own knowledge is that although it can be experienced in many ways, all forms of mysticism involve a personal apprehension of the Living God, and all involve an awareness shift into another dimension—the spiritual dimension. In essence, every mystic lives with one foot in this physical reality and one foot in the eternal reality. We peep over the edge of this life, get a glimpse of the next, and promptly fall in love with it.

Many mystics have written of their own experiences, and they are quite beautiful and helpful in explaining this concept. I can't help but to include a few here:

"Primary break with the sense-world. The 'new' birth and development of the spiritual consciousness on higher levels. Ever closer and deeper dependence on and appropriation of the fullness of the Divine Life; a conscious participation, and active union with the infinite and eternal." – Evelyn Underhill

"To be Christian," wrote Thomas Merton, "is to be committed to a largely mystical life."

"Mysticism has been understood, in the main, in terms of direct union with God. It is thought to be a rare, indeed extraordinary, occurrence. The individual soul meets and, gradually and progressively, is united with the one God. The goal of mystical journey is the immediate apprehension of the deepest recesses of divine life. The mystic is usually a solitary, often eccentric figure, someone not like the ordinary Christian. Many traditional approaches to mystical experience affirm that the mystical life is not the normal outcome of the baptismal call to the life of holiness and pursuit of virtue. The mystical life was judged to be extraordinary life, made possible by special graces." – Michael Downey

Okay, so maybe I am not your average Christian, according to Michael Downey, but then who wants to be average?

In order to relate to you as fully as possible my own mystical adventure—

and to validate it for you as much as I am able—in addition to my own spiritual journal entries, I have included many quotes from various mystical and spiritual writers. These writers contribute from various eras, from the time Moses wrote the book of Genesis to the more contemporary writings of sections from my first book *Pandora's Story*. God inspired an insatiable need, a desire, a craving to read spiritual writings after my awakening in 2002, and during that time I read hundreds of books, pamphlets, online works, stories, and, of course, the Bible to gain some sort of understanding of my experiences. They were so beyond my past frame of reference that I needed some answers. Thank God that others throughout the centuries have also been inspired to write down their own awakenings and spiritual experiences, for without them I would not have had very much of a leg to stand on to inspire faith, hope, and joy.

Because mystic writings have survived many centuries, it was possible to relate my own experiences to theirs. God's Holy Spirit inspired me, and as we read the books and writings together, He would highlight sections of the books for me that held a special meaning. Many of those highlighted sections are contained in this book. Using as many passages from past spiritual greats as possible is my way of telling these beautiful, deceased souls how much I appreciated their advice and wisdom. They are still with us today, helping us to understand the eternal dimension of life in which they now reside.

My first book, *Pandora's Story*, was really an exploration into my past mistakes and life journey thus far. There are many sections of *Pandora's Story* that were truthful recollections of my own past. These sections are not included. My past sins have been purged from my soul, totally forgiven by His mercy—ancient history that I needed to get over. We must learn to forgive ourselves—befriending our mistakes, putting our arms around them, and kissing them good-bye. But there were also many other passages that were stimulated by God as a way of teaching me in incredibly creative and innovative truths about His eternal kingdom. These passages that I have included, I hope you will clearly see, prophesied my own leap into eternity.

After beginning to write *Pandora's Story*, I noticed that the Lord began the first steps to awaken my soul. The journey held many spiritual gifts. Describing these gifts is another main focus of *The Mystic In Your Midst*. All strike a cord deep within your soul that are unmistakable. When you receive them, no matter how much you might try and rationalize them and write them off, you will not be successful. Every experience of the Lord causes you to reflect over and over, at the same time continuously thinking of Him. Of course, you may not be able to describe them to anyone else and what they mean to you, but they are given as supernatural understanding to fathom what is going on in your own heart and God's promptings and interaction inside you. Other people's hearts will receive the Love of God in totally different ways. Yet, when you have received a gift, mysteriously you may be able to connect with another person's story regarding their similar spiritual gift.

Some of you may wonder if you have missed your own spiritual awakening from the Lord. No way; put that doubt right out of your mind. An awakening is about as easy to miss as a violent thunderstorm passing directly overhead.

Pandora's Story, as I mentioned earlier, held many of the keys to explaining my own particular awakening. Clues were all over the place in that book. God's inspiration, particularly in key chapters, was His own creative way of explaining my new life and direction in great detail. Originally, I had written it with the hope of publishing it, but I soon realized that it was not God's purpose at all for having me write it. I know now that it was an exercise that God sent so that I could gain self-knowledge.

Self-knowledge is one of the most critical steps on any spiritual journey, and mine was no exception. All the greatest saints and mystics have known this fact. They are eloquent in their emphatic praise of self-knowledge.

Really, there is no going forward without a good hard look back, no progress toward wisdom without understanding. And it is amazing what looking into your own inner universe brings to your awareness. Self-knowledge is like taking a long look into a magical mirror held up by God Himself. All your errors, blindness, selfishness, and laziness meet you eye-to-eye during this first upward step on the spiraling and winding journey to the Lord. And just like Alice in Wonderland and her fall through the rabbit's hole, understanding and acknowledging those sins takes you full speed ahead into another land very different from this present one. In that new place in your heart, things that seem familiar—like birth or gifts—operate in a refreshingly different yet wonderful way.

You don't have to take my word for how important self-knowledge is. Here are several quotes from the "experts":

> *"Self-knowledge puts us on our knees, and it is very necessary for love. For knowledge of God gives love, and knowledge of self gives humility."*
> — MOTHER TERESA

> *"This virtue of self-knowledge ... is so excellent and so necessary."*
> — ST. JOHN OF THE CROSS

> *"I do not know if I have explained this clearly: Self-knowledge is so important that, even if you were raised right up to the heavens, I should like you never to relax your cultivation of it; so long as we are on this earth, nothing matters more to us than humility."*
> — ST. TERESA OF AVILA

"Before the Lord grants a soul these favours (I refer to them as gifts) He always gives it a high degree of self-knowledge."

— ST. TERESA OF AVILA

❧

I have divided the book into three main sections: The Pre-awakening, Awakening, and Post-awakening Blessings. In the pre-awakening you will begin to see what is largely hidden from my view emerge and shout for my attention, then promptly return to the eternal dimension, until God knew I was ready for the next experience. In contrast, in the awakening, my perception takes a quantum shift to the eternal and largely remains there for the duration of the week that this chapter relates. In the blessings section, which takes place from the end of the week of my awakening in February 2002 to August 2003, I relate a broad and varied range of experiences—really more of a collection of short stories in seven broad religious categories: The Trinity (Father, Son, and Holy Spirit), Nature, The Blessed Mother, Prayer/Charity, Saints, Angels, and Demons. In August 2003, as a crowning achievement, I am given a vivid vision, which is the ultimate for all Christian mystics.

Of course, life continues on after August 2003 with spiritual adventures to the present day, but not in the intense, everyday way of the post-awakening period. I know now to welcome every glimpse. I believe that God sends them as reminders that as His child, I am called to a higher life. Frankly, I just can't wait for the absolute, final shift. I can assure you that I will not be looking back.

❧

And now, as you are about to step into the part of my life I call my pre-awakening, I bid you welcome. Step onto my magically, mystical royal purple and passion red flying carpet and let me take you for a whirlwind tour of an incredible land, my very own inner universe, in hopes that I will encourage you to take a soaring flight into your own. Remember that you can step into it any time, any day, any place. In this new world anything can happen. And things you are sure you know the meaning of will take on a whole new meaning. Be not afraid. For the Fearless Master goes always before us and though we pass through raging water or the fires of hell, we shall come to no harm. To the Father, He will lead us. That is where I received the divine gifts, along with my mission and message. The Son will also give you the keys to the narrow door and to the treasure house of the divine gifts. And the Spirit will keep the wind always at your back.

Take a seat while I pry open the corner of the lid to the box of my life—to give you a small peek. Take the steps with me as I begin climbing my own stairway to heaven. Remember that small steps usually precede a major spiritual awakening and there is always a test—a test of faith ...

THE MYSTIC IN YOUR MIDST

BY

IRENE B. MANIAN

Trafford
PUBLISHING™

PART I

THE PRE-AWAKENING

1

Musical Test of Faith
Pandora's Story—God's Idea for a New Beginning
Locutions—The Beautiful Voice of God
New Sensations
Renamed—Pandora
Sister Saints from the Past Mirror My Past, Present, and Future
Left Behind "Godincidence"

My lowered eyes caught glimpses of bended trousered knees, mahogany wooden benches, and the worn navy blue carpet as I quietly walked toward the back. Quickly, I glanced over a sea of heads to make sure my children had remained in the pew as I had just asked them to do. The soft rustling of people shifting in their seats and palm branches being waved by little hands whispered into the momentary hush within the church walls. Diffused sunlight from the opaque dimpled windows seemed to illuminate my chosen path, and my rose floral skirt swirled unsettling dust motes from their suspended state. I turned right at the end, past the confessionals, walking the length of the church before taking another right to walk toward the altar. The Lord's words settled into my heart traveling through my consciousness and diving into the deepest depths of my soul, returning to their source. Only His final words and command lingered: "Sing it for me."

STEP 1

I had had a very difficult series of days leading up to Palm Sunday 2001. It was late Friday afternoon when I received a call from a doctor who was sending Sam, my husband of sixteen years, to the emergency room. She was a young doctor, and when she called to tell me that she had sent him directly to the hospital, her voice trembled. After the call, I couldn't help but wonder: was my husband dying? After all, doctors are usually composed when they call people.

I rushed home from work then pulled my children—Patrick, 10, and Christina, 8—out of after-school care and left them with my close friend, Karin. After I knew the children were safe, I headed straight to the emergency room. Sam was in great pain with kidney stones. He ended up being fine, but the entire Friday evening was a great strain.

On Saturday night I received a call from Jack Carraway, one of the members of a family singing group which I had joined several years ago. Together we had been bringing music into the Mass at St. Paul's. Pam, his wife, had had a relapse of her multiple sclerosis and needed to go in for a treatment that would end up lasting the weekend. I was very worried by the call because the Carraways and I were scheduled to sing at the Palm Sunday Mass in the lower church at St. Paul's, and now they wouldn't be able to make it. Without them, I knew there wouldn't be any music for the Mass.

Jack, Pam and Jill had, as a family, inspired parishioners in various local churches for close to twenty years together, bringing their unique brand of lively worship songs to all who came to Mass. They were all very special and not your "run of the mill" Catholics—a far cry from those extremely common types who only showed up for Easter and Christmas. Jack, the guitarist, was the rock of the group. Tall, with graying hair, a beard, and glasses, he was soft-spoken and gentle. He played and took direction from Pam, his wife, and was basically there to sound off against. Being the sweet man that he was, he had visited the children's Mass one Sunday during the fall several years prior, and he was the one who told Pam that they were needed there. And he was right.

Pam was so full of God's holy energy that she radiated it. She was a lovely woman in her fifties with a beautiful, serene expression on her face. Her eyes, light blue like her daughter's, were lively and kind. And her strength of character was evident in how she handled herself. Although you would never know it, she was blind and in a wheelchair for three years after suffering from multiple sclerosis, yet her faith was unshakable because God worked a miracle through her. By His power she was able to see and walk again and resume a normal life. As normal as it gets with raising nine children, completing her master's degree, joining the Coast Guard, crusading for the whales, becoming a DARE officer, all while continuing to sing at Mass. She was a woman of great faith and prayer, and she effortlessly inspired others with her passion for devotional music.

Jill was Pam's daughter. A more bouncy, lively twenty-five-year-old you will never meet. She was pretty in a soft doe-like way, with large gentle blue eyes hidden behind horn-rimmed glasses. Her perfect, radiant skin and shoulder-length light brown hair only enhanced her beauty. Jill once spent a year in and out of the hospital due to a very serious seizure disorder that was caused by a head injury, while experiencing up to twenty seizures a day; at the time she was totally incapacitated. Even the doctors did not know how to treat her. But luckily one doctor eventually did come along that could cure her. That experience changed her, and you can tell when you hear her sing that she has great faith in God. I suspect that her long illness helped shape her strong faith.

Jill had a beautiful alto voice, and I took great joy in teasing her about this since I was a soprano and she had always wanted to be able to sing high notes. Because she can sing them so well, she constantly asked for low songs and I, of course, always wanted songs with lots of great gutsy high notes. Luckily for us, though, our voices blended perfectly as we evened each other out. When a song called for especially low notes, we counted on Jill to sing them loud and strongly. Although I could sing those alto tones, no one could hear them since they were out of my range. I carried all the high notes.

On Palm Sunday morning in 2001, at 9:55 am, my children, Patrick and Christina, and I made our way to the lower church Mass at St. Paul's in Hingham. The lower church at St. Paul's was a place for parents and young children. Ever since I had two young children of my own, I attended the 10:00 am lower Mass. The children's Mass was a fun, high-spirited Mass for those days when the children were a little noisy; no one turned around and glared at you. Not decorated in the grand style of the upper church since it was used specifically for the children's Mass, it has a homey appearance, well worn with light-caramel colored walls and a white plaster ceiling that peeled in some spots. The royal blue carpet was faded due to traffic; the pews, plain and serviceable. There were eight frosted glass windows, each permitting in a few rays of light, and in between them stood sculptured plaster of paris scenes of the Stations of the Cross.

The altar was simple, but there were some very beautiful statues of Mary and Jesus that were recessed into the semicircle shape of the altar. My favorite statue was not actually in the altar but on the right-hand side of the church. It depicted Jesus just being taken down from the cross, and Mary's arms holding Him up so that He was in a semi-reclining position. Mary, as His loving mother, was dressed in a pale blue headscarf and sky blue robe. Her face emanated her love and her acceptance of God's will, but the love and acceptance did not totally mask her sadness. The Savior's eyes were closed, but His expression was beautiful, like He had accepted His suffering. There were marks on His forehead from the crown of thorns, a gash under His left breast, blood dripping from His hands and feet, and even His knees were scraped raw from falling with His cross. It would be a sad sight if the Lord had not risen from the dead three days later, canceling out all the horror of His death. Thank heavens He is now with His Father in heaven and will never suffer again.

All the children who attended Mass at the lower church at St. Paul's Parish were actually quite fond of this statue; they loved to venture up to it and place their little hands in His cool plaster one, which extends from the edge of the base of the statue. They seemed very drawn to Jesus' still form, just as He was drawn to them in His earthly life. Even though some people might think the statue too graphic, for me was a beautiful testimonial of God's love and suffering for all His people. The statue was perfect for the Children's Mass, as it reminded the children and their parents of God's love for all His own children.

At the back of the church were a couple of steps up to a landing with doors to the confessionals. Bordering this area was a wooden railing where countless children climbed delightedly, looking as content on their perch as a sparrow sitting on a maple tree branch. Often have been the times when the Mass stopped mid-service so that the priest could kindly ask a parent to remove their child from the narrow wooden bar before they came crashing down in tears.

I have a great love for the lower church.

"Zeal for your house will consume me," (John 2:16–17).

Usually, I would be there by 9:30 to warm up with the Carraways, but since we were not singing, there was no need. I thought that Sherri, St. Paul's Children's Mass music director, would have been able to locate another group to sing, but when I arrived I could see that she had been unable to do so. Sue, a lovely woman with three boys, and a very active parishioner, bravely took a seat behind the keyboard alone trying to bring some music into the church. Christina, Patrick, and I sat in the far right-hand corner near the back of the church—a spot about as far away as I could get from our usual first row pew on the left-hand side of the church. I felt so sad that we were not singing, but I didn't know what else to do. The opening song was played, and from where I sat, I could only hear three people singing—Father Raffey, Sue, and myself. The lack of musical enthusiasm only depressed me further. It was Palm Sunday, after all, and Jesus' passion should have been framed with inspirational devotional music.

Apparently, our Lord agreed that Passion Sunday should have music, exactly reading my thoughts. For just after we all finished the opening song and

I settled uneasily down in my seat, I heard His voice asking me to go up and help sing the Mass. How did I know it was His voice you may wonder? Well, from deep within my soul a voice of great majesty and authority arose and parted the waves of my thoughts, clearing away all that swirled in my mind. It was unmistakably God—clear as a bell.

I didn't know the name for it then, but it is called a locution, and I would have several similar gifts in the future. In a location, the Lord speaks to you from deep within your spirit. His voice interrupts your thoughts and resonates through—rather like He flips the dial on a radio to another channel. You might have been listening to your own thoughts on old troubles, or to a song that just happened to pop into your head, when suddenly the frequency changes, goes blank for a second, and then His voice comes through. Perhaps it was a combination of my love for Him, my ability as a medium (more on this aspect of my journey later), and my absolute belief in Him, which allowed me to hear His voice. And then again, maybe when He decided it was time for me to be guided by His will, I couldn't help but hear Him.

With utter splendor, grandeur, and power, the King of my soul spoke. At first He asked politely, and then as the authority came through, my heart heard the command in His tone. It was impossible to ignore. But still I was reluctant to approach the altar, even though Sue obviously needed some help. My reasons were all valid. I knew that because I had never sung with Sue's accompaniment, we would probably sound awful. Also, I hadn't warmed up because I had not expected to sing. Not to mention, the church was packed, which always makes me nervous. On top of all of the other doubts, I would be alone without the rest of my group to support me.

But God's voice kept insisting. "Go up and sing. Sing 'Be Not Afraid' and do this for Me. Remember, it is Palm Sunday."

Silently I answered Him in my head. "Dear Lord, this is really a lot to ask. I will make a fool of myself, and I am afraid."

God said: "Do not be afraid, I am with you. Prove to Me and to the church your faith and your love for Me. Get up and go now. Leave the children where they are. They will be alright. Sing it for me."

What choice did I really have? How could I deny my Lord His wish? It would be far better for me to be mortified and never be able to show my face in town again than to ever deny my Lord. And in my heart I believed that at least once in every person's life there comes a time when one's faith will be questioned, and I hope when this happens to you that you, too, will choose to show your faith.

"Oh that you would listen to his voice today. The Lord says, 'Don't harden your heart.'" (See Psalm 95:7–8.)

"We should desire him and strive after His companionship that He calls us ceaselessly, time after time, to approach Him; and this voice of His is so sweet that the poor soul is consumed with grief at being unable to do His bidding immediately, and thus, as I say, it suffers more than if it could not hear him." – St. Teresa of Avila

"So, like a good Shepherd, with a call so gentle that even they can hardly recognize it, He teaches them to know His voice and not to go away and get lost but to return to their Mansion; and so powerful is this Shepherd's call that they give up the things outside the castle which had led them astray." – St. Teresa of Avila

"I am the good shepherd, and I know mine and mine know me, just as the Father knows me and I know the Father; and I will lay down my life for the sheep. I have other sheep that do not belong to this fold. These also I must lead, and they will hear my voice, and there will be one flock, one shepherd" (John 10:14–17).

So I left my children in the pew and made my way down to the back of the church, then up the end aisle. Trying hard to avoid any familiar faces as I passed in the back of the church, it felt better not knowing who was there because, for better or for worse, I had made my decision. My legs shook with each step, and I knew that my singing would probably mirror my legs. Although I had been singing the Mass for years with the Carraways, I had never sung practically a cappella and alone in front of a large congregation. Never having memorized where to sing the various parts of the Mass, since it had always been Jack's job to cue us when and what to sing, I was going to be at a loss.

When I almost reached the spot where Sue was playing, I heard His voice again—this time comforting me, supporting me, loving me. "Be strong in your faith. I have given you your musical gift for a reason. Give the people some of your faith and love for Me." In my heart, as if the songs of the heavenly choir had come through, I could hear the familiar responsorial psalm playing in my soul, singing: "If today you hear His voice, harden not your heart." Today I had heard His voice, and I did not harden my heart.

Happiness and thankfulness lit up Sue's face as she watched me traipse up the aisle to help. Once I sat in the front pew next to her, she exclaimed, "Oh Irene, thank God."

Yes, I thought, *Sue, you should definitely be thanking God.*

By that time the offertory song would be coming up, so I told Sue that I would like to sing the song that God had asked for: "Sue, for the offertory I would like to sing 'Be Not Afraid.'"

Sue's son, Jack, approached the altar and retrieved the microphone. Sue whispered to her son to announce the next song.

Jack announced in his small eight-year-old voice: "Our next song will be, ah—"I quickly rushed up and whispered in his ear, "'Be Not Afraid' on page 613 in the music book."

Jack finished the announcement and handed me the microphone. I took a deep breath and looked down at the words printed in the missellette.

You shall cross the barren desert,
But you shall not die of thirst.
You shall wander far in safety
Though you do not know the way.
You shall speak your words in foreign lands
And all will understand.
You shall see the face of God and live.

Be not afraid, I go before you always.
Come follow me,
And I will give you rest.

If you pass through raging waters
In the sea, you shall not drown.
If you walk amid the burning flames,
You shall not be harmed.
If you stand before the power of hell
And death is at your side,
Know that I am with you through it all.

Be not afraid, I go before you always.
Come follow me,
And I will give you rest.

Blessed are your poor,
For the kingdom shall be theirs.
Blest are you that weep and morn,
For one day you shall laugh.
And if wicked tongues insult and hate you
All because of me, blessed, blessed are you!

Be not afraid, I go before you always.
Come follow me,
And I will give you rest.

As I began singing the words slowly and prayerfully, I noticed that Sue's keyboard playing did not exactly match my voice, but I tuned it out and sang the song as my heart told me it should be sung. My voice shook only the tiniest bit in the beginning, but I overcame it, and by the second verse I felt that the song danced off my lips in a pleasing melody. Behind every word and expression I hoped the people could hear as well as feel my faith. My every word sung only to praise God.

Of course, I did not know that the Lord would use the very words of this song as a prophecy as I sang it, nor that He would ask me to sing it as a way of underlining these spiritual possibilities for every true Christian, but within the next year, two of the verses of this song would take root in vivid detail. The third verse would also come true, painfully, through my own family. This verse reflecting quite accurately the Lord's own experience with His extended family in Nazareth.

As I sang, my heart and soul were filled with God's incredible love. The love that I felt for everyone in the church exploded in my heart. The feeling was so intense that I knew it meant that God was pleased with His servant. Later, I would remember and take that incredible feeling of love away as the best and happiest moment of the day. I ended the song and turned off the microphone, then took my place in the front pew. I listened to the church. Absolute silence rang in the church from every man, woman, and child. I wondered at the time if the silence implied everyone's shock and embarrassment.

The rest of the singing at Mass did not go nearly as well as "Be Not Afraid." Sue's timing and mine were off for some of the small parts like "The Gospel Acclamation" and the "Hosanna." When it came time to sing the "Lamb of God," Father Raffey was singing the song in a totally different way, and I had a hard time following him. I blanked out the first bars of "The Our Father." My mind couldn't pull out the correct opening bars of the usual one our group sang since I had about three versions of this sung prayer in my head. Father Raffey, Sue, and then the whole church ended up helping me out with the first chords so I then had to hurry to catch up.

For the communion song, I sang "Amazing Grace," which was okay with only one note that really didn't sound quite right to my ear. There were so many people that day that four verses of "Amazing Grace" were not enough, so Sue asked me to sing our old standby: "I Love You Lord."

> I Love you Lord, and I lift my voice
> To worship you, oh my soul rejoice.
> Take joy my King in what you hear,
> Let it be a sweet, sweet sound in your ear.

Halfway through the song, someone's foot must have pulled out the microphone cord after they had received communion, because the sound went dead. One dad from a couple of pews over sent his little girl up to tell me this.

Yes, it was a difficult Mass, but I knew that I would survive its various trials. After all, I went up knowing that it would not be easy, and I also knew that when God asks you to do something for Him, it usually isn't effortless. That is why we revere all our saints so much, because they did the things God asked. They took the hard road, and those who did not understand did unspeakable things to them. But having God's love was all that would ever matter to them, and they never wavered.

Even after all the flaws, I felt pretty proud of myself for doing the Lord's will, even if no one else in the entire church understood. For the recessional Sue wanted to bring the children up to the front and have them sing "This Little Light," so I gathered up my courage and stood tall. I walked up to Father Raffey and asked him for his microphone, since the other one was broken. I bravely smiled at the children, whose tender faces reflected openness, kindness, and acceptance, took a deep breath, and sang the recessional in unison with all their sweet voices. Mass was finally over, and we could all go in peace.

I collected Christina and Patrick, and together we walked out of the church. Happily, neither my leaving them nor my singing the Mass had particularly upset either child. As soon as I got home, I left the children with my husband, changed out of my blouse and skirt and into jeans and a sweater, and took a long walk on the beach. The wind, crashing waves, bright blue sky, and darting seagulls did much to sooth my aching heart. I needed to talk to God—to tell Him that I was incredibly grateful for the gift of His calling, but also to ask for comfort, since the experience had been very trying and I didn't know how I was going to face everyone next week.

"Your worst humiliation is only someone else's momentary entertainment." – Karen Crockett

"Come on now. It's all right that God created human beings for amusement and entertainment. That idea even amuses us. But our humiliations being other people's entertainment? We'll have to think long and hard about that one. In fact, if we just think of the loving teasing we have experienced over the years, we were always able to be amusing to someone. We don't have to see it as at our expense. We really are much more entertaining that we had realized. When we shift our perception ever so slightly, new possibilities always appear." – Karen Crockett

And St. John of the Cross mentions: "The soul is truly humiliated in preparation for the exaltation which it is to experience."

Someday I would look back and see the Palm Sunday Mass as the test of faith that it had been—a "spiritual entrance exam" sent by God. If tested, what would my answer be if the Lord made a very difficult request? My only answer needed to be "yes"; not "possibly" and definitely not "no."

Even though He already knew what my answer would be, because we have free will, He (being a perfect gentleman) asked. And I am so glad I said "yes" because if I hadn't, I would have been exactly as I was before the Lord asked. And even worse, I would have missed the greatest adventure of my life! So if you ever hear His voice, answer His call. You will never be sorry!

During the next several weeks, as I had suspected, people were, in general, embarrassed and avoided eye contact. "Oh well," I thought, "at least I do not have to apologize to the Lord for not obeying Him."

Eventually, I lived down the embarrassment of that Mass. I kept on singing with the Carraways and held my head up as high as I could.

> *"I believe deeply that God wills something for us, and if we do not bring ourselves to will that thing, then we condemn ourselves to a frustrating and frustrated existence."*
>
> — ST. IGNATIUS

❧

Step 2

After Palm Sunday 2001, I went through a very quiet introspective period. My usually effervescent personality all but disappeared throughout the rest of the spring and into the summer. They say that a depression can be useful, sometimes even therapeutic. Looking back now, I can see that the Lord was just beginning to make the first few corrections to my soul. What I noticed especially during this time was that my past mistakes and sins were starting to surface from the deep recesses of my mind where they usually lived, where I had stuffed them, and they began to haunt me. All my life I had tried hard to live life at breakneck speed in an effort to prevent them from becoming visible to my consciousness where I could dwell on them. God, of course, had noticed this trait of mine. And much to my horror and discomfort, He began raking up my old dirt, tilling everything to the surface, much like you would take a pail of part mud and part clear water and stir it up. The dirt was ugly, but He made me look at it in order to get me to accept my past mistakes, own them, and stop running away from them. But He wasn't done there. Then He was going to do a wonderful thing. He was going to strain my pail of dirty water through cloth and charcoal so that no dirt would remain. I would become as clear and as beautiful as water from a pristine, mountain stream.

By September 2002, the sifting process was coming to an end. But there would still be five more steps until the fireworks began—first a heart-to-heart talk with the Source of all Wisdom, then the first signs of a new hypersensitivity. Next a new name would accompany these changes, along with a new deep longing and direction in my life, and finally, a glimpse in a creative way that I would have a personal revelation of the Living God.

Just after 9/11/2001, a day that still echoes its immense horror, I headed toward Squantum Beach in Quincy, MA during my lunch hour. As I walked along the sidewalk, watching the cracks go by underfoot, I was too preoccupied with my own thoughts to appreciate the wonderful view of the Boston Harbor skyline, the darting seagulls overhead, or the surreal blue hue of the ocean water. It was during that walk that I talked to the Lord. We had a long conversation. I was going over and over all the old and more recent painful and sinful events in my life, and also the tremendous collective pain that I shared with the rest of the U.S. and the world over the terrorist attacks. I remember asking God for a way to finally get past my pain and also for some—even if very small—way of helping my people. His Fatherly advice suggested I write a book—that it would help me to heal and perhaps there would be a nugget or two of wisdom for others. From that intimate talk, the idea to write *Pandora's Story* was born.

Part of *Pandora's Story* is imbedded here in this book. You will see scenes crop up from time to time because some of the sections were inspired directly from God. He used them to illustrate all the changes He was going to bring about in my life. Of course, as I wrote many of these scenes, I had no clue that God was going to use them in helping me understand my awakening. In fact, I found some of them very awkward to write, and too fantastic to be believed by the average reader—especially the parts about Jacques. (There is much more to come on Jacques later, I promise.) Many of the passages are about future spiritual events He would later work in my soul—predictions of the future that have all come true.

Writing *Pandora's Story* was also the Lord's way of helping me gain something absolutely necessary: self-knowledge. As you have already read in the introduction, this tool is the first step of any spiritual journey.

As soon as I took God's advice and began writing *Pandora's Story*, I had an irresistible urge to write all the time. The first draft of the book was finished in three months—early January 2002. Practically every day, as I sat at my computer, I felt a numbing, a pulsating throb over my left shoulder blade. The touch acted in such a way as to pull me toward my computer for writing, signaling that creative inspiration was now available. I would only have to wait a few seconds for the words to flow from my fingers onto the computer screen. It was better than magic since it was divinely inspired. This feeling continued throughout the writing of the book and has persisted beyond.

I never fathomed that inspiration was a pure emotion like love and that it could be given to me in this way. I always thought that inspiration would come as actual words, but I can see that it is more like pure thought. From time to time, I envisioned the feeling of inspiration as coming from a muse who stood at my shoulder feeding me inspiration directly from the eternal world. I could sometimes see her in my mind—a beautiful female fairy dressed in light lavender chiffon, with pearl gray filigree wings, flowing blond hair, and a mix between pixie and drop-dead-gorgeous facial features. Surely this was how all great art, music, poetry, and theatre have come into being. I don't doubt that there really are muses—God's creative, inspirational divine beings, because I am positive that heaven is teeming with all kinds of wonderful divine spirits.

One of the most wonderful by-products of taking the Lord's advice was that writing the book produced the most ecstatic joy I have ever felt. Those endless hours spent writing gave me the most supreme high. Even writing the difficult sections of the book, which spurred tears and some sadness, couldn't stop the river of mind-altering joy that the Lord continuously fed me.

Joy is truly one of the surest signs that God is sending you a gift.

As I typed away in a cloud of joy on *Pandora's Story*, I came to understand God's involvement through each part in my own past and His intense love for me (as well as for everyone else). It was this intense love that motivated me to press on with writing the book because with every page there was always some sign of this wonderful treasure.

In September 2001, the Carraways gave me a new CD to memorize. They often did this to encourage integrating new music into our worship. The words of the song "I Live Simply For You" struck a chord deep within me. God seemed to speak directly into my heart through the title and words of the song, telling me that I would live from this point on simply for Him. Love welled up into my heart, and God was close to me listening to the fountain in my depths overflow.

Step 3

In church one Sunday, in the early fall of 2001, I was listening to a visiting priest give a wonderful sermon in the lower church at St. Paul's, when

I noticed something new. My hands were vibrating whenever the priest spoke—"hearing" what he said by feeling these vibrations and picking up the inflections from his impassioned voice. I could feel the sound waves going through the missellette and into my hands. If I had been deaf, I think that I would still have understood the sermon—like his voice was bypassing my ordinary sense of hearing and directly penetrating my soul. My hands picked up not only the words but also the sound of his feet as he paced near the altar. Later, I would understand that my senses were being gradually intensified and heightened.

Mystics are most known for their beyond normal sense perceptions. And there have also always been others who are known as "sensitives"—people who can sense spirits and ghosts, give palm readings, get in touch with deceased family members, and predict the future.

Step 4

During a weeknight in November 2001, I received another locution—just as I had during the Palm Sunday Mass. The Lord spoke just two words that day: "Trust Me." Two words from God can have millions of meanings, so I found myself meditating on these words during the weeks of Advent leading up to Christmas Day. "Of course, I trust You, my Lord," I thought. I tried to imagine what a person might mean if he or she were to say these words. Usually, common sense would suggest that something would happen in the future to make you doubt the person. But since God is completely trustworthy, I couldn't even imagine how I could ever lose faith. Not until February 2002, in the throws of a terrifying, soul-shattering awakening would I truly understand the meaning of His words "Trust Me."

In my later research I was to find out that St. Teresa of Avila had much to say about locutions. Here are some quotes from her book *Interior Castles*, which may help to explain what they are and why the Lord might give them:

"The surest signs ... are, in my opinion, as follows. The first and truest is the sense of power and authority, which they bear with them, both in themselves and in the actions which follow them."

"They can be ... a single word of this kind—just a 'Be not troubled.'"

"The soul is effected by means of locutions, which are of many kinds. Some of them seem to come from without; others from the innermost depths of the soul."

"The genuine locution is so clear that, even if it consists of a long exhortation, the hearer notices the omission of a single syllable."

"Within the soul itself there is a certainty, which cannot be overcome."

"There still remains within it such a living spark of conviction that they (meaning the words) will come true."

"The soul has not been thinking of what it hears—I mean that the voice comes unexpectedly, sometimes even during a conversation."

"These words do not vanish from the memory for a very long time: some, indeed, never vanish at all. Words, which we hear on earth—I mean, from men, however weighty and learned they may be—we do not bear so deeply engraved upon our memory, nor, if they refer to the future, do we give credence to them as we do to these locutions." (There is also in the Bible a similar saying by Jesus: "Heaven and earth may pass away, but my words never will.")

"In a genuine locution one single word may contain a world of meaning such as the understanding alone could never put rapidly into human language."

"Frequently, not only can words be heard, but in a way which I shall never be able to explain, much more can be understood than the words themselves convey and this without any further utterance."

St. Augustine further adds: "Not by these, then, does God speak, but by the truth itself, if any one is prepared to hear with the mind rather than with the body."

Step 5

On Christmas Eve 2001, He spoke again. Since it was Christmas Eve, I knew that somehow this new locution simply had to be a gift. This time He told me that the Pandora from my book that I had been working on since September was not just a made up character—but that I was Pandora, that this was my true eternal name. In the Bible there are many instances when the Lord gives someone a new name. For example: Abram to Abraham, Simon to Peter, and Saul to Paul. In all these cases, the new names were given when the person was about to embark on a totally new life direction. Abraham was to become the father of many nations, Peter became the rock of the church, and Paul took the life of a Christian missionary.

My new name, Pandora, would somehow reflect my role in His eternal kingdom. But how, I didn't have any idea. I understood, though, that the knowing sometimes comes much later, even beyond a person's lifetime. The name, Pandora, is a Greek name meaning "all gifts." Who was this woman really? Had she ever really existed? And above all, how could I possibly be her? Questions and uneasiness sprang into my heart. The meaning of the word is beautiful, but the legendary character of Pandora is another story altogether. Here is her story from *Bulfinch Mythology*.

"The first woman was named Pandora. She was made in heaven, every god contributing something to perfect her. Venus gave her beauty. Mercury persuasion, Apollo music. Pandora was seized with an eager curiosity to know what this jar contained; and one day she slipped off the cover and looked in. Pandora hastened to replace the lid! But alas! The whole contents of the jar had escaped." (She, of course, is attributed to having let out all the bad things from that jar that mankind can ever experience, especially on a spiritual level, such as hate, envy, greed, etc.)

"Another story is that Pandora was sent in good faith, by Jupiter, to bless man; that she was furnished with a box containing her marriage presents, into which every god had put some blessing, She opened the box incautiously, and the blessings all escaped, hope only excepted. This story seems more probably than the former; for how could hope, so precious a jewel as it is, have been kept in a jar full of all manner of evils?"

> More lovely than Pandora, whom the gods
> Endowed with all their gifts; and O, too like
> In sad event, when to the unwiser son
> Of Japhet brought by Hermes, she insnared
> Mankind with her fair looks, to be avenged
> On him who had stole Jove's authentic fire."

Milton, Book IV of Paradise Lost

The one grain of hope I clung to when looking at her story was her ability to give mankind just that: hope. The new name, while flattering in some ways, would take some growing into, and much meditation. I often found myself in tears, as thoughts bombarded me that maybe God was really making a joke in naming me this based on my past sins (sorry, reader, I will not satisfy you here, for my past is dead and buried). After all, she is the Greek myth equivalent of Eve. She was another way of explaining the downfall of mankind on a woman. The devil had a field day for several months sending me uncomfort-able thoughts on my new name—telling me that I was really evil and that God was simply acknowledging the fact. Trying to rob my new name of all its beauty, it made me even more positive that he was much more to blame than Eve in that incident in the garden.

Satan made me so mad. He made me want to erase her mythical past with a new myth. This time, my mind fought back, if God was willing, Pandora would show mankind how to retrieve those lost gifts directly from the hand of God Himself. And it would serve Satan right. Eventually, I was able to still his awful, singsong voice just by accepting it. I left my new life's direction to the Lord. Surely, God knew what He was doing.

After the first draft of *Pandora's Story* was done in mid-January 2002, I allowed myself free rein to research religion and other related subjects to fit into my book. I had purposely waited until then so that what I was reading would not taint or color any of the writing. Almost immediately I began no-ticing that the Holy Spirit was speaking to me through passages in books and through the sermons of the priests and deacons at Sunday Mass. I became open to spoken or written words. The words that the Holy Spirit wanted me to particularly see would almost jump off the pages; they couldn't have been more clear than if He had taken a pink highlighting marker and colored over the passage.

During a lunch hour at work in late January 2002, I obeyed a strong urge to venture to Arch Street in Boston to buy several items at a religious shop—a set of rosary beads, a hymnal for my daughter Christina, and a prayer book. As I was walking through the aisles letting the books pick me, so to speak, something compelled me to pull a slender dark brown volume from among hundreds on the shelf. When I opened the cover, I knew why this book had chosen me. It was all about the ways of knowing God. As I devoured the pages of the slim volume, I discovered that nothing that the author talked about was surprising—in fact, what the book contained seemed to unearth similar knowledge already hidden deep within myself. Like I already had detailed blueprints outlining all the ways that God talks or makes Himself known to all His human creatures.

Two other books, one of which I also picked up that day, struck deep cords inside me for a totally different reason. The reason is centered on my given name, Irene. One of the books was a dictionary of all the saints—approximately 5,000 were listed. The other was, of all things, the first book in the *Left Behind* Series, a fictionalized story based on the book of Revelation from the Bible.

Step 6

If I had read Thomas Merton's *Seven Story Mountain* I might have recognized the Lord's next grace. (By the way, another name for a spiritual gift is a "grace.") The grace the Lord sent instilled in me the beginnings of a strong and distinct urge to become a saint. According to Thomas's friend Lax, all you have to do to become a saint is to want to be one. So God's next move was to make me want to become one of His Elect.

I never would have guessed how He would pull this off, but God, who is so creative and original, had absolutely no difficulty. All He had to do was to get me to pull the dictionary of saints off its shelf and then let my natural, human curiosity take over. Upon opening the thick, hardbound secondhand book, I did what was expected. I looked my name up. With my finger going down the I's, I finally found the only Saint Irene listed. Quickly, I read her entry:

"(d. April 1, 304) Agape and her sisters, Chionia and Irene, Christians of Thessalonica, Macedonia, were convicted of possessing texts of the scriptures despite a decree issued in 303 by Emperor Diocletian naming such possessions a crime punishable by death. When they further refused to offer sacrifice to pagan gods, the governor, Dulcitius, had Agape and Chionia burned alive. When Irene still refused to recant, Dulcitius ordered her sent to a house of prostitution. There, when she was unmolested after being exposed naked and chained, she was put to death either by burning or by an arrow through her throat. April 3.

"She was only a young teenager when she became along with her two sisters, Chionia and Agape, a Christian. The girls were from a wealthy family in Thessalonica. They were born, unfortunately, in the decade between 280 and 290 A.D. They were martyred because they refused to sacrifice to pagan gods, and Irene was further punished because she was hiding some sacred scripture about our Lord. Their refusal to sacrifice to pagan gods really means that they refused to take part in offering sacrifice or to eating any of the food so offered.

"The girls took to hiding in the mountains. Others, who were secretly helping the Christians, supplied them with food. But eventually, they were found and brought into the court of the time for a trial. The two older sisters were burned to death right after their trial, but Irene, because she was only fourteen was given another chance. She was stripped naked and put in a brothel for any man to molest. God protected her, though, and no one bothered her for the day or two that she survived her sisters. She was either shot with an arrow through the throat or burned to death.

"St. Thomas the Apostle Roman Catholic Church further mentions that Agape, Chionia and Irene's father remained firmly pagan and in the mountains, apparently in the company of others, they spent their time in prayer. Although they had abandoned willingly their own possessions, and were without funds, God took care of them."

With something resembling shock, I noticed a detail about Saint Irene right away, a common thread we shared. We both had two sisters. My sisters are Caroline and Anne, and hers were Chionia and Agape. Not only did we each have two sisters, but the first initials of both the sisters were the same. How weird and strange, I thought. *What is the likeliness of that?* I wondered.

That one similarity hooked me. The more I read and researched on Saint Irene and her sisters, the more fascinated I became with her. For the next month, I was obsessed, constantly pulling up searches in Google. Something in me was driven to understand her state of mind and why she had decided to die for her faith. I wished to go back into time to the year 303 A.D. and have a conversation with her and talk about Jesus. No doubt I would have died with her, if I could have returned, because 303 A.D. was the height of the persecution of the Christians. Within months, though, I didn't have to go back to Saint Irene's time to experience a wave of Christian persecution. When the scandalous behavior of a number of parish priests broke out in all the newspapers and TV, anyone with a strong love for the Catholic Church was attacked—verbally. Many of us felt as if we were on trial. It was a tremendously difficult time, especially for St. Paul's parish that had a past pastor accused. But luckily for us present-day Catholics in the U.S, burning, crucifying, beheading, and getting shot by an arrow were not allowed. However, many non-U.S. Catholics are still physically persecuted in many places throughout the world.

The more I read the facts and legend of the sister saint's story, the more that I wanted to become like them—a saint with unshakeable faith and conviction. Believe it or not, the actual words from their trial with the magistrate, Prefect Dulcitius, still exist. I was amazed that their defense and words had been recorded; that the transcription had survived over 1700 years is miraculous. Odd as it may sound, it seemed to me that they survived so that someday I could personally read them. God with His long-range knowledge had protected their words for future "saints-in-the-making." Through those preserved words it was possible to see just how wonderful and brave the sisters were—especially Saint Irene. My wish to get to know them had been granted, I was able to touch the brave souls that they once were and their immortal souls today. The entire trial proceedings are in the appendix at the back of this book for those who are curious.

With a growing hunger for wisdom, I then decided to delve into the political and historical situation of ancient Thessalonica during the decade of St. Irene and her sisters' childhood. Here is what I found from the book *The Faith: A History of Christianity* by Brian Moynahan:

"The final wave was the most devastating, and came to be known as the Great Persecution. Diocletian, a soldier from Illyricum, modern Dalmaria, was declared emperor by the legions at Chalcedon in 284. A ruthless man who killed the Praetorian prefect with his own hand, he reorganized the empire and restored it to health, securing the frontiers against barbarians and Persia. His wife, Prisca, and her daughter Valeria were thought to be Christian sympathizers, and the Church prospered during his first two decades. He was concerned, however, at the decline of paganism and the growing Christian influence at court, among governors' wives, and in the army. The last was a direct threat to discipline, as cases of men refusing to serve proved.

"The oracle of Apollo at Didyma recommended that Christian impertinence be punished. Diocletian issued a decree on February 23, 3003. Services were banned, places of worship destroyed, and scriptures burnt. All privileges were ended, including Roman citizenship and the right to be executed by the sword. A further edict in 303 ordered all Christians to sacrifice to pagan gods."

The website of St. Thomas the Apostle Roman Catholic Church reads that "Christians were punished because they refused to take part in offering sacrifice to the 'strange gods' or at least eating of the food so offered. Diocletian, last of these persecuting Roman rulers, went further. He decreed that even the possession of New Testament texts or other Christian literature was treasonable, and therefore punishable by death."

Next I found some intriguing background from Web sites on the Roman holidays that occurred in March and April, mere weeks before their deaths and during the month they actually died. 303 A.D. Greece was part of the Roman Empire.

"March is the first month of the year. This makes good sense, because the earth is finishing with winter, and life begins to grow again. This month is the beginning of the eternal cycle of life and death. March is named after the divine Mars, the patron of Rome."

March 6 - The festival of venerating the Lares. Small images of men and women are placed at crossroads: lamps are burned to honor the gods, doorways are decorated and wreathed, the Pater Familias sacrifices to the Lares. Tarquin offered heads to the Lares, but Brutus thought it proper to offer poppy heads and straw men after the expulsion of the Tarquins. Slaves minister the celebration, and during this time they are treated as free men, incense is burned to Vesta.

March 14 - Annual horse race in honor of Mars.

March 15 - A white lamb is sacrificed to Jove. Festival of Anna Perenna, the faithful sit in the sun and drink on the riverbank with a partner; they sing and dance indecently and as they parade home, they are pronounced 'fortunate.' Drink as many cups of wine as years you wish to live.

April: The Month of April is probably named after a form of the word Aphrodite.

April 1 - There is a sacrifice to Juno. Veneralia: A festival for Venus Verticordia and Fortuna Virilis is celebrated women only. Remove ornaments from the holy idol and wash it. Offer flowers, especially roses. Garland the temple in Myrtle. All must be nude. Incense is offered. A potion of poppy, milk, and honey.

April 4 - Ambarvalia: This is the festival of the Magna Mater. Cymbals, flutes and drums sound. Eunuchs parade with self-mutilation. She delights in noise. The idol is carried in procession around the fields three times. Fresh flowers are scattered. A heifer innocent of work and mating is sacrificed. A white haired priest in purple robe washes the idol.

Is it any wonder that the sisters chose Jesus? Just the thought of having to participate in these activities was enough to turn my stomach. Just imagine being forced to offer flowers nude or watch eunuchs in a parade openly displaying themselves. Horrible.

During the weeks of my research, many similarities that St. Irene and I shared surfaced and struck me. St. Paul preached and wrote a letter to the Thessalonians, the same place that St. Irene and her sisters lived. As a member of St. Paul's parish in the South Shore of Boston, this especially touched my heart. Coincidentally, Boston's South Shore and ancient Thessalonica have similar climates. Mountains and the ocean border both cities. My sisters and I all love camping out, especially in the mountains. In fact, my sister, Caroline, is a talented wilderness cook, almost like she has had a lot of experience in her past. When I want to get away, I always enjoy heading to the mountains.

Mountains have always welcomed me. I remember once taking a three-day road trip up to the New Hampshire Mountains solo just so that I could be immersed in this wonderful, tender affinity I feel for their soaring peaks.

When I was around thirteen, I experienced for about six months an incredible anxiety, a dread and fear of death that came from out of nowhere. The feeling just one day surfaced, and for half a year I had uncontrollable crying fits and fell asleep with tears drying on my cheeks night after night. The feeling did not spring from my childhood. After all, I had a conventional, safe, and secure childhood. We had lived in a two-story contemporary house that my dad designed and had built. I grew up surrounded by four brothers, two sisters, and two loving parents. I shared a room with my two sisters—one sleeping on either side of me in twin beds in our cheerful red rose floral bedroom with ruby red wall-to-wall carpet. Halfway up, the walls turned to windows for three-fourths of the room. There were sixteen in all. On the ledgers we displayed our huge joint Breyer's horse collection. Every night from our beds we could see the stars, and every morning our room was as bright as the outdoors.

We were not wealthy, but we were comfortable. We lived in a small town on a quiet street. Our house was surrounding by manicured pine trees, and instead of grass there was a thick bed of soft pine needles. My dad had decided that he was not going to plant any grass. That way he would save himself countless hours of mowing. Instead he spent all his outdoor time trimming all the branches on the white pines up to 20 feet with a long-handled branch saw and picking up all the sticks that fell from higher above. Once I can remember asking dad if he would pay me one penny for every stick I picked up. I felt terribly rich when I collected my one-dollar bill—the payment for 100 picked up sticks.

All seven of us children were robustly healthy. There was absolutely no reason for my overwhelming unease. But now I understand this as a very significant connection between Saint Irene and I because at age thirteen she was living in incredible fear, and went into hiding throughout much of her thirteenth year and must have felt constant dread. In the months before her death at age 14, I somehow seemed to be in a parallel mindset with her even though we lived 1669 years apart in this physical dimension.

Also, I relate to her in another way. I have always been super-modest and embarrassed about my body—especially as a teenager. It was like I picked up her shame upon being chained naked and stared at by all types of men on their way to taking their pleasure with a prostitute.

My name, Irene, somehow instilled in me her feelings and deep loves. There is so much in a name. In her honor and because she gave her life for the sacred scripture, I became a lector at St. Paul's Parish. All Christians in this present time, although the thought probably never passes through their minds, owe an incredible debt of gratitude to all the men and women who gave their lives to protect the writings—writings of such power, wisdom, beauty, and yes, magic. With the Holy Spirit's help, reading them can transport you to God's eternal kingdom to learn of the secrets that very few take the time to find.

Just as Saint Irene did, I began to truly appreciate how much you can come to love God, hear His call, and have every thought be of Him—her courageous decision to die rather than offend God was now understandable. She would have realized then, as I do now, that offending God when He resides in your heart in such a beautiful way as He is for me and was for Saint Irene would be much worse than death by any form.

St. Paul's conversion of the Thessalonians is vividly illustrated in their story. The sisters' brave death no doubt testified to the Thessalonians that the Spirit of the Living God, Jesus, was at work in their city.

> *"If we consider what a large number of people God can draw to Himself through the agency of a single soul, the thought of the thousands converted by the martyrs gives us great cause for praising God."*
> — ST. TERESA OF AVILA

After that research I branched off to try and find the meanings of the names Irene, Chionia, and Agape. I looked up my own two sisters first. Caroline means "a man's strength," and Anne means "favor, grace, or graceful." Our name, Irene, means "peace." It is a Greek name, and Irene was the goddess of peace in ancient Greece. St. Irene's sister Agape's meaning was very easy to find. It means "beloved or love of God." Agape is the meaning of one of the four types of love as defined by C.S. Lewis. Agape is the highest love—the true love of neighbor.

In contrast to Agape, Chionia's meaning proved more difficult to find. Someone told me that they thought but could not confirm that the name Chionia means "snow." In fact, I never did find out the actual meaning of Chionia, but I did find out some interesting facts about the name, which are very telling as they relate to my sister, Caroline. There is a Greek legend about a Chionia. In that legend she was married to Poseidon. Poseidon, besides being the god of the sea, was also the creator of horses. Another interesting close association of Chionia is the name Chinon. In Greek mythology, this is the centaur—half man and half horse.

My sister, Caroline, currently lives in a large house with a view of Cape Cod Bay. The house is at least a couple of hundred years old and in the dining room there is a massive fireplace with a carved head and shoulders of none other than Poseidon. Caroline's main passion in life are her horses—currently she owns three. In fact, she spends her entire day, every day with her horses. They are her life.

The next time we sang "Be Not Afraid" at Mass, I was thunderstruck by the words from the second verse. Through my new knowledge of St. Irene and her sister saints, the words seemed to leap from the page. Here her faith vividly came to life in a song. Though her sisters faced the burning flame, they knew that the Lord walked by their side. He told them not to be afraid, only follow Him and they would gain eternal rest and peace.

The first prophecy of the song came true for me in a unique way through St. Irene's life. She and her sisters had literally faced and walked through the burning flames after their trial:

**If you pass through raging waters
In the sea, you shall not drown.
If you walk amid the burning flames,
You shall not be harmed.
If you stand before the power of hell
And death is at your side,
Know that I am with you through it all.**

Be not afraid I go before you always, come and follow me and I will give you rest.

Another Saint Irene later turned up through my research from the Web site www.coptic.net/boston/heros/irene. This Saint Irene is known for her vision of a dove. As you probably know, the dove is a symbol of peace, and Irene means peace. Later I reveal how an image of a dove also played a large part in my own story.

"At birth St. Irene was called Pina Louis. She was the daughter of King Lincinius of Macedonia. When she was thirteen years old, she started thinking of the idols, which her father left in the palace. One day while she was awake, she saw a vision: a dove entered the room and dropped an olive branch on the table, then a eagle brought a crown in his beak, and left it on the table also. Finally, a crow carrying a snake entered the room and left the snake in the same place. Irene was puzzled and asked her old teacher to explain the meaning of that vision.

The old man prayed for a long time, asking for God's help. Then he said, 'The dove signifies the knowledge of the true God through His Word. The branch of the olive is the baptism that you will receive. The eagle symbolizes the victory of the almighty God. The crown is the glory of the saints. The crow refers to your father and the snake designates the persecution of the believers.'"

Through St. Irene, just as God had wished, I was inspired to become one of His saints and able to deeply associate myself with them. He pointed out some interesting connections with the real Saint Irene, and assured me that I had indeed been correctly named. Names have a very real affect in people's lives. They transcend time and space, and bring out amazing connections in our lives. Being named for someone who has passed away is a special way to bring the deceased back to life. Many cultures already know this and have passed this tradition on through the centuries. The Jewish people, especially Zechariah, the father of St. John the Baptist, come to mind. When Zechariah told his relatives that the baby's name would be John (an angel told him that would be the baby's name), they questioned him saying that there were no Johns in the entire family tree. Yet not naming little St. John the Baptist by an accepted family name was the right thing to do in this case, since St. John was the one-of-a-kind preparer for the Lord. As a matter-of-fact, an angel also named Jesus. There would be no need to rename Jesus or John, since their names were in sync with their eternal roles.

Step 7

Along with establishing my desire to become one of His saints, my name also gave me a small but vivid glimpse of where my path would lead.

As I mentioned earlier, there was another book that proved significant in my personal journey. This other book came to me from my singing friend, Jill. She absolutely insisted that I read the Left Behind Series books. My first inclination was to pass when I found out they were based on the end times, and specifically about the Antichrist, but in order not to upset her, I reluctantly agreed. I didn't have long to read (about two paragraphs) before I noticed that one of the main characters in the beginning part of the story shared my name, Irene. The Irene in the book was shockingly similar to me. She was forty-ish, and I was forty-two at the time. She was attractive and vivacious. And she had lately been very into church, had found God, and was now trying to save souls for God. Well, this also described me.

In the story she was a lucky woman. God enraptured her before sending the seven-year tribulation period. How I also hope that when the last days are upon the earth, I shall be taken up to heaven to be with Jesus and the saints. But what is most significant about her as she relates to my own story is that her character appeared at the beginning of this fictionalized account of the Book of Revelations. You will see that God was about to bestow on me a revelation of His Holiness—a personal revelation.

Those, and a few incidents that I might have forgotten in lieu of what was to happen next, were constant questions that circled over and over in my mind. Thomas Merton said, "God makes us ask ourselves questions most often when He intends to resolve them. He gives us needs that He alone can satisfy, and awakes capacities that He means to fulfill. Any perplexity is liable to be a spiritual gestation, leading to a new birth and a mystical regeneration." As you will soon see, Thomas's statement explains perfectly the whole next section of my faith journey—The Awakening.

So let us now open wide the lid, full speed ahead. Fasten your silk tassel seat belts and prepare for a glimpse of the most glorious sight—the longing of every heart. St. John the Baptist: "Hit it." (Thanks.)

PREPARE YE, THE WAY OF THE LORD
PREPARE YE, THE WAY OF THE LORD
PREPARE YE, THE WAY OF THE LORD

BLAST OFF

PART II

———⟨⟩———

THE AWAKENING AND
THE DIVINE GIFTS

2

EYES LIKE LIGHTNING
LOVING CLOUD

"I am the Alpha and the Omega, "says the Lord God, "the one who is and who was and who is to come, the Almighty." – Revelations 1:8

"Write on a scroll what you see and send it to the seven churches." —Revelations

"For often when a person is quite unprepared for such a thing, and is not even thinking of God, he is awakened by His Majesty, as though by a rushing comet or a thunderclap."

— ST. TERESA OF AVILA

"More to the point, William James calls the kind of change that occurs when cold beliefs become hot and central, conversion: "To say that one is "converted" means, in these terms (heat and location) that religious ideas, previously peripheral in the consciousness, now take a central place, and that religion aims form the center of one's energy."

— JOANMARIE SMITH

As if a golden blazing lightning bolt had struck the inside of my brain, the revelation of the Lord appeared. His magnificent face—a truly human, living face—filled my entire mind and stilled it into ecstasy. Radiant golden skin and long flowing white hair were noticed only for a split second. Like a mesmerizing force, His glance pulled my inner attention with the drawing power of a galactic black hole, and it became impossible to change my focus—amazing, compelling, and yet kind and noble. Beyond any doubt I knew I looked into the eyes of a great Ruler with eons of wisdom, who had seen the birth of the universe and the birth of my own children.

Blazing a silvery light teal, gray-green fire in sword-like fashion, his eyes filled and spread beyond His golden, light-filled face. The fire blazed forth, sparkling and dancing like a flickering candle moved by the wind—-more brilliant than a million-carat diamond in full sunlight. His Holy Spirit emulated from his eyes. Thankfully, as his gaze kindly met mine, the fire calmed, but they were easily recognized for what they truly were: judgment eyes.

> *"I can tell you truly that, wicked as I am, I have never feared the torments of hell, for they seem nothing by comparison with the thought of the wrath which the damned will see in the Lord's eyes—those eyes so lovely and tender and benign. I do not think my heart could bear to see that."*
>
> — ST. TERESA OF AVILA

> *"Yes, the eyes are windows into the soul. But the eyes of holiness are also reflectors. Holiness reflects the radiance of Someone Else's loving eyes. Just as Jesus knew the gaze of a dear Father's eyes, Walter Ciszek experienced God's loving gaze in the depths of his despair and helplessness. The same loving gaze blesses us all, each and every one, with a freedom and a trust that does not take all suffering out of our lives, but does enliven our hearts, our souls, and our eyes."*
>
> — WALTER CISZEK

> *"An eye can threaten like a loaded or leveled gun, or it can insult like hissing or kicking; or, in its altered mood, by beams of kindness, it can make the heart dance with joy."*
>
> — RALPH WALDO EMERSON

"May God bless you and keep you. May the Lord smile upon your face and be gracious to you. May the Lord show you his favor and give you his peace." (Numbers 6:22–24)

As abruptly as the intellectual vision from deep within my hidden self began, it ended. Once again I found myself surrounded by the walls of my tan office cubicle slightly disoriented. I glanced over at my desk clock. The time was 2:30 p.m. I shook my head, clearing it of the experience that was vividly real. With powerful certainty, I knew that my vision was the risen Lord's face—otherwise known as the Beatific Vision. How had I earned such an unimagined, splendid gift, I wondered. As I spend the rest of the afternoon tying contract information into the company billing system at my computer, my mind relentlessly returned to the vision still intact in my memory.

How beautiful and amazing He is—the Lord of Life. Volumes could be written on His visual image. Even though it had only lasted for a second, His face was to become an indelible memory in my mind and a true knowing, strengthening gift. It left in its powerful wake another gift—a lasting conviction that no one should die while unprepared to see His holy face and be judged on their earthly lives and all their past sins. With it I felt an absolute knowing that there were many souls that upon death see His eyes blaze up in a consuming fire—hell was just as possible for a lost soul as heaven is for a saint. I was left with this truth as I sat at my desk that afternoon.

During the week of Monday, February 4 through Friday, February 8, 2002, I spent every spare moment typing up all the details of the heaven chapter—listening to the inspiration being feed into my mind from the Creator, and envisioning the heavenly scenery image by image. What delight I had found in writing that chapter. To me it was the most beautiful part of *Pandora's Story*, which oddly enough was of my own death and journey to God. Somehow just imagining it produced the most mind-altering joy, while waves of ecstasy, deep peace, wellness, and wholeness washed over me all week long. The joy that exploded from my solar plexus in the area of the heart Chakra was not just a mind joy, but a body joy as well. (A *Chakra* is an energy center. Much more about Chakras can be found in the "Blessing" section of this book.)

My heart was delighted, and that enchantment embraced my entire being. I walked through that week in a cloud of such inner joy that not a single negative thought entered it. If I had had the ability to levitate, I would have walked six inches above the floor, my spirit was so light. Many were the hours I lost without being aware of a passing moment, so engrossed was I in the scenery from heaven. I could barely stop writing to come back to reality. Although I went through the motions of work and caring for my family, my mind was elsewhere—somewhere over the eternal rainbow.

Then wonder of all wonders, the Lord decided to provide His own version of a grand finale of that spiritually magical week—His face. The vision confirmed that through my writing I had found the key that opened the door to heaven, a key hidden deep in my own heart all along. Somehow a seismic crack had opened to reveal our Lord. "It must be the 'Narrow Gate' that leads to heaven straight from the Gospel of Matthew (7:13)," I thought. All the substance, light, and joy had leaked out and surfaced and suffused throughout my spirit. Truly I had experienced the reality that heaven exists deep within us, just as I had always heard from so many sermons throughout the years.

"The human heart travels by a sure road when God calls it."

— ST. TERESA OF AVILA

47

At that very moment, the connection between the writing and the Lord became clear, but eventually many other reasons for the vision would emerge. For one, although I could never have guessed, I would soon learn that seeing His face was the beginning of the end of my old existence—just as if I had died and gone before Him for judgment, only to be given His divine mercy. Looking back, I know that it was also a strengthening gift, for I was about to live through the most trying week of my life—the beginning of a total transformation process difficult beyond belief.

Perhaps you are curious about what I had been writing that could produce such a treasure. Take a peek at heaven (excerpt from *Pandora's Story*):

Black, it is so black. Infinitely far away there appears a tiny pinprick of light. I watch, as it grows bigger; it is a moment until I realize that I am moving towards it—flying, gliding, glissading, toward a living luminosity—forward and upward, slowly, and gently. So this is death. Excitement fills my spirit and my energy fields swirl and dip and sashay toward God. Hurray, I am finally going to meet God face to face.

My spirit arms reach around my aura and encounter something. I take a second to look down at my chest, and see by the light entering through the portal, the many cords radiating from the spot where my physical heart used to be. They must be pure emotion, energy. I pass my hands through them and feel their electric charge. I pick one out of the group and hold it between my two fingers. I immediately get a strong mental picture of Jill. These cords must be the emotional connections I have had to all the people who were in my life. I pick up another one. This time I see my old high school best buddy, Debbie. Even though the cords are not made of matter, I can still touch and feel them. They pulsate and vibrate, and are as soft as a daisy petal. Some of my connections lead through the portal to the people I have loved who have passed into eternity, while others are pointed back to the earth plane. Some cords seem thicker than others. The more love you feel for a person, the larger the cord must grow. Maybe, God judges us by the weight and number of our cords. Maybe this is why you can see them when you die. It must be very plain to God how much you loved others by their number and size. They illustrate vividly how we have loved others in our life, and how others have loved us.

There is one central cord that seems to be activated. It is tugging me, pulling me. This cord must take me directly to God. He is calling me to his side.

> "Lack of devotion to the Sacred Heart is the reason for frequent relapses into serious sin, because people pay scant attention, and are not sufficiently encouraged to acquire the love of Jesus Christ, which is the golden cord which unites and binds the soul to God."
>
> — ST. ALPHONSUS LIGUORI

The light expands and swallows me in its brilliant, piercingly electric, yet somehow loving depths—bathing me, enriching me, and cherishing me. A song from the musical "Tommy" is playing in my head because I know this is a healing light, and I am going to be healed.

> *See me, feel me, touch me, heal me.*
> *See me, feel me, touch me, heal me.*
> *See me, feel me, touch me, heal me.*

I step into a place of such beauty I can hardly describe it. Magnificent flowers banked in all directions—many with unearthly colors—fill my vision and like a kaleidoscope change constantly as I move. The music, from layers and layers of choir members, penetrates my spirit. Here music can be heard, smelled, tasted, and felt. Its dancing waves are alive with energy and drama. Memories buried when I lived on earth return. Home sweet home.

> "As these Mansions are now getting near to the place where the King
> dwells, they are of great beauty and there are such exquisite things to
> be seen and appreciated in them that the understanding is incapable
> of describing them in any way accurately without being completely ob-
> scure to those devoid of experience."
>
> – ST. TERESA OF AVILA

The journey was short, yet infinite. I am utterly at peace. There is no hurry. I am going to God, but He wants me to enjoy the scenery of my new home. How wonderful He is. I pass through incredibly scenic vistas of breathtaking beauty, cascading waterfalls that fall in all directions some that swirl before reaching the ground. Rocky mountains smile gentle granite grins, and happy lions lounge while pure white lambs play a game of tag in their midst. Clouds of carmine, chartreuse, robin's egg blue, sea foam green, and violet whirl wrapping their misty presences around me, and giving me kisses of affection as I go by.

Every bit of everything is alive. That is the difference between earth and heaven. Every inanimate object and every place is alive. Pure, happy, joyous emotion emanates from every surface. Oh, it is so wonderful to be here. I never want to leave. No one would ever want to leave. Being in this place is worth all the pain and suffering that one must live through on Earth, believe me. I know someday, God willing, you will all agree.

> "The experience of God, then is just right; it fits you to a 't.' It is the thing
> that you have been waiting for. While nothing will be fully satisfying un-
> til you get to heaven, still, through the spiritual senses, this experience

*strikes us as being the perfect coming home; something which always
should have been there and which we suddenly realize is there. 'Taste
and see.' If we get through our trials we will sing the same song."*

— FR. THOMAS KEATING

*I could feel myself slowing down. It was so brilliantly bright that my eyes
take a moment to adjust. Then I see him—The Creator. He is truly magnificent. Totally awed, but oddly not overwhelmed, the white, crystal, sparkling
rays that emit from him, wrap me in a loving embrace. His body is not sharply
defined, but radiates out in all directions, although his hands are visible. My
spirit is bathed in love. He is seated, and motions me to come forward. His eyes
hold mine. They were so gentle, so incredibly full of depth and wisdom, and are
not a color that you can see here on earth. Perfectly symmetrical, his features
are strong, not too harsh, not too gentle, inspiring absolute trust and devotion.
His hair was long and white. I kneel by his side ready to stay here forever—
never to leave again. Somehow I know that I see him as I want to see him, as I
want him to appear. Everyone, who sees him, must see his or her own ideal of
God. I believe this is because God wants us to have our heart's desire.*

"I turned, I saw seven gold lamp stands and in the midst of the lamp stands one like a
son of man, wearing an ankle-length robe, with a gold sash around his chest. The hair of
his head was as white as white wool or as snow, and his eyes were like a fiery flame. His
feet were like polished brass refined in a furnace, and his voice was like the sound of rushing water. In his right hand he held seven stars. A sharp two-edged sword came out of his
mouth, and his face shone like the sun at its brightest." (Revelations 1:12–16)

*I can hear the perfectly sung notes of the heavenly choir as they sing a lovely
melody in the background. The music is breathtakingly, heart-stoppingly lovely.
The most magnificent, perfect sound one could ever hear.*
*"My child, your eyes are full of questions. Ask anything you would like to
know." The Creator says …*

⚜

After I finished the heaven chapter that week, *Pandora's Story* was almost
complete, and several weeks would go by before I received confirmation of
the truth of my vision in a totally different way. One of the members of St.
Paul's decided that a framed picture of the Holy Shroud of Turin showing the
Lord's face would be a wonderful addition to the lower church, so they hung
the picture on the left-hand side of the altar boundary. It was fixed to the wall
in front of the same spot where the Carraways and I sung every week, and I

couldn't help but notice it the first time I stepped up to sing. Immediately, I was struck by the resemblance of the bone structure of the face on the Holy Shroud of Turin and the Lord's actual living face from my vision. They were the same. In fact, the face of God's Son, Jesus, as shown on the Shroud of Turin is remarkably like the Creator's face that I had envisioned while writing the heaven chapter of *Pandora's Story*. How appropriate—the Son looks just like His Father. Every time I looked at the picture I smiled, cherishing the memory of my amazing vision of Him.

Within a short amount of time, as we sang it for the Lenten season, it hit me that the first verse of "Be Not Afraid" had come true:

> *You shall cross the barren desert,*
> *But you shall not die of thirst.*
> *You shall wander far in safety*
> *Though you do not know the way.*
> *You shall speak your words in foreign lands*
> *And all will understand.*
> *You shall see the face of God and live.*

Singing that song for Jesus on Palm Sunday was producing the most wonderful blessings in my life—the second prophecy fulfilled.

I was on "cloud 9" on Sunday, February 10, 2002, three days before Ash Wednesday, and two days after I experienced the vision of the risen Lord. While sitting in a wooden pew in St. Paul's upper church, surrounded by the pearl-gray columns, soaring ceiling, the beautiful medieval gothic altar, amongst the familiar faces of the congregation, I received another startling revelation.

Over and over a familiar devotional tune played in my head all morning. Unable to conjure up the name of the song, I was certain that God resonated that particular song in my mind for a reason. As soon as I settled Patrick, Christina, and myself in the pew, I reached for a missellette to try and find the song, which I was positive was in the music section. So I half listened to the Mass and half thumbed through the hymnal in search of the song title. It took me about fifteen minutes into the Mass to find the song, and I only needed to read the title to understand God's significance. When I read it, my heart almost stopped:

"You Are Mine" it said.

I knew with absolute certainty that God was telling me that I was His. With that news I was overjoyed.

I stared up at His image on the stained glass windows above the altar that depicted His risen image in all its magnificence, and my heart overflowed with love. In the stained glass windows He was actually looking to the side, but as I examined the glass picture, His face turned and He looked directly at me. He looked down from his image straight into my heart and told me directly that He loved me.

That very night both my watches stopped at the same time—8:06 p.m. on Sunday, February 10, 2002. I know this because the next day when I was going to work I noticed that the first watch I picked up was not working so I reached into my horse head-shaped glass mug, given to me as a six-year-old by my Aunt Marguerite, and pulled out my other watch only to find that that was also not working. They both read exactly 8:06 p.m. "How odd," I thought. I didn't really get the message behind the stopped watches then, that I was now dead to my old life. Only in hindsight would I realize this. Death is just a point in time, you know. Nor could I have really ever understood then that it was also simultaneously a message of the beginning of a wonderful new life. But that is exactly what happened.

> "That soul has now delivered itself into His hands and His great love has so completely subdued it that it neither knows nor desires anything save that God shall do with it what He wills. Never, I think, will God grant this favour save to the soul which he takes for His very own. The soul shall go thence sealed with His seal."
>
> — ST. TERESA OF AVILA

⚜

There are so many beautifully written passages from the Bible, and from the saints and mystics of the ages, on the "Beatific Vision" of our Lord. Together they confirm that we do not have to die to see God—at least not physically. The following passages will hopefully convince you that, in fact, many people have witnessed the risen Lord in this life:

The Sermon on the Mount: "When he saw the crowds, he went up the mountain, and after he had sat down, his disciples came to him. He began to teach them, saying:

> Blessed are the poor in spirit, for theirs is the kingdom of heaven.
>
> Blessed are they who mourn, for they will be comforted.
>
> Blessed are the meek, for they will inherit the land.
>
> Blessed are they who hunger and thirst for righteousness, for they will be satisfied.

Blessed are the merciful, for they will be shown mercy.

Blessed are the clean of heart, for they will see God.

Blessed are the peacemakers, for they will be called children of God."

(MATTHEW 5:1-9)

"When Our Lord is pleased to bestow greater consolations upon this soul, He grants it, in whatever way He things best, a clear revelation of His sacred Humanity, either as He was when He lived in the world, or as He was after His resurrection; and although He does this so quickly that we might liken the action to a flash of lightening, this most glorious image is so deeply engraven upon the imagination that I do not believe it can possibly disappear until it is where it can be enjoyed to all eternity. I speak of an 'image,' but it must not be supposed that one looks at it as at a painting; it is really alive." – St. Teresa of Avila

"The brilliance of this vision is like that of infused light or of a sun covered with some material of the transparency of a diamond. Almost invariably the soul on which God bestows this favour remains in rapture, because its unworthiness cannot endure so terrible a sight. I say 'terrible,' because, though the sight is the loveliest and most delightful imaginable, even by a person who lived and strove to imagine it for a thousand years, because it so far exceeds all that our imagination and understanding can compass, its presence is of such exceeding majesty that it fills the soul with a great terror. It is unnecessary to ask here how, without being told, the soul knows Who it is, for He reveals Himself quite clearly as the Lord of Heaven and earth." – St. Teresa of Avila

Definitions of Mysticism: "Mysticism in general refers to a direct and immediate experience of the sacred, or the knowledge derived from such an experience. In Christianity this experience usually takes the form of a vision or, sense of union with God." — The World Wide Web

The great Sufi philosopher, Al-Ghazzali, insisted that upon entering paradise the true lover of God would receive a "Vision of the Divine Countenance," which, he affirmed, is "none other than the gnosis (ma'rifa) already given in an inferior and more fleeting fashion to the saints of this world."

"And there I saw One who had a head of days, and His head was white as wool, and with Him was another being whose countenance had the appearance of a man, And his face was full of graciousness, like one of the holy angels. And I asked the angel who went with me and showed me all the hidden things, concerning that Son of Man, who he was, and whence he was, (and) why he went to the Head of Days? And he answered and said onto me: This is the son of Man who hath righteousness, with whom dwelleth righteousness, And who revealeth all the treasures of that which was hidden." – Book of Enoch, Chapter 46

53

The definition of the "Beatific Vision": "Those who die in God's grace and friendship and are perfectly purified live for ever with Christ. They are like God for ever, for they 'see him as he is, face to face.'" – The Catholic Answer Bible

⚜

As we move on to His divine justice to share in the joy of my awakening, never doubt that although you are "saved" because you believe in Him, that you will taste of his justice. Its length, of course, will depend on the number and severity of your sins.

(In my own case, whatever sins, imperfections, wrong choices, blindness or laziness had attached themselves to my soul became alive and hauntingly I became aware of each and every one. For whoever reads this passage and lives through a similar spiritual journey, the experiences will differ because what was wrong with the soul would not be identical.)

3

FEAR OF THE LORD—ASHES TO LIFE

I turned my attention from the odd fact that both my watches had stopped at the same time, to getting ready for something I had been absolutely dreading. This morning, a chilled February 11th, I was going to Brigham and Women's Hospital for a colonoscopy, which my primary care physician had ordered due to bleeding. I was a nervous wreck, since I had heard horror stories of this procedure. As it turned out, what I heard was correct.

My husband, Sam, drove me into the hospital and helped me find the waiting room. As soon as possible, he excused himself and headed to the cafeteria for a cup of coffee and the sport's section of the paper to pass the time while he waited for me. I watched his lean, medium-framed body head for the door. Just before he left, he turned around and smiled, his green eyes framed with deep laugh lines, and he told me that I would be just fine. Only a little bit reassured, I found an empty chair, gingerly sat on it, and allowed my eyes to scan the room full of equally nervous patients. The décor was the standard hospital office look in cream and dark blue. Trying to distract myself, I pulled out a romance novel. Within a half an hour, a nurse called me into a small curtained cubicle and asked me to undress and put on a "johnny." I did, and the wait continued.

When the doctor swept in along with his female nurse assistant, he was all smiles and reassurance. He instructed the nurse to give me a painkiller. As I looked at the syringe just as it was about to be inserted into my vein, I noticed it only contained about one-half an inch of fluid. Somehow that didn't look like enough "stuff." And I was right. When the time came for the scope to be inserted, the drug, which was supposed to ease the pain, did not. Agony surged through me as the doctor pushed the tube up. At one point he hit a kink in my bowels and for three attempts pushed with all his might to get around the kink. My mind's eye still stores the memory of his intense, excited expression. He reminded me of a plumber faced with a particularly nasty plugged up drain. He had inserted his snake and no matter what was going to get his instrument through it. I have delivered two babies, never once uttering a scream, but the pressure was so intense that against my will the sounds erupted from my throat. The memory of the white-walled privacy curtain and the forty-something nurse's sympathetic face became etched in my memory because of the trauma. It was a wonder that he did not perforate my colon—I doubted I would forget the intense pain for a long, long time. But I was grateful that they had found nothing wrong.

Dutifully, even after that awful morning, I went back to work for the afternoon. I fervently hoped to push the memory out of my mind as fast as possible. As I sat at my desk in my cubicle, my thoughts turned toward God and filled with all the love in my being. My mind was so drawn to Him. I now had His image vividly implanted in my mind to call up whenever I needed Him, and yesterday He had told me I was His. The awful morning was soon replaced with joy as my mind floated up to God. So powerful was the emotion I was now feeling for Him that it leaked out from my soul and my mind into my body; as I kept my thoughts on Him the love translated into waves of sensual passion. God, as a wonderful comforting friend, seemed to want me to feel His love to help me override my painful morning.

Doubtless St. Augustine and St. John of the Cross would have seen this as a bit of a conflict with a relationship with God, but my body seemed to be experiencing and enjoying my intense mental ecstasy, almost totally in line with it. As much as I enjoyed the intense feeling, I felt it was inappropriate given my location. So I tried to get up and walk around to distract myself, but the wonderful, sensual feeling lasted throughout the entire afternoon.

That night I quickly feed everyone dinner, read the children a story, and picked up the stray shoes, coats, newspapers, and toys scattered on the floors of most of our seven-room street-front colonial. After I finally picked up the last item, I dragged my exhausted body up the stairs into my red floral and paisley wallpapered room with its large windows overlooking the street that I shared with my husband, Sam, and closed the door. On my knees, I prayed the Joyful Mysteries on my rosary beads and gratefully climbed into bed. As I settled the blankets and comforter around me, I thanked God in prayer, silently, for the amazingly enchanting afternoon, and for having survived my morning procedure. Sleep couldn't come fast enough.

Just as I was starting to drift off, I was awakened by what felt like a cloud of spiritual energy descending on me—my spirit and my body were surrounded by a "loving force field," the type sometimes depicted in sci-fi space movies. I lay immobile, not really frightened, but not understanding either. I could feel a definite non-physical presence holding me, comforting me. Why, it felt like a cloud had come down from the night sky and was embracing me in a hug—loving me. I could feel a touch where nothing was touching me. I could feel pressure points of what felt like hands on my body. No matter which way I turned, the caress just kept coming back. If it wasn't physical, or only in my mind, then the only other possibility was that the presence was a spiritual one.

With acute awareness I began to detect an energy flow traveling up my legs, settling in my body cavity. Somehow I could tell that it was not penetrating my physical body, but some other part of my essence. The spirit was merging, passing into, and blending with my own spirit. A feeling expanded between my legs. The spiritual stream moved up into my lower stomach region and seemed to stop there, and remained there for the next hour as I lay quietly unmoving, confused and uncertain. Yet I was certain that this presence was of God and although nothing in my Catholic upbringing had prepared me for this experience; as strange as this may sound, it was as if God had become my lover.

> *"But since the mind, itself, though naturally capable of reason and intelligence, is disabled by besotting and inveterate vices not merely from delighting and abiding in, but even from tolerating His unchangeable light, until it has been gradually healed, and renewed, and made capable of such felicity, it had, in the first place, to be impregnated with faith, and so purified."*
>
> – ST. JOHN OF THE CROSS

Later, I was to read this quote and understand that this was exactly what God was doing on this night—impregnating me with faith.

As quickly as the cloud had descended, it left. I felt a fleeting flow of energy exit my soul, passing down my legs, and then … nothing. I gave the entire experience a little more thought but found no logical conclusion. I was so tired that it was not long before I fell asleep into a dreamless slumber. The next morning, as I awoke and watched the sun filter through the sheer white cotton curtains, I found myself still very confused and uncertain about the experience, but it was not fear I felt. As I headed to the shower, I decided that the best thing would be for me to chalk the whole incident up to an overly active imagination, with the possibility that the drug I had received in the hospital that day had had a rather bizarre side effect.

Tuesday, February 12th, was a normal day at the office. From time to time my mind turned to God as I input data onto spreadsheets and loaded billing information into the company billing system in preparation for doing our monthly invoice run. I was busy trying to finish up all my work before our February family ski vacation, which would begin the following weekend. That night at home, after I finished folding laundry and praying a rosary for one of my family members, I climbed into bed. I had a split-second thought about last night, but resolutely closed my eyes and said a quick "thank you for the day"-type prayer to God hoping that sleep would come instantaneously. After I had pulled my red and white rose comforter up to my neck, though, I again felt the energy descend all over my body as soon as my body relaxed. This time the spirit cloud held me in its embrace for several hours. There was no pain or discomfort, but just an absolute awareness of energy movement, touching, probing. Somehow, I was perceiving and feeling beyond this physical world. My sense of touch was awakened to the point where my flesh was stimulated although there was nothing physically making contact with my skin.

During those hours, I weakly tried to understand what was happening, yet nothing could explain the phenomenon. Fear crept in. Was this an experience I was going to have every night? The spirit felt like a man, and it felt man-size. How could this be God? My mind could not grasp the answer. I avoided thoughts of any of the stories I had read that spoke of demon lovers—frightened that if I went there, I would go insane. Perhaps I had already crossed the line of insanity. Had my pain from yesterday's experience turned my mind somehow?

That night I struggled immensely with my faith. This spirit descent in contrast to last night's brought an image of the devil to my mind. For by the end of this night, I was certain that this experience, in contrast to last night's "loving cloud" experience, was not about evoking love. If anything, it felt neutral. There was something different, and I couldn't put a finger on it. Without love coming from the cloud, I doubted it could be God. So I prayed and called out to Him with all my might. I begged Him to not abandon me, to examine what was going on down here, and to help me. I told Him that I didn't understand what was going on, but I was now intensely afraid that the manifestation was not Him, but instead His archrival, the devil. I later learned that my confusion was exactly what the devil hoped to create.

After three hours of rummaging through circular questions that chased through my mind, my mental search evoked the beginning of intense fear. Somehow I managed to drift off. Upon waking the next morning, I felt weakened physically, mentally, emotionally, and spiritually. But I was immensely grateful that that day was Ash Wednesday, and I could go to church and pray with all my heart. I tried to enjoy the day, the bright sunlight, and the average people around me—anything and everything that was normal and regular in my life. I was beginning to dread the coming night.

*"They tasted the sweet exultancy of the fear of God, which is the first in-
timate touch of the reality of God, known and experienced on earth, the
beginning of heaven. The fear of the Lord is the beginning of heaven."*

— THOMAS MERTON

(This quote from Thomas Merton would particularly strike me later because these nights had been very frightening and incomprehensible. How I
had wished I had known that the first intimate touch of the reality of God is
"fear of the Lord.")

*"We do what we can to find the peace of Christ, and he does the rest.
But this does not mean that there is no price to be paid. Almost certainly we will need to leave behind much that we have clung to, the
familiarity and comfort of being self-sufficient, our reassuring self-con-
fidence, our abounding self-love. It will be painful. As the scriptures say,
to separate us from our self-love he will bring 'not peace but the sword.'
His sword will leave our hearts raw. We will resist with our whole being
the wrenching that precedes peace. It's true however, that in the end, if
we remain committed to find the will of God, and do our own small bit,
faithfully and courageously, he will do the rest. His promised peace will
come. 'Let not my will, but yours be done.' Our peace will be found in the
midst of warfare, our serenity will be bought at the price of surrender."*

— ST. FRANCES DE SALES

(Frances de Sales, and the Lord Himself, hit the nail on the head with this
quote, which is tough to understand until you live though the part of your
life where the Lord's sword begins to penetrate your heart for its own eternal
good. It not only leaves your heart raw, but full of holes, and in immense pain
as well. It is much like a battle over your very soul.)

*"All these complaints Jeremias makes about these pains and trials, and
by means of them he most vividly depicts the sufferings of the soul in this
spiritual night and purgation. Wherefore the soul that God sets in this
tempestuous and horrible night is deserving of great compassion."*

— ST. JOHN OF THE CROSS

"Jesus said, 'Blessed is the man who have suffered and found life.'"

— THE GOSPEL OF THOMAS

"Humility, in accordance with the doctrine of Richard of St. Victor, he identifies with self-knowledge; the terrible vision of the soul as it is, which induces first self-abasement and then self-purification—the beginning of all spiritual growth, and the necessary antecedent of all knowledge of God."

— DIONYSIUS THE AREOPAGITE

At 7:30 p.m. I went to Mass at St. Paul's in the upper church and received ashes. Ash Wednesday is always in a way a sad Mass. We begin the preparation for the Lord's Passion with a period of sacrifice and meditation to strip away all the things that clog our spiritual pores. The period of Lent mirrors Jesus' forty days and forty nights of His supernatural fast and reminds us of His struggle with the devil who had followed him into the desert to tempt Him from His mission. The great Old Testament Prophet Elijah had also fasted for forty days and forty nights without food or water during his journey to the mountain Horeb. The fast for forty days is, I am sure, one of the reasons that the people wondered if Jesus was the reincarnation of Elijah. This Lent I, too, was destined to experience a small taste of what they had both endured—a very difficult Lenten period with immense struggles as I grappled demons and the evil one.

"Then as before, I lay prostrate before the Lord for forty days and forty nights without eating or drinking, because of all the sin you had committed in the sight of the Lord and the evil you had done to provoke him. For I dreaded the fierce anger of the Lord against you."

— DEUTERONOMY 9:18–19

Since it was evening, the beautiful stained glass window of Jesus above the altar was dim and difficult to discern. I could not see His beautiful face clearly. At all the Lenten season Masses, the processional is not sung, but all the rest of the music is. When I found myself straining to sing, I noticed that my encounter last night had somehow weakened me. I was nearly fainting all during Mass. I felt ill all over; my heart sickened. I wondered if my heart would turn into a pile of ashes, leaving an empty cavity in my chest. This experience was new to me since church had always been my shelter and it had always strengthened me. I felt a door open and close in my mind, reminding me about the spirit of the last two nights. The unease kept its hold on me.

As soon as I lay down to try and sleep that night, again the energy descended, but this time I was immediately uncomfortable as it overcame me. My mind had a moment of vivid clarity. *No, oh no,* I thought. I knew without a shadow of a doubt that the energy was of a demon or the devil himself. My instinct was to fight him. I kept my body in constant motion to try and stop the awful awareness that he was trying to settle into my spirit. But every time I stopped moving the feeling would come back. At one point, I began shivering uncontrollably, and asked Sam to hold me, which he did a little reluctantly. Sam, if he is not about to have sex, does not like to touch me. I got into his arms and continued shivering. He noticed my state. "You are shaking all over."

"I know." I said. Then I felt a cold wind seep through Sam and settle around me. My shivering grew even more violent. I quickly released myself from Sam's arms and moved to my side of the bed again. There would be no help from him, but I didn't fixate on this. I had other problems—a distant, cold, marital relationship was the least of them.

After two hours of tossing and turning, and fighting the energy that had built until it felt like not just one demon but a whole army of angry enemy spiritual warriors attacking, I gave up any hopes of sleep that night. I took down my crucifix from the wall over my bed and held it in my hands, suffering mentally as my eyes looked at my beloved savior—Jesus suspended on the cross in excruciating pain. The thought crossed my mind of our connection across the ages. Jesus had descended to hell for three days after his crucifixion, and it seemed to me that this, too, was my destiny.

I traipsed downstairs and settled myself in the light-blue armchair in our bright and cheerful living room. I pulled a multi-colored hand-knit afghan, which Sam's Aunt Lou had crocheted years ago, from the recessed wall cabinet. Sitting down in the chair, I tucked the afghan around me and prepared mentally for the spiritual battle that seemed to be raging around me. I spent the night holding my Bible and crucifix across my lap in our living room with the light on and continually repeating in my head: "I reject you, Satan."

This went on all night long. I spent from 11:30 p.m. to 4:00 a.m. this way. I don't think Satan was in any doubt by the end of the night that I was not going to give in.

"Those who have the disposition and greater strength to suffer, He purges with greater intensity and more quickly."

— ST. JOHN OF THE CROSS

"In those who have afterwards to enter the other and more formidable night of the spirit, in order to pass to the Divine union of love of God (for not all pass habitually thereto, but only the smallest number), it is wont to be accompanied by formidable trials and temptations of sense, which last for a long time, albeit longer in some than in others. For to some the angel of Satan presents himself—namely, the spirit of fornication—that

he may buffet their senses with abominable and violent temptations,
and trouble their spirits with vile considerations and representations
which are most visible to the imagination, which things at times are a
greater affliction to them than death."

— ST. JOHN OF THE CROSS

(Dear St. John of the Cross, a spiritual writer that many think too harsh, is right on the nail here for me. The angel of Satan, the spirit of fornication, how true, how very true. Lust, sex, sensual pleasure—removed from my heart, painfully, frighteningly. I have often wondered if I should ask God to send the same spirit to certain priests in the Boston Area.)

I prayed, and then I begged with my last ounce of strength for God to come to my rescue. No way was I going to fall into a spiritual crevice and somehow end up in the devil's camp. My longing and passion focused on God, and I refused to believe that my Jesus would abandon me. That somehow, someway God would help me overcome whatever spiritual menace had decided to attack me. Anything it took, I would do. In my mind I could see myself being pulled into the black abyss. A great tug—a spiritual struggle persisted. The enemy had descended on my spirit and a raging war felt as if it was being played out. My soul was more terrified than if I had simultaneously fallen off a mile-high cliff, watched a thirsty vampire emerge from my closet, and been startled by an ax murderer chopping down my bedroom door. Nothing compared to the fear I felt that night.

I could not see anything different, just my own physical surroundings, but I intensely felt a new dimension devoid of my physical existence. The images were not in my mind's eye either—but instead all the knowledge was in my sense of touch. My senses understood that I was on the edge of an immense spiritual void, and at the bottom of that blackness—orange flickering flames—hell's armies and the absence of God awaited me. I could sense a tug pulling me into that abyss. I planted my spiritual feet in the mud at the edge and dug them in; they held fast for the moment, but I knew that I had better not let my guard down or I would loose the fight.

"It is saints, not common people, who experience the 'dark night.'"

— C.S. LEWIS

"This greatest of all blessings should be won by the soul at some cost to itself."

— ST. TERESA OF AVILA

"Oh, my God, how great are these trials, which the soul will suffer, both within and without, before it enters the seventh Mansion. Really, when I think of them, I am sometimes afraid that, if we realized their intensity beforehand, it would be most difficult for us, naturally weak as we are, to muster determination enough to enable us to suffer them or resolution enough for enduring them, however attractively the advantage of so doing might be presented to us, until we reached the seventh Mansion, where there is nothing more to be feared, and the soul will plunge deep into suffering for God's sake." – St. Teresa of Avila

"The soul feels itself to be perishing and melting away, in the presence and sight of its miseries, in a cruel spiritual death, even as if it had been swallowed by a beast and felt itself being devoured in the darkness of its belly, suffering such anguish as was endured by Jonas in the belly of that beast of the sea. For in this sepulcher of dark death it must needs abide until the spiritual resurrection which it hopes for." "For indeed, when this purgative contemplation is most severe the soul feels very keenly the shadow of death and the lamentations of death and the pains of hell." – St. John of the Cross

It also felt like the specter, Death, ran his fingers across my flesh, telling me that there is no life after death. "This is the black void you now feel," it seemed to say. "There is nothing to look forward to. You are nothing. You will die, and that will be the end of you." Horrible inner voices coarsely whispered from the shadowy dark corners of my soul— despair, doubt, and hate. On the edge of hopelessness, my own fictional death scene from *Pandora's Story* that God had inspired as prophecy in a truly bizarre, unforeseen way seemed to be coming true; it kept playing over and over in my mind. Jacques, my executioner, was chasing me in Luddom's State Park. It was the scene just before the heaven scene. The place in the book where I died ...

꧁꧂

Married with a three-year-old daughter, Jacques Fournier's condition has been worsening and his marriage was suffering. The depression was sinking him into the pit of despair. The enjoyable moments, the ones that made his live bearable, had all but disappeared. His wife, Linda, had lately born the brunt of his foul temper. She had been begging him to go to the doctor, get some help, and try some of the new medications that are out there for depression. She had been reading all sorts of publications and knew that there was hope. As an optimist—who has lately had a tough time living with Jacques—what keeps her going is her love for her husband and her deep faith in the Lord; that and her memories of their happy years together. It is only in the last two years that that love has been very sorely tested.

Jacques decides that he needs to get away from everyone and everything. Since money has been in very short supply lately, he comes up with the idea of getting away on a camping trip—a small one. There is a local park in the next

town over that allows camping. Once he makes up his mind, he decides there is no reason to wait so he packs up his gear and heads out. He doesn't want to tell his wife where he is going. There will only be an argument. Since his mood is worsening, he doesn't know how he will handle his wife's nagging. Better to just get away before he does something he regrets. He focuses on packing his pickup truck, driving to the park, and finding a quiet spot to set up camp.

Jacques arrives at the park at 6:00 p.m. on October 24th. He starts unloading his camping items. The campsites are some distance from the road, and he must make several trips before he has all his gear. Because it is the fall and drizzle has begun to fall, no other people have set up campsites, which is just fine with Jacques. In the fading daylight, he is blind to the beauty of the golden, crimson, and tangerine leaves, the tingling sound of the crystalline stream as it falls over granite and mica stones, and the comforting forest feel of the tight stands of white pine, maple, and oak.

He searches the ground looking for a good spot to set up the tent. He finds a level clearing, then sets about clearing the area of rocks and twigs. Next, he lays out his ground sheet, unrolling his tent onto it. Taking the tent poles, he begins to insert each piece into the matching fitted end of the adjacent section. When the poles are fully expanded, he inserts them into their tent pockets, then goes around the tent and inserts the poles into their pegs. When the last pole is inserted into its peg, the tent springs up as if by magic—the effect of both tension and balance. He finishes staking the tent, opens the fly, and unrolls his sleeping bag.

With that task done, he takes the bundle of dry wood he has brought and begins a campfire. Next he takes out his food, camp stove, and cooking gear and sets about making dinner.

Once everything is ready, he takes a Miller from the case he has unpacked. He flips the lid and takes a long swig. His depression held at bay momentarily while setting up his campsite, returns. The quiet, peaceful night in the woods doesn't work any magic on his mood. Thoughts of unhappiness, helplessness, sadness, and worthlessness overwhelm him. He can't seem to get ahead in his job. He boss is always on his case. There are bills piled up. He knows he should get a bachelor's degree, but he can't bring himself to undertake the effort. His wife is continually bugging him, and the marriage has gone sour. Life looks bleak and no real change looks like it will ever occur, and Jacques does not have the energy or ambition to put into making changes. The depression is so bad at times that lately he has thought about suicide. More and more suicide is beginning to look like the right thing to do.

Jacques continues to sit, drink, and think negative thoughts for the entire evening and early morning hours until his eyesight starts to fade and the beer bottles pile up. He staggers to the tent and passes out. He awakens at 10:15 a.m. to a chilly morning. A slow, steady rain is still falling. His head is killing him, his eyes are bleary, and his mood dismal. He rolls over and sits up. He gets up to relieve himself.

He is just leaving the tent when he sees a woman. She is looking at him, curious. He trips over the tent stake line, which rattles his head and makes him nauseous. With a bad hangover, he is in no mood for chitchat and angrily yells, "What are you looking at? Leave me alone. Get out of here." The woman still doesn't move. This makes Jacques furious and he screams, "Did my wife send you to see if I was OK? That's it! She sent you. Damn woman always interfering. Get out of here."

He picks himself off the ground and starts walking toward the woman. The woman turns and starts running, finally understanding his anger. Jacques, on impulse, starts running after her. It has suddenly become important to know if his wife sent this woman.

◦ᘏᓄᘏ◦

Two trees squeak together in the gusting wind, and they startle me. I decide to try a new path. Why not? Today I feel the need to try a new direction. There is a lone campsite up ahead. There is a man coming out of his tent. Roughly around 35, of average height, chestnut hair, with eyes, which are nearly closed in a deep, pre-maturely wrinkled face, the stranger looks up to see me. For some reason he seems very startled and upset when he notices me. I wonder why? He begins shouting at me to get out.

What is his problem? What is he saying? Is he asking me if his wife sent me? What a dumb question. For a moment I am too startled to move. Then he starts walking toward me. I am suddenly very afraid. I turn away. Every one of my instincts says "run." I obey, and I run for all I'm worth. The umbrella I have been carrying, dropped and forgotten.

I can hear him start running after me. Already out of breath, I can't seem to keep the screams from forming in my throat and erupting. There seem to be branches to slap me, and roots to trip me everywhere I turn. Briars pull at my clothing as I turn off the main path onto a small foot trail. I look behind me and see he is still chasing me. Soon he will catch up. I leap into the underbrush hoping to lose this mad man, but no such luck.

As fast as I am running there is a force interfering with my escape—a supernatural force weakening me, making me slow down, giving the attacker the advantage. I trip and fall over a couple of weathered granite boulders. I gash my knee, but the gaping wound goes unnoticed. The mad man is on top of me. He pulls out a knife. He begins stabbing me. The pain is overwhelming, I scream for my life. Blackness.

65

"We can only get to Heaven by dying for other people on the cross. And one does not die on a cross by his own unaided efforts. He needs the help of an executioner." – Thomas Merton

"To enter into the realm of contemplation one must in a certain sense die: but this death is in fact the entrance into a higher life."

Joel's Through Death's Gate: A Guide to Selfless Dying:

"There are four ways to find out what happens during and after death:

1. Nearly 50% of people who undergo a clinical death and are later revived remain lucid and have a NDE.

2. The world's great religious traditions. Virtually all of these traditions have attested to the continuity of consciousness beyond physical death and offered some description of what takes place in the afterlife.

3. Finally, we now have available in the West a growing body of literature from those spiritual traditions, which have made a specialty of cultivating meditative techniques that actually mimic the dying process. Perhaps the most sophisticated of these is the Tantric Buddhist tradition of Tibet. For more than a thousand years, Tibetan Buddhists have been making increasingly refined observations of the mental states, which occur during such simulated death experiences.

4. The Mystics of all traditions unanimously agree that death will offer you're a 'golden opportunity' for attaining that Gnostic Awakening which has been the supreme goal of your spiritual quest.

"According to both the Christian and Islamic cosmologies, if you have led a virtuous life, you will enter into paradise following the world's destruction at the end of time. Now on the face of it this sounds quite different from the Tibetan, Hindu, and Kabbalist conceptions, which insist that the opportunity for Gnosis comes immediately after physical death has occurred. But if we read the 'world's destruction' as a mythological description of what an individual experiences during the death process, these accounts are quite compatible. From the point of view of the dying person, the progressive eradication of all phenomena from consciousness will, indeed, seem like the 'end of the world.' In fact, this is precisely how Tibetan master, Kalu Rinpoche, describes it."

(Way number five: write a story about your past, which ends up in your own death, and see what happens.)

I shook my head to clear the fictional scene from *Pandora's Story*, but it stuck nonetheless. The resemblance to what I was now feeling was close to that scene. I was feeling a combination of Jacque's despair and my own helplessness over a very threatening—if non-physical—situation. A menacing power was overtaking me, and I could not escape. In fact, I felt like I was being pulled into death or a beyond life dimension, and I was almost outside of my own strength to stop it.

As the sun peeked over the horizon, indicating early dawn's arrival, my husband came down the stairs to ask me if I was all right. I guess he must have noticed that I was missing from my side of the bed. It told him very bluntly that I felt like I was being attacked by the devil (I think I said that exactly). He gave me a neutral look, but did not say anything except to ask me to come back upstairs. I have often wondered why he didn't ask for an explanation of my startling statement, but perhaps he was really still asleep and walking at the same time. I told him, "No, I can't go back there right now. He seemed to accept my statement and quietly walked back up the stairs and left me to my own battle. I could hear him walk around our bed and climb into his side.

As the first sunrays poked over the edge of the bushes in the neighbor's backyard, signaling the end of that horrid night, I had an inspiration to go and see Father Raffey, our parish priest. As I tossed the idea around, it formed into a very strong and powerful urge. I needed to talk to someone—someone who might be able to understand, someone who could give me direction, someone to help me go on and give me some tips for this spiritual battle. Yes, Father with his tall spare frame, his salt-and-pepper hair, hearty laughter, kind, happy expression and smile, and his open friendliness, would surely help me.

As I drove into the office that same morning, I mentally rehearsed over and over in my mind exactly what I would say to get Father to meet me. When I made the call from my cell phone en route, I got his answering machine. "Father, this is Irene Manian. I have situation that I don't know how to handle, and I really need to talk to you, today, if at all possible. Could you please call me back? It's really urgent." By mid-morning Father had returned my call; his open heart had heard my pressing need. Praise God. He told me to come to the rectory, and he would meet me in the small den in the front of the building on the first floor at 12:00 noon.

To say that I was grateful would be an understatement. In his kind and caring way, he saved my life that morning. God does send just the right people to you when you are in great need. You can trust that God knows just when to throw you a lifeline as you feel you are about to drown. That morning, God was truly with me in the form of one of His most faithful servants, Father Raffey.

After I arrived at the rectory, he led me to his small study. The warm wood-paneled walls and the many religious icons enclosed us in a warm, comfortable feeling. I wasn't sure how to begin my story—it was such an uncomfortable topic—so I just plunged in. Giving him a quick synopsis of my spiritual history, I began with my early experimentation in the ESP Class and finishing with last night. He listened to my story and did not deny the possibility of what had happened to me. He asked me instead how my marriage was going—was Sam treating me OK. I guess that he thought our marriage was on the rocks again. True enough, but Sam was not the focus of this latest struggle.

> *"Catherine of Genoa, who seems to have possessed from childhood a religious nature, was prepared for the remaking of her consciousness by years of loneliness and depression, the result of an unhappy marriage."*
>
> – EVELYN UNDERHILL

> *"The conversion of Madame Guyon to the mystic life, as told by herself in her Autobiography. (Her conversion) followed upon a period of mental distress; also the result of an uncongenial marriage."*
>
> – EVELYN UNDERHILL

After I told him that the marriage was OK, he insisted that God loved me so very much, and that He would never abandon me in my struggles. That I only had to place all my trust in God's hands and all would be well. Then I watched as the Holy Spirit took over the familiar form of Father, and used his voice and body to say an inspired prayer over my crucifix—the one I had brought with me from home, which I had originally bought at Saint Anne De Beaupre in Quebec, Canada. How did I recognize the Holy Spirit take him over? His eyes glazed over and his voice became melodic and a bit higher in pitch. He took my crucifix in his hands and uttered the most wonderful words in the form of a blessing, which denied Satan any power over any that Jesus had made His own. His blessing was elaborate and powerful—lasting at least ten minutes. Oh how I wish I had been able to record it in my memory. The words settled on my cross and the wood seemed to glow with an extra luster—as if its essence had changed and the wood became holy and immeasurably stronger than ordinary wood.

> *"People have no idea what one saint can do: for sanctity is stronger than*

the whole of hell. The saints are full of Christ in plenitude of His Kingly and Divine power: and they are conscious of it, and they give themselves to Him that He may exercise His power through their smallest and seemingly most insignificant acts, for the salvation of the world."

— THOMAS MERTON

After he was done, I took my crucifix back and looked at it. I realized that it had become my holy weapon. From that moment forward, it became my cherished friend at night. Many would be the endless, difficult nights that would be made easier because of its comfort. Certainly, I believe now that the cross made an enormous difference in the night to follow.

"Left blind by the light, which he understood to be Christ himself, he was taken to Damascus and sat for three days in the darkness. Baptized by Ananias, his sight restored, he left the city to spend several years in Arabia in prayer and Meditation." – Acts 9:8 and 9:18

4

The Birth Of The Eternal Word

DAY 1

February 14, 2006 (Valentine's Day). After dinner that night, Sam presented me with a box of chocolates and half-dozen beautiful roses in white, lemon, and fuchsia. In two white envelopes were cards from the kids and him. They were beautifully written, and for a few moments I felt happy. The rest of the evening was typical, filled with dirty dishes to clean, rooms to pick up, and children to bathe and get ready for bed. I was busy enough to focus only on the present moment. I wanted to delay my getting into bed as long as possible.

Although I was more exhausted than I'd ever been, and desperately wanted to just lay down and fall into a coma, as I looked at my bed, all sorts of awful feelings arose. A question volleyed in my mind: should I give up and sleep on the sofa, or should I again try to overcome and fight whatever was happening to me? I decided to give the bed another chance. I gingerly pulled the sheets and comforter aside and arranged myself under them. I had my crucifix by my side and was wearing my rosary beads. I had the light on and was trying to relax while reading my Bible. As soon as I lay down, though, I could feel spiritual energy all around me, bumping into me, touching me, and jostling me. I tried hard to concentrate on what I was reading, ignoring all the spiritual sensations. Yet it proved difficult to ignore the touching, holding, grabbing. I couldn't see anything, but my skin was crawling with all the invisible touching sensations. I thought I would go mad.

My perceptions told me that I was in an intense struggle with a spiritual monster. I could sense that the beast was very large. I denied my mind its usual ability to conjure up images of anything that it might want to see. I knew who it was; it didn't matter what form he was in. I didn't need to see what he so dearly desired—a vivid image that would haunt me in my nightmares for countless future months. He was back to violate me just like the last two nights. Terrified, I desperately wanted to go back to only last week when I had been writing my beautiful heaven scene and experiencing God so vividly.

> *"Origin of the Nephilim (prehistoric giants of Palestine). When men began to multiply on earth and daughters were born to them, the sons of heaven (the celestial beings of mythology) saw how beautiful the daughters of man were, and so they took for their wives as many of them as they chose."*
>
> — GENESIS 6:1–4

> *"I cannot exaggerate the night of my soul. When I sing in my verses of the happiness of heaven and the eternal possession of God, I feel no joy, I sing only of what I wish to believe."*
>
> — ST. THERESE OF LISIEUX

I got up from bed and walked into my children's bedrooms, then took the crosses down from their walls. I hated to do this, because they would not have Jesus' presence for the night, but I entrusted them into their guardian angel's hands. Somehow I knew that I was going to need every ounce of spiritual blessing I could find.

Very panicky, I lay down and arranged the three crosses between my legs and around my torso under the white cotton sheets. It felt like a major battle was going on centering around my lower abdomen. A monstrous beast felt so close that I could feel his rancid breath. I had slept not one wink last night, and I accepted with quiet resignation that tonight would probably not hold any of the wonderful bliss of oblivious sleep. All around me energy fields swirled. The energy was so strong that I could feel it trying to shake off the crucifixes where they lay, but thankfully although they vibrated and trembled, they stayed where they had been placed. I struggled into the late hours of night, staring at the red-flowered wallpaper on my bedroom walls as shadows from my bedside table lamp spread soft light across my bedroom. Sam, who loves sleeping in the dark, allowed the light to stay on after one look at my face. I thought of the blessing that Father had given me earlier and I prayed and kept hope foremost in my heart.

> *"Therefore, that I might not become too elated, a thorn in the flesh was given to me, an angel of Satan, to beat me, to keep me from being too elated. Three times I begged the Lord about this that it might leave me, but he said to me, 'My grace is sufficient for you, for power is made perfect in weakness.'"*
>
> — 2 CORINTHIANS 12:6–9

*"For our struggle is not with flesh and blood but with the principalities,
with the powers, with the world rulers of this present darkness, with the
evil spirits in the heavens."*

— EPHESIANS 6:12

"Come, let us return to the Lord, For it is he who has rent, but he will heal us; he has struck us, but he will bind our wounds. He will revive us after two days; on the third day he will raise us up, to live in his presence. Let us know, let us strive to know the Lord; as certain as the dawn is his coming, and his judgment shines forth like the light of day! He will come to us like the rain, like spring rain that waters the earth. What can I do with you, Ephraim? What can I do with you, Judah? Your piety is like a morning cloud, like the dew that early passes away. For this reason I smote them through the prophets, I slew them by the words of my mouth; For it is love that I desire, not sacrifice, and knowledge of God rather than holocausts." – Hosea 6:1–6

"Destroy this temple and in three days I will raise it up."

— JOHN 2:19

*"But not finding him, they returned to Jerusalem to look for him. After
three days they found him in the temple, sitting in the midst of the
teachers, listening to them and asking them questions."*

— LUKE 2:45–46

Every so often I would glance over at my husband who was sleeping peacefully on the other side of the bed. He had pretended not to notice the crosses and rosary beads as he simply turned over and went to sleep.

My daughter, Christina, had woken up at about 10:30 p.m. frightened because of a nightmare. She was now on the floor on my other side—my left-hand side—in a sleeping bag because she didn't want to go back to her room. With her dark curly hair fanning out from her face against her pillow and her deep brown eyes closed, she appeared a picture-perfect angel. I wondered if her spirit was troubled without her crucifix on the wall, then dismissed the thought. Since she had many nightmares, her sleeping on our bedroom floor was not unusual. She, at least, was comforted by my closeness.

At some point around midnight, I must have drifted off, because I woke up startled. Something had happened, but I could not figure out what. As I lay awake I noticed that my stomach area began to have a spasm. It was odd, but I felt no pain, so I ignored it. About five minutes later, it happened again. Then the spasms became regular—occurring at five-minute intervals for the next thirty minutes. They vaguely reminded me of something, something in my past. With shock, I entered into the memory of my first labor with Patrick. The spasms were very reminiscent of labor contractions—false labor contractions—the type that don't cause any pain.

As soon as I made this observation, my weary eyes turned to the clock and I started to time them. They started out at five minutes, but then dropped to four minutes, then three minutes apart. Now I was completely at sea, because my stomach was flat, and I was not pregnant. Terrified, and nearly out of my mind with fear, I held back tears. "I must stay strong and keep hope in my heart," I told myself over and over. I closed my eyes and realized that with my eyes closed, I somehow felt the sensation of being hugely pregnant. I opened them again to see that, sure enough, I still had a flat stomach. While my physical body was not pregnant, something else about me was. The only other possibility was my soul. My soul was pregnant? What?

"Since the soul, according to mystic principles, can only perceive Reality in proportion, as she is real, know God by becoming God-like, it is clear that this birth is the initial necessity. The true and definitely directed mystic life does and must open with the most actual, though indescribable phenomenon, the coming forth into consciousness of man's deeper, spiritual self, which ascetical and mystical writers of all ages have agreed to call Regeneration or Re-birth." – Evelyn Underhill

> "He it is also that is born each instant in our hearts: for this unending birth, this everlasting beginning, without end, this everlasting perfect newness of God begotten of Himself, issuing from Himself without leaving Himself or altering His one-ness, this is the life that is in us."
>
> — THOMAS MERTON

> "In the beginning, the spirit-wind of God moves across the face of the deep. The deep is not barren but pregnant, an emptiness teeming with the promise of life."
>
> — WAYNE MULLER

> "Since the birth of the human heart is an ongoing process, love is the continuous birth of creativity within and between us."
>
> — JOHN O'DONOHUE

> "But to those who did accept him he gave power to become children of God, to those who believe in his name, who were born not by natural generation nor by human choice nor by a man's decision but of God."
>
> — JOHN 1:12–13

My spiritual "labor" continued for two more hours. As it continued on and on I could feel my heart pounding, as if at any moment it would rip out of my chest. It was beating so hard that it practically shook the bed. The contractions accelerated in continuous increasing rhythm.

Around 2:20 a.m. a new sensation occurred. I could feel energy on my lower left leg. A spirit, an angel? Then the image of the Blessed Virgin Mother popped into my head, and I knew beyond any doubt that it was the Blessed Mother. She was standing at the edge of my bed rubbing my leg in a circular motion, just as if I was really delivering a baby; it was at the excruciating climax that I needed reassurance that it was going to be all right. Over and over again, the rubbing continued like a gentle circular vortex of energy on my left lower calf. It was such a loving and gentle touch. From it I could feel the strength coming from Her—telling me to hold on just a little bit longer. My dear mother from the eternal world was on my side and was with me in my greatest hour of need. Helping me give birth. My memory returned to Patrick and Christina's birth. Both times there had been nurses by my side to hold my hand through the climax of pain.

> "The Buddha described the seed of mindfulness that is in each of us as the 'womb of the Buddha' (tathagatagarbha). We are all mothers of the Buddha because we are all pregnant with the potential for awakening."
>
> — THICH NHAT HANH

> "In Isaiah 66, the woman's birth pangs are followed by the messianic age of salvation. Here they bring on an attack of the dragon, which is still not yet the final showdown between good and evil."
>
> — PHEME PERKINS

> "Amen, amen, I say to you, no one can see the kingdom of God without begin born from above." Nicodemus said to him, 'How can a person once grown old be born again? Surely he cannot reenter his mother's womb and be born again, can he?' Jesus answered, 'Amen, amen, I say to you, no one can enter the kingdom of God without being born of water and Spirit. What is born of flesh is flesh and what is born of spirit is spirit. Do not be amazed that I told you, "You must be born from above." The wind blows where it wills, and you can hear the sound it makes, but you do not know where it comes from or where it goes; so it is with everyone who is born of the Spirit."
>
> — JOHN 3:3–8

Finally, the contractions reached their climax and I felt a great release, and an immediate, incredible respite from fear. Elation, bliss, happiness, euphoria, and joy rose up from my own spirit and surrounded me. From totally distressed, frantic, and desperate to ecstatic and rapturous in one minute. It was approximately 2:30 a.m. in the morning. I breathed a deep sign of relief and turned over onto my stomach, something that just minutes before would have been totally impossible.

As soon as I turned over, I noticed something that reminded me of my children's births. I had a painful feeling of hemorrhoids flaring up, and this time there was pain. As soon as I thought about the pain, I felt a spirit gently touch my back. Sure that this one meant to help, I was unafraid. Perhaps it was some kind of a "nurse angel" sent by God. Normally, I would have been embarrassed about this, but I think I was way past any normal, regular human emotion. As I lay on my stomach, I could feel a feeling of intense heat over my rectum. The heat was so soothing. I was being spiritually healed from my spiritual labor and birth. The healing lasted for about ten minutes, and then the pain from my hemorrhoids disappeared. The "nurse spirit," having fixed the minor spiritual discomfort, left. Strange that the labor and birth itself had been painless, but my hemorrhoids had flared up in pain.

Then there was nothing left; no dark shadows remained in my spirit, only clouds and energy swirling, bringing with them euphoria and upwelling feelings of love that drifted all around me and throughout my entire being. Like a tidal wave, the emotion overcame me. As horrid as the last two nights had been, the feeling of delight, enchantment, bliss, and joy surged in and swept away all the terror, unhappiness, uncertainty, hopelessness, and evil and carried them far, far from me.

As I continued to lay on my stomach, I was strengthened by a gift directly from God. I felt a great spiritual wallop hit my back right between my shoulder blades. My mind's eye filled with light, and I was given the knowledge that I had just received a softball-sized hit of light. You might expect that a ball of light hitting your mid-back would hurt when it entered, but instead, my entire soul from the crown of my head to the tips of my toes experienced utter delight and extreme pleasure. Just as I was about to beg the Lord to please "hit me again," I again felt another ball of light penetrate my soul and fill it with utter rapture. Then the third and final ball of light splashed into my soul like a loaded water balloon that exploded and drenched my spirit with light. It felt so good that I wished that the Lord would keep sending them. In less than five minutes, I had become an addict of the light. The Lord had "enlightened" me with His own essence—pure uncreated light. Because there had been three balls, I had an immediate association of the Holy Trinity: the Father, Son, and Holy Ghost—a gift of God, in three distinct separate spheres.

I talked to God. He was pleased with me. On my left cheek, the lips of His Spirit touched my skin and I knew that He was giving me a kiss. The kiss felt exactly like a human lover, friend, or even my own child had actually swept my cheeks with his lips.

"He also gives the soul that kiss for which the Bride besought Him; for I understand it to be in this Mansion that that petition is fulfilled."
— ST. TERESA OF AVILA

> *"The spiritual sense of touch is more intimate than the sense of smell and the attraction to the delightful perfume of God's presence. The divine touch, like the divine perfume, is not a bodily sensation. Rather it is as if our spirit were touched by God or embraced. The divine touch might feel as if God were descending from above and enveloping us in an embrace, or embracing us from within, and placing a great big kiss in the middle of our spirit. The delight may overflow from this deep spiritual source into the external senses, and then the body also rejoices. The Spirit of God, can transform the entire organism into an immense celebration of love, peace, and joy—'an alleluia', to use the well-known phrase of St. Augustine of Hippo."*
>
> – FR. THOMAS KEATING

When I asked God if all was well and if the worst was over, He did not say anything, but at least He did not disagree, which at that moment I took to mean yes. Then the Lord gave me another amazing gift. Because I was so excited and had had very little sleep (it was approximately 3:30 a.m. by this time), and God knew how much I needed to rest, He gave me a little help. His Holy Spirit touched my head, and my eyes sank deeply into my head and then I felt them go rapidly back and forth in deep REM sleep. I was awake and aware during this unusual sleep period, recognizing that the REM sleep was a divine substitute for my lost night's sleep. After this, relaxed and exhausted, with God's Spirit hovering over me, I did let go and drift off.

My alarm clock went off at 6:00 a.m., but I was very groggy, almost in a daze, and I didn't immediately jump right out of bed and go to the shower. Instead I drifted in and out of slumber. For once I knew that I needed to allow myself some extra time in bed, so I suspended the guilt and let my body take its time to awaken. One and a half hours later, at 7:30 a.m., I dropped my legs to the floor and headed to the shower. I would be late for work, yet I couldn't have cared less. I had been to hell, heaven, and back, and the office would just have to wait.

> *"Meister Eckhart speaks often of the birth of the eternal Word of God in the soul. It is the silent soul that becomes the womb in which the true God can dwell."*
>
> – FREDERICK BAUERSCHMIDT

> *"We intend therefore to speak of this birth as taking place in us, as being consummated in the virtuous soul, for it is in the perfect soul that God speaks his Word."*
>
> – MEISTER ECKHART

Jesus said: "Amen, amen, I say to you, you will weep and mourn, while the world rejoices; you will grieve, but your grief will become joy. When a woman is in labor, she is in anguish because her time has arrived; but when she has given birth to a child, she no longer remembers the pain because her joy that a child has been born into the world." (John 16:20-22)

One evening while reading the Gospel of John months later, this passage struck a deep cord inside my soul. Vividly it would transport me back to this night. I had truly wept and mourned, and also labored, but afterwards I was filled with immense joy. My labor was spiritual, but, after all, the entire Bible is a spiritual document, and my Lord is the King of the spiritual world, and not the physical world. I also realized that if for the last three days I had been dead, in hell feeling the total absence of God, or in the throes of dying, now I was resurrected or reborn just as the Savior had been.

After that night, I was left to ponder the events that took place. There has been much written about rebirth throughout all time. After the season of Lent was over in 2002, I hit upon many references. In the Book of Revelations, there is a central figure of a woman giving birth while a dragon attempts to swallow her baby. This place of Revelations is used in the Catholic Church to describe Mary. Of course, it does describe the Virgin Mother who had the mission of giving physical birth to the Savior. But what I came to discover, little by little, is that anyone who has a revelation of God is also called to give birth to the Savior in a spiritual way. Here are the Revelation passages that relate to the woman giving birth and also several passages by authorities on this section of Revelations:

> "The Woman and the Dragon. A great sign appeared in the sky, a woman clothed with the sun, with the moon under her feet, and on her head was a crown of twelve stars. She was with child and wailed aloud in pain as she labored to give birth. Then another sign appeared in the sky; it was a huge red dragon, with seven heads and ten horns, and on its heads were seven diadems."
>
> – REVELATIONS 12:1–3

> "Then the dragon stood before the woman about to give birth, to devour her child when she gave birth. She gave birth to a son, a male child, destined to rule all the nations with an iron rod. Her child was caught up to God and his throne. The woman herself fled into the desert where she

had a place prepared by God, that there she might be taken care of for twelve hundred and sixty days."

— REVELATIONS 12:4–6

"But the woman was given the two wings of the great eagle, so that she could fly to her place in the desert, where, far from the serpent, she was taken care of for a year, two years, and a half-year."

— REVELATIONS 12:14

"The story of the woman and the dragon draws upon a wealth of symbolism from the myths of the ancient Near East, and from Jewish and Greek sources. The 'woman clothed with the sun' would easily remind the audience of the Roman use of the story of the sun god, Apollo. Roma, the queen of heaven, was worshiped as mother."

— PHEME PERKINS

I felt shock when I came upon this next quote from Pope Paul VI and his prayer. Here is his prayer acknowledging the spiritual birth that I had just experienced. By no means is he alone in using labor and birth to describe an actual experience of God. Other writers who have also used this same language follow Pope Paul VI:

"The hour is coming, in fact has come, when the vocation of woman is being acknowledged in its fullness, the hour in which women acquire in the world an influence, an effect and a power never hitherto achieved. That is why, at this moment when the human race is undergoing so deep a transformation, women impregnated with a spirit of the Gospel can do so much to aid humanity in not falling."

"Dear Lord, Impregnate me with the spirit of the Gospel and let me bring Your life to the world. I want to birth You in the lives of the poor, the downtrodden, the weak and maligned. I want to birth You in the hearts of the fearful, the distraught, the grief-stricken and desolate. I want to birth You in the souls of the wounded, the troubled, the lonely, the bereft. I want to birth You to the proud, the arrogant, the sophisticated, and chic. I want to birth You in moments of pain and confusion, doubt and disillusion, trial and travail. I want to birth You in abortuaries and prison cells, in research labs and legislative caucuses. I want to birth You in grade schools and high schools, in college classes and think-tank sessions. I want to birth You in my family and parish, my community and country. The hour has come. Let my labor begin. May Your life infuse the world. Amen"

(Please note that there are seven I "birth yous" quoted here! That will be important to remember soon.)

St. Therese Lisieux said, "Suffering alone gives birth to souls." The birthing process is painful. What kinds of pain can I expect if I set out to birth Jesus Christ to the world? Am I willing to endure it? Why or why not? What can I do to prepare for it?

> *"The spiritual journey consists of an ongoing transformation of consciousness, a continual conversion, which is the Light of Christ shining upon our minds and hearts with ever-greater intensity. He who is 'the light of the world' enlightens and transforms our conscious with his very own light, poured into us by the Holy Spirit under the loving gaze of the father. Thus the spiritual journey can be understood as a continual 'birthing of Christ' in us until we come 'to maturity, to the measure of full stature of Christ' (Ephesians 4:13). In a true sense, like Mary, we become 'bearers of Christ'; by the power of the Holy Spirit, we 'give birth' to Christ as he grows in us."*
>
> — FRANK X. TUOTI

> *"I give, then, but one example: that which is referred by mystical writers to the Nativity, and concerns the eternal Birth or Generation of the Son or Divine Word. This Birth is in its first, or cosmic sense, the welling forth of the Spirit of Life from the Divine Abyss of the unconditioned Godhead. (Ruysbroeck) – An eternal Ray, the which is the Birth of the Son. Saint Augustine says this Birth is ever taking place. Eckhart "But if it takes not place in me, what avails it. Everything lies in this, that it should take place in me."*
>
> — EVELYN UNDERHILL

> *"This awakening, from the psychological point of view, appears to be an intense form of the phenomenon of "conversion"; It is a disturbance of the equilibrium of the self, which results in the shifting of the field of consciousness from lower to higher levels. All conversion entails the abrupt or gradual emergence of intuitions from below the threshold."*
>
> — EVELYN UNDERHILL

> *"The Tao may be within him, but he is completely out of touch with it, just as he is out of touch with his own utmost self. Recovery of the Tao is impossible without a complete transformation, a change of heart, which Christianity would call metonoia. Zen, of course, envisaged this problem and studied how to arrive at satori, or the explosive rediscovery of the hidden and lost reality within us."*
>
> — THOMAS MERTON

Jesus said, "That which you have will save you if you bring it forth from yourselves. That which you do not have within you will kill you if you do not have it within you."

— THE GOSPEL OF THOMAS

5

A Seven-fold Bundle of Baby Gifts
Remade in Seven Days
Personal Demons and the
Underworld Ruler

What is in a Name?
Where Do Legends Begin?

DAY 2 AND DAY 3

On February 15, 2002, wonder of wonders, nothing spiritual happened. I spent the day taking care of office paperwork and the evening packing for the annual family ski trip to Southern Canada. As anyone who has children and has taken them on a ski vacation knows, this takes up hours. While I worked, thoughts of God spurred wonderment and peace, filling all my inner thoughts and feelings. That night I slept soundly and was up very early that Saturday morning to do all the things that mothers do to get their families off to vacation. I cooked the kids breakfast, put on light timers, feed the pets, did the dishes, took out the garbage, finished packing, and generally did all the last-minute details necessary before our ski trip

During the long drive through Massachusetts, New Hampshire, and then Vermont, I thought constantly about God and my love for Him. Sam was driving so I was able to drift in and out of sleep, exhausted from the week and all the spiritual ordeals. At one point as my spirit mentally reached toward the divine, I lost all awareness of my surroundings, including my physical body.

About one hour from our destination to the Owl's Head area of Southern Canada, a ski resort halfway between Montreal and Quebec, as we were passing rolling snow-frosted hills and picturesque, colorful Canadian homes in coral, sky blue, and lilac, I felt what I can only describe as a vortex of energy. The energy was suspended over my stomach area and penetrated into my lower abdomen. It seemed to fill me, and somehow I was aware of again being spiritually pregnant. The image of God the Father's outstretched finger touching Adam from the work of Michelangelo's "The Creation of Adam" on the ceiling of the Sistine Chapel popped into my mind. The penetrating touch of the vortex I had felt was his Holy Finger. The next divine gift—selfless love—had arrived.

As we reached our destination, and checked into the hotel, a lethargic, languid, dreamy state came over me. I was really out of it—exhausted and so heavily spiritually pregnant that I found myself waddling instead of walking. The children and I stood in the lobby behind Sam as he headed for the front desk.

My next spiritual labor was eminent, and I needed get to our room so that I could lay down with my cross and my Bible.

There were no regular rooms left at the hotel, due to all of the skiers flocking to the mountains. But this was never a problem when you have my husband along because he is without a doubt one of the world's shrewdest negotiators. So unlike Mary and Joseph in long-ago Bethlehem (too bad Sam wasn't along on that trip), we were given a room that Sam would never have consented to pay for, but obtained anyway—the presidential suite.

The suite was on the top floor in one of the corners of the hotel. It was a splendid place with a double-sided fireplace, Jacuzzi tub, off-white furniture and fixtures, and a white marble bathroom. It was high luxury, and I wondered at the time if the room wasn't a special gift from the Lord.

Within a half an hour I was growing more uncomfortable and turned the TV on for the children so that I could lay down on the king-sized bed with its ivory satin down comforter. Contractions came for about an hour, and then I felt another spiritual release, which left me feeling much better. Almost like myself again; in fact, there was a small rush of joy. This birth had not been at all difficult and really was nothing like the first. Shortly after it was over, our family decided to take a wonderful horse-drawn sleigh ride through the woods. A local farmer owned the Belgian draft horse and sleigh that the hotel had hired to delight all the tourists. As we traveled in the silent, dark forest with only the sound of the tingling of the sleigh bells around the horse's neck and its heavy hoofs slamming into the snow, I looked up at the amazing number of stars in the sky above, and I was filled with awe and wonder that the King of the Universe loved me so much that He had descended from so high above to be with me.

Perhaps you are now really wondering what was happening to me. One spiritual birth was perhaps understandable given all the good references I have listed above, but two? I was curious, too, but I knew something that you don't know—that there would be seven births and not just one. How did I know? You guessed it. Let us return to the heaven chapter of *Pandora's Story*, to the place where God asks me to explain which gifts I would choose to give the world and why:

"Mankind is under the mistaken impression that there are only two categories—free will or fate. These two both exist. Man has free will in the small choices. Things such as jobs, spouses, homes, friends, etc. fall under free will," said the Almighty

"For the big picture there is fate. All men must bow down to My Plan and meet fate eventually. But there really is a third choice. If man will come to know me, accept me into his heart and soul, then I will talk to him. I will tell him personally what I would like him to do. This is called guided will. When a person is tuned in to me, listens, and does what I ask him/her to do, then they are using guided will. Guided will is the best choice because you will have an idea of where your life is going and how you fit into the bigger picture of fate. As you know, Irene, guided will is only possible after a person actively seeks me and goes on a spiritual journey. A person must have a thirst for me first.

"Irene, you are now ready for your mission. You have passed your test of faith and developed a soul capable of unselfish love and compassion. Henceforth, you will be my Pandora. Pandora means all gifts, and you will be my instrument of change. You will mark the beginning of a new faith-filled era."

After God spoke these words to my soul, He gave me a vision of Pandora. I do not know for sure whether I ever existed as this woman, this Pandora of Greek legendary fame. Or whether she was truly a real woman or just a legend given as a glimpse into our present time. I do know that the impossible becomes possible when you are referring to God, and that the stories about her are close but not exact. She had a good heart, and did try to do as God had requested. Only, she was waylaid by the enemy, and was persuaded by a man to go against what she knew she should do.

The Creator waved His wondrous palm to reveal a glimpse into the ancient story: "Once, eons ago in man's time, Pandora was placed on the earth with gifts for mankind. I gave her a jar as her marriage gift. While she was walking down the stairs to earth, the devil tripped her, and she fell. Let's go back and revisit that time."

꧁꧂

Frothy clouds cleared to reveal a window-sized patch of brilliant blue sky. As I watched, the blue of the sky changed, and I saw a young woman dressed in a Grecian-Toga style wedding dress, which shimmered as she moved. Raven's wing black, with a ruby-studded band woven into its heavy masses, her hair framed an oval of rose cream. Eyes and eyebrows matched the hair. A straight aquiline nose set in between high cheekbones and a small rosebud mouth were her features. She bore a close resemblance to me, although not exact.

Suddenly, I wasn't just looking down at her through an opening in the sky, but I was her. I looked down at my feet, clad in soft-doe skin slippers, and at the dress, under my fingers, softer than the underside of a bunny's belly, the material was radiant and sparkly; it seemed alive. In my arms was a beautiful crystal jar; its mouth stoppered with a golden angel figure. Then the echo of God's final words to me rang back in my head.

> *"Listen, my daughter, and understand; turn your ears to what I have to say." – Psalm 44(45)*

"Your name is Pandora. Pandora, you are my first, and in many ways my most wonderful gift to man. I am giving you this jar to give the man you will meet at the bottom of the stairs. It is filled with all my gifts. You will love the man you meet instantly and forever. You will have many children together. I love you, Pandora. Remember you always have my love; it will be in your heart. Be careful to guard your steps as you walk down the stairs. Be sure and give the man, named Prometheus, the jar as soon as you see him. It is very important. Go now my Pandora." God waved to me and pointed His finger to a circular white marble staircase about ten feet away.

> *"It does seem as though you do have to find the God that is in love with you before you can really begin your journey. This part was written in the Fall. Perhaps remaking the Eve story, when you are a woman is critical to finding God because woman do have to contend with Eve's fall and how women are seen as bad and sinful. We need to have God reach out and tell us just how much he loves us. God must have all the perfect virtues whether we see these as feminine or masculine. After all God is perfect compassion, love, understanding, empathy and these are all seen as feminine. In fact, God is much more reflective of all virtues which are womanly and soft than the harder, more aggressive male 'virtues.'"*
>
> — PATRICIA LYNN REILLY

"I often use the example of the spiral staircase as a symbol of the purification that gradually takes place through contemplative prayer. In doing this I mean to suggest that every time we move to a new level of recognition of our weakness and dependence on God for everything, we experience a kind of inner resurrection."

— FR. THOMAS KEATING

I turned toward the staircase, and waved good-bye to the Creator. My heart surged with love. I took a moment before I began my descent just to look at God. The sight of His Beauty was nectar that I eagerly drank in.

"There is something very special about the love which is the beatitude of heaven; it makes us resemble God, because God Himself is love. The more we love Him as He loves us, the more we resemble Him; and the more we resemble Him, the more we come to know Him."

— FR. THOMAS MERTON

After a moment, I turned my attention to the enormous circular stairway. It was mind-boggling huge. Wherever I was going was a long way from here. "No small jaunt, this descent," I thought, "why it was so far that it seemed to descend into another dimension, another time, a whole new world." As I glided down the steps, billowing clouds drifted about me. At times they blew in fast, and then left; at times their fluffy substance would cling onto the fabric of my dress, like sticky cotton candy. They danced and broiled and swirled with abandon, having fun just being weightless.

With patience and steady walking, I eventually reached a place where I could see the bottom. A lush emerald carpet of ivy vines were climbing up the other way, but had thus far only made it up about four steps. At that point, a man with blond hair and colorless eyes in a black tailored suit appeared out of nowhere. Was this the man I was supposed to love instantly? I didn't think so. Looking into his eyes sent shivers down my spine. I could see all the way through into a void. He had no soul.

"God created man in his image; in the divine image he created him; male and female he created them.

The Lord God then took the man and settled him in the Garden of Eden, to cultivate and care for it.

The Lord God said: 'It is not good for the man to be alone. I will make a suitable partner for him.'"

— GENESIS 1:27, 2:15–16, 2:18

"So the Lord God cast a deep sleep on the man, and while he was asleep, he took out one of his ribs, and closed up its place with flesh. The Lord God then built up into a woman the rib that he had taken from the man. When he brought her to the man, the man said:

This one, at last, is bone of my bones and flesh of my flesh; This one shall be called "woman", for out of "her man" this one has been taken.

That is why a man leaves his father and mother and clings to his wife, and the two of them become one body."

— GENESIS 2:21-24

"Hi there, going to meet someone special? What's that you are holding?" the stranger asked.

I hesitated; who was this? "Yes, I am on my way to my wedding. I think Prometheus must be wondering about me. So I must go."

"What is in the beautiful jar you are holding?" the stranger asked again. He was standing right in front of me blocking my way.

"This jar contains all of God's most wonderful gifts. It is for my husband-to-be. Excuse me, but I must be going." I walked around him, and didn't look back. One moment later he materialized in front of me and tripped me, and the beautiful glass jar from God was shattered. I tried to pick up the pieces; but the only thing that was salvageable was a round amber oval, which read "Hope." I tenderly picked it up. The rest of the gifts were smashed; but as I watched, the smashed bits lifted and floated back up the marble steps. Magically, they seemed to reassemble together, gaining upward speed, as they headed back to God. I was so upset; I didn't know what to do. The stranger had done that on purpose, and now he had disappeared. "Hopefully for good," I thought.

What should I do I wondered? Should I go back up the stairs and ask God for a new set of gifts? Or should I go through the leafy entrance to what looked to be a beautiful garden and meet my intended. I decided that I should just go into the garden and find the man; after all, the entire garden was now very close and God was so far away up the mountainous spiral. Perhaps my husband could give me some advice.

So I walked into a garden riotous with flowers so vivid that they were almost fluorescent. There were trees everywhere and most were loaded with fruit—perfect and unblemished. I saw the man almost immediately. He was seated on a stone bench patiently waiting. His back was ramrod straight; his expression was kind and gentle. I walked over to his side and touched him. At my touch he looked up and into my eyes. I fell in love with him instantly. He was the most beautiful man with dark hair and large emerald green eyes. His smile lit up his face. He reached for me and pulled me into his arms. I remembered the gift then and handed it to him. I tried to explain that there were other gifts that

God wanted me to bring, but because of an accident, I had lost them. He listened for a moment but then he leaned toward me as if magnetically attracted. He brought his lips to touch mine, and I lost my train of thought. The next moment I was snuggly held in his arms and being passionately made love to.

> *"When you find the person you love, an act of ancient recognition brings you together. It is as if millions of years before the silence of nature broke, your lover's clay and your clay lay side by side. That in the turning of the seasons, your one clay divided and separated. You began to rise as distinct clay forms, each housing a different individuality and destiny. Without even knowing it, your secret memory mourned your loss of each other. While your clay selves wandered for thousands of years through the universe, your longing for each other never faded. This metaphor helps to explain how in the moment of friendship two souls suddenly recognize each other. It could be a meeting on the street, or at a party or a lecture, or just a simple, banal introduction, then suddenly there is a flash of recognition and the embers of kinship glow. There is an awakening between you, a sense of ancient knowing. Love opens the door of ancient recognition. You enter. You come home to each other at last."*
>
> – JOHN O'DONOHUE

I pulled away for a moment and whispered a question. "Do you want me to go and ask God for the gifts lost? I will be happy to go if you want me to? I think they were very important."

"No don't leave. I don't think I could bear it. Don't worry we will do just fine with this one gift."

⁂

From Bulfinch Mythology, here are some references for Prometheus. Prometheus also gave gifts to mankind, but please notice that while Pandora's gifts are spiritual, his are physical.

"Prometheus was one of the Titans, a gigantic race, who inhabited the earth before the creation of man. He, took some of this earth, and kneading it up with water, made man in the image of the gods. He gave him an upright stature, so that while all other animals turn their faces downward, and look to the earth, he raises his to heaven, and gazes on the stars. Athena breathed life into his clay figure.

Prometheus loved man more than the Olympians.

Prometheus, who, with the aid of Minerva, went up to heaven, lit his torch at the chariot of the sun, and brought down fire to man. With this gift man was more than a match for all other animals (sounds like the Holy Spirit).

Prometheus gave the mortals all sorts of gifts: brickwork, woodworking, telling the seasons by the stars, numbers, the alphabet, yoked oxen, carriages, saddles, ships, sails, healing drugs, seer craft, signs in the sky, the mining of precious metals, animal sacrifice, and all art.

Zeus decided to inflict a terrible punishment on both man and Prometheus. He had his servants, Force and Violence, seize Prometheus, take him to the Caucasus Mountains, and chain him to a rock with unbreakable adamantine chains."

⚜

The scene ended and I was with God once again.
"So you see, mankind did not get all the intended gifts. The one gift left in the jar that you could truly give every man, woman, and child was hope—which you did. If you had not been tripped, then every man, woman, and child would have known all the great good gifts of knowledge, wisdom, love, joy, peace, happiness, compassion, empathy, and kindness—plus the many other wonderful pleasures found here in heaven. All the other gifts returned to heaven."

> *"He (the Holy Spirit) not only brings to us divine gifts, but is the author of them and is Himself the supreme gift, who, proceeding from the mutual love of the Father and the Son, is rightly considered and called 'the gift of the most high.'"*
>
> — POPE LEO XIII

"Instead of just having them always, every man and woman who desires a particular gift, such as wisdom, must reach upward toward me for it. Sometimes a gift is granted, but sometimes it is not. It is not impossible to achieve receiving a gift only it can be a long hard struggle. Sometimes the devil will fight an individual to wrestle away a gift. At times, fate will eliminate the possibility of obtaining a particular gift."

> *"In the great moments of existence, when he rises to spiritual freedom, these are the things which every man feels to be real. It is by these for these that he is found willing to live, work, suffer, and die. Love, patriotism, religion, altruism, fame, all belong to the transcendental world. Hence, they partake more of the nature of reality than any fact could do."*
>
> — EVELYN UNDERHILL

"On the same manner shalt thou do with this little word 'God.' Fill thy spirit with ghostly bemeaning of it without any special beholding to any of His works—whether they be good, better, or best of all—bodily or ghostly, or to any virtue that may be wrought in man's soul by any grace; not looking after whether it be meekness or charity, patience or abstinence, hope, faith, soberness, chastity or willful poverty."

— THE CLOUD OF THE UNKNOWING

"Understand that the devil is out in the world promoting his great evils. Sometimes, he succeeds in making men and women think they are really good gifts instead of the evils that they really are. Some of these are closely related to love—envy, jealousy, lust. Pandora, these love-related negative gifts were your downfall. When you return to earth, be careful and guard yourself closely in the future."

Then God asked me, "If you could give mankind any seven gifts now, in the present time of 2002, what gifts would they be?" I looked at the Almighty and tried very hard to put into words what was in my heart—which gifts and why they seemed the most important to me. Understand that I knew that God wanted me to ask, even though He already knew everything I would say. You must ask God for whatever you really need, and then you will receive.

"I would give mankind Faith. Faith is such a wonderful gift, and it is one that gives gifts just for accepting it. It is so needed now that the devil is inspiring terrorism throughout the world."

"Next, I think, Selfless love, which is necessary so that people will put the 'me' generation behind them."

"Charity, of the kind that doesn't advertise itself, but is truly an act of kindness rooted in love, so that more gentleness and kindness will be present to the needy instead of just money."

"Empathy is extremely important because it is always so necessary to understand others' plights.

"Trust, so that all men and women will learn to lean on one another, and to listen and believe their inner voice, which is You, Lord.

"Perseverance and patience are very necessary because almost nothing happens instantly, and there is a lot of work to be done to help make the world a little closer to resembling heaven."

"Well said. When you arise and awaken, I will send you the seven gifts that you requested—the ones that you feel are most needed now—Faith, Selfless love, Charity, Empathy, Trust, Perseverance, and Patience," the Lord responded. He is so gracious.

"Eventually, you will write another book about your life and spiritual journey. In your book you will show others how to achieve guided will, and through the book you will give others the faith to find me as well as the understanding

that they might also seek any gifts which they believe are most needed now.

"You will be one of my candles—to dispel the darkness in a dark time. You will be my candle, and I will be your flame—your inner illumination. Do no feel that you will be alone. I will be lighting many candles to help the world, and you will be one of many. The world needs healing and comfort. I hear all my people's pleas. Mankind will more than stem the current wave of evil and terrorism," said the Divine one.

⚜

Yes, this birth had not been at all difficult nor as frightening as the first. However, it, along with the next five gifts to come, were all going to release horrible spiritual things from inside me—things that I would have to fight to defeat, or have them enter back in.

> *"The Appearance to Mary Magdalene. When he had risen, early on the first day of the week, he appeared first to Mary Magdalene, out of whom he had driven seven demons."*
>
> – MARK 16:9

Almost as soon as the final spiritual labor pain was done, I noticed something strange about the space around me. Searching the meticulously designed, spacious, sumptuous suite, I saw nothing in the air. But I could feel something new. Energy flows passed all around me into the surrounding area. Ominous, bad vibes and negativity that I could sense emerged—like the energy I had released was, for lack of better word, a demon. Releasing his evil into the room in such a way that it permeated into every dark corner was bad enough, but the worst part was revealed in his cold touch. His spiritual touches were like needles, sharp and stabbing. His aura was painful, and my soul was quickly lacerated. His absolute delight seemed to be in my pain and fright. My fear rose quickly; it almost felt like another presence and was so difficult to control, that at any moment I felt like I would just start screaming and not be able to stop. Luckily, I did have my children with me, and I realized that I would not be able to explain uncontrolled screaming to my little ones, so I was able to keep a grip on myself—just barely.

At that point I did not allow myself the thought that the evil I sensed had come from within me. God does protect you from knowledge that you are not yet ready to handle. Knowing that I was fighting a demon on the outside was very different from understanding that this horror had been inside me just seconds ago, that he had been inside my heart and had probably caused me to do all sorts of awful things. Months later, now understanding that the labor has been symbolic of the release of a demon, I would try and piece together what had actually been living in my heart. The first gift that I had asked for was faith, so possibly what I had felt for the three days leading up to the first birth was doubt or disbelief, despair—or that other "D" word—the devil himself.

I could only guess what selfless love would have driven out of my heart. Was it vanity, pride, arrogance, or selfishness? I would never know for sure. They never tell you their names, nor in any way draw attention to themselves. That way you never notice them. Only other people have the ability to see them clearly lurking in your soul. Usually, though, people are too polite to tell you that the demon of arrogance, for instance, is peering out from your eyes.

I would also realize that not only was God giving me the divine gifts that I had asked for, but He delivered me from the spiritual menaces that threatened the gifts. Only Jesus, His Son, as the amazing demon fighter that He is, could drive out whatever was in my soul/spirit that would neutralize or destroy the gift being given. In order for selfless love, my second asked for gift, to be born in my soul and grow to maturity, there needed to be a cleansing. The spiritual labor was the release of the negative energy that had been living inside me. I hadn't realized that I had any demons. How wrong I was. Sin of any kind must produce them.

The seven deadly sins according to the Roman Catholic Faith:

- Pride is excessive belief in one's own abilities that interferes with the individual's recognition of the grace of God. It has been called the sin from which all others arise. Pride is also known as vanity.
- Envy is the desire for others' traits, status, abilities, or situation.
- Gluttony is an inordinate desire to consume more than that which one requires.
- Lust is an inordinate craving for the pleasures of the body.
- Anger is manifested in the individual who spurns love and opts instead for fury. It is also known as wrath.
- Greed is the desire for material wealth or gain, ignoring the realm of the spiritual.
- Sloth is the avoidance of physical or spiritual work

Due to haunt me for the rest of the week, my personal demons were definitely part of the negative spiritual soup simmering in the atmosphere, but they were not the only ones. Several of the events that were about to occur would spark from a must stronger, far more ancient source.

"Terrible are the crafts and wiles which the devil uses to prevent souls

from learning to know themselves and understanding his ways."

— ST. TERESA OF AVILA

"In the afternoon I brought up the unrestful subject of demons! A house is a symbol of the self. But the self is seldom without problems. Our lives are always threatened by disintegration, from within and without, and we can talk about that in the language of demonology. In a weaker interpretation than Antony of the Desert, we can say: your demon is that part of yourself that has become your enemy, shadowing and threatening you always. Your demon is you and not you; it is something disowned, perhaps, out of fear. Because it has the look of not being ours, it has leverage over you; but because it is you, it knows you intimately and never leaves you alone. It peeps through your windows, darkening your moments of joy, crippling your freedom."

— DONAGH O'SHEA

6

The Birth of Charity

Day 4

After a hearty breakfast complements of the hotel, Sam, Patrick, Christina, and I headed for the pristine slopes of Mount Orford in Southern Canada. What a wonderful, strengthening day it was for my soul—the air so beautiful, the snow so white, and the winter scenes so intoxicating. My spirit breathed in the panoramic winter vistas on the mountain that day like a strong gin and tonic. Nature is such a balm for my being.

The lifts lines were light, so the children and I skied every green circle trail on the mountain and quite a few more daring blue ones. As we flew down the trails on our waxed skies, I thought only of God as He appears in His splendid creation—the mountains, the snow and ice, the wind, and the intoxicatingly frigid air. I tried hard to put the thought of the next gift and its eminent arrival out of my mind. I would live only in the moment for today, and enjoy every second.

After the sun set behind the mountain in a cascade of brilliant orange, we decided to call it a day and head back to the hotel. After helping the children take off their ski gear, I jumped into the shower to relax and then dressed in forest green corduroys and a matching sweater for dinner. Since our dinner reservation wasn't for another half hour, I allowed the children to watch TV while I sat down on the ivory brocade chair to do a little reading.

Only a couple of moments had gone by after I had settled into the recliner when I felt again a vortex of energy hovering over my abdomen. Then, like a finger with a lightning bolt on the end or a loaded canon, God sent the next gift, charity, and I felt it penetrate my being. Immediately my spirit became pregnant with its beauty and essence. There was no pain, only a sensation. At the same instant as the gift had penetrated, I heard a small pop—a sudden rush or buzzing—sound in my mind. "How wonderful. She has arrived.

Thank you, dear Lord." Then, "I wondered what beauty she would bring into my life, and what new directions she would take me. An act of kindness derived from love is her formal way of being known. Why, that could be almost anything done from a loving heart," I thought.

Almost as soon as she had been sent it was time to make our way down to the dinner room. Knowing that my spiritual labor contractions would begin shortly, I hoped that I would make it through dinner before they became too uncomfortable. I would have to wait and see.

Seated in the restaurant, amid crisp white linen and sparkling crystal, I read the menu and looked at my real physical children, trying to enjoy the leisure of having dinner prepared by someone else. We read the menu and soon a waitress arrived and took our orders. As we waited for our food, we talked about our wonderful day of skiing—the brand-new memories were taken out for everyone to enjoy.

I particularly wanted to revisit them since I needed the distraction. Although, I was happy to be pregnant with God's divine gift, as the minutes ticked by, I realized that something else was not at all pleased. There was a definite building sensation and an expanding presence coming to my awareness—either from out of the air molecules or from below them. *How did he always know?* I wondered. *Can they see everything here from there?*

As the minutes passed, the ominous, threatening, and enlarging being flooded the spiritual surrounding air with his rancid presence—getting harder and harder to ignore. I looked around. In blissful oblivion, no one else seemed to be aware of his presence. *Oh, how I wish that I, too, could totally ignore him. What or who will it be tonight?* I worried. *What would be sent to fight God's divine Gift? Was it the demon of miserliness, stinginess, blindness, greediness, or indifference?* Hard to tell.

By the time our meals finally came, the labor contractions had begun in earnest. Though I remained seated and casually ate my meal, as the minutes passed I inwardly winced at the intense uneasiness. For some reason I felt totally vulnerable without my cross. Instinctively, I knew that whatever it was would be impossible to defeat without my blessed crucifix. The negative vibes from the spiritual dimension swept over me like six-foot ocean waves, and the anxiety within me compelled me to leave my dinner, go back up to our suite, and retrieve it.

"Sam, I need to go back to our room. There is one thing I really need to get, but as soon as I get it I will come right back," I told my husband.

"Patrick and Christina, enjoy your supper. Mom will be right back," I told my angels.

I made my way out of the restaurant straight to the elevator banks. Taking the steps crossed my mind, but the urgency kept building and so I decided on the elevator as the fastest means to my cross. My rosary beads, ones I had had blessed by St. John Paul the II in St. Peter's Square on my honeymoon and which I had begun wearing around my neck as protection, stung and burned my flesh—especially the medallion of the Pope's face. I was sure that I would forever carry his face branded on the skin between my breasts. I had to remind myself that what I was feeling was spiritual and not physical—that my spirit was alive and could feel again.

As I waited at the elevator bank, impatiently tapping my foot and pacing frantically back and forth, my hair rose on the back of my neck and waves of dread washed over me. My stomach churned and my senses warned me that this time instead of a demon it was the devil himself right at my heels. The ding of the elevator startled me as my mind raced. The doors opened, releasing other casually dressed vacationers into the lobby. As soon as the last one exited, I jumped in. Hitting the button repeatedly to the fourth floor, I willed the doors to close, and the elevator began its climb upward.

It was then that it hit me, dawning on my awareness like a spiritual solar eclipse, that I was alone in this enclosed space with the archenemy. I almost cursed myself aloud. "How stupid. What if the elevator broke down," I thought. "You will be trapped indefinitely with him until a repairperson is summoned. You should have made a bolt to the stairs," I sharply reprimanded myself. Then I reminded myself that stairways are also very lonely places. My fear was rising to a dreadful level adding to the thick, negative spiritual energy. "Oh, what does it matter? Dear Lord, just get me to my crucifix on time." To distract myself I frantically jabbed the button praying to Jesus to help me reach my room as fast as possible.

Praise God, the elevator did function normally, and what had seemed to take an eternity in truth only lasted about thirty earthly seconds. As the elevator hit the floor, sank into its spot, and the doors opened, I turned to start down the corridor. And I realized for the first time just how long this hallway was—why, it appeared to have been at least a quarter mile long from my frenzied vantage point, and very unfortunately, our room was at the very end.

When the knowledge of my distant cross dawned, immense waves of mind-numbing terror washed over me. I doubted that I could tolerate this horror for another second. But since I had no choice, as rapidly as I could, I raced down the sand brown carpet, down the infinite semi-dark corridor papered by the hotel decorator in a floral, paisley Persian blue design.

When I was about halfway down the corridor, and just as I was beginning to feel hopeful that I would actually get to my cross, the being at my heels begin using his negativity as an energy force, pulling me backwards. His counter energy acted like a spiritual vacuum cleaner, sucking me back into the dark and away from the Light. My own spirit began bending and stretching backward like I was a rubber band that someone was stretching. My spirit was beginning to halt, and my physical progress began to slow. Like a greedy miser, ready to snatch God's gift away with both hands, he sought to pull it out of my spirit.

Then as if that wasn't bad enough, the devil began feeding me its own despair, misery, and futility. Flung like poison darts into my soul, his thoughts flew into my mind and penetrated my consciousness. I cannot bear to remember them—polluted, repulsive, and petrifying. The stuff nightmares are made of.

Realizing that I desperately needed help, I prayed to Jesus. "Jesus, HELP. This hallway is so long, I don't know if I am going to make it." Mentally, I envisioned my beautiful cross from St. Anne De Beaupre, which Father had blessed, so near, yet so far. In answer to my prayer, help arrived. Something like a shield descended and blocked the void and the force. It was just enough.

With shaking hands, I inserted the key in the lock and pushed open the heavy, wooden door. I felt faint, barely able to walk, and overcome by the intensity of my awareness. Quickly, I scanned the room as my eyes latched onto my wooden holy weapon. Without another thought I lunged for it, and instantly the spiritual storm passed—leaving me in a spiritual calm. Taking deep breaths, and leaning against the closed door for a moment, I gathered myself together. Blessings emitted from its surface. With resolve and my chin in the air, I calmly walked back to the restaurant with my crucifix tucked away in my black leather purse. I sat back at the table and tried to finish some of the dinner that I was forced to abandon. Sam, upon looking at my face, asked with a certain concern in his voice, "Are you alright? You look pale."

"Yes, I am just fine. Thanks. I got what I needed," I softly answered him. After five minutes, I abandoned any attempt at eating. The birth was eminent, the contractions were building, the gift was about to be born, and I knew that I must go back to the room and lay down to have the birth.

"Patrick and Christina, are you done?" I asked them.

They answered, "Yes."

"Good, let's go back to the room, and you can watch some T.V. OK?" Then I turned to my husband. "Sam, I don't feel really well; I think I am going to lie down." The three of us took the same walk back to the room I had just left, leaving Sam to pay the bill.

Normally, I would have enjoyed staying in such a beautiful accommodation as night progressed, however, I found myself barely able to stand it. The relatively fast one and one-half hour labor had finished in a strong almost fluid feeling of spiritual release. Having already fought the archenemy, now I wondered what evil had been released from my spirit—evil that I had allowed to live in my heart that would try to kill charity. That was the worst, knowing that I had things in my own heart that had killed other gifts that God sent through the years. I accepted my fate and worked to strengthen my resolve because the dark side would be present, strong, and active all evening long, and I knew that it would be able to affect everyone in the room—not just me.

The first signs appeared as I was putting the children to bed, and they got into a sibling squabble. Then Sam got into the act, his fury instantly rising in response to them. I stood back from the scene, looking at it from a different perspective. I thought back to all their childish fighting—aggression, hitting, neediness, clinginess, fear, and screaming—wondering how influential the devil was in even these childish things. Not just in my children's lives, but in all of us.

How able he is to unharness all that is negative in us and unleash it into the world we live in and through the people around us. Intuitively, I understood as I watched my family yelling at each other that I must not show or even feel negative emotions or display them now. Anger, rage, and frustration were out of the question. I knew I must slam the door on all these negative emotions to defeat him. It was too soon after the birth of the gift and the release of the demon; he was lurking and looking for a way back into my heart. Giving in to yelling over their petty issues would allow him access. The devil and I were in some kind of a battle. A battle I could only win by clinging onto the Savior, not just in the tangible symbols of things like crosses and rosary beads, but in all the beautiful ways He taught us to live—the gospels and His actual words.

> "Don't let anger get the smallest foothold in your heart. Exclude absolutely, as Augustine advises, even its slightest presence, however justified and reasonable it may seem. For once it gets into your heart it is hard to uproot. A mote rapidly becomes a beam. It will stay and harden into hatred. Constantly fed by imaginings and delusions, it will become all but impossible to set yourself free of it. As soon as you are aware of having given into anger or whatever, repair your mistake immediately with an act of kindness to the person you have hurt. The best cure for anger is an immediate act of gentleness."
>
> – ST. FRANCIS DE SALES

> "Then the dragon became angry with the woman and went off to wage war against the rest of her offspring, those who keep God's commandments and bear witness to Jesus."
>
> – REVELATIONS 12:17

"God gives these souls the keenest desire not to displease Him in any respect whatsoever, (the gift of Fear of the Lord) however trivial, or to commit so much as an imperfection if they can avoid doing so. For this reason alone, if for no other, the soul would like to flee from other people, and greatly envies those who lived, or have lived, in deserts."

— ST. TERESA OF AVILA

"Manual For Conducting Truth Encounters" on the Demon Possession Web site— "We want to make sure that what is revealed is from the Holy Spirit, and not the product of our suggestions. Another thought to keep in mind is that 'things revealed, such as a spirit of anger could be an attitude of anger (or harbored sin of anger), or a literal spirit of anger that we've allowed to oppress us.'"

During that long Sunday night into Monday, as I lay in bed, I tried to gather my strength. I thought deeply. The battle and my awareness of the spiritual reality of evil tonight had been horrible. No longer just living in the physical realm and oblivious to the other spiritual one, now I seemed to be caught between them in a place of great tension, stretched to the breaking point not totally in either place. The spiritual plane had been far stronger during the last week than the physical realm.

For the rest of the night I felt whatever evil presence had been released hanging around me all night long. Even as I lay in the king-sized bed with Sam loudly snoring at my side, I could feel its presence all around me, touching me, running its hands over me, occasionally stabbing me, and reminding me that entry into my spirit was possible—that charity, only just beginning to live, could be snuffed out. I shuddered contemplating such a horrible possibility.

I intensely disliked that the other side had access to me, and I could not do anything to stop its bitter caresses. I was defenseless against it. It could see as well as touch me—a physical being. But I could not do likewise—I could not see or touch it. Not that I would ever want to do either thing. God created His angels with spiritual bodies, and spiritual bodies are a higher form of existence. But just then it did feel very unfair that the "higher form of existence" of both angels and demons should have such an advantage. I was a spiritual "Helen Keller" with the added disability of not being able to feel them. I might have been spiritually blind, deaf, and dumb, but I could sense them.

"When the good angel permits the devil to gain this advantage of assailing the soul with this spiritual horror, he does it to purify the soul and to prepare it by means of this spiritual vigil for some great spiritual favour and festival which he desires to grant it, for he never mortifies save to give life, nor humbles save to exalt." - St. John of the Cross

To distract myself, I read the Bible and I prayed to God. After only three gifts—faith, selfless love, and charity—I was nearing the end of my rope. I hadn't a clue how I would live through the next four, and whatever subsequent evil planned to attack me. I was terrified and doubted that I had the strength to get through the next nights. In the gospels, Jesus tells us that we should only live for today, that today has more than enough cares by itself—how very, very wise this advice is and how true. I realized, though, that possibly for the rest of this week I may need to live minute by minute, and hour by hour. Thinking about the whole day and night was immensely overwhelming.

"Perhaps," I said to God, "You have chosen the wrong woman to bring Your message and gifts to the world, my Lord. Oh, dearest, I don't know if I can get through the rest. Empathy, trust, patience, and perseverance are still to go. How am I to survive? Please help me."

And He did. A memory from my talk with Father Raffey just last week surfaced. Father had said that during times of troubles, he always found the Psalms especially soothing and strengthening. Turning the pages of my leather-bound Bible, my eyes fell on the very first of the Psalms. From that one, I continued on to the end of that book, and as I read I began to understand why Father had particularly recommended them for me.

Attributed to King David, I could well imagine that he had written them down in between frays with various enemies. Many seemed to spring from the depths of his soul when he was feeling the need of God's protection. In the deepest, darkest part of that night, they inspired me to keep placing one foot in front of the other.

> "As the ordinary man is the meeting-place between two stages of reality—the sense-world and the world of spiritual life—so the mystic, standing head and shoulders above ordinary men, is again the meeting-place between the two orders. Or if you like it better, he is able to perceive and react to reality under two modes."
> — EVELYN UNDERHILL

Psalm 3

Threatened but Trusting

How many are my foes, Lord!
How many rise against me!
How many say of me,
"God will not save that one."
But you, Lord, are a shield around me;
My glory, you keep my head high.

Whenever I cried out to the Lord,
I was answered from the holy mountain.

Whenever I lay down and slept,
The Lord preserved me to rise again.
I do not fear, then, thousands of people
Arrayed against me on every side.

Arise, Lord! Save me, my God!
You will shatter the jaws of all my foes:
You will break the teeth of the wicked.
Safety comes from the Lord!
Your blessing for your people!

As dawn filtered through the gauzy white fabric of the curtains, with a little help from above I turned the corner between despair and hope. A great surge of delight welled up in my soul, and my early morning joy started to return. I dismissed all thoughts of the future and dark presences in the night and called forth thoughts and remembrances of the immense blessing of the divine gifts that God was bestowing, and the awe and wonder that He loved me enough to help me overcome whatever had been burdening me.

Because the gifts had come in the form of spiritual pregnancies, I let my mind envision them all as babies—my own divine cherubs. How I wished that I could see what they looked like. Were the "girl gifts" of faith, selfless love, charity, and empathy wrapped up with silver angelic wrapping paper and pretty pink bows? What about the "boy gifts" of trust, patience, and perseverance? Were they chubby baby blue gifts with suspenders and patches instead of bows?

Obviously, the devil was really furious over these divine gifts. I could only think that he was trying his best to scare me to death and to interfere and take away all my joy in God's amazing way of bestowing them on me. How creative and loving God had demonstrated Himself to be. Imagine God giving birth to the gifts that I had asked Him for in my book *Pandora's Story* in my very soul. It was miraculous!

Months later I would reread the listing of the seven spiritual gifts that the Holy Spirit bestows on Jesus' close followers to arm them for all the difficulties of living in the physical world, but also simultaneously dwelling in the spiritual dimension. I had not asked God for these particular gifts, but then I remembered that I had already received them during the sacrament of confirmation when I was thirteen. As the week went by, I noticed some of these long-buried gifts emerging from under the pile of rubbish, which my life's sins had covered and trampled.

The Novena of the Seven Gifts, Second Day—The Gift of Fear: "The gift of Fear fills us with a sovereign respect for God, and makes us dread nothing so much as to offend Him by sin. It is a fear that arises, not from the thought of hell, but from sentiments of reverence and filial submission to our heavenly Father. It is the fear that is the beginning of wisdom, detaching us from worldly pleasures that could in any way separate us from God. They that fear the Lord will prepare their hearts, and in His sight will sanctify their souls."

The Third Day—The Gift of Piety: "The gift of Piety begets in our hearts a filial affection for God as our most loving Father. It inspires us to love and respect for His sake persons and things consecrated to Him as well as those who are vested with His authority. His Blessed Mother and the Saints, the Church and its visible Head, our parents and superiors, our country, and its rulers. He who is filled with the gift of Piety finds the practice of his religion, not a burdensome duty, but a delightful service. Where there is love, there is not labor."

The Fourth Day—The Gift of Fortitude: "By the gift of Fortitude the soul is strengthened against natural fear, and supported to the end in the performance of duty. Fortitude imparts to the will an impulse and energy which move it to undertake without hesitancy the more arduous tasks, to face dangers, to trample under foot human respect, and to endure without complaint the slow martyrdom of even lifelong tribulation. He that shall persevere unto the end, he shall be saved."

The Fifth Day—The Gift of Knowledge: "The gift of Knowledge enables the soul to evaluate created things at their true worth—in their relation to God. Knowledge unmasks the pretense of creatures, reveals their emptiness, and points out their own true purpose as instruments in the service of God. It shows us the loving care of God even in adversity, and directs us to glorify Him in every circumstance of life. Guided by its light, we put first things first, and prize the friendship of God beyond all else. Knowledge is a fountain of life to him that possesseth it."

The Sixth Day—The Gift of Understanding: "Understanding, as a gift of the Holy Spirit, helps us to grasp the meaning of the truths of our holy religion. By faith we know them, but by Understanding we learn to appreciate and relish them. It enables us to penetrate the inner meaning of revealed truths and through them to be quickened to newness of life. Our faith ceases to be sterile and inactive, but inspires a mode of life that bears eloquent testimony to the faith that is in us; we begin to 'walk worthy of God in all things pleasing, and increasing in the knowledge of God.'"

The Seventh Day—The Gift of Counsel: "The gift of counsel endows the soul with supernatural prudence, enabling it to judge promptly and rightly what must be done, especially in difficult circumstances. Counsel applies the principles furnished by Knowledge and Understanding to the innumerable concrete cases that confront us in the course of daily duty as parents, teachers, public servants, and Christian citizens. Counsel is supernatural common sense, a priceless treasure in the quest of salvation."

The Eighth Day—The Gift of Wisdom: "Embodying all the other gifts, as charity embraces all the other virtues. Wisdom is the most perfect of all gifts. Of wisdom it is written 'all good things came to me with her, and innumerable riches through her hands.' It is the gift of Wisdom that strengthens our faith, fortifies hope, perfects charity, and promotes the practice of virtue in the highest degree. Wisdom enlightens the mind to discern and relish things divine, in the appreciation of which earthly joys lose their savor, whilst the Cross of Christ yields a divine sweetness according to the words of the Savior."

There are several more "seven-gift listings" that holy souls have asked for and been given from the Spirit of Love.

"The Seven Contrary Virtues: Humility, kindness, abstinence, chastity, patience, liberality, diligence.

"The Seven Heavenly Virtues: Faith, hope, charity, fortitude, justice, temperance, prudence.

"The Seven Corporal Works of Mercy: Feed the hungry, give drink to the thirsty, give shelter to strangers, clothe the naked, visit the sick, minister to prisoners, and bury the dead."

God seems to give everything in seven. I remembered how God had guided me to ask for seven gifts while I had been writing *Pandora's Story*. He really loves that number. Much later I would wonder how many things of seven there were in the Book of Revelations. I was astonished at how many. Open any bible and see for yourself.

⚜

Eventually, though exhausted from the day's skiing, the birth and spiritual battles, the reading and endless circling questions in my mind, God had pity on me and lulled me to sleep.

7

A Cloud of Empathy

Day 5
At around six o'clock the following morning, with only two or so hours of sleep, I got up out of bed, walked over to the door of the balcony, and opened it. The new day had arrived and I needed to face it. Leaning over the railing and looking at the early morning sky, I absorbed the rarified, cold Canadian mountain air and its freshness. It brought peace, healing, and strength.

After everyone was up, showered, and dressed, my family and I enjoyed another wonderful breakfast at the hotel's restaurant on the main floor. I tasted and thanked God for every morsel as I chewed, understanding now more than ever before that every good thing we are given in this life is a blessing. After breakfast, we felt ready to hit the slopes, so we packed up our various ski gear and headed for the minivan. We were venturing to a new mountain about an hour away called Owl's Head.

When we were fifteen minutes from the mountain, I again received the feeling of a vortex of energy going into my midsection. Number four was on the way. But this time God had decided to use the bright hours of day instead of the night, and I was so grateful. I was so much stronger in the daytime and the evil one was weaker—although certainly I could feel him all around. But the day is always an easier time for a battle of this nature, and I thanked God with all my heart for giving me this gift in the day. *Empathy, welcome to the world,* I thought. She is a such a tremendous gift with her great depth of understanding into how everyone feels.

When we arrived at the mountain, we unloaded the car and trekked to the ski lodge. My contractions were mild, and although I was uncomfortable, I could bear them easily while I was walking, riding the chairlift, and even skiing down the mountain. I received guidance to stay in the light as the contractions came on, so I skied only in the bright beauty of the sunshine. As the children skied down the slope ahead of me, the snow blew up from the back of their skies and the sunlight hit the crystal prisms and produced beautiful snow rainbows.

My daughter, Christina, had lately been very moody and unhappy—possibly because she sensed her mother going through some kind of emotional and spiritual upheaval. But that morning as I spiritually labored while skiing down easy, breezy, green-circle trails with her, she also seemed to get some part of the divine gift that God had sent. She made several remarks that were rather stunning in their depth of empathy and understanding toward several strangers and even her dad, which were totally uncharacteristic of her ten-year-old self. I marveled in amazement that her spirit was absorbing some of God's gift, much like a rose's perfume fills an entire room, and even if those roses were not sent to you, you can still enjoy and appreciate them. So it is with empathy. In fact, the gift of empathy must be more of an airy, cloudy spiritual gift. For the gift had the ability to give everyone who only passed by me its lovely essence, as you will see.

My final contraction and the spiritual release came while I was in the line for the ski lift. We were standing in full, strong sunlight, so I was able to follow God's advice. It was about half past eleven. That was so easy, I thought. I was over the hump. Suddenly I had great hope that I would persevere; only three left!

As the morning passed into afternoon, we took a Canadian-style lunch break, which means French, elegant, with a wonderful assortment of meal and dessert choices, and even wine if one desires. Then we returned to the ski mountain. As we rode up the chairlifts and got off at the top of the mountain, my spirit sang. I thought of Moses with the burning bush on the top of Mount Sinai, and of course my Lord during His transfiguration with Peter and John. And as we skied down, I sang John Denver's "Rocky Mountain High" (slightly altered to fit my vocal range) until the children were tossing me embarrassed looks over their shoulders. I didn't need to worry about Sam. He was far upslope looking down on us. The children were much too fast for him.

> She was born in the winter of her 42nd year
> Coming home to a place she'd never been before
> She left yesterday behind her; you might say she was born again
> You might say she found a key for every door
>
> When she first came to the mountains her life was far away
> On the road and hanging by a song
> But the string's already broken and she doesn't really care
> It keeps changing' fast and it don't last for long

And the Southern Canadian rocky mountain high
I've seen it raining' fire in the sky
The shadow from the starlight is softer than a lullaby
Rocky Mountain High Hi Hi Hi

She climbed cathedral mountains, she saw silver clouds below
She saw everything as far as you can see
And they say that she got crazy once and she tried to touch the sun
And she lost a friend but kept his memory

Now she walks in quiet solitude the forest and the streams
Seeking grace in every step she takes
Her sight has turned inside herself to try and understand
The serenity of a clear blue mountain lake

And the Southern Canadian rocky mountain high
I've seen it rainin' fire in the sky
You can talk to God and listen to the casual reply
Rocky Mountain High Hi Hi Hi

Now her life is full of wonder but her heart still knows some fear
Of the simple thing she cannot comprehend

And the Southern Canadian rocky mountain high
I've seen it rainin' fire in the sky
You can talk to God and listen to the casual reply
Rocky Mountain High Hi Hi Hi

The sun and God's influence was very strong until after the sun descended from its overhead spot to a place on the other side of the mountain. Then my euphoria began to dissipate, and for the rest of the afternoon, just as with the other gifts, I battled with unseen energy forces, which seemed to strengthen considerably whenever I was in the shadows of the surrounding forest or shaded by rocky overpasses on the chairlift. When the sun could no longer be seen as I skied down the mountain, I suddenly sensed a hitchhiker. He was standing on the back of my skies holding onto me for dear life all the way down the ski slope. As soon as I realized that he was camped out in this rather tenuous spot, I decided to have a little fun and give him the ride of his life. This was the first spark of humor over my bizarre situation that I had felt. I was so happy to see it return that I began thinking of all sorts of fun things I could do to this particular demon.

First I tried swerving drastic rights and lefts, then I purposely detoured over a few small ski jumps and fell into some deep snowdrifts to try and freeze him out. I must admit I did get a little satisfaction knowing that he must really hate the ice and cold since it is not his natural element. It must be a form of torture for a devil to be freezing on a ski mountain on a crystal, clear day in February. I heartily hoped that the devil and all his minion of demons suffered mightily for what he had been doing to me, and what he had inspired others to do on Sept 11th. Of course, I had conveniently forgotten that a spirit would feel none of these things, but on this day thinking those thoughts seem ed to help me cope.

In my head I talked to the demon while I skied. Then I made a mistake. I told him that I would make a bargain with him not to write a book about my encounters with him, if only he would leave me alone. After I had that thought another raced into my head. "It is always a mistake to make any bargain with a demon," I heard a gentle voice say inside my head. My guardian angel must have decided that I needed a small bit of advice. But the demon wasn't having any part of my bargains anyway, because he was with me on those skies for the rest of the afternoon. All in all it was a fun day despite all the spiritual interference the other side tried to pull. Just being in a winter wonderland, gliding down snowy hills and watching my children have a wonderful time was heavenly for me, and my heart was happy despite the demons.

As I have mentioned, it would not be for several months that I would really understand what was happening to me—when the Lord inspired an unbelievable, uncontrollable urge to read everything that I could get my hands on that related to the spiritual life, specifically mysticism—so that day I did not have a very good idea of how I should attack the evil spirits I sensed. All I knew was that I had to live in the present and deal with the present using the tools I had—waiting and praying for the time when I would get through the negative side of these gifts. I would never give up loving the Lord. My faith, always strong and loving, was now unshakeable no matter what shadowy, evil spirit might emerge next. I believed in Jesus' incredible power absolutely.

> *"What are we to do with our demons after we have seen the whites of their eyes? Well, let's not be in too much of a hurry. To look at them is already an act of great courage. Yes, but what then? Let your meditation tell you. Study how the devil's work in you can be repaired. 'Don't be afraid.' Anthony kept repeating, you have much on your side. The demon is always solemn, humourless; he is the spirit of gravity, the enemy of joy, or music, he is the spoiler the maker of discord. But make him sing! It will drive him out of his mind ... or rather, out of your mind!"*
>
> — DONAGH O'SHEA, OP

On the drive home, though, the other side was a bit more successful than they had been on the mountain. But the havoc they inspired was not going to be the ultimate final word. In fact, God was going to use the very thing they pulled off—hoping to bring me despair. Instead, probably infuriating those underworld spirits, the Lord used the incident to show how He can bring something very beautiful out of even trying circumstances. After all, He is the master of the universe and the evil ones really have only limited power.

As we approached the small town where our hotel was located, Sam took a wrong turn and while making a U-turn ended up in what we thought was a snowbank. Ordinarily, I would have been angry, but I remembered that the devil would only be too delighted if I gave rise to any emotion, so I held my tongue and smiled sweetly at Sam as I tried to help him free the car. This would eventually prove impossible, because while it looked like an innocent snowbank, it was really a huge mound of snow over a six-foot drop off the road and the tire was suspended in midair with nothing beneath it to grip.

There we were in the frozen Canadian wilderness in zero and dropping temperatures on a lonely road as the evening approached in a disabled vehicle with no cell phone to call for help. Sounds disastrous, doesn't it? Instead, though, it turned out to be one of the more heart-warming memories of that fateful ski trip. The thought of it still brings joy to my heart because it proves that all things work together for the good of those who love God.

Empathy, as I mentioned, emanated off my spirit in cloud-like waves, and everyone, I mean *everyone*, who drove by our car that evening stopped to try and help. It was a truly remarkable display of this divine gift.

The first couple to stop had five people in the car—two kids, a grandparent, and husband and wife. They were on their way back after several hours spent in the emergency room at a local hospital. Their son had had a skiing accident that morning and had broken his arm. He was sitting in the car all bundled up. The husband got out first and came over to my husband to talk over possible ways to get the car out. Then his wife came over and talked with me. She could sense that I needed a woman's support, and so even though they had a very trying day themselves, they stayed with us and offered assistance.

They spent at least two hours with us, talking and staying with us, trying to get us out of the snowbank. I could not ever think of a time when I had seen total strangers show so much empathy. In their situation, after a long wait at the hospital, I doubted very much (to my shame) if I would even have stopped, and here they were taking on our problem as if it were their own.

Many others also saw us, pulled over, and offered help. For a while there were five or six strong men trying to lift the wheel back onto something solid. We had been stuck in different situations before, and we had always been lucky enough to have at least one person stop and offer help. But that late afternoon, which stretched into early evening, at least thirty-five people stopped to ask us if we needed help; some stayed longer than others. But in the end, no amount of shoveling, rocking the car (putting the engine continuously into forward and then reverse), or just plain old brute human pushing would propel us out of the ditch, and we finally used a friendly stranger's cell phone to call a tow truck.

During the several hours that this played out, I grew anxious and tried to hide my fear. I was pretty upset about being out on a cold Canadian road with two tired, unhappy children in the middle of nowhere as dusk smothered us with darkness. But God in His loving caring way provided assistance through the many people who had come by. Instead of the expected indifference that most would have shown, they revealed only their best truest selves. It was the first time I could ever recall that I vividly understood how God might call other people's hearts to respond in ways that would not have been natural given the circumstances when He wanted to show His loving providence. In my heart I knew that God sent all those lovely people as support. By no means are all God's gifts on the supernatural level.

•

8

Distrust Takes the Wheel

Day 6

Very early the next morning, around four o'clock, I again felt the now familiar feeling of the energy vortex to my lower abdomen—God's gift was on its way. God was really keeping me on my toes as he mixed up all the times when He sent the gifts. I believe that He did this purposefully so that my anxiety level would be lower, since I would not be prone to anticipating His next move. It later occurred to me that perhaps He was trying to thwart or hinder the devil.

It was a very easy birth, but I could sense that this gift was very large, feeling like it could be a boy baby gift. The contractions and birth were done by the time any of the kids or Sam even stirred in their beds. That was a great gift in itself. I now felt incredibly free for the rest of the day—knowing that God was probably not going to send another today. With number five, trust, here, I began to believe I might live and even get some use out of these incredible, divine gifts after all. On the way up the mountain, I noticed a very unusual cloud formation that held my gaze. This two-pronged cloud had long finger-pointed ends. I knew in my gut that it was important, but I couldn't figure out why. (As I write this now, four years later, I know that the cloud was sent by God, the Father, to illustrate that the Holy Spirit is really His own fingers. It was the finger of God who touched my spirit and sent that vortex of energy I felt just before the labor began. Often, in the past, saints have described the Holy Spirit as God's finger in the world.)

The day was again a beautiful, clear one. We chose to ski at a different resort area that day at a spot called Sutton Mountain. Like the day before, the demon of the day spent all day long freezing on the back of my ski tips. I am sure that he didn't enjoy the majestic views of the rolling hills covered with snow and the perfect robin-egg blue sky splashed with marshmallow fluffy cumulous clouds. Nor did he appreciate the wonderful crunch of the newly packed powder, or the happiness on my children's precious faces. He was really missing out. Some days truly are like heaven on earth. Of course, when did a demon ever enjoy heaven?

While we escalated up the mountain on the chairlifts, this one became particularly strong. As soon as the chairlift rose above the slope by over twenty feet, I could feel it come up from under the seat of the chair, under my backside, and give a mighty spiritual push, which seemed to actually lift me from my seat by an inch or two. Good thing I was wedged in tightly on the four-man quad with my husband and two children, as well as secured by the safety bar holding me in place. Its plan was very easy to figure out—it was trying its best to push me off onto the frozen, rocky ravines below. It was trying its best to bring about my accidental death. Even though it was not successful (of course God would never have allowed it to win here), it nevertheless jabbed me and ran icy ghost fingers up my legs, strokes I could feel even through my long thermal underwear and ski pants.

Even with you-know-who shadowing my every move, it was still a very wonderful, near-perfect skiing day, and the kids, Sam, and I enjoyed ourselves tremendously. On the way home that night, though, I did a very foolish thing. I guess I was feeling so good after that day that I let my guard slip. After all, even though the dark side had tried, nothing, not even a bad fall, had happened. If there is any advice I would give to someone experiencing life in the unbelievably supernatural way that I was, it is not to let your guard down. I offered to drive home while Sam, with exhaustion etched in his weathered face, took a nap. (I can't imagine why he was so tired! But then perhaps he was being put to sleep by the evil side for his own purposes).

Our hotel was about an hour away, but I was sure it would be a breeze, since I was wide awake. However, as soon as I got comfortably settled into the driver's seat and exited the small access road onto the highway, I felt the devil become increasingly strong. The energy swirled so strongly that I could almost visualize its waves, much like you can see waves of heat come off sun-baked pavement on a hot summer's day. Fighting fear, which threatened to become panic almost every mile of the drive, I don't know why I didn't wake up Sam to take the wheel, but I guess I just wanted to feel that I was still in control; plus, I did trust God to get us there. I prayed fervently throughout the entire ride home—Our Fathers, Hail Marys, Glory Bes, Acts of Contrition, and anything that came to mind.

When we were within ten to fifteen minutes of the hotel, I could feel the steering wheel drift on its own. I kept my hands locked on it, trying with all my might to counter whatever I felt to do an immediate correction. I didn't want to scare the kids, and Sam slumbered in his seat. Locked in a battle with the devil over the steering wheel, I didn't figure out right away that the gas pedal on the car was also moving without my pressing it. The devil was trying his best to turn trust into distrust before twenty-four hours of receiving the gift.

Using the brake an awful lot more than would have been normal on a highway drive, I did eventually win in the end. As we drove up the driveway to the hotel, I praised God mightily, thanking Him for all the strength He had sent. As you might guess, I was rather shaky as I exited the car and nearly collapsed as my knees gave way. But luckily I was able to pick myself up before anyone could notice.

> *"Do on then, and travail fast awhile, I pray thee, and suffer meekly the pain if thou mayest not soon win to these arts. For truly it is thy purgatory, and then when thy pain is all passed and thy devices be given of God, and graciously gotten in custom; then it is no doubt to me that thou are cleansed not only of sin, but also of the pain of sin."*
>
> — THE CLOUD OF THE UNKNOWING

9

Patience/Perseverance And
Fear Of The Lord

Day 7

In the early morning hours of Wednesday, February 20th, 2002, as I lay in the luxurious king-sized bed surrounded by fine linen sheets snuggled under an ivory down comforter, I sensed a spiritual presence in the bed with Sam and I. Instinctively, I knew that the presence wanted entrance to me. The spirit was asking my permission. What was really odd was that this presence didn't seem bad. I couldn't sense the usual negative vibes and pins-and-needles sensation that had been prevalent with the other demons, nor the evil my intuition perceived in the past week. In fact, I wasn't sure, but I thought it might have been the Holy Spirit or at least an angel or good spirit. I talked to it mind to mind. It seemed to be friendly, but I didn't want to chance being deceived by the devil again, so I told the spirit that it would have to wait until morning. And anything it wanted to do would have to be done through the cross, which was going to be on top of my stomach.

Two hours later, at approximately six o'clock as the dawn peeked its yellow head from the bottom of the landscape as I could see it through the sheer curtain panels, I consented to what the spirit proposed. I turned off the light that was on and waited patiently. (Never give the devil an opportunity like this. If you invite him in, he will be happy to come whether or not a cross is on top. Once permission is granted, the cross is overcome.)

I didn't have long to wait. I felt again the feeling of fullness between my legs, and then the most incredible feeling of heat. I seemed to be getting burned from the inside out. I put up with the feeling for about a minute when I realized that, of course, I had been deceived. It was again the devil wearing sheep's clothing. Very fearful that I had made a dreadful mistake, I turned the light back on and grabbed my Bible and read the Psalms continuously to ease my fear.

That was my impression at the time, but later I realized that I was wrong. The feeling of fire is of God and the Holy Spirit. The feeling of coldness is of the other side. God is warmth, fire, light; and the devil is the opposite. I know now that this was the Holy Spirit with His purifying fire. He had come to give me a charismatic gift called the fear of the Lord. Fear of the Lord is given to inspire a repellant feeling about sin and offending God. This trial had been sent for a special purpose to give me an extra dose of this gift before I received the last two gifts I had asked for: perseverance and patience. Since by my many past sins I had shown the Lord that I didn't have enough of this grace given at my confirmation, He sent me an extra dose—like a giant injection into my spirit. It was not given to make me fear God, but only fear offending Him.

> *"The fear of the Lord is glory and exultation, and gladness and a crown of rejoicing."*
>
> — (SIR 1:11)

> *"From this there arises another and a second benefit, which is that the soul habitually has remembrance of God, with fear and dread of back-sliding upon the spiritual road, as has been said. This is a great benefit, and not one of the least that results from this aridity and purgation."*
>
> — ST. JOHN OF THE CROSS

Within a half hour, I felt the power of the Lord descend and touch my abdomen. The sixth baby gift of perseverance was born in an hour. Then unbelievably, I felt the finger of the Lord with its electric spiral vortex energy touch the skin over my uterus and send the final gift, patience. As I labored, I realized that the last two gifts I had asked for were twins. Delivered one after the other, they would walk hand in hand and help me in many a crisis. With perseverance I would never lose my faith and would have the strength to overcome obstacles with constant striving. And with patience I would be able to wait for others and events to happen in their own eternal time.

"To those who by the mercy of God have overcome in these combats, and by dint of perseverance have entered the third Mansions, what shall we say but 'Blessed is the man that feareth the Lord'? We shall certainly be right in calling such a man blessed, for, unless he turns back, he is, so far as we can tell, on the straight road to salvation." – St. Teresa of Avila

> *"We were told to ask God to give us the strength we needed to stay in religious life. Looking back on this practice, I see a positive side: praying for perseverance reminded us that perseverance was, indeed, a gift from God."*
>
> — MELANNIE SVOBODA, SND

"That the saying of Isaias may be fulfilled: 'In Thy sight, O Lord, we have conceived, and we have been as in the pangs of labour, and we have brought forth the spirit of salvation.'"

— ST. JOHN OF THE CROSS

"And those who combine the things which Allah has ordered to be joined (truth with virtue, prayer with charity, and patience with perseverance) hold their Lord in respect and fear and ever terrible penalty (if they do wrong)."

— SURA 63 AR-RAID

After I delivered the twin gifts, I lay in bed utterly overjoyed and praised the Lord. Even though my lower spiritual abdomen and uterus ached, just imagine laboring and delivering seven babies in seven days. I was so thrilled my heart sang a joyous Alleluia. I had made it. I was sure I was past most of the worst of my spiritual difficulties. (Yes, the awakening was about to come to a close, but it would actually be a year and a half before the entire remaking of my heart was complete and the spiritual effects began to decrease.)

"When this house of sensuality was now at rest—that is, was mortified—its passions being quenched and its desires put to rest and lulled to sleep by means of this blessed night of purgation of sense. It is set out on a road called the way of illumination or of infused contemplation, wherein God Himself feeds and refreshes the soul, without meditation, or the soul's active help." – St. John of the Cross

"Peace does not mean living without pain. You lose peace not when you are trouble free, but when you cease to be dependent on God and fail in your duties. You must expect pain and not be disturbed by it. Our set ways of doing things are not let go of easily. They give way to the 'new person' in God with great reluctance. Don't be disturbed. You have not lost favor with God."

— ST. FRANCIS DE SALES

We had a leisurely morning packing up the room before eating a fattening but satisfying breakfast from the buffet spread out on the crisp white linen— eggs Benedict, home fries, bacon, fresh fruit, muffins, and Danish. I don't think I missed a single item. Yesterday had been our last day skiing, and today we had to drive home. Right before we left the room, I took a good look around. This room would live in my memory forever, and I would never forget how it looked and how I felt living through the delivery of God's gifts. In a way I looked forward to going home, but I had large dose of anxiety over sleeping in our bedroom, so I tried not to think about it. Instead, I would look forward to the long drive—reading my novel and working on my angel embroidery.

"How very many are the pleasures, Lord, that you have stored up for those who fear you."

– PSALM 30: 31

Just before we crossed the border of the Canada/Vermont line, a powerful feeling penetrated through me. Inside my mind came the absolute sureness that I would find something I needed in the duty-free shop. Suddenly, I had the strangest sensation in my hand—right in the center of my palms there felt like a big opening, just like where I imagined those iron nails had pierced Jesus' hands so long ago on that hill in Calvary. They didn't look out of the ordinary, but they felt strange.

As soon as we pulled into a parking spot and turned off the engine, I walked into the shop, followed closely by Sam who wanted to get the refund due on the taxes we had paid for our room. The kids, who can never pass up a chance to get a souvenir or candy whenever we are on vacation, tagged along behind. Aimlessly, I wandered around the various glass cabinets and shelves; I didn't have the faintest idea what I was looking for. As I stooped over to look at a very pretty yellow-gold Swarovski crystal cross enclosed in a waist level glass case, I pressed my hand against the glass right over the cross pendent. Then something happened that I have never felt before. Just as if my hand were a divining rod, a strong pulling sensation targeted the center of my palm. I pulled my hand away and the feeling disappeared. Tentatively, I hovered my hand back to the same spot and felt again the strong tug. My hand felt an "attraction" to the cross. How odd. Was I supposed to buy this cross, I wondered.

I decided to contemplate this for a moment and walked away. Next, as I was examining an upright stand with little wooden pegs on it and all sorts of glass/crystal ornaments hanging from the pegs, I noticed a beautiful crystal angel. Slowly, I brought my hand up close to the angel; the same strong pull sensation came out of my hand again. The sensation seemed to be drawing my hand to the angel. Looking over the entire shelf, I passed my hand over every other item, but the pulling sensation occurred only on the angel. So I was meant to buy the angel and the cross. *OK*, I thought, *why not?* They were both beautiful and strong Catholic religious symbols. I would love to own them.

Sam impatiently paced the store waiting for me, so I decided that if there was anything else here that I was being guided to purchase I had better find it quickly. As unobtrusively as I could, I held my right hand up and walked up and down all the aisles. I was finishing up with the last aisle, when a strong spiritual tug stopped me in my tracks. The item was a silver-colored neck-lace and pendant in the form of a familiar Indian theme—a totem pole. In the center of the totem pole was a small round piece of a shiny black stone. I looked at the necklace, puzzled. Ordinarily I would never have looked twice at this necklace; it looked like something a child of seven might wear. But the energy pull in my hands was strong, and I knew that I would somehow regret leaving this item here. So I picked it up and went back and got the angel and cross, and proceeded to the checkout—my credit card in hand—and bought all three items.

When we got back into the car, I immediately took out my new crystal cross and put it on. I was already in love with it; it was so beautiful. About an inch long and a half an inch wide, round golden crystals were set in a gold metal cross. The crystals were inlaid on both sides of the cross as well as on the top. Next, I removed the angel from its packaging and held it in my hands; its weight was heavy and comforting. It was a beautiful crystal-clear female angel with gold metal filigree wings. She was praying and flying at the same time. I admired her tiny detailed praying hands and the folds of her long gown for a while, and then I returned her to her tiny blue velvet box so that she would not get broken, heaven forbid.

But the other silver necklace was not as pretty to my eyes, and I questioned why it had been on the shopping list, so to speak. It even looked mysterious. On the top was a bird with outstretched wings appearing to be in mid-flight. Nestled in the pendant was a small oval of a shiny, reflective black stone, which the off-white jewelry boxes' black tag touted as genuine hematite. Just below the bird was a square human face, and below that was another slightly larger square human face. I put it back in the bag, puzzled, hoping that some-day I would learn the answer.

I took out my embroidery of a guardian angel crossing two children over a breaking bridge and reflected in awe at how incredibly imaginative the whole shopping trip had been. It had been impossible to miss the items; the spiritual attraction had been unmistakably strong. An angel in human form guiding me around the store and pointing out items wouldn't have worked better. This had been an amazing spiritual adventure of the type that I would not mind having all the time. In fact, I hoped it happened often in the future. I never would have guessed that God sometime uses even man-made items to show His love and creativity. What a tremendous gift this event was. I thought to myself, *Wow, every once in a while even God goes shopping!*

❧

Spiritual answers may take a while to come, which was the case with the silver necklace. One day in the office, about two weeks later, I decided to look hematite up on the Web. Here is the what the site said: "Hematite is a fasci-nating stone. Black or dark gray, it has a deep luster that seems to glow from within. On the Mohs hardness scale hematite rates 5 1/2 to 6 1/2. Ancient peoples sometimes used hematite crystals as mirrors. Indeed, the Latin name for hematite, *specularite*, means 'mirror'. The word hematite derives from the Greek work for 'blood', because when the stone is cut, the coolant is colored red. In fact, hematite is often found with reddish bands of other materials. The stone is found in England, Germany, Scandinavia as well as Spain, Brazil, and New Zealand. Hematite has been used to decrease inflammation, drawing out heat from a feverish part of the body. It is said to dissolve negative energy and to work as a shield of armor for any person or thing."

After reading the last two lines of this Web site, it was clear to me that the necklace was to help dissolve all the negative energy that I might be the focus of and work as a shield against future outbreaks. So, I guess the Lord had directed me to it for this reason. The fact that the stone also means "blood" reminded me of Jesus. Here was an item that would be very useful when fighting demons from Hades.

About one year later, I was given another answer to the puzzle of the necklace. I was reading some Web sites on Pacific Northwest Indians and what totem poles represented in their culture, when I came upon a piece of information explaining that totems represent families. Then the real meaning of the necklace hit me directly in the solar plexus. God had meant me to understand that He considered me part of his totem or family. Then the entire necklace and the symbolism and message became crystal clear. The bird was the Holy Spirit, Jesus was the middle face, and the Father was the larger bottom face. What God had wanted me to know that day through the purchase of this particular necklace was just this: "Welcome to the Family." I had officially been accepted into the heavenly rank or Chorus of Saints. My name was written in the Great Book, as St. Paul would say. I was now adopted as God's own child.

"For those who are led by the Spirit of God are children of God."
— ROMANS 8:14

In seven days, God had begun the long-term project of remaking my soul. Seven days—just like in the Genesis creation stories of how God created the world. God had given me a new Genesis twist with my name, Pandora, a legend from the beginning of time. As you will remember, I also received the last book, which is the Book of Revelations. But He was really just beginning. From this point I still had a long way to go, as you will see in Part III—The Blessings. If we think of an ordinary Bible, we know that there are a lot of pages between Genesis and Revelations with a lot of different stories. The next section of the book will take you to the experiences that comprised the rest of my own spiritual book from God spanning the next year and a half of my life. My enlightenment was about to be turned over to continue with a whole choral spectrum from heaven.

In this section there are experiences from all the members of the Holy Trinity, the Virgin Mother, the Saints, and the Angels. Through them I was taught the wonders of the next life. Aided always in this highest of high learning by His Royal Highness—The Holy Spirit Himself.

> *"The first thing that emerges as pattern as we relate to the Spirit as Counselor is the need to change or modify our behavior. The Spirit teaches us how to behave in the Father's house. We are like a youngster brought off the street into a very cultured family that decides to take him in out of charity. He does not know how to behave. When he sees the dining-room table, he puts his muddy shoes on top of it. Someone has to tell him that this is not the way to behave."*
>
> — THOMAS KEATING

Also included are some experiences that teach using the negative aspects of spiritual life—the demons. Since these sections are all about experiences, perhaps it might be good to define the word "experience." An experience is defined as: "the apprehension of an object, thought, or emotion through the senses or mind." True knowledge of God is always derived from experience.

My metamorphosis from an ugly caterpillar to beautiful butterfly was just beginning. God had mentioned in *Pandora's Story* that I would be formed into a diamond from carbon, and then shaped into a beautiful gem. The first step of the purging process had begun by blasting away at the old bedrock of the surface of my life to tap into the deep inner core. Intense heat and pressure would then be exerted, along with the chipping, chiseling, sanding, smoothing, and polishing necessary to perfect the surface of my soul to expose the hidden light, depth, and beauty.

Eventually this process would lead to "foreknowledge of the future, understanding of the mysteries, apprehension of what is hidden, distribution of good gifts, the heavenly citizenship, a place in the chorus of angels, joy without end, abiding in God, the being made like to God, and highest of all, the being made God (that is, sharers in the divine nature)" according to St. Basil the Great. Oh joy, the difficult climb would be well worth the view at the top.

But before we can shift gears for Part III, we must first travel through that Lent of 2002—a tremendously difficult period in my life.

City of God
by Dan Schutte

Awake from your sleep
Arise from your slumber
A new day is dawning for all those who weep.

The people in darkness have seen a great light
The Lord of our longing
Has conquered the night.
Let us build a City of God.

May our tears be turned into dancing.
For the Lord, our Light and our Life
Has turned the night into day.

We are sons of the morning
We are daughters of day.
The one who has loved us
has brightened our way.
The Lord of all kindness has called us to be
A Light for his people
To set their hearts free.

10

LENT 2002

Poor Souls
Darkness Into Brilliant Light

"More courage is required of those who set out on the road to perfection than of those who suddenly become a martyr, for perfection is not
attained overnight. You are traveling by the royal and safe road along
which our Lord, all the elect, and the saints have passed. Put aside the
misgivings that the world would impose upon you. Take no notice of
public opinion. This is no time to believe everything you hear. Be guided
only by those who conform their lives to the will of God."

– St. Teresa of avila

"The Temptation of Jesus. Filled with the Holy Spirit, Jesus returned
from the Jordan and was led by the Spirit into the desert for forty days,
to be tempted by the devil. He ate nothing during those days."

– Luke 4:1-2

And the pendulum swung back from the heights of heaven into the depths
of hell. Scathing whispers quickly evaporated my delight over the divine shopping expedition. Like drops of rain running down a windshield, the voices
came one after another sending me horrid mental letters. As I sat with my
angel embroidery, silently making stitches into the fabric, glancing up occasionally to check on the children and to admire the rolling snow-covered hills
and mountains of Northern Vermont as we passed by in our silver minivan,
their words filled my mind:

"You are crazy, insane," they said. "You will no longer be able to function
nor raise your kids." On and on they droned. "You are mentally unstable and
unbalanced ... You belong in the loony bin."

After about twenty noisy minutes had passed, panic replaced it. Panic attacks had been part of my young adult life, and I could see that now they might return. Instead of totally dismissing the frightening thoughts of insanity, I let them ramble on. Then I stilled them. The best defense is a strong offense for most attacks, even spiritual ones. I mentally outlined a plan to schedule an appointment with a counselor, then I quickly added another one: "I've got to see my primary care physician to get another prescription for Xanax." A drug I had taken in my early twenties to combat almost continuous panic attacks, it had worked wonderfully well. "Perhaps I had crossed the border of sane," I thought. But then I dismissed it. It was too pat of an answer, insanity. I knew that something else was going on here. What exactly, I didn't know. But I prayed that somehow, someway, I would soon find out. The conviction that God was behind every supernatural effect persisted. Then again, would one necessarily know if they had gone insane? I didn't know the answer. However, I knew that I must eliminate that possibility from my thinking.

At some point during the rest of the three-hour drive home, I received another inspiration. This time I was sure it came from the good side. The message was having an awfully hard time getting through the static produced by the demon. "Begin writing everything down that happens to you on a spiritual level," the angel whispered into my ear. Good advice, I guessed. Why not? Perhaps someday I would need to remember each and every incident. I made a promise to myself that I would start as soon as I could, and I would begin with all the events that had just occurred since I had finished the heaven chapter of *Pandora's Story*.

Writing the experiences and feelings down as honestly as I could was instituted into my daily routine. It became a driving force. Believe me, there were many mornings when I would be driving into work with a pad of paper and pen writing at every stoplight from Hingham to North Quincy jotting down every detail I could remember after each amazing supernatural event at night—all the beautiful and the sublime as well as the horrendous. Journaling became as automatic as brushing my teeth. I am so glad I carried out that task, since I would never have remembered all the events to be able to share them in such detail with you.

> *"The inspirations of the Gift of Counsel are usually practical, concrete, and down to earth—suggesting what to do in practical affairs. They may suggest at times some long-range project. But most of the time they suggest what to do right now and often in great detail, such as what to eat or what not to eat, what journey to take or not to take, when to go to bed and when to get up."*
>
> – THOMAS KEATING

The incessant negative inner chattering was my first ominous inkling that not only were my spiritual woes not over, but they were about to descend to a new low. I was about to be pushed into a fiery furnace for my soul's own good because it badly needed reshaping. This place, often called purgatory, is really God's diamond-making factory. I guess I should have been able to guess that. After all, being raised Catholic includes much talk and speculation about this realm. But it was still a shock. It is considered a place we reside after death before entering into final eternal bliss. But even if you only die spiritually, you will enter. (For me dying spiritually means that my old patterns of thinking and behaving for the last forty-two years would undergo an abrupt halt and radical change would occur.) It was now to be my fate to spend the next month and a half in this place—to undergo purification before all of heaven would open up to share its amazing secrets with its newly adopted daughter.

"The word mysticism is connected to the mystery cults of the ancient Greeks, which revealed the knowledge of things divine to an inner circle of initiates. Mystics are sometimes called the 'elect of the elect,' or the 'friends of God.' The human being is endowed with a spiritual sense that opens us inwardly, just as our physical senses open us outwardly."
– Ursula King

As our minivan pulled into our driveway, the sky was already darkening. Night made haste upon us, and my body and mind in turn began to tense up. For the next several hours, I found distractions to aid in pushing these thoughts from my mind as I unpacked our loaded family car. Depositing skis, poles, and boots in the cellar, collecting dirty laundry from the suitcases, cleaning up all the paper and Styrofoam from the assorted fast food containers left in the car, and putting away my newly purchased gifts in a safe location occupied me for a while. After my exhausted children settled into bed, feeling utterly spent as well, I went into our master bedroom and gingerly sat on the bed. In that moment of stillness I felt overwhelming spiritual energy swirling all around me; the energy seemed angry and agitated. Deep inside knowledge struck, telling me that sleeping here was out of the question for the immediate future.

This thought had been lurking under the surface all week long, and now I knew I must deal with it. I had no choice but to alter my lifestyle in a number of ways to cope with my new "sixth sense." I made a decision and immediately began gathering my things. When Sam came upstairs, I was heading downstairs with blankets, my rosary beads, my crucifix, and my prayer books to make up my bed up on the sofa in the living room. Getting a good night's sleep looked now about as likely as climbing Mt. Everest. In fact, during Lent 2002, it was going to prove extremely difficult to get more than three to four hours maximum of interrupted sleep at night.

That first night I slept on our blue and pink floral sofa with my back tightly pressed against the back of the sofa. The blankets were tucked tightly around me, securing me in my self-made cocoon—like a caterpillar that must weave a tight cocoon around itself as it is being transformed. Somehow this made me feel safer, more protected. I hung my crystal angel from the lamp and kept the lamp on. During this time I noticed that I could not stand any darkness in my surroundings. In the bright sunlight I was fine. At night, I panicked if rooms were not brightly lit. I realize now I was instinctively trying to illuminate the darkness that had invaded my mind. Purgatory as a mind state is definitely a dark and gloomy place—not a place to reside for long.

Rosary beads and my crosses adorned my neck. My greatest fear was that the devil was trying to possess me, and if he succeeded I would lose myself. My personality would turn evil, twisted, horrible, demon-like. I couldn't let this happen—I wanted to go to heaven with no possible chance of getting sucked into hell.

For hours into the pre-dawn I read prayer books and meditated on Scripture until my heavy eyelids drifted me into a restless sleep. Praying and reading the Bible offered the only solace I could find, the only thing that worked to help calm and relax me. My last act of the night was to drape the Bible across my chest and fall asleep. This was my routine every night in Lent. Although each night would be a little different, most would be extremely tense battles just to win enough sleep to get me through the next day. There would occasionally be nights when, because I was so exhausted, I would be asleep before my body stopped moving. The oblivion of those nights was so wonderful that if I could have had any wish granted it would have been to enjoy sleep like that forever. Throughout all the nights of Lent 2002, that is how I coped and endured the enormous mental and psychic trauma.

When dawn broke the night, I cried tears of utter joy. I had made it through another night. Daytime was better. There was distraction, sunlight, people, noise, and nature. I lived through the days hour-by-hour—focusing on just coping within each hour. Sometimes, it was minute-by-minute.

My life had drastically changed, and I didn't know if I would ever be my carefree, normal self again. Functioning at work and with the children became very tough. My focus was so shifted. I would need a lot of time to make the adjustments of being able to simultaneously function in both the natural plane and spiritual plane. For now the spiritual plane overrode everything else going on inside me and around me.

According to St. John of the Cross, whose book *The Dark Night of the Soul* I read within a couple of months, the stronger and harder the spiritual trials, the quicker the Lord is able to remake your soul—so more and harder is better. God purges the weaker souls very slightly and over a long period of time. Looking back now at this extremely difficult time, I am somewhat comforted that according to St. John of the Cross, I was in the category of being spiritually strong, but at the time going through this process with no idea that God was making me into a mystic, I could find nothing to hold onto except my simple trust and faith in Jesus.

> *"Indeed, the truth that many people never understand, until it is too late, is that the more you try to avoid suffering, the more you suffer, because small and more insignificant things begin to torture you, in proportion to your fear of being hurt. The one who does more to avoid suffering is, in the end, the one who suffers most: and his suffering comes to him from things so little and so trivial that one can say that it is no longer objective at all. It is his own existence, his own being, that is at once the subject and source of his pain, and his very existence and consciousness is his greatest torture. This is another of the great perversions by which the devil uses our philosophies to turn our whole nature inside out, and eviscerate all our capacities for good, turning them against ourselves."*
>
> — THOMAS MERTON

Beyond the sleepless nights, the worst part of this intense new feeling was the touches. This spiritual effect was an every night and every day occurrence. I could perceive all sorts of new things groping me through my spiritual skin. My senses were overwhelmed by what felt like hordes of spirits having a field day on my newly awakened soul. What an assortment there were—pestering demons, departed souls, devils from Hades. (Your guess would have been as good as mine at that time.) The spirit touches were the overwhelmingly prevalent experience during these weeks.

In my more compassionate moments, I pictured the souls causing these touches as lonely, naked, alone, and in purgatory. Finding me with them, even only spiritually, they seemed to want to communicate with me. Having died into this place, with no escape but other people's prayers until they were purified, they were, at the same time, both asking me for help and giving me their observation of the other side, which was an awful black void in their perception. Often my mind was in sync with these poor souls. I seemed to find myself mentally in a silent unhappy place with no help. Since they could see I was one of them, they wanted to share their horrible knowledge with me. Much as I would have liked to remain deaf and dumb to their insistent pleadings, it was impossible to do. And eventually I would learn what they really wanted. What they had died without discovering but now were in great need of—prayer. As soon as I unleashed this harsh reality, I readily gave it to them.

Whichever they were, demons or poor souls, they were persistent. Their stroking, poking, and pinching caused me to constantly look at my arm, hand, or leg where I would feel a sensation, only to find that nothing was physically touching me. Sometimes the touches were jabs into my side or subtle pinpricks—displaying their restlessness and discomfort. Sometimes I sensed their anger at their fate as painful stabs, like a yellow jacket's sting, landed on my spirit skin. Touches of intense heat to one part of my body (or soul) were common—like their enflamed hand was trying to hold my hand or touch my cheek or brush my thigh. Sometimes their fingers stroked my hair, and they felt like bugs crawling through and around my scalp. I had nowhere to flee from them.

On the sofa at night my blankets, already tightly wound around my body, would mold by themselves to outline the spaces between my legs and between my arms and body—like a lonely soul just wanted to lie on top of me or by my side for comfort. Often whatever they touched tingled and went numb. Sometimes there was a feeling of pressure from their spiritual hands touching one of my body parts—especially my head, above my heart, my legs, hands, and arms.

The spiritual pinches were often overwhelming in the late afternoon at the office. One day I had the inspiration to surround myself with red Bic pen crosses. These were made by laying one red Bic over the other at right angles, which made them look like little six inch by six inch square red crosses. I arranged a whole box of them in different spots on and under my desk with hopes of stopping the constant barrage of spiritual sense manifestation. It helped only the tiniest bit; I had to learn to live with whatever came my way.

Amazingly, this excerpt from *Pandora's Story*, which I wrote sometime in late fall 2001, eerily mirrors my Lent 2002 experiences. It was yet another premonition that God bestowed to illuminate my new life's path. It is situated just after the heaven chapter in the book. At the time of writing this, I had just been sent back from God into a place that humans usually never awake from. Notice especially the words of God, the awful bug crawling sensations reminiscent of the touches of the spirits, the feeling of being below the surface in a conscious level with purgatory, and the original gifts exploding into the many blessings which are to come:

I am fighting for life, clawing, struggling. Fighting against the walls all around. There is air though. Where is this place? Smells like a fresh dug grave. There is pain, dull pain radiating from my abdomen. There is no way to move.

Can't turn around. Waves of panic surface and surround me. My body vibrates with terror. Must calm down. Must calm down. Think. Think. I can breath at least. Try to relax. I feel bugs crawling on my body. One crawls in my ear, up my nose. Feels like one is chewing on my earlobe. Another wave of panic surfaces. I want to scream, but can't open my mouth. One minute you are with God and the next—in hell or purgatory?

The voice is calling—the voice in my head. God is talking—reminding me, calming me, loving me.

"Pandora, do you hear me? You are back on earth. You are in the ground, but help is coming. You don't need to panic; you now know that death is nothing to be afraid of. You must find a way to occupy yourself. I know that you have always loved the song 'Be Not Afraid.' If you listen very carefully, you will hear the heavenly choir singing it—just for you."

In the far distance, I really could hear them singing, and it was absolutely beautiful—much more beautiful than I could ever sing the song. Perfect, every note. In my head I sang along with the choir.

Sorrow that I had had to leave returns and fills me. But then I think of my children, my sisters, my brothers, Mom, and even Sam, and know I can bear it. God, who is my beloved dear Father, is always with me. It is neither for Him nor I that I return. My soul belongs to God and no power in heaven, hell, purgatory, limbo, nor earth can change that. No, it is for all the souls in question. The souls who are uncertain about which side they belong to. Of course, God wants them all with Him, but because man has free choice, some decide they want the evil one. I will never understand why, and it is my job to go to battle for these undetermined souls.

God's voice continues: "Think of your beautiful children; soon you will see them again. I have sent you back, but I have not abandoned you. Do you remember your old gardening buddy, the woodchuck—the one you rescued? I have sent one of his kind to guard you. Be strong. Ignore the insects. They can do little. You will soon emerge from the soil, and you will be just like a diamond, which is also formed under the earth, hardened and beautified as no process above the ground could ever do."

God is right. Wait … I sense the place I am in is vibrating. The place I am in is shaking. Something is around me and above me. I try and flex and move my arm all the way down to my fingers. I can move it just a little, just enough, I think. I move my arm, extending it, bringing my lower arm upwards. My hand grabs the dirt above. I can feel the air above with my pinky. Thank goodness that I felt like painting my nails a couple of days ago. I feel waves of dizziness overtake me. The evil one's minions are playing havoc with my brain. I feel myself drift in and out of consciousness. I will myself to stay focused, awake, and aware. The minions are very strong. Below the earth is their domain. I can't hold on much longer. Hurry, hurry. Find me. Oh, find me. See me. Please, see me. Blackness.

༻✿༺

"What's the matter, Whist? What moved?"

"It's just your imagination," says Officer Patterson.

"Look, look for yourself," Whist manages to stammer out.

All three portly, balding middle-aged small town police officers look at the human-sized mound in the dirt. There is one pink-painted fingernail protruding from the ground. It is definitely a human fingernail. It slowly moves upward as all three officers' eyes are watching. The three officers look up at each other—incredulous expressions apparent on all three. The next moment, all are on their knees side by side flinging dirt away from the mound as fast as their arms will work. Gingerly, McGory steps over the entire width of the mound and removes the 30-lb granite rock from its spot on the top of the dirt mound. The wildflowers, which were leaning against the stone, are flung, broken and quickly buried as the officers scoop the forest humus away. The well-trained German shepherd, its leash released, is whimpering, but it is too well trained to touch the dirt mound.

It doesn't take the officers long to unearth the woman. It is almost as easy as uncovering a child who has willing been buried in beach sand. She is lying on her stomach against a hard ledge of granite. It is difficult to tell what color her hair is. She is wearing very dirty blue jeans and a blue sweater. Blood stains the edges of the surface of the rock she is laying on. Her filthy white sneakers are also bloodstained.

Trained professionals that they are, they all reach for the victim's arm to feel for a pulse. McGory brushes the other two men aside and encircles his fingers around the women's wrist. A faint but definite pulse can be felt.

"My God, she's alive." Very gently McGory reaches under the victim's face, feeling for air movement under the nose to see if she is breathing. "And she's breathing. Patterson, call for an ambulance; Whist, take the dog. Go to the parking area and direct the EMTs here." Both officers quickly trot back to the path. They know that the EMT unit will be at the access lot within five minutes.

Officer McGory turns back to the victim. He is finding that he is having a very hard time understanding how anyone could survive being buried alive. As he looks closely at her face, though, he notices there is a three-inch wide hole in the ground below her left cheek. Air is flowing upward from the hole. There must be another hole leading to this one for air to flow this way. He begins walking in circles around the woman looking for the hole. It doesn't take him more than two minutes to locate the other one. It is only ten feet away. As he watches, a small brown roly-poly creature darts up from inside. It stares directly back into McGory's eyes. The creature seems to be telling him something, *and then it turns and runs quickly into the thick underbrush.*

McGory shakes his head to clear it. His imagination is on overdrive. He returns back to the woman; she is unchanged. He wishes that the emergency crew would arrive faster, but knows that it has only been less than six minutes since they found the woman. He would love to move her, tenderly lift her from the rocky bed she is on to a more comfortable spot, but knows that this would be a mistake. She could have back injuries or injuries to her abdomen lying against the rock she lay on that could be worsened by moving her. He must leave her be.

Patiently waiting by her, not touching her except to assure himself that she is still breathing and alive, he wonders as he waits how it is that she is still alive. What happened to her? Who did it, and why? With all the blood, it looks like she should have died from blood loss long ago. He wonders if she has been buried here for many hours.

Far off in the distance McGory hears a guitar playing which is very odd since the closest house must be a third of mile away as the crow flies. Some guy must be on his deck playing, and by some weird effect the sound is carrying much farther than normal. The words are clear as day and as he listens to them, they send a jolt through to his solar plexus. How bizarrely appropriate.

You're worried my son about people hating
And how this world is run, and how this world is run.
You say it ain't true, its dirt that we're made of and often return to, often return.

But don't search too long for that gold that you seek,
It's too deep to dig for and your arm's too weak.
That man long ago, with his low-down birth, found his glory planted in the earth.

But don't search too long for that gold that you seek,
It's too deep to dig for and your arms too weak.

Don't you worry my friend about people hating.
Love is still the Lord, love is still lord.

But don't search too long for that gold that you seek,
It's too deep to dig for and your arms too weak.

Don't you worry my friend about the dirt in the soil
Flowers still grow there, flowers still grow.

A sudden, very strong gust of wind blows through the forest. The dirt in piles is scattered along with the sodden leaves. Soil, ground into the woman's shirt, is being blown up in a vortex above the woman's body. As McGory watches the vortex elongates, lifting up until it reaches the top of the tree canopy. After it crests the treetops, it remains stationary for a moment, and then impossibly it seems to explode and disappear. The forest echoes with the clap from the explosion. Still looking up at the strange phenomena, McGory feels a couple of grains of dirt fall into his eyes.

(April 6, 2003 - Special insight gained at Mass during a sermon on seeds. Father was telling us that a seed must die to produce a flower or a tree, that the seed's death is a beautiful thing because it ends up in a much more beautiful form. I realize that I was the seed that God has planted. My old self is now dead, but the new one emerges to grow into a far more beautiful form. That was His message to me with this scene.)

> *"Says the Lord Almighty. For I am planting seeds of peace and prosperity among you. The grapevines will be heavy with fruit. The earth will produce its crops, and the sky will release the dew. Once more, I will make the remnant in Judah and Israel the heirs of these blessings."*
> — ZECHARIAH 8:11–12

Gradually over that trying period I came to understand that God was also working to release past sins and difficult experiences from my soul in addition to exposing to me the souls that dwell in this in-between place. My soul, chained and bound by my past errors, needed to be released. Or perhaps I was really breaking out of, shedding, that tight dry husk that incased my soul. Eventually I would stumble upon this quote from Thomas Merton that would really speak to this part of my journey: "Wish not to be happy but to be free." Looking back now, I see that part of the sensations I could feel was my soul releasing spiritual garbage into the atmosphere. As my spiritual chains were snapping with bangs and cracks, my soul felt released and sprung away from its bindings. Perhaps it depended on what the problem had been as to how it felt being released.

One thing that I became convinced of was that somehow these chains were a by-product of my sinful past. Instinctively, I knew spiritual pain was necessary to get rid of whatever had stained, twisted, and disfigured my soul. Even my memories produced nothing but pain. (I didn't know this at the time, but I would have been greatly comforted to know that according to the "experts," upon death, having enduring purgatory as a physical being, I would be able to pass right through the cleansing fires of purgatory and onward to heaven, all my spiritual dross already burned off.)

As God drew me closer and closer, I noticed that the days of desolation seemed to shake out past incidences like a saltshaker. The harder the shaking, the faster the salt of my past came out. It was a time for deep reflection for me. Past sins that had haunted me, regrets of things I had not done, my past pettiness and impatience rose up from the deep recesses of my mind and with enormous spiritual shaking were released from my spirit. At times instead of coming out from my spirit, they revolved over and over again until I was so sick of them I wished for an injection of mental Novocain that would stop them from attacking me inwardly.

From the Charismatic Orthodox Church Web site: "Nepsis is a Greek word which means to be watchful, alert, vigilant, and to basically keep a look out. Attention must be so united to prayer as the body is to the soul. Attention must go forward and observe the enemies like a scout, and it must engage in combat with sin, and resist the bad thoughts that come to the soul. St. Symeon, the New Theologian, regarded the struggle of Nepsis thusly. Our whole soul should have at every moment a clear eye, able to watch and notice the thoughts entering our heart from the evil one and repel them. The heart must be always burning with faith, humility and love. Do not fear the conflict, and do not flee from it; where there is no struggle, there is no virtue. With Nepsis and watchfulness, comes a charismatic gift, discernment." (Discernment as it relates to charismatic gifts means to be able to detect when a spirit is evil or good.)

Those attacking thoughts of my past taught me a great deal about humility, and how I had practically none of this wonderful "saint characteristic." As soon as this mood hit I learned to recognize that darkness was setting in, and there was only one tonic that worked: prayer. Prayer became my mental anesthesia. It was the balm that my mind needed to sooth it from its past sinfulness and to open it up to God. The nights that I strung prayers together until the early morning hours were many. My mind needed prayer to relax enough to fall asleep. Prayer books of many various kinds filled my top dresser drawer to overflowing. I began to fall in tune with the saints through them, and I drew incredible comfort from these ancient prayers. The Jesus prayer became my mantra: "Lord Jesus Christ, Son of God, have mercy on me." My mind became capable of reciting this prayer as a continuous background to my other thoughts.

> *"I had been getting up and saying the Rosary in the middle of the night, as a sort of night office, for several months past. I asked God to wake me up at Galion, Ohio, so that I could do this, and so, in the middle of the night, I woke up, and we were just pulling out of Galion."*
>
> — THOMAS MERTON

As the weeks went by, the intense feelings dissipated. But prayer, more and more, filled my quiet night hours. There were many nights when I prayed straight through, particularly when I felt overwhelmed. Now I knew at least one possible reason why many of the saint's stories mention that they often prayed throughout the night. Spiritually speaking, they needed to—for the souls that surrounded them that they could sense and for any semblance of personal peace. They were quick studies and learned that prayer was the answer.

Eventually it occurred to me to wonder if the Lord doesn't send these kinds of periods in our lives in order to teach us just how elevating prayer is, how much it can help both ourselves and others. The souls that had come to surround me also needed my prayer; in fact, they were quite desperate for it. Prayer is what they had been lacking in their lives, and now my prayers were a soothing balm to their tormented souls. I prayed for all sorts of things for myself and for them: strength, energy, and patience. I told the Lord exactly how I was feeling, and soon, usually only the next day, my mood would shift even if only for one day into a much higher, happier place.

> *"He learned the love of God was inseparable from suffering, and was the path by which the soul must make its spiritual ascent toward God. Prayer became for him more passive and his knowledge of the greatness of God and man's poverty grew."*
>
> – FRANCESCO (PADRE PIO)

Prayer, at its basic element, is conversation with God. Just as sitting and talking to an intelligent scientist will cause you to gain a greater understanding of science, prayer opened me up to my origins of comprehending the eternal side of things. God looks at the big eternal picture and when you have many conversations with Him over a period of time, you begin to find yourself much more focused on His view, and much less consumed with this temporary place.

Until God gives you spiritual experiences, you may never be able to understand your soul or how God might communicate through it of the wonderful experience of the eternal life. Perhaps among all the gifts given, prayer should have a special asterisk next to it. Prayer is open to everyone, just like faith. And just like faith, special gifts are born of a rich prayer life.

"Each of us possesses a soul, but we do not prize our souls as creatures made in God's image deserve and so we do not understand the great secrets which they contain." – St. Teresa of Avila

"God is joy, joy is prayer. Joy is a sign of generosity. When you are full of joy, you move faster and you want to go about doing good to everyone. Joy is a sign of union with God—of God's presence."

— MOTHER TERESA

On the following Tuesday morning after our return from skiing, just as I had promised myself, I went to see my doctor. During the quick appointment, I updated her on my overwhelming stress and fresh rounds of panic attacks. I also mentioned that Xanax had worked great when I experienced this problem before. So without any hesitation she promptly prescribed the drug. I didn't go into any other reasons I might have for the panic attacks, and she didn't ask. No doubt she chalked it up to hormonal changes or family issues. When my anxiety built to a mountainous level throughout the rest of Lent, particularly at night, I took ½ a tablet. It was just another tool in my tool chest, and it did help with some of my anxiety, but by no means did it close down my awakened sixth sense.

Next I set up an appointment with a counselor. When I met her for my first appointment, she quietly listened to my story and promptly prescribed some Prozac. I decided to give it a try. After all, a lot of people called Prozac a wonder drug. I must admit I was a little curious. But I learned very quickly that taking this drug was going to go against my physical/spiritual makeup. After just three days on it, I felt an unbearable burning sensation inside my entire body. It was an awful feeling, and each day I took the drug the intensity grew until I could not stand it anymore. So I stopped taking it. God seemed to be discouraging me from using crutches (drugs, alcohol, and the like). What a sharp contract this terrible feeling was from the beauty of the delightful fire sensation that the Holy Spirit would eventually send my soul.

Over the course of a year of counseling, other than the offer of a drug, the therapist offered me little real help and seemed lost as to what to make of my story, although she was a wonderful listener. Our counseling sessions were helpful for my stress but provided no answers to any of my most pressing spiritual questions. Obviously I was going to have to seek help elsewhere. Shortly after this momentous Lent ended, I would find a totally different kind of "counselor" who could help. And the answers to many of my questions would begin to find answers.

Having given up sleeping in the master bedroom with my husband, I also abstained from having sex with him. I just could not handle the association with those three nights in mid-February. Perhaps to some extent my intuition told me that I needed to "fast" from lovemaking.

"Hence our former compulsive reaching out for security, affection and esteem, power and status symbols cease. In particular, there is no energy for sexual activity apart from commitment and genuine love."

— THOMAS KEATING

"Oh, how happy a chance is this for the soul, which can free itself from the house of its sensuality! None can understand it, unless, as it seems to me, it be the soul that has experienced it. For such a soul will see clearly how wretched was the servitude in which it lay and to how many miseries it was subject when it was at the mercy of its faculties and desires, and will know how the life of the spirit is true liberty and wealth, bringing with it inestimable blessings."

— ST. JOHN OF THE CROSS

"Those who will want to be more devoted and signalize themselves in all service of their King Eternal and universal Lord, not only will offer their persons to the labor, but even, acting against their own sensuality and against their carnal and worldly love, will make offerings of greater and greater importance."

— ST. IGNATIUS OF LOYOLA

Upon pressure from Sam, I eventually gave lovemaking another try, only to find that afterward when I settled down for the night back on the living room sofa, I felt a very strong spiritual "cloud" descend. The cloud hovered and swirled and rocked back and forth over my genital area, which really frightened me. That night I prayed the Act of Contrition over and over, begging for God's forgiveness, sure that He was chastising me. After that one try, I gave it up totally for about one year.

"This night, contemplation, produces two kinds of darkness or purgation, corresponding to the two parts of man's nature—namely, the sensual and the spiritual. And thus one night or purgation will be sensual, wherein the soul is purged according to sense, which is subdued to the spirit, and the other is a night or purgation which is spiritual, wherein the soul is purged and stripped according to the spirit, and subdued and made ready for the union of love with God." – St. John of the Cross

Perhaps, I thought later, *God is really doing me an enormous favor*. There is a Bible passage in which the Lord says that even if a house is swept clean, there is still a possibly that the problem could become sevenfold. Heaven knows that would be a disaster in light of my past.

133

"When an unclean spirit goes out of a person, it roams throughout regions searching for rest but finds none. Then it says, I will return to my home from which I came. But upon returning it finds it empty, swept clean, and put in order. Then it goes out and brings back seven other spirits more evil than itself and they move in to dwell there." – Matthew 13:43–45

I hate to admit that my sins, my offenses against the Lord, were mostly in the area of the passion of lust. I got on that path at a young age and never was able to reconcile what I knew to be right, and what my body craved desperately. Would my one terrible demon of lust have become seven even worse ones? Hard to tell, but I am so glad now that I was never to find out. Total fasting—abstinence—proved quite necessary.

After the end of the year, we resumed normal marital relations; eventually making love (physically) was allowed After I had defeated this particularly (for me) thorny, horny demon, I noticed a big change in myself. The fasting had done a world of good. It would allow the act to go from just a physical act to one of great spirituality. Whereas before sex used to be fun, urgent, but almost animalistic, now it was gentle and beautiful. The Lord had elevated the act of sex to the much higher act of love. Now my soul was involved much more than just my body. I had regained my long lost spirit of chastity.

> *"The soul will certainly suffer great trials at this time, especially if the devil sees that its character and habits are such that it is ready to make further progress: all the powers of hell will combine to drive it back again."*
>
> – ST. TERESA OF AVILA

Many were the days when I lived just going through the motions, trying to stay afloat. Sadness seeped from my pores; depressing, horrifying, frightening, shame-filled thoughts invaded my mind. I wondered how I could ever be happy again. True, the bad, scary days did predominate, but there were times I could feel the pendulum swinging back and then invariably the Lord would send an incredibly happy day when He knew that I was close to the breaking point.

This spiritual effect of swinging from the highest peaks to the deepest valleys, I would soon learn, is very common in the purging and to some extent in the illuminated way of a mystic. The unsettling effect of going from the heights of rapture into the depths of hell has a way of reshaping a human soul into a more divine pattern. It definitely forces a soul to turn away from the physical dimension and into the uncharted territory (from a human perspective) of the spiritual dimension, and to place themselves totally in God's hands with utter trust and humility.

"The purgative way is the way, or state, of those who are beginners, that is, those who have obtained justification, but have not their passions and evil inclinations in such a state of subjugation that they can easily overcome temptations, and who, in order to preserve and exercise charity and the other virtues have to keep up a continual warfare within themselves." – New Advent Web site (online Catholic Encyclopedia)

> "*Suffering, pain, sorrow, humiliation, feelings of loneliness, are nothing but the kiss of Jesus, a sign that you have come so close that He can kiss you.*"
>
> — MOTHER TERESA

When the pendulum swung back, and joy entered my heart, I was able to perceive sensations of a vastly different nature. In fact, they felt just like God was touching me—loving, gentle, tender hugs. Other times, some felt as if a lover was running his hand gently through my hair. Those times I knew with assurance that they came from the Lord. Once when I was singing "I believe In You" with my singing group at the 10:00 children's Mass at St. Paul's surrounded by the Carraways and facing the congregation, I felt a gentle squeeze upon my hand just when I was singing the words "I believe in you." Jesus was standing there by my side telling me that because I believed in Him, He believed in me. Countless times the touches have conveyed a meaning. There will be several examples in the upcoming blessing section.

In just a few short months I would be able to understand a lot better what was happening. According to St. Teresa of Avila, spiritual touches are an everyday, normal part of the spiritual awakening. She says not to worry, that ultimately everything comes from God.

> "*I believe that all trials would be well endured if they led to the enjoyment of these gentle yet penetrating touches of His love. This, sisters, you will have experienced, for I think that, when the soul reaches the Prayer of Union, the Lord begins to exercise this care over us if we do not neglect the keeping of His commandments. When this experience comes to you, remember that it belongs to this innermost Mansion, where God dwells in our souls, and give Him fervent praise, for it is He who sends it to you, like a message, or a letter, written very lovingly and in such a way that He would have you alone be able to understand what He has written and what He is asking of you. On no account must you fail to*"

answer His Majesty even if you are busy with exterior affairs and engaged in conversation."

— ST. TERESA OF AVILA

"It knows God by seeming to touch him. Or rather it knows Him as if it had been invisibly touched by Him ... Touched by Him Who has not hands, but Who is pure Reality and the source of all that is real! Hence contemplation is a sudden gift of awareness, an awakening to the Real within all that is real. A vivid awareness of infinite Being at the roots of our own limited being."

— THOMAS MERTON

"Searching through anthologies and histories exposes still more surprises in this unique spiritual way of life. Genuine mystics—and this applies to all religious traditions—live with a vivid awareness of God's clear and overwhelming initiative in their life. This initiative results in a profound feeling of being loved as well as a heightened sense of their own sinfulness and need for divine mercy. Mystics respond by a gradual and painful shaping of their entire life and prayer around these intense experiences. After an arduous process of self-cleansing, there occurs the holistic merging of one's entire life with the Divine Mystery. Mystical prayer, an engaging contemporary issue in itself, accents all these qualities through a variety of visions, locutions, and intense ecstasies that eventually pass into sublime interior forms of prayer. These heightened experiences dominate all the other aspects of the lives of mystics. The qualities and characteristics of the mystical experience flow into and shape even life's daily routines."

— FATHER HARVEY EGAN

Fortunately, God does understand just how difficult a newly awakened soul is going to find the purging process. Why, it was just as if God Himself was pruning my spirit. Pruning would probably hurt an apple tree tremendously if the tree had nerves. After it is pruned, it is much more capable of bearing a huge harvest, much more than would have been possible without the cutting away. Just as in pruning, the light could shine into the deepest depths of my soul where it was absorbed, thus driving darkness out. My relief was huge. My spirit became lighter than ever before.

When He saw that I needed a spiritual "pick-me-up," He interspersed the days and nights with some wonderful gifts. And every so often amazing joy periods came through, allowing me clear vision of the horrendous trials I endured, but not without great gain. Sometimes He sent an experience that was so incredible, so sublime, and so wonderful that my soul was transported into ecstasy. These are called consolations, and as a rule they are given to lighten the burden, to reward the soul, and to keep it on the straight and narrow path followed by our Lord.

When my mind broadened, expanded, and filled with light, on those wonderful days and nights, I was able to mentally operate above all the small things that used to bother me. My spiritual burdens slowly became unknotted, and even though ridding these burdens reaped growing pains, afterwards my soul felt periods of lightness, peace, and joy. As you might have already noticed from my awakening, God can sometimes give the most sublime spiritual gifts just before or just after some extremely difficult spiritual trials. This was true for the Lenten period also. Days when consolations rule are days lived in heaven, even if your feet are still planted on the earth. Not because of anything physical, but because of how beautiful your spirit makes you feel from the inside and how happy these feelings are.

Alongside the consolations was the unshakeable surety that I would live on forever; my name was written in the great book, and I would be constantly by Jesus' side. During these two months, I became totally focused on my spirituality. Unbelievable as it may seem, I began to notice that my feelings for God grew and grew as my heart became unbound by past sins. I was now capable of feeling incredible joy and love for God. As time passed I felt better and stronger, and I came to realize that I was being transformed, remade into a new, better self. I was no longer the same person that I once was.

One of the most prevalent consolations given during this period was something I call "inward light explosions." These were explosions of light into my soul that I could see in my mind's eye. The light came from deep within me—exploding to my outer skin from inside my deepest hidden self. The light is internal but can be seen behind closed eyelids. The experience is like someone turning on the light in the room where you are resting with your eyes closed.

You will have heard the term to become "enlightened." This term is not just a touchy-feely modern word, rather it is a very "true" action verb. One of the times the light came, I foretasted heaven. Exquisite music rejoiced into my heart from what could only be the choirs of angels singing—the kind of melody that only heaven can produce. I experienced incredible rapturous peace and joy. My heart seemed to strain toward the light with all its fiber; it lifted and sought to merge with the light. I came to understand much later that Jesus had sent His own light to me, and as the words of the "Our Father" describe, thy Kingdom (had) come. Jesus as the light of the world had come bringing me His Kingdom. When He was here on earth with us, the Kingdom of Heaven walked on earth. The Kingdom of Heaven is truly within us and arrives from within our deepest hidden depths, because Jesus dwells as the King of our souls.

> *"Asked by the Pharisees when the kingdom of God would come, he said in reply, 'The coming of the kingdom of God cannot be observed, and no one will announce, 'Look, here it is,' or 'There it is.' For behold, the kingdom of God is among you (or in you, never apart from you).'"*
>
> – LUKE 17:20–21

> *"Matthew described the Kingdom of God as being like a tiny mustard seed. It means that the seed of the Kingdom of God is within us. If we know how to plant that seed in the moist soil of our daily lives, it will grow and become a large bush on which many birds can take refuge. We do not have to die to arrive at the gates of Heaven. In fact, we have to be truly alive. The practice is to touch life deeply so that the Kingdom of God becomes a reality. This is not a matter of devotion. It is a matter of practice. The Kingdom of God is available here and now. We read in The Lord's Prayer that we do not go to the Kingdom of God, but the Kingdom of God comes to us."*
>
> – THICH NHAT HANH

Several other times, however, the experience was different. The light began to descend, but then before the feeling became strong, it withdrew. I thought that it might be something like an angel popping in to check on me. On a couple occasions I experienced a disappointing flat feeling. I wondered about those. My research would eventually turn up that Satan is also a being of light that can reveal himself this way.

"For such people are false apostles, deceitful workers, who masquerade as apostles of Christ. And no wonder, for even Satan masquerades as an angel of light." – 2 Corinthians 11:13–15

One day the song from the musical *Peter Pan* started playing in my head, and it seemed to me that my guardian angel was showing me the beauty and similarity of the words to my understanding of the Kingdom of God. I came to experience the light in a place in my heart where all dreams are born: Excerpt from the Song "Never Never Land," slightly altered.

> "There is a place where dreams are born
> And sunlight never ends.
> It's not on any chart,
> You must find it with your heart.
> Forever Forever Land.

It is not miles beyond the moon,
But right there where you stand.
Just keep an open mind,
And then suddenly you'll find
Forever Forever Land.

You'll have a treasure if you stay there,
More precious far than gold.
For once you have found your way there,
You can never, never grow old
Forever Forever Land."

"There is no cage for the soul. The soul is a divine light that flows into you and into your other."

– JOHN O'DONOHUE

"The natural strength of the intellect is transcended and overwhelmed by its great supernatural light."

– DIONYSIUS

"According to Gregory of Palamas, the prayer of the heart leads eventually to the vision of the divine light, which even in this present life can be seen with the eyes of the body. This light is identical with the radiant splendor that surrounded Jesus at his transfiguration on Mount Tabor, for it is none other than the uncreated energies of the Godhead. Palamas distinguished specifically between the essence of God, which remains unknowable, and his divine energies, which permeate all things and can be directly experienced by the human being in the form of deifying grace."

– URSULA KING

"When this Divine light of contemplation assails the soul which is not yet wholly enlightened, it causes spiritual darkness in it; for not only does it overcome it, but likewise it overwhelms it and darkens the act of its natural intelligence."

– ST. JOHN OF THE CROSS

"True emptiness is the realization of the underlying prajna-wisdom of the Unconscious is attained, when the light of prajna (the Greek Fathers would say of the 'Logos'; Zaehner would say 'spirit' or 'pneuma') breaks through our empirical consciousness and floods with its intelligibility not only our whole being but all the things that we see and know around

us. We are thus transformed in the prajna light, we 'become' that light,
which in fact we 'are.'"

— THOMAS MERTON

❧

The collection of eclectic experiences left me thoughtful. I had experienced Gnostic awakening, given birth to seven divine gifts, fought my personal nemesis (demons of seven types) and the archenemy of the friends of God, and traveled to purgatory. Yet God was far from through with my soul. Lent was only the beginning. Experiences both frightening and magical awaited me. In a very short time, God was going to send some help through both His living and eternally living saints and none too soon since I was at the point of really needing some answers.

A central theme running through Part III is the beauty of the wonderful world of faith and the many unique and wonderful gifts that were in turn born from all the divine gifts of faith, selfless love, charity, empathy, trust, perseverance, and patience that the Lord had bestowed. Receiving these gifts of faith allowed me, just as if I was a hot air balloon, to rise about the surface of the earth, then pass above it. These gifts are different from the ones I received in the awakening section. In a way they are second generation gifts or fruit of the original gifts—all born of God's wonderful treasures.

The section is broken up into the following parts:

The Father, Nature, the Son and the Holy Spirit, the Virgin Mother, Prayer, Charity, the Saints, Angels, and Demons. Each one contains my experiences of God that reflect one of the cherished parts of the Roman Catholic faith. Each section is chronological, so you may see the same weekend reflected in several sections. This is because it is possible for the Heavenly Father to teach a lesson, and then have the devil immediately attempt to counter or neutralize it. Many are actual supernatural encounters, but there are also teachings given through dreams, inspirations, music, nature, and other people. Written in short story format, most reflect one particular experience. I hope that you will enjoy them and remember the many blessings that God sends to His children.

"Faith is the realization of what is hoped for and evidence of things not
seen. By faith we understand that the universe was ordered by the word
of God, so that what is visible came into being through the invisible."

— HEBREWS 11:1–3

"*Faith is a gift of God. Without it there would be no love. Love and faith go together. They complete each other.*"

— MOTHER TERESA

"*The mystical way stands alongside the ordinary gospel way of conversion and love as both complement and catalyst. The path of the mystics points to the end of God's plan for all people. We might say that God's salvific plan is fast forwarded in their lives with the purpose of helping the majority keep in sight the true end of their daily efforts.*"

— FATHER HARVEY EGAN, SJ

PART III

––––– ❧❧ –––––

THE BLESSINGS

THE TRIUNE GOD

"The Father is made of none: neither created, nor begotten.
The Son is of the Father alone: not made, nor created but begotten.
The Holy Ghost is of the Father and of the Son, neither made nor created, nor begotten,
but proceeding." – Thich Nhat Hanh

"The Buddha is often described as having 'three bodies': Dharmakaya, Sambhogakaya, and Nirmanakaya. Dharmakaya is the embodiment of the Dharma, always shining, always enlightening trees, grass, birds, human beings, and so on, always emitting light. It is this Buddha who is preaching now and not just 2,500 years ago. Sometimes we call this Buddha, the Buddha at the center of the universe. The Sambhogakaya is the body of bliss. Because the Buddha practices mindfulness, he has immeasurable peace, joy, and happiness, and that is why we can touch his body of bliss. Nirmanakaya, the transformation body, a light ray sent by the sun of Dharmakaya." – Thich Nhat Hanh

"The One engenders the Two, the Two engenders the Three and the Three engenders all things." – Tao Te Chi'ing.

"Friendship is the nature of God. The Christian concept of god as Trinity is the most sublime articulation of otherness and intimacy, an eternal interflow of friendship." – John O'Donohue

11

THE FIRST PERSON

THE FATHER

Father Who Is a Universe
Love Eternal
Always Making Sons and Daughters
Experience The Fire, The Darkness, The Light
An Ocean of Uncreated, Unchangeable Goodness
Strengthening, Caring
Knowledge Emerging
Eternal Melody of the Soul

AT THE BASE of all existence lies the Father. Even though He is in you and around you, always surrounding you, you may never get a glimpse of Him. And if you do, you may not recognize Him. That is just the way He is. However, someday He may arrange an introduction, and you may find yourself surprised at who does the introduction—a very good reason to remain open to everyone. In my case it was, of all people, my senior year high school boyfriend, Gary.

An average looking boy—5'9", slightly overweight, with lovely large green eyes and pleasant facial features, even if his skin was usually broken out—Gary expressed great wisdom at age seventeen that he wanted to pass along to me. Gary received good grades in school because he was very smart, but that was not what made him special. It was his unique outlook and what he considered necessary to living a good, enlightened life. He was into all sorts of things that I found at the time quite strange but alluring. And whatever new thing he discovered, he strong-armed me into trying.

When he finished reading *The Hobbit* and *The Lord of the Rings* trilogy, he insisted I read them. We had long discussions on *The Magic of Findhorn*. Findhorn is a spiritual center in Northern Scotland that began in the late 1960s. God guided the three people who founded the center to tap into the spirit world of "Devas" and elemental or nature spirits to help them grow an incredibly lush garden that defied every gardening law known to man. A "Deva," by the way, is a spirit who is responsible for a certain type of vegetable, fruit, or nut tree. In other words, there is a pea "Deva," an apple tree "Deva," and so on. An elemental/nature spirit is an elf.

The garden grew in almost pure sand with only two inches of compost on top. Yet the vegetables were enormous, perfect, and bug free. One cabbage was 42 pounds. Experts travelled from all over the United Kingdom to see for themselves. The experts concluded that the gardening results seen in Findhorn were unexplainable as far as soil or climate. Rather, an "X Factor" was responsible; i.e., the elemental spirits/Devas were demonstrating what mankind could achieve with their cooperation.

One of the kookier things that Gary decided to try was something called EST training. He was so intrigued with his own experience that he insisted I needed to try it too. The very next day he called and told me he had signed me up for a trial EST session. Under mild protest, I allowed myself to be driven to the hotel in Boston where the "training" was being held. I found out immediately, though, that the whole thing made me uneasy. So I put my foot down on attending the whole session. Next, he signed up for transcendental meditation, was assigned a teacher and a mantra, and he ended up becoming a practitioner. Of course, he immediately concluded that everyone should learn this—that it was very important. So against rules from his teacher, he taught me his mantra and the technique. (The mantra was "om." I was just recently reading a book on Hinduism that claimed the mystical syllable "om" is considered the beginning sound of the universe and a manifestation of the Supreme Being. No wonder ...)

This was the one thing that he insisted on during the year that I dated him, and admittedly I was glad because I ended up really enjoying it. I wouldn't have been able to tell you what I specifically enjoyed about it. Certainly it was not because it allowed me to get in touch with my inner being or that it brought me deep peace. Who cares about inner peace at seventeen? No, I couldn't have explained what it did for me, but I was drawn to it. I must have had good inner discipline at that young age because for the next year, morning and evening, I "religiously" meditated, sitting in a quiet place (not an easy thing to do when you have six brothers and sisters) and repeating my mantra over and over again for twenty minutes twice a day.

Toward the end of that year, I achieved one of the major gifts that is often given when you practice through Eastern meditation techniques. I, of course, had no way of knowing that I had achieved something considered to be a pinnacle of meditation practice then. Only much later after my awakening while looking for answers would I find that my experience matched some of the great Eastern mystics. I only knew the experience was utterly wonderful, and I came to look forward to going there through meditation. I was able to achieve it probably only a handful of times.

With something like a flip of a switch, my mind would transport me to a very different inner world. I would find myself suspended in a beautiful golden space. It stretched on forever. There were no objects or anything to see. There were no "things" as we think of things, but still I knew that everything was there anyway. My inner vision beheld a totally loving—but empty of all physical reality—beautiful, gigantic, inner galaxy but with no stars. The feelings that the vision invoked were of love, acceptance, peace, and trust. It never felt empty or desolate, even though to describe it, it might seem that I am saying that. It was more like I was a cherished child being held in loving, fondling hands—or that the universe was holding me in invisible arms, and I was suspended in its immense being. Literally, I believe that the Father wanted me to know that I was a child of His universe.

I can't recall now why I ever gave up the practice, nor how I could ever bear not to go back to that inner splendor. But when my family moved to Cape Cod when I was nineteen, my relationship with Gary ended. Perhaps out of spite I gave up everything associated with him, when the rose-colored glasses came off. I really can't recall, but I found my thirst for the supernatural and the psychic realms unquenched, as you will later read about in the angel section.

One thing I do know for certain now. God the Father meant me to experience Him in that way so that I would someday recall it and tell about it. He moved my life in different directions after that year but eventually all the spiritual puzzle pieces would fit together.

> "One afternoon, completely unbidden, came emptiness. I felt a spaciousness beyond measure. For no reason I could fathom I felt how all things dissolve into nothingness, and arise again—people, buildings, the blanket covering my legs, thoughts, feelings, passion, ideas, my body, my loved ones, the earth itself, all simply forms that would, in their time, inevitably dissolve again into emptiness. The terror of the void was not there; I felt more liberated than frightened. In a way, everything was already over, all life destined to disassemble into emptiness. Suddenly, there was nothing left to worry about. Kabbalists call this place the most intuitive and intimate relationship with God-the ein sof, literally, no limit, or infinite. It is that place that is both full of God and completely empty—because at that level there is no 'thing' for God to be. There is

only quiet, spaciousness, being. As the poet Paul Valery said, 'God made everything out of nothing, but the nothing shows through.'"

— WAYNE MULLER

"It considers itself as having been placed in a most profound and vast retreat, to which no human creature can attain, such an immense desert, which nowhere has any boundary, a desert the more delectable, pleasant and lovely for its secrecy, vastness and solitude, wherein, the more the soul is raised up above all temporal creatures, the more deeply does it find itself hidden."

— ST. JOHN OF THE CROSS

"The best of these kinds of beginnings is a sudden emptying of the soul in which images vanish, concepts and words are silent, and freedom and clarity suddenly open out within you until your whole being embraces the wonder, the depth, the obviousness and yet the emptiness and unfathomable incomprehensibility of God. This touch, this clean breath of understanding come relatively rarely."

— THOMAS MERTON

"Through turning inward, the heart must be freed of all images. Sinking into an 'imageless nudity', inward freedom is achieved through which union with God can be found, a life of secret or inward friendship wherein the 'true sons and daughters of God' are rapt out of themselves and 'burned up in the flame of love.' This highest union is attained only by a few and remains momentary in the present live. After losing or finding oneself in an immeasurable abyss above reason, melted into union, light and truth, the vision ends and the human being 'falls back into reason' and the ordinariness of daily life."

— RUUSBROEC

After the Awakening ...

For the July 4th holiday weekend in 2002, Sam, Patrick, Christina, and I planned a trip to Fire Island, NY, where my husband's family owned beach houses. The trip typically consumes an entire day of driving. From New London, CT, we boarded the first of two ferries that would eventually get us to Fire Island. The ferry from New London crosses to the outer tip of Orient Point, New York. From there we were less than two hours from Bay Shore.

Then the final ferry trip from Bay Shore to Fire Island lasts about twenty minutes.

During the last evening hours, Sam and I walked the children and our luggage to one of the beach houses and settled in for the night. We passed whispering marsh grasses that danced in the wind and late night bikers on their way home from a late dinner. That night, after my body fell into a narrow single bed in one of the four bedrooms of the beach house, I slipped under a thin cotton sheet. The bedroom were sparsely decorated with old, faded yellow cotton curtains, one end table between the two twin beds, and a simple wooden dresser with a couple of knickknacks on it. Sam was peacefully sleeping in his own twin bed four feet away. I was trying to sleep amid the laughter, shouts, and loud rock music coming from one of the two restaurants in Kismet that doubled as nightclubs until 4:00 a.m. every weekend.

Suddenly I felt overwhelmed with fiery heat. One instant my body sustained a normal temperature, and the next I felt like my skin would melt off my hot molten internal body parts.

It was the worst in a series of what I came to call "heat attacks" to date. For a couple of months I had been overwhelmed by sudden flashes of intense heat often during prayer or while laying in bed praying, which somehow I was sure were not physical premenstrual "hot flashes." My body was cool to the touch, but my soul became superheated. Needle pricks came next and covered my body—my legs went totally numb. I pictured my soul and could see it in my mind's eye totally overwhelming my physical body, like I had become not a physical woman but a cloud of gaseous heat, similar to that of a miniature sun. The feeling was very uncomfortable, bordering on painful.

I prayed in the darkened room for about an hour trying hard to accept the burning sensation. After about an hour or so, though, I gave up any hope of sleep and proceded into the living room where I sat on the hard sofa, turned on the light, and read my Bible. So intense was the feeling that afterward I would wonder if I glowed and gave off light. Finally my suffering eased sometime around 1:30–2:00 a.m. Then I returned to my bed and was finally able to sleep.

At this point I was just beginning to understand "heat attacks" as some type of inner purification. I also had another insight into this experience much later. The Gospel of Thomas shares a passage where Jesus tells His disciples that He will make all the women "sons" so that they might also enter heaven. Perhaps during translation the passage got a bit mixed up and Jesus really said that He would make all men and women "suns," not sons. Because that is exactly how intense this feeling of heat was. (Or maybe the Father was detonating firecrackers off inside my soul to commemorate my independence day!)

Sometime later that night after I fell back asleep, another feeling awakened me. In contrast to the earlier heat attack, this was a beautiful feeling. It was a sensation of being wrapped in a warmed blanket, my spirit essence stilled into deep peace. Somehow I had submerged into His pure essence of spiritual energy, which vibrates below the surface of all life into the furthest nooks and crannies of the universe. There was a sensation of my soul humming with an eternal note. In a paradoxical way it hit me that I was experiencing God the Father as the ever present, ever unchanging, but also as a tingling, vibrating energy force. And it felt as if my soul was drinking in the love and acceptance that seemed to be pouring into it. How marvelous this all felt. I don't know how I understood this, but somehow my soul became strengthened and more real or solid (if such a thing can be said of a soul). Unfortunately, I didn't stay in this state for more than a few seconds, just enough to get an understanding of how wonderful it was, and then it was gone. Twice more before dawn the Father bestowed on me the experience, though, rather as reinforcement to His message of one God but three beings—just as He had done with the light balls in February after my awakening. (Later my research would call this state "union" or infused contemplation—a mystical state of oneness with God.)

> *"We must perceive in it, as some mystics have done, 'the beating of the Heart of God.'"*
>
> — EVELYN UNDERHILL

> *"She does not, of course, mean that every one of her nuns who prepares herself as far as she can to receive mystical favours does in fact receive them: she could not presume to pronounce upon the secret judgments of God. But she evidently believes that, generally speaking, infused contemplation is accessible to any Christian who has the resolution to do all that in him lies towards obtaining it."*
>
> — ST. TERESA OF AVILA

Catherine of Siena wrote a beautiful prayer about the Father, which describes Him very well: "He is all. O eternal Father! O fiery abyss of charity! O eternal beauty, O eternal wisdom, O eternal goodness, O eternal mercy! O hope and refuge of sinners! O immeasurable generosity! O eternal, infinite Good! O mad lover! And you have need of your creature? It seems so to me, for you act as if you could not live without her, in spite of the fact that you are Life itself, and everything has life from you and nothing can have life without you."

The next morning I woke feeling utterly wonderful. I looked forward to a wonderful full day having fun with the children riding the surf, making sand castles, reading a spiritual book, sunbathing, and daydreaming. The Father must have been listening to my thoughts, because today He would give me another lesson in total contrast to last night's "sun" from the fire-of-the-Father's-love-type experience or His essence as a universe. As I was swimming in the crystal clear three-foot breakers on one of the magnificent open ocean beaches on Fire Island, He gave me another inspiration of how much He can be compared to the ocean.

Coming up from my deepest self, He began by pointing out the similarities. First, He pointed out how we are all submersed in Him, swimming in Him. "Just as the stingrays, seahorses, bluefish, and schools of minnows that are passing by you this very moment somewhere in the depths of the Atlantic Ocean are unaware that they are actually living in the ocean, you have been oblivious that you are living in Me at every moment," He said to my heart. "Even though you are living in the environment of air with only the soles of your feet on the ground, you have always, wherever your feet may carry you, been immersed in Me."

Next He instructed me to "notice that the ocean has an infinite number of creatures in it, and they come in all sorts of shapes and sizes and colors. The vast seas are ever changing, ever non-changing, ever new, ever old, and are immense. Even the color reflects me—colorless, blue or green, or any color of the rainbow depending on the sky, the depth, and the bottom that lies below it at the particular moment in time you are looking at it. The next hour the seas may be a different color even in the exact same location." I smiled inwardly.

"Father, you are reminding me of my own dad, taking me for a walk on the beach and all the while explaining things when I was a young child," I told Him. Then I thought that finding the Father was rather like having the air, wind, and surrounding space come alive and talk, respond, touch, and listen to you.

"As we continue to take Romuald's advice and just 'sit' with it, the waters of our inner life begin to clear and we begin to discover what is going on within us. Like a placid sea, our quiet mind begins to reveal its depths to us. With additional practice, the energy we get from this experience can be immensely helpful in weathering life's most terrifying storms. In the beginning, however, it is important for us just to learn how to become inwardly still so that we may experience what is going on in the depths of us. Jesus gives us similar advice when he says, 'Whenever you pray, go to your room, close your door, and pray to your Father in private. Then your Father, who sees what no one sees, will repay you.' Learning to live with ourselves is important for inner listening." – Francis Dorff

"The ocean," He continued, "can be incredibly gentle letting you float, swim, play, and become uplifted in its motion—its waves playful, fun. It is full of surprises and delights. Conversely, it can inspire awe and wonder. Think of the power displayed in storms, undersea earthquakes, and tsunamis. There are also many hidden vortexes, undertows, and currents. It forms the clouds. Its constant movement transforms the objects on the shore it interacts with, such as rock and driftwood, removing their sharp edges and making them rounded. In every seashell you can hear My infinite echo. Yet most rounded beach stones still retain something unique. The ocean can take life or it can give it. The very first life forms were born in it. It is deep and really only partly knowable."

> *"Her mysticism was mainly Theo centric, not Christ centric. She speaks of the absorption into the totality of God as if immersed into the ocean. 'I am so submerged in his immense love, that I seem as though immersed in the sea, and nowhere able to touch, see, or feel but aught water.'"*
>
> — ST. CATHERINE OF GENOA

> *"If I try to examine what happens when I am thinking, it stops happening. Yet even if I could examine my thinking, it would, I well know, turn out to be the thinnest possible film on the surface of a vast deep. The psychologists have taught us that. Their real error lies in underestimating the depth and variety of its contents. Dazzling lightness as well as dark clouds come up. And if all the enchanting visions are, as they rashly claim, mere disguises for sex, where lives the hidden artist who, from such monotonous and claustrophobic material, can make works of such various and liberating art? And depths of time too. All my past; my ancestral past; perhaps my pre-human past. Here again, if I could dive deeply enough, I might again reach at the bottom that which simply is."*
>
> — C.S. LEWIS

"You can't put your arms around the ocean, but you can feel it and totally appreciate its beauty and immerse yourself in it. But you must always respect it. No man will ever totally be able to harness or control it." From His gentle loving inspiration, I understood that the Father is the ocean around us and within us. This "Ocean" is part of us all. Resting in it, you can contact His living, divine being.

> *"In Him we live and move and have our being. Consider that you are in God, surrounded and encompassed by God, swimming in God."*
>
> — MOTHER TERESA

> *"Ultimately love is gratuitous; it is sweetness and delight, and gives one new energy. But in order to ascent to the highest form of love, suffering and denial are an integral part of the way. She describes the freedom at the summit of love as the immensity of love, a sense of spaciousness that make her spirit roam around the depths and heights of love, just like the fish explores the vastness of the ocean and the bird the heights and vastness of air."*
>
> — BEATRIJS

That night I slept as peacefully as a sunbather lying on a float in the middle of a mirror-still, deep ocean. The next morning, I again woke up with a sense of wonderment. I headed to a small store down the street to pick up a coffee and bagel, followed by a two-hour walk on the magnificent beach. Just as I was nearing the edge of Kismet on my way back from my walk, I felt the Father touch me, administering within me a sudden impulse to pick up a stone, then another prompt to pick up another, and then several more. As far as I could tell the pretty polished stones that I was picking up were mostly of the quartz family—rose, smoky, white, pale purple, and greenish. Then I received the signal to stop, that I had collected enough stones. As I examined each stone in my hand, ready to go up the boardwalk toward the beach houses, I again felt God's gentle touch, and I knew He was trying to get me to notice something about the stones. Immediately I knew right away what it was. There were seven of them. That reminded me of the gifts that I received and wrote about in the awakening section and *Pandora's Story*, so I named them according to the order that I had picked them up.

I closed my hand around them and felt the warmth in each from the summer sun. Picking up each one individually, I held it up to the sun so that I could see its crystalline depths and wonder of its birthplace deep in the earth or its length in years. Each one was differently hued and together they formed a gentle pastel rainbow in my hand. I know that He meant me to know that they were even more powerful since they had come from and been weathered, smoothed, and rounded by the ocean that I had likened to Him.

Those stones would be my reminders of our long heart-to-heart talk on the ocean and all the wonderful things that the Father taught me through it. When I returned home from our July 4th long weekend, I was curious about why the Father had had me pick up quartz stones—that maybe their meanings would have more to say for Him. Pulling up the Healing Properties of Gemstones and Crystals Web site (www.gems4friends.com), and the Crystal Healing and Metaphysical Properties of Quartz Crystals Web site (www.ka-cha-stones.com/quartz_crystals_properties.htm), I found loads of interesting nuggets:

Quartz crystals naturally structure, energize and literally expand the subtle bodies, this has been proven through Kirlian photography. The Chakras, our energetic connections to our environments both near and far, can be activated, cleansed, balanced and energized and all the psychic abilities, in their many shades, can be initiated and strengthened by the use of quartz crystals.

Quartz: One of the seven precious substances of Buddhism, set in the breastplate of the Hebrew high priest in the Bible, power stone of the shaman and revered as brain cells of Grandmother Earth to Native Americans. In the oldest writings on Earth, the Sanskrit literature of ancient India, quartz is named, bhisma-ratna, the gem that removes fear.

The quartz crystal is the connection between the physical and mind dimension. It can be used to communicate with minerals, plants, animals, and intelligent forces outside the physical dimension. In early times, when all things were thought to be parts of a greater living consciousness, the quartz crystal was believed to synchronize the individual and total consciousness with that of the heavens and advanced life-forms.

Channelling Crystal: The main, front face is large and seven sided. Its opposite, rear face is a smaller triangle. Seven indicates wisdom and mysticism. Three indicates understanding what appeared irreconcilable, by the introduction of another factor/deeper vision. This crystal facilitates a connection between both our conscious mind and innate wisdom, as well as other planes of existence.

Amethyst: Spiritual upliftment, a very spiritual stone, the purple colour is associated with the 3rd eye and crown Chakras and helps in spiritual development.

Selenite: Is a Crystal form of gypsum. Could be considered as the sword of awareness cutting through assumptions and promoting re-connection between the conscious self and the inner mystic. Selenite allows direction of energy into the body and energy system to remove blockages, which result in disease. Superior for psychic development and intuitive processes. As a bridge to altered states of consciousness. Selenite is an excellent tool for visualization, meditation and working with the subconscious.

Rose Quartz: Rose quartz emits a beautiful calming energy, which works on the whole system to gently remove negativity and reinstate soft loving and gentle energies. It is particularly helpful to bring back peace and love after emotional traumas. It is quite simply the soft gentle nurturing love of the mother. Brings healing to the heart and crown Chakras.

"Ruusbroec's most famous and most systematic work is The Spiritual Espousals, probably written about 1346, although some of his shorter works such as The Book of Supreme Truth or The Sparkling Stone are perhaps more accessible. According to Evelyn Underhill, the latter in particular reaches 'the high water mark of mystical literature.' The books takes its title from Revelation 2:17: 'To him who is victorious, I will give a sparkling stone, and on the stone will be written a new name, known to none but him that receives it.' For Ruusbroec the sparkling stone is a symbol of mystical union and also of Christ's humanity. The stone is white and shining, radiating the glory of God, a flawless mirror in which all things are alive. Its roundness signifies that truth has no beginning

or end; its smoothness means that truth is equitable; its slightness shows that although truth is immaterial, it bears upon heaven and earth by its strength."

— URSULA KING

✣

Perhaps the wonderful peaceful interlude of those early morning walks with the Father on that holiday weekend sparked the long-buried memory of my transcendental meditation experiences, because later in July I had an inspiration to begin again after the over twenty-five-year lapse. Only now instead of one of the Eastern meditation techniques, I knew I would try instead something called "centering prayer." Reading our church bulletins at St. Paul's, I had seen many notices about centering prayer and decided if I was going to attempt a meditation technique, I would go with this one. Although used by members of the early church and as late as St. Teresa of Avila's time, the practice lost favor and remained largely hidden from the main body of the Catholic Church for centuries until Fr. Thomas Keating, among others, were inspired by God to resurrect this ancient practice.

Centering prayer differs from Eastern meditation in a number of small ways—depending on which tradition one adopts. Like Eastern techniques, it is very simple to practice. Pick a comfortable chair in a location with as little noise or distraction as possible, close your eyes, and repeat a holy word, such as "Jesus" or "Love" or "Joy" over and over. The idea is to empty the mind of all thought so that eventually when you are past all thought, you will notice that God waits just beyond.

The next three mornings as I semi-reclined on the yellow and blue cornflower sofa of our sunny spare bedroom with my new mantra "Jesus," I begin centering prayer. Those first mornings I sank into myself to a place so deep and so restful that upon returning to normal consciousness, I knew that I had again visited my inner universe that I remembered from so long ago—my deep inner space brimming with utter peace—although this time without the spectacular view. Three definite yet separate times upon wakening those mornings I found myself immersed in the feeling of God's love, similar to being wrapped in an electric blanket with a vibrator attached, something I now identify as union with the Father. This feeling reflected the immense peace and comfort of the deep depths of my soul, and as soon as I awoke, I couldn't help but long to go back to that place and never return to this dimension again. It was akin to ascending (or descending) to heaven.

Coming back up from that deeper reality, eventually I would come to understand that the words of the song "You are Mine" (words and music by

David Haas, arranged by Donald Neufeld, and the very same song that the Lord had called me to find that Sunday morning in early February just before my profound awakening) reflect this aspect of union with God. In addition to becoming God's own, His message to me was a call to contemplation. Read the following words to that song, and reflect on how the writer has portrayed God in the beauty of His eternal silence:

I will come to you in the silence,
I will lift you from all your fear,
You will hear my voice,
I claim you as my choice,
Be still and know I am here.

I am hope for all who are hopeless,
I am eyes for all who long to see.
In the shadows of the night,
I will be your light,
Come and rest in me.

Refrain: Do not be afraid, I am with you.
I have called you each by name.
Come and follow me,
I will bring you home.
I love you and you are mine.

I am the word that leads all to freedom,
I am the peace the world cannot give.
I will call your name, embracing all your pain.
Stand up now walk and live.

"At the foundations of physical reality, the nature of material things reveals itself as non-material ... The elementary components of real things partake of a kind of reality that is different than that of the things that they form."
— PROFESSOR SCHAFER; IN SEARCH OF DIVINE REALITY

"In the gift of divine union, the Spirit, through the Gift of Wisdom, grasps our imagination and reflective apparatus and suspends them temporarily, so that we may be filled with divine presence without any

*hindrance from our fragile nature and the false self. This is like a kiss.
One is totally absorbed in the delight of God's presence."*

— THOMAS KEATING

*"When the attraction to prayer and interior silence endures whether we
feel consoled or not, that is a good sign that we are receiving the grace
of contemplative prayer. That grace attracts us to the daily practice of
prayer regardless of psychological content."*

— THOMAS KEATING

*"If we are really very fond of vanities the devil will send us into trans-
ports over them, but these are not like the transports of God, nor is there
the same delight and satisfaction for the soul or the same peace and joy.
That joy is greater than all the joys of earth, and greater than all its delights, and all its satisfactions."*

— ST. TERESA OF AVILA

Meister Eckhart's teachings are at one level very dualistic whilst ultimately celebrating the highest unity. To find such unity, we must retreat from the world and its images to an inner state of utter denudedness in order to experience the "birth of God in the soul."

*"Blessedness consists primarily in the fact that the soul sees God in her-
self ... Only in God's knowledge does she become wholly still. There she
knows nothing but essence and God."*

— MEISTER ECKHART

Dionysius the Areopagite describes the Spiritual Heaven as a "state" rather than a "place.'"

There were to be countless "special divine Fatherly effects" and a variety of experiences that flowed directly from my morning meditations. On a Wednesday morning in mid-July, I noticed a slight burning sensation in my shoulders and back as I began centering prayer; the Father's love was touching me as I sank into myself. After that very deep meditation session, I felt refreshed. When I went to work that day, as I sat at my desk, an inner light came on and struck me with the similarity of my spiritual journey and the Book of Revelations. I remember at the time being fearful of this knowledge. After all, the biblical Book of Revelations is a frightening book.

Again and again I would notice that sometimes during morning meditations my soul would grab and bring back to the physical dimension a new knowledge. The knowledge came directly from Him during my meditation and seemed to travel from my subconscious level to full conscious awareness. From time to time, instead of experiencing the contemplation of sinking into the essence of the Father, He would pursue a heart-to-heart conversation with me. In these conversations, there are no words but a silent knowing that is so rich and satisfying that you fathom the spiritual feeding just as surely as you might eat a slice of double cheese, sausage, and mushroom pizza. The Father can transfuse you with His wisdom and understanding without any conscious thought ever passing into your mind. This process happens all the time to all people without their knowledge. Ever wake from a satisfying slumber with a new solution to a problem that you have wrestled with? Praise God the Father, because during the night He fed you the inspiration.

Because you are with God, you are handed this "super-knowledge" as well as being left with incredible peace and joy. I didn't know yet how to relate myself to the Book of Revelations, but eventually more and more hints and inspirations would be given, and like puzzle pieces that fit together to make a glorious sunrise, I would eventually have a fullness of knowledge based on my love and relationship with the Father.

> *"The Father says: 'I will lead her into the desert and there speak to her heart.'"*
>
> — MEISTER ECKHART

> *"Blessed are the pure of heart, for they will see God" (Matthew 5:8). This "seeing" is the gift of contemplation, which our Lord promised those who would become his disciples: "Those who love me will be loved by my Father, and I will love them and reveal myself to them" (John 14:21b).*
>
> — FRANK X. TUOTI

> *"Authentic contemplative prayer leads to a continuous increase in the Christian virtues. We become more detached and disinterested in the things of this world that formerly entrapped us. We become attracted to silence and solitude, and to quiet prayer; more and more aware of God's presence and love for us.'"*
>
> — FRANK X. TUOTI

The future held many more moments of surreal enlightenment. On a particular day in August during a deep meditation I made a connection. Such a wonderful meditation could be given just before a very difficult day—as a strengthener, a prelude, and as a reminder to keep everything in perspective.

Upon arriving at work that morning, my inbox contained a follow-up e-mail from the Writer's Edge telling me that they had looked into the manuscript of my book, *Pandora's Story*. The Writer's Edge is supposed to be a critique service helping first-time writers correct errors in their books in order to make them publishable. They have a listing of publishers that they release book proposals to after you pay a fee, and they look over your proposal. *Pandora's Story* had been sent to thirty-three publishers and was rejected by them all. I had been rather devastated, but I still wanted to know if they could provide any clues as to why.

There initial response had been that while the synopsis was quite exciting, the actual plot of the book was practically non-existent. This did not seem to make any sense, and my e-mail inquiry asked how this could be possible. Seeking answers, I asked point-blank if their writing service sent form letters to authors that they turned down. In other words, were they a legitimate writing service or a fraud. I never heard back from them after that.

It was very good that the Father had sent that deep Meditation, because otherwise, I might have stayed angry. Instead, I accepted it. Eventually, the Father had seemed to say that all things work out for the best, for I was later able to incorporate the prophecies contained in the pages of *Pandora's Story* into the story I now share. They were inspired scenes that only with time and searching would I come to understand.

Later that fall of 2002, I had a strikingly deep and strengthening meditation, and as I rose from the sofa, I felt robust and utterly happy. That day was a Saturday, the day I always take my daughter to her horseback riding lesson.

Traveling in the minivan with her in the front passenger seat heading for home from the horse barn at half past eleven in the morning, I was momentarily distracted. I closed in on an approaching stoplight, unable to stop before slamming into the green vehicle in front of me. No one was hurt, thankfully, but the impact caused a leakage of antifreeze into a growing puddle on the ground beneath my vehicle As I called Sam and listened to his tirade, arranged to have the car towed, tried to calm my upset, crying daughter, and humbly and profusely apologize for my dumb error to the other driver and her son, I remembered my deep meditation of that morning ... and I realized something. Since God always knows what is going to happen to us, He will send extra strengthening when He realizes that we are going to need it—and just in the nick of time. The car incident eventually worked out better than I could have hoped. Despite the damages, we are still driving that same minivan, and it now has 190,000 miles on it. I believe its longevity is largely due to having much of its mechanical components replaced after that accident.

❧

Of course, not all my meditation sessions are that incredible. Sometimes they are filled with only my own thoughts and nothing happens. But often, two or three times a week, the Father reaches out and grabs me, like a giant spiritual ocean wave with arms, and I sink into Him. Just before this happens, I have often noticed a loud ringing in my ears. I love it when He does this because it is such an amazing feeling, like being submerged into a vibrating, tingling pool without getting wet. The force of God is warming, exciting, invigorating—well, just like swimming in an ocean.

In mid-August I had four wonderful sessions—a flood of feeling. Some early mornings, as I drift in and out of sleep, spiritual "warmings" or "heat waves" would surface and fade and surface and fade. The waves of God's energy force embraced me on those mornings.

Sometimes upon returning to myself, I had the feeling that I had attended a wonderful party. But I could never remember a single memory or concept. Perhaps that is because since you can't take anything with you when you die or when you go to heaven, the same rule applies and nothing can be taken back to reality—only the bliss of the experience.

Contemplation is wonderful, but I have to be careful not to long for any particular experience because whatever rush of feeling that comes will quickly subside when I actively long for it.

On August 29th during the early morning hours, I drifted in and out of sleep. As I surfaced, I noticed that I was in that place of union with God. All my body quivered and tingled. As I fully woke up, I felt the gentlest loving spiritual touches, and my whole body felt a tender spiritual bliss—a cloud of love. It was just as if I was falling in love for the first time—so loved, so special, and so beautiful to the Father.

Un Lugar Celestial
Sung by the Daughters of St. Paul

Sometimes I realize when I gaze in the sky, this spinning world is not my home.
A place of mystery, a land of destiny is where I know someday I'll go.
I dream of beauty I have never see, I know the arms of Heaven wait for me.
And yet I feel its sweetness here and now. In this life on earth I have found.

Un Lugar Celestial, just a little bit of Heaven sent from up above.
Un Lugar Celestial, where the presence of my father holds me in his love, Un Lugar Celestial.

When all my skies are grey, I simply steal away into my secret hiding place.
When hearts are cold as ice, the breath of Paradise is warm and gentle on my face.
I know I need my time alone with him, His healing waters flowing deep within.
Don't have to wish upon a distant star, cause a light of love fills my heart.

Un Lugar Celestial, just a little bit of Heaven sent from up above.
Un Lugar Celestial, where the presence of my father holds me in his love, Un Lugar
Celestial.

On the mornings of September 7th and 8th, the Father gave me the wonderful grace of the descent of His love, again in a spiritual cloud. Feeling His love in this special way is overwhelming but wonderful. I am positive that this is exactly how wonderful heaven will feel for every second for the rest of eternity. It was so powerful that I felt on the edge of exploding with joy. My soul was filled and filled and filled.

After those meditations, my soul produced utter, total, all-day-long joy. This period was a wonderful, bountiful, abundant gift of God. Even though my feet touched this physical earth, I lived in heaven. The "joy" period lasted for months, and the days passed by in a haze of joy. During these months, my heart and mind produced nothing but joy, for now my soul was cleared of much of the mental and spiritual garbage that had been blocking it from God's radiant blessing.

The sensation of fire and light, which I knew to be the Father's love, became common in late fall 2002. The infusions resembled the warmth garnished when sunbathing, and the illumination felt like God was lighting me up. I was becoming one of His candles in order that I might shed His heavenly light and love on those around me. The heat and fire of the Father seemed to melt away all my past impulses toward sin. Sometimes I felt positively un-solid, or not at all physical, but semi-liquid like a partially melted caramel warmed.

"Why do you call it 'scorching love'?"

"Because the love of the Eternal Father for each creature of His, and especially for us His children, is so immense that the mere awareness of it ignites a flame in our hearts."

"A flame in our hearts?"

"Yes. The flame of love becomes so intense that it extinguishes all fear, all fatigue, all self-love." – Janice T. Connell (from an interview of one of the visionaries at Medjurgje)

Please note that this effect was a combination of meditation along with many other types of spiritual healing treatments from the other members of the Holy Trinity and heaven. Those healings are elaborated on in other spiritual blessing chapters.

Because contemplation and meditation are experienced by each individual in unique ways, I have included a sampling here from other mystics who have experienced the Father in this special way:

> *"It is a great and very rare thing for a man, after he has contemplated the whole creations, corporeal and incorporeal, and has discerned its mutability, to pass beyond it, and, by the continued soaring of his mind, to attain to the unchangeable substance of God, and, in the height of contemplation, to learn from God Himself that none but He has made all that is not of the divine essence."*
>
> — ST. AUGUSTINE

> *"Souls of prayer are souls of deep silence. We cannot place ourselves directly in the presence of God without forcing ourselves to an inner and outer silence. Therefore, we have to get used to the silence of the spirit, of the eyes, and of the tongue."*
>
> — MOTHER TERESA

> *"The union of God with the soul is so great that it is scarcely to be believed. And God is in himself so far above that no form of knowledge or desire can ever reach him. He also speaks of jubilation, of the joy of those who know God."*
>
> — MEISTER ECKHART

> *"For, as it is an entirely supernatural thing, we cannot acquire it. It may last for a whole day, and the soul will then be like one who has drunk a great deal."*
>
> — ST. TERESA OF AVILA

After reading a book by Madeline D-Engle in which she praised Bach's symphonies (they were, in her opinion, the most holy, devotional music ever to be created), I made a decision to purchase a CD of some of his different masterpieces while in a book store with my daughter mid-October. After listening to the music, I agreed with Madeline that some of the melodies were very invocative of God, and that they spoke utterly of His love.

The "Air in the G String" symphony, particularly, reflects the ability of music to transport the soul. The melody gently climbs the scale, peaks, and then descends into silence. The next piece of the symphony peaks higher on the scale and is slightly louder, then descends. This wonderful feeling of a musical spiral is reflective of the spiritual journey. The Father seemed to lead my soul to higher and ever higher peaks with a rest or a space of time where there are no signs of Him, and then He sweeps me into the next part of the journey to bring me higher still. In the highest most intensive peak of the symphony, my spirit soars to God. Every time I hear that symphony, I felt my spirit lift with the music, like I am a small child and the Father is throwing me in the air and, with a thrill, I land safely back in His strong arms, only to quickly be joyfully catapulted to another spiritual peak immediately after. The notes and the melody invoke the thought of the Father actually playing with my soul, just as any physical father might play with his child, producing a rhapsody of perfect love with the power and intensity of Bach's symphony. I am struck by an eternal echo that the symphony produces in my heart. The dear Father is this eternal melody in my soul.

So awakened by this song was I that from that point on, songs that never before struck me as being particularly "religious" all seemed to remind me of Him. Love songs, particularly, seemed to reflect His love. It really didn't matter if it was a popular Broadway song or a romantic love song. To my ears they all spoke deeply of Him—spoke of His love, brought special blessings, gifts, and deep messages of understanding.

> "Sometimes audition assumes a musical rather than a verbal charac-
> ter: (in the mystic) a form of perception which probably corresponds
> to the temperamental bias of the self, the ordered sweetness of Divine
> Harmony striking responsive chords in the music-loving soul."
>
> — EVELYN UNDERHILL

Sitting in the Hingham High School auditorium in May 2003, listening to the seventh and eighth grade students play strings and band instruments one evening, I could strongly sense the Father. I could feel Him reach in through my left shoulder blade and then step in. He seemed to be enjoying the music just as much or more than any of the physical dads watching their kids on the stage. I felt His joy in the beauty of the children's gift of music. It reminded me of the scene from the "Little Drummer Boy" when Aaron goes up to baby Jesus and plays for Him. The newborn King responds by smiling with joy to the gift of the rat-a-tat-tat of his drums. Through our connection I could feel my whole body vibrate with the music, my soul swept away by the notes; it seemed to dance in rhapsody with joy at the children's renditions of familiar songs—tingling and in tune with the notes.

> "As you enter that city, you will meet a band of prophets, in a prophetic
> state, coming down from the high place, preceded by lyres, tambourines,
> flutes and harps. The spirit of the Lord will rush upon you, and you

will join them in their prophetic state and will be changed into another. When you see these signs fulfilled, do whatever you judge feasible, be- . cause God is with you."

— SAMUEL 10:5−6

The musical inspirations lasted well into 2004, when I woke up with a beautiful song playing in my head, "Michelle, My Belle," and a lovely feeling stayed all day. I looked up Michelle in my name book and it means "Who is like God," while Belle means "beautiful." The Father was singing a beautiful meaning directly into my heart. A few months earlier I had arisen from my morning meditation with an inspiration that every person possesses a beautiful harp in his or her soul; when the string is plucked, a melody from God arises and can be heard in the heart. God Himself places the harp there. But sometimes another person can pluck the string and bring His music into your soul.

⚜

Other times I noticed that the Father would bring me reassurance in a creative new way that I could now physically feel. The comfort reminded me of my own beloved dad, but His methods are all-spiritual as they soothe and reassure. They bring understanding that He is by my side in whatever difficulty may present itself.

October 29, 2002, was a day that I had not been looking forward to. It was the day of my MBA Statistics Midterm at Babson College where I had been attending as a part-time graduate student. Located in Wellesley, Mass Babson College is the number one college for entrepreneurship in the world. As you might wonder, I will tell you that I began my MBA just two weeks before my awakening. And during the duration of the coursework, which spanned five and a half years, I often felt like a fish out of water. My mind and heart were full of God; compared to Him, business is so dull, yet I persevered. Throughout my time there, an internal nagging prodded me to continue, saying that the skills that I would take away would be helpful in a future direction. Perhaps not in the boardroom of some corporation, but in some yet undefined direction. As I left class at night for the hour-long drive home, a conviction lingered saying that someday I would understand why the Father wanted me to attend Babson. Was it because He wanted me to bring to the world a spiritual innovation, or an entrepreneurial bent to worship? Or perhaps like any physical father, He just wants me to be my best.

The night of the exam I was a nervous wreck, hoping I had studied enough, but not confident. In order to stay calm, I did a lunchtime meditation in my car parked along Wollaston Beach in Quincy. The feeling of fire and love came with a rush and left in its wake gentle touches centered around my head—a special touch from the Father that had the effect of taking away most of my anxiety about the exam. It was my own personal miracle. My life was chock-full with raising two children, completing an MBA degree, working a full-time job, writing two books, doing works of charity (elaborated on in a coming blessing chapter), and running a moderately large home and the surrounding gardens. The Father was my energy source through His gift of contemplation to sustain the immense energy level needed to maintain my current life. God will not necessarily eliminate the busyness of your life when He reveals Himself, but He will sustain you.

That night while I took the exam, the Father visited my awareness and produced an intense fire in my lower legs only. It felt like an electric blanket was turned up high over and under my legs. I could tell that the Father wanted to keep me warm, remind me of His constant presence, and comfort me during my minor ordeal. This was an especially wonderful gift, since I can get so nervous that my legs shake as if they were freezing cold.

> "We are in conversation with God at every moment. Nothing we do is too trivial for God, nothing beneath his notice. If we truly believed this, our lives would be immediately transformed."
>
> — MICHAEL DUBRUIEL

> "This true possession of God depends on the disposition, and on an inward directing of the reason and intention toward God, not on a constant contemplation in an unchanging manner."
>
> — MEISTER ECKHART

"Loving you as I loved My Son, Who am I Myself, I say to you, My creatures, as I said to Him: You are My beloved children and in you I am well pleased. Because of this I rejoice in your company and I desire to stay with you. My presence among you is like the sun on the earth. If you are well disposed to receive Me, I will come very close to you, enter into you, light you up and warm you with My infinite love." – Taken from The Father Speaks to His Children, a revelation given to Sister Eugenia Elisabetta Ravasio, recognized as valid by the Catholic Church. The Eternal Father speaks directly to Sister Ravasio and gives her His message of love.

As you will soon see in the charity blessings chapter, I found incredible happiness in doing works of charity and nearly had a fit of delight whenever I could do something that I felt would bring someone closer to God—whether it be the children, my co-workers, a stranger—it didn't matter who. I felt like the Father had printed me out spiritual business cards with the name of the Lord on top, the Kingdom of Heaven as the address, and the message "To put

Joy into your Life" printed along the bottom, and my job was to pass them out to everyone around me. Its fiber was faith—the strongest spiritual paper you could ever find. If I was successful in getting people to take one, that meant that another person could walk right up to the pearly gates and join in the dance of the Lord with the communion of saints and the choir of Angels.

Some time in November I was inspired with the thought that the Father and I were playing a game of heavenly tennis. I would lob a good deed or a work of charity over the net, and He would return my stroke with infusions of love during meditation. Then the love would grow in my heart, and with a smash volley I would send it out into the world. That is surely how all the saints have operated, having received gifts of immense love, which their own souls were much too small to contain; they were driven from deep within themselves to find new ways to share the Father's love—so, so often their stories contain amazing feats of service and prayer.

> *"The man who has God essentially present to him grasps God divinely, and to him God shines in all things; for everything tastes to him of God, and God forms himself for the man out of all things."*
>
> — MEISTER ECKHERT

> *"For contemplation is naught else than a secret, peaceful and loving infusion from God, which, if it be permitted, enkindles the soul with the spirit of love."*
>
> — ST. JOHN OF THE CROSS

> *"Exceeding lofty is this step of love; for, as the soul goes ever after God with love so true, imbued with the spirit of suffering for His sake, His Majesty oftentimes and quite habitually grants it joy, and visits it sweetly and delectably in the spirit; for the boundless love of Christ, the Word, cannot suffer the afflictions of His lover without succoring him."*
>
> — ST. JOHN OF THE CROSS

During my morning meditation sessions in the month of December, I noticed a new spiritual effect. I began my prayer for my session as usual: "Lord, Jesus Christ, Son of the Living God, have mercy on me." But what came next was anything but usual. I experienced a very strong sensation of pins and needles. In the beginning it started with my right arm and hand but then traveled all over my body, producing a numbing effect. The numbness was akin to my body falling asleep, but when the meditation was over, there was no painful sensation to endure for five minutes or so because the nerves had been compressed. Instead what seemed to be happening is that the Father was numbing my physical body so that I could feel and understand my spiritual body. My body needed to be put to sleep so that it could not intrude. When my entire body was numbed, I could feel an occasional sharp needle sensation in one small point in the center of my chest where my ribs covered my heart. By April 2003, the small pinpoint had expanded to a much larger area. My heart Chakra was so wide open now that it could be infused with a larger amount of the Father's grace. I experienced this heat/light/fire penetrating into my chest area. My heart was receiving God's light/love directly—being purified and cleansed.

> *"That his prayer was nothing else but a sense of the presence of God, his soul being at that time insensible to everything but Divine Love."*
>
> — BROTHER LAWRENCE

> *"One of the paradoxes of the mystical life is this: that a man cannot enter into the deepest center of himself and pass through that center into God, unless he is able to pass entirely out of himself and empty himself and give himself to other people in the purity of a selfless love."*
>
> — THOMAS MERTON

> *"The yearnings for God become so great in the soul that the very bonds seem to be dried up by this thirst, and the natural powers to be fading away, and their warmth and strength to be perishing through the intensity of the thirst of love. This thirst David had and felt, when he said: My soul thirsted for the living God."*
>
> — ST. JOHN OF THE CROSS

From the Web site: near-death.com/forum, attributed to "Susan": "During her near death-experience, Susan kept remembering the verse in the Bible that says to be absent from the body is to be present with the Lord."

In January of 2003 my morning meditation reaped something new. I was able to stop all my thoughts, my mind becoming a blank screen. Instead of seeing my busy mental to-do list and worries, I concentrated on the blank screen behind my eyelids, knowing that many of the saints saw God as infinite darkness. As I sat there utterly quiet, the darkness changed, or rather my perception of it changed like a picture that can be seen in two ways. Suddenly the blankness (although unchanged) became God in all His reality, beauty, and love. It was a feeling of incredible knowing, a look at the ultimate reality:

blackness, nothingness, and conversely everything at the same time.

Tears of joy rolled down my cheeks unheeded as I gazed at the Father's absolute everything/nothingness. I wished that I could bask in that feeling forever. When I came out of my twenty-minute meditation, the physical world—the one we are bound by—seemed totally unreal, false, and ridiculous. That day, instead of opening my eyes to our physical reality, I opened them to find myself in a foreign land, although I was still surrounded by the familiar white walls, blue flowered sofa, and cornflower blue rug of my living room. I had entered into an altered consciousness far, far away ... an eternity from ordinary existence.

Understanding dawned that everything we feel, see, and hear is directly related to our inner mind workings. Our minds may relate the same to a particular physical space, but the perception of our world is unique to each of us. Our experience of reality—even outer reality—is related to our inner journey. Life is really lived from the inside out. The deeper the life experienced within you, the greater the complexity, joy, and love that is felt and can be given to everyone around us.

> *"Behind their bright surfaces is the dark and the silence. Words are like the god Janus, they face outward and inward at once."*
>
> — JOHN O'DONOHUE

> *"Interior silence is very difficult, but we must make the effort. In silence we will find new energy and true unity. The energy of God will be ours to do all things well, and so will the unity of our thoughts with his thoughts."*
>
> — MOTHER TERESA

> *"Of course, it is not necessary to wait for physical death to attain Gnosis. This process of absorption ... does not occur only at physical death, it also happens in an extremely subtle manner when we fall asleep or when a thought is removed from our mind. The Atman or Divine Self is experienced in the intervals between two states or between two thoughts ... Its true nature is known when it is out of contact with objects or thoughts. You should realize this interval is the abiding, unchangeable Reality, your true Being. The reason it is difficult to notice this abyss of nothingness is that, first of all, its appearance is exceedingly brief. Secondly, our attention is conditioned to focus only on things, but the abyss of nothingness is not a 'thing.'"*
>
> — JOEL: THROUGH DEATH'S GATE—A GUIDE TO SELFLESS DYING

Beyond my post-awakening period, in the fall of 2005 I went to the eye doctor for a routine eye exam. During that exam the doctor decided to dilate my pupils to get a better look inside the eye itself. My eyes checked out fine. As I left the doctor's office with sunglasses in hand and opened the door to the outside, the light profoundly struck me. I was blinded by the light, yet I could see part of true reality. When your pupils are wide open, you can truly see that the world is absolutely flooded with intense light—similarly, the light of God is clearly visible every day, all day. We tend to overlook this fact because our pupils function (purposely in this life) to filter some of the light because we would be overwhelmed by it, as I was that day. But in reality the world is super bright all day, everyday. I realized that the reality of the place we call home, earth, is that it is a place of brilliant light. God's presence is blinding while here with us, shining out of every object right here and right now.

> *"Our God also is a consuming fire. And if we, by love, become transformed into Him and burn as He burns, His fire will be our everlasting joy. But if we refuse His love and remain in the coldness of sin and opposition to Him and to other men then will His fire (by our own choice rather than His) become our everlasting enemy, and Love, instead of being our joy, will become our torment and our destruction."*
> — THOMAS MERTON

Throughout all human history, the Father has been identified by many names. From the experiences I have just shared of the Father, perhaps you can now understand why. The following listing from the Mustard Seed Web site is by no means an exhaustive one:

Adonai: (Lord) means "master, sovereign ruler or Lord" and generally denotes the authority and position of God.

El Elyon: "God most High" and pictures God's strength and sovereignty.

El Olam: "Everlasting and Eternal God" and pictures God's eternality and infinite strength.

El Roi: "God who sees" and denotes God's personal care and presence.

El Shaddai: "God Almighty" and pictures God as the all-powerful source of blessing and comfort.

Elohim: "Might or strong one; it denotes the power and pre-eminence of God and is especially used in relationship to creation and strength."

Yahweh or Jehovah (Lord): means most likely the self-existent one (I am who I am or I am the One who is) and denotes God's personal name and His eternality. It is often used in relationship to God as redeemer and covenant keeper.

A look outward into the physical world is meant to inspire thought of the spiritual world. The Father created it all to remind us of our eternal home. All of nature begins with a seed. According to the Big Bang theory, the universe began from a tiny object about the size of a pinhead or a small seed about the size that comes from a cosmos flower. Seeds are the blueprints for just about every living thing on the planet, which should point to something for you. The same Divine Architect who created the universe is the very same One who created all living things. There is nothing random about any of it.

The next chapter is all about nature and all its bountiful beauty—both physically and spiritually—that can be seen by an awakened soul.

Orthodox Scholar Anthony Coniaris states that "many of those who are baptized have in them the seed of theosis but have never made an authentic act of personal faith. Seeds create things, both physical things and spiritual things."

12

NATURE

Masterpiece of the Divine Architect
Window Into The Eternal
Awe Around Every Corner
Clouds of Majesty
Emotional Animals
Rainbows of Meaning
Nature in "Cross" Formation

"He asserts that the universe is filled with 'signposts.' Like the 'starry heavens above and the moral law within'—Immanuel Kant's phrase—all pointing with unmistakable clarity to that Intelligence. Lewis advises us to open our eyes, to look around, and understand what we see. In short, Lewis shouts, 'Wake up!'"

— DR. ARMAND M. NICHOLI, JR.

GOD USES NATURE to bring us closer to Him. Just as He used a creature, a woodchuck, to inspire me during my "burial period," He finds ways to encourage His children using the masterpiece of creation around us.

You might remember from the Lenten chapter, God mentioned that the woodchuck in the scene was an old friend of mine. Well, we certainly didn't start out that way! But sometimes animals can help bring about prophecies. I have found that God can lift portions of my life to give them much greater meaning—no encounter with another human or animal is unintended from the beginning of time. God notices all; nothing is below His notice. And never doubt that what you send out into the universe will be returned in amazing yet sometimes bizarre ways. Life is like a boomerang in that way.

Every summer for the past twenty years I plant a vegetable garden. This is one of my summertime joys. As a New England gardener, I have had to contend with all sorts of issues that crop up. By far the biggest challenge that I have ever encountered in growing vegetables was the large extended family of woodchucks that live in holes they dig in our rocky ledge backyard.

That large family produced one genius, a very intelligent woodchuck that could outthink me by miles as far as finding ways into my garden. Most woodchucks would have been deterred from entering my garden by the sight of my three-foot-high wire mesh fence. That was nothing to him; he simply dug under it. That was the end of all my vegetables that summer. Next spring, in preparation for our next battle of wills, I dug the fence down one and a half feet.

That was the year he decided to learn how to climb. One day as I raced out to the garden in the early morning to check on my plants, I spied his large protruded belly halfway up the fence with one paw clinging on for dear life, his inch long claws wrapped through the chicken wires. As he caught sight of me, he rustled up the energy to pull his fattened body the rest of the way up the fence and over the top; not bothering to climb back down the other side, he propelled himself from the top into the dense raspberry patch on the other side. I had read that woodchucks are not supposed to be able to climb. Huh.

Every morning he would get up at 5:00 a.m. and proceed directly to my garden where he would have a leisurely breakfast dining first on the lettuce, which would be only a stubble top and roots by the time he finished. Next the broccoli would entice him, but since he only liked the very top, he would take a huge bite of the choicest spears just starting to emerge from the tough stalk. Eventually, he got around to all the plants—none managed to survive his constant hunger—except the tomatoes.

I don't know how those tomatoes ever set with no leaves on the bush, but they did. As soon as they turned that wonderful, perfect vivid red, he would decide that possibly he should take a bite. Every morning as soon as I got up I would race out to the garden, hoping against hope that at least I would get a tomato or two, only to see that beautiful tomato with a large tooth-marked edge hole in the side.

I used to get so mad. After all, I love my fresh vegetables just as much as the woodchuck apparently did, and I did all the work. When I looked at the rows of pea plants that I had tenderly staked that were now only pale green chewed-up stubs, I wanted to cry. No one loves the taste of a pea from a freshly snapped pea pod more than I do. But Farmer McGregor I am not. It is unimaginable to me what he did to those poor bunny rabbits. So when everyone else said to shoot the creature, I just couldn't—he was one of God's creatures and had a right to live. He was born free and had a right to all that good stuff that hit song from the '60s talks about.

So I decided to trap him instead. I filled the steel mesh cage with all sorts of his favorite goodies—lettuce, broccoli, carrot tops. For a few days he was able to elude me, passing up his favorite goodies because he smelled a trap. But one day he just couldn't resist, and I caught him. I went out that day to check the trap and found him inside. I felt triumphant at last, vividly imagining how wonderful next year's garden would be, until I knelt down and peered closely at him. His fur was dark brown, and the individual strands were so large they closely resembled porcupine quills. His mouth was red and bleeding where he had tried to chew his way out of the trap. He was so terrified that he had defecated all over the cage, and the whole area reeked (this woodchuck demonstrated his relation to skunks).

Looking into his eyes I finally saw him for what he really was—not an enemy sent to wreak havoc on my garden, but a beautiful, frightened creature and my heart melted. His eyes were a luminous brown and soft as puppy dog eyes. I packed the cage, woodchuck and all, into the minivan and drove him to a local park so that I could release him far from my garden. Since somehow the whole encounter had brought back memories of my uncle playing the hit song "Born Free" on his piano every time we visited my grandmother's house in Buzzards Bay, Massachusetts, I sang the lyrics of the song to him on the way to the park. Of course, I know that he could not understand the words, but possibly he might understand that I meant him no harm.

> Born free, as free as the wind blows
> As free as the grass grows
> Born free to follow your heart.
>
> Live free and beauty surrounds you
> The world still astounds you
> Each time you look at a star
>
> Stay free, where no walls divide you
> You're free as the roaring tide
> So there's no need to hide
>
> Born free, and life is worth living
> But only worth living
> 'cause you're born free.

(Sung by Andy Williams, words by Don Black, and music by John Barry)

When I found a safe spot deep in the forest far, far away from traffic, I took out the trap and set it on the soft pine needle bed. As I lifted the trap door, he skidded right out with a funny rolling kind of a gait. For fifty feet he ran as fast as his short legs could take him, then he turned and looked back at me. Our eyes met. I could tell he was thanking me and saying good-bye. I stared after him until he disappeared in the brush, then I went home. My heart was just a little sad as I thought I would never see the creature again. Somehow I knew that gardening would no longer hold the challenges that a lively, intelligent woodchuck can impose on a gardening enthusiast.

> *"Of all other living creatures you shall bring two into the ark, one male and one female, that you may keep them alive with you. Of all kinds of birds, of all kinds of beasts, and of all kinds of creeping things, two of each shall come into the ark with you, to stay alive. Moreover, you are to provide yourself with all the food that is to be eaten, and store it away, that it may serve as provisions for you and for them. This Noah did; he carried out all the commands that God gave him."*
>
> — GENESIS 6:19–22

I believe that all wild animals are wonderful and beautiful, and all of them remind me of God. I have always loved getting close enough to see into an animal's eyes because I believe that by seeing into their eyes you can glimpse into their souls. Always I have believed that animals have souls just as people do.

Even as a young child, I was a close observer of nature. When I was a young girl, my younger sister Caroline and I used to spend our summers searching for and taking home all sorts of small creatures that we would find near our home, which was close to both Mann's Pond and Hyland Lake in Norfolk, Massachusetts. We knew just where to look every spring to find all the creatures that would fill our summer backyard zoo.

The animals in the "zoo" ranged from snakes, frogs, crayfish, freshwater fish, salamanders, turtles, tadpoles, and fairy shrimp. Crayfish could always be found near the shallow dam that regulated the water flow in Mann's Pond. There were always schools of minnows under the grassy clumps at the water's edge near the bathing beach of Mann's Pond. If you went to visit the pond early in the morning on a particularly sunny, warm day, you could find coiled three-foot black water snakes on the sandy beach's edge ready to dive into the water at the first sign of humans. We had many favorite fallen logs that we would turn over on a regular basis to uncover salamanders and snakes hidden in the moist decaying environment. Our family home had cellar window wells that we would check everyday to see if any animals had fallen into them overnight. On different occasions, we found a baby water snake, a star-faced mole, spring peepers, and salamanders.

One summer I remember filling up our old "kiddy" pool with water, rocks, and duckweed, going out in a rowboat on Hyland Lake, and netting twenty-eight painted turtles. They lived in their makeshift pond for the entire summer, and when summer was over, we returned them to a small vernal pond near our home. During the next four summers, we went to that vernal pond and visited our old turtle friends.

All summer long we tended to and enjoyed our animals, and then when summer was done, we returned them to where we had found them. Nowadays keeping all these wild pets would be taboo. But as a young girl, my summers were filled with enjoyment from observing all my summer animal friends. I would talk to them and ask them how they were each day. Caroline and I both loved examining them and caring for them, and we were very good at it too, for we lost very few of our wild pets. I used to think that every child spent their summer in just the same way—enjoying nature's creatures.

As a grown-up I continued to feel that same awe and connection with animals that I had felt as a child. Whenever I was out walking and encountered wildlife, I was always thrilled. The sighting of any animals added a special luster to any day. It didn't matter if it was a red fox darting away deeper into the forest, a garden snake leisurely winding its way in my rows of planted corn, an owl in the forest during the daytime, the sleek blue-black crows peeking out of the grass in groups of fifty or more, the stately white swans escorting their yearly offspring around our backyard pond, or the darting eels in the shallows of the saltwater estuaries near our home.

As my children grew, instead of wild pets, I allowed them to talk me into keeping many small domestic pets. Without exception, no matter how small, l fell in love with each one. Patrick had two gerbils when he was six. Unfortunately, while Christina was holding one, she squeezed it too tightly and poor Nuzzles was crushed in her small four-year-old fist. Oh, the guilt I felt at letting such a sweet creature into the hands of a rough preschooler. I know she wasn't old enough to know, but I felt such sadness at the needless loss.

The other gerbil lived to the ripe age of three, when he suffered a stroke. I should have had him put down when it happened. But he could still hobble one-sided about his cage and seemed to enjoy eating and playing with his toys, so I cared for him especially tenderly, and he lived for six months longer. I knew the end was near when he couldn't move any longer, so I took him to a vet to be put to sleep and cried my eyes out for a day.

To replace the gerbils, next we bought two parakeets—Dommie and Blanchie. Dommie was the sweetest turquoise bird, the prettier of the two. We enjoyed them for three years until one day we found Dommie half-lying on his side on the bottom of his cage. I was heartbroken. I called half a dozen vets that day, but since it was a Saturday, no one would see him. Finally, in desperation, I drove him up to Angel Memorial Hospital in Boston. There was nothing they could do, so they put him to sleep and gave his tiny body back to me so that I could bury it in the backyard—right next to Nuzzles. I cried for two days over him.

We also have, and thankfully they are alive and well, a pair of aquatic frogs, a beta named Sky, and our Bichon Frise named Al. Our beautiful white dwarf bunny that Christina named Duchess just recently passed away at age nine. Blanchie has also passed away, but you will read all about her soon. Although I bought all the pets for the children, I take care of them, so they seem like mine.

My love of nature extends to trees, flowers, and all kinds of plants as well. I guess it was reading *The Magic of Findhorn* that did it. But I also love all the perennials, annuals, trees, and wildflowers in my yard. Every year I look forward to spring because all the flowers and bulbs I have planted put on their annual show. I know just when they will come up and where, and I am sad when one fails to return the next year. Every evening, when I return home from work, I stroll around the yard visiting my flower friends.

In fact, since they are really my friends, I painted an oil collage of them all. Starting at the upper left-hand side of the canvas, I took a specimen of each flower and painted them overlapping. The later in the spring the flower blooms, the further over to the lower right-hand corner it is shown. The painting shows snowdrops first and roses as some of the last. I called the painting "Flower Friends" and hung it in a prominent place in the hallway. That way, even in the winter, I can get a taste of springtime anytime I want.

I treat the houseplants almost like they were animals—talking and touching them often as I pass by them. They have rewarded me by living very, very long lives. I think I have only lost one houseplant in twenty years, and some of my plants are over twenty years old.

◦⁅❧⁆◦

When I was a little girl, nature held such magic; fairies seemed to sparkle under each bush. The earth was an enchanted place. I don't remember just when the transition from magical to simply beautiful began. Probably it was when I was just around seven or eight, when my mind shut out the enchantment of the view of the world as a realm of wonder and delight, or heaven as I now know. But when you are spiritually awakened, the magic of the world returns to you, and you can glimpse with awe things that just seemed flat if very pretty. Suddenly nature begins to glow again with supernatural radiance. The universe, as my own lovely parent, began to talk to me again. And the magic returned.

Right around the beginning of the summer in 2002, as the heat was just beginning to intensify in New England, God began delivering the most wonderful, colorful, and very biblical gifts—gifts of rainbows and amazing cloud formations, gifts in the trees and flowers, and the animals—particularly birds. Nature began to speak deeply of my own beloved Catholic faith. All the natural elements of sunlight, clouds, birds, trees, and flowers seemed to form into an element of my faith that was truly mesmerizing. It was like all of nature was praising God. God can teach His lesson through any medium—and after all, nature ultimately reflects Him. Coupled with the gifts was the feeling of a remembered "last day of school freedom," a brand new horizon to discover, and perhaps even new eyesight—gifts that finally allowed me to see again how amazing and full of meaning nature really is. When you are on a vacation or trip, the scenery around you constantly changes from what is familiar, but on a spiritual journey the very same landscape becomes different.

One Saturday as I was taking a walk in the forest at Luddum's State Park in Pembroke, MA, I turned the corner of the thick pine forest. A shaft of sunlight shot down from between the pines trees and, just like a spotlight from the sky, illuminated three monarch butterflies as they danced and hovered over a patch of daisies, wild anemones, and fiddler ferns. The scene was so sublime, it touched my heart with pure heavenly joy, and I held my breath in awe that such a simple natural scene could transcend the ordinary forest into a slice of eternity.

> "At other times it wonders if it is under a charm or a spell, and it goes about marveling at the things that it sees and hears, which seem to it very strange and rare, though they are the same that it was accustomed to experience aforetime. The reason of this is that the soul is now becoming alien and remote from common sense and knowledge of things, in order that, being annihilated in this respect, it may be informed with the Divine—which belongs rather to the next life than this."
>
> — ST. JOHN OF THE CROSS

> "I believe that every flower created by him is beautiful, that the brilliance of the rose and the whiteness of the lily do not lessen the perfume of the violet or the sweet simplicity of the daisy. I believe that if all the lowly flowers wished to be roses, nature would lose her springtime beauty, and the fields would no longer be enameled with lovely hues. Our Lord has created great saints who are the rose and the lilies of his kingdom, but he has also created lesser ones, simple daisies and violets growing at his feet. His love is as manifest in the small as in the great."
>
> — ST. THERESE OF LISIEUX

The sky, decorated with clouds, sunshine, moonlight, and twinkling stars drew my eyes like magnets after that awakening. Rich meaning and new beauty suddenly became clear. Our view of the sky shows eternity but also holds all the symbolic presence of God that you could ever need. The clouds are symbolic of the Father. This theme is clearly spoken of in the Old Testament, as God appeared to the Israelites as a cloud. And Jesus is called the Son and the light of the world. Think of how closely the word "son" is to "sun." This cannot be happenstance. How often have the rays of the sun warmed your skin on a summer's day?

The Virgin Mother has often been seen as having her "blue cloak" covering the world. This is our very own sky. Wind as gentle as a summer breeze or as gusty as a Nor'easter is the Spirit of God or the Holy Spirit. If your mood needs a lift, look up and envision them embracing and touching you through the sky.

> *"The skies tell the story of the glory of God, the firmament proclaims the work of his hands; day pours out the news to day, night passes to night the knowledge. Not a speech, not a word, not a voice goes unheard. Their sound is spread throughout the earth, their message to all the corners of the world."*
>
> – PSALM 18 (19)

> *"When trumpeters and singers were heard as a single voice praising and giving thanks to the Lord and when they raised the sound of the trumpets, cymbals, and other musical instruments to give thanks to the Lord for he is good for his mercy endures forever, the building of the Lord's temple was filled with a cloud. The priests could not continue to minister because of the cloud since the Lord's glory filled the house of God."*
>
> – 2 CHRONICLES 5:13–14

One morning in January an astonishing cloud formation drifted overhead as I began my morning commute. It had been a cloudless sky that morning as I drove into work, but the newly approaching one in the deep blue sky was really something beautiful to see. As I drove into work, my eyes gravitated toward it, for it reminded me of something. Suddenly it came into focus. The cloud resembled the crèche figure of Mary in my own Christmas nativity scene that had just been displayed all Christmas season.

In our manger scene she is in the kneeling position, with her hands folded over her chest, and her face turned slightly to the left. Her gaze is fixed adoringly on her divine Son. Her sapphire robe extends out slightly from the back. Throughout my drive to the office following 3A through Hingham, past the shipyard, and into Weymouth, I kept the "Virgin Mother cloud" in view. Around all the bends in the road, the cloud remained just above and to the front of my car. When I drove into the work parking lot in North Quincy, the cloud of the Virgin Mother was sitting center overhead, just as the Star of Bethlehem had done so long ago. As I left my car and walked to the building, I watched the cloud gradually dissipate into the brilliant blue sky.

On another occurrence—a brisk Sunday in October—there was an enormous whale cloud sitting in the blue sky. With gaping open mouth it was threatening to wholly swallow another cloud also shaped like a fish. Luckily for the fish-shaped cloud, they remained at the same distance, and the whale sailed backward in the sky with the fish cloud following it. The whale cloud never did get to eat the fish cloud, at least not that day. The next day I saw the exact same cloud formation again, only this time the fish was much closer to the mouth of the whale. The second appearance of the whale and fish clouds reminded me of the book of Jonah, and I was inspired to reread the book. You might know that a very large fish in the ocean swallows Jonah because he wants to escape. God has called Jonah to be a prophet to the people of Nineveh, and Jonah is reluctant, yet he ends up with no choice. So after three days, Jonah is regurgitated onto the shore by the whale that probably is left with a bad taste in his mouth.

After I read it I could not come up with any clear answers about what Jonah and the clouds were supposed to inspire within me. Jesus does speak in the gospels about the book of Jonah, instead telling those who want a sign that He will give them no sign except the one from the book of Jonah. He was referring, of course, to the three days he spent in hell in the tomb of Joseph of Arimethea after he died on the cross. In *Pandora's Story* I stayed buried in the earth three days, and just before my awakening (in real life), I spent three nights in deep spiritual darkness just before my rebirth. The sight of those clouds caused me to do a lot of thinking. Connections traveled from my subconscious mind into my consciousness. I didn't have all the answers yet, but eventually the meaning became clear. At the very end of this book is a final story, and there the whale cloud's message will be spoken again.

> "He said to them in reply, 'An evil and unfaithful generation seeks a sign, but no sign will be given it except the sign of Jonah the prophet. Just as Jonah was in the belly of the whale three days and three nights, so will the Son of Man be in the heart of the earth three days and three nights.'"
>
> — MATTHEW 12:39–40

One Sunday in June dawned as a perfect summer day, breezy and beautiful and in the 70s—a picture-perfect day for the annual St. Paul's picnic. We couldn't talk the children into joining us, so Sam and I packed our lawn chairs into the minivan and drove to the Hingham Bathing Beach. I picked out a good spot to put out our chairs between two trees on the spacious lawn and then sat down to enjoy a leisurely, lazy afternoon. Those hours spent with my parish family were very enjoyable and I believe everyone thoroughly enjoyed the day. Sam and I helped ourselves to grilled sausage, pepper and onion subs, soda, pasta salad, watermelon, and a strawberry shortcake ice cream treat. After lunch we reclined and I walked around talking with other parishioners, then concluded my day with a book under the pitch pine trees in the shade. Sometime in mid-afternoon, I looked up to see overhead a beautiful sign from God—the sign of the cross formed in the clouds. God the Father and Son were with us quite literally. They had provided all the beautiful weather and were watching from the sky enjoying their children's obvious happiness. As the afternoon drifted on I felt such deep peace. I was safely nestled in the wonderful spiritual oasis of my church.

Later, when Sam had the pictures developed from that day, the large cross was clearly visible in the photos.

Photo of cross which appeared in the sky over the
St. Paul's Parish picnic in summer 2003

"For I will not dare to speak of anything except what Christ has accomplished through me to lead the Gentiles to obedience by word and deed, by the power of signs and wonders, by the power of the Spirit (of God), so that from Jerusalem all the way around to Illyricum I have finished preaching the gospel of Christ."

– ROMANS 15:18–19

*"Tradition uses many images to illustrate the Spirit's actions: Water, sig-
nifying the Spirit's saving action at baptism; Oil and Seal, by which the
Spirit anoints us at confirmation; Fire, by which the Spirit transforms us
into Christ; Cloud, the shining glory that led Israel in the desert, dwelt
on the Ark of the Covenant, overshadowed Mary at the Annunciation,
and was present at Christ's baptism and transfiguration. The cloud image emphasizes how the Spirit helps us experience the effective Divine
presence."*

– ALFRED MCBRIDIE

October was filled with cloud gifts from God. Every time I looked up I
saw new images. On the 14th of October I witnessed another beautiful set of
clouds. Fluffy cumulus clouds clustered together appeared to be three large
swans flying closely together. Two were neck and neck and the other was a bit
behind. The clouds were comprised of thicker ones in the back, some clouds
going sideways, and lighter, feathery clouds going up and down. The sideways
clouds made up the head and neck and the feathery clouds the wings. The
two layers of clouds made the birds appear three-dimensional. The distant
moon was also in the sky right next to the birds. The cloud formation was
straight ahead of my eyes the entire drive into my office. Then it shifted directly overhead of the office parking lot. As I parked my car, the last swan was
fading. The swans reminded me of a beautiful swan funeral I had witnessed
at our neighborhood pond just a few weeks ago. I seemed to be developing a
keen insight into how birds felt. Often depicted as a dove, I wondered if the
Holy Spirit hadn't awakened this affinity, which I seemed to see as a pattern
during the years after my awakening.

In August, I noticed that our white and speckled blue parakeet, Blanchie,
was not eating and had started to look sickly and puffed. My son, Patrick, had
named her—appropriately enough—Blanche, which means "white" in French.
(What a smart boy!) I opened the door on her blue wire cage, and she flew
out—straight into me and landed on my back. The next day, Friday, she did
the same thing. "How odd," I thought. "She has never wanted this kind of attention. In the six years we have had her, she has never once flown onto anyone. In fact, since we had moved her out of Patrick's room about a year ago,
she had not once come out of her cage to strut around on the top, which she
had always loved to do. I think she really missed being with Patrick at night
and had been sulking. Now, as she sat on my back, clinging tightly to my t-
shirt, somehow I knew that she was trying to tell me that she wasn't feeling
well and needed help.

I called a vet at Angel Memorial Hospital who thought she would have to be seen. I drove an hour's ride into Boston to the hospital and was overjoyed when they saw her and told me they could make her well. She was admitted and stayed two nights. We just saved her. The cost was $760. I tried to not think about all the starving children that the money could feed as I paid the bill. But I just had to help her since she had asked.

A month later, I was taking Al, our Bichon Frise, out for a walk to the pond when I noticed the most beautiful scene enacted by the birds that live on Foundry Pond—a small pond about one acre across and one acre wide, bordered on one side by the old Greenbush railroad tracks, and the other by the damn that spills into the saltwater river that rises and falls with the tides. It is a very quiet meditative place, where at intervals during the day you can hear the bells at Glastonbury Abbey through the woods. A couple of weeks ago I noticed that the larger male swan was no longer accompanying his mate to the edge of the dam, and I wondered at the time if he had died, was sick, or was no longer able to swim to the other side of the pond. I had been worried about him, but there was little I could do for my long-time swan friend.

The pair of swans had arrived at Foundry Pond many years before and always had their babies at the pond. They fly south together and return every year, and have carried out this routine for at least ten years. Unfortunately, although they had hatched many babies over this time, the signets have always met with an early death. I have always supposed that the babies were pulled under the water and eaten by the snapping turtles that also inhabit the pond.

On this afternoon as I walked along the embankment leading to the dam edge, I was struck by the number of birds sitting on the dam edge. The edge of the dam, usually under water during spring, in early summer was exposed. There were six or seven ducks, six or seven Canadian Geese, and the lone female swan. As I got closer and closer, I watched as the group of ducks left the dam edge and swam into the pond. They were so silent. Next the Canadian Geese swam away from the edge and followed the ducks. They were separated by about ten feet.

The lone swan stood by herself. Her back was turned toward me. On her beak, clinging to it, was a single feather from her deceased mate. The water pulled to the edge of the dam had washed in a white row of swan's feathers, which lapped on the water's edge at her webbed feet. Her neck and head moved from side to side as if looking for her mate. She never turned her head to give Al and I a glance. She looked distracted and caught up in her own thoughts.

Suddenly, it struck me just how much the scene resembled a funeral procession, from the slow, silent procession of the ducks and geese to the lone female mourner. My heart was saddened, and I felt a moment of real empathy. Swans mate for life, and now her mate was dead. She must be having thoughts of all their years together, all the babies they had tried to raise, and how she would manage the long flight south without her loving, protective mate. I wondered if she would come back to Foundry Pond next summer, or if a new pair of swans would try their luck against the ever present, hungry turtles.

How clearly I saw God in this scene, and I truly believe that witnessing it was a glimpse into the Almighty's plan for His non-human creatures. All wild animals follow the will of God, and He seemed so clearly to be present in the sad scene and to speak through them of eternal truths for animals as well as humans—a mate mourning her partner's loss along with the groups of other birds that also nested at the pond joining in her mourning for their friend. My Catholic faith teaches that animals do not have souls, but after seeing them that afternoon, I have really wondered if they do. They seemed so clearly able to feel for each other. The Almighty's beautiful love and empathy painted the scene poignant through their body language and utter silence.

Later I was to wonder if this gift from God the Father was at all related to my saving Blanchie at great cost. It did seem as if God was thanking me for caring for one of His birds with this beautiful dramatic scene, especially emphasizing their feelings and evident care of one another.

> "Dread fear of you shall come upon all the animals of the earth and all the birds of the air, upon all the creatures that move about on the ground and all the fishes of the sea; into your power they are delivered."
>
> — GENESIS 9:2

One of the most beautiful stories written up in the Islam faith, in my opinion, is about Jesus. When he was a child, according to their tradition, he used to make clay figures of birds, and then when they were finished, he used to bring them to life.

> But ask now the beasts, and they shall teach thee; and the fowls of the air, and they shall tell thee. Or speak to the earth, and it shall teach thee; and the fishes of the sea shall declare unto thee."
>
> — JOB 12:7–8

A year later, Blanchie was again not eating, was extra quiet, and her feathers were all puffed up. Several days before I noticed that she was sick, I had a dream. In the dream there were a couple of cages and Dommie, our deceased blue parakeet, as well as Blanchie were in the cages. I realized that the message of the dream was that soon Dommie and Blanchie would be together again.

Even so, I did try to save her. I rushed her up to Angel Memorial Animal Hospital in Boston because I knew once birds get sick you don't have a large window if you want to save them. The vets ran some tests on her and found that she had an enlarged liver. The condition was treatable with medication that would have to be given twice a day so she could live for a while longer. I was so happy to hear this because I really loved her. She ended up staying in the hospital for five days, mostly because she still was unable to eat on her own.

It was a difficult week handling all the "bird" problems. The hospital wanted me to call in for progress reports. They would tell me when I could pick her up. But she swung from eating to not eating, so the vet was hesitant to send her home. After five days, I received the call from the vet that she could finally come home. Alas, all my care this time around really didn't matter. On the fifth morning of her stay, a Sunday, as they were administering her daily medicine, Blanchie aspired it and it asphyxiated her. I would miss her a great deal, but in my heart, with the seriousness of her condition, I knew that it was time for her to pass out of this life. I knew then that my dream was God's way of preparing me for her loss.

Earlier that morning before I received the call that she had passed away, I was in the hallway near her room and oddly I could hear her chirping away just as if she was not thirty miles away in the city at the hospital. Moments after that was when I received the phone call from the vet at Angel's telling me that she had passed away that morning. After the phone call, I understood that her spirit had returned one last time, and that she herself had come to say good-bye to thank me for all her care and my love.

> "We're arrogant if we believe we're the only animals with thoughtful intelligence and an ability to solve problems. Intelligence also includes feelings, doesn't it? I mean empathy for others and sadness, also a sense of humor."
>
> – JANE GOODALL.

> "Perhaps it can suffice to say that anyone who has never been in a long-term relationship with an animal has endured and suffered great poverty of the spirit. Nothing is more healing than a warm cat on our laps or a big dog greeting us as we come through the door. Animals can be, and usually are, some of our most brilliant and patient teachers. If we want to learn love, devotion, trust, loyalty, responsibility, and many other characteristics we attribute to humans, we can just humbly ask an animal to be our friend. One who has been chosen for friendship by an animal is a lucky person indeed."
>
> – ANNE WILSON SCHAEF

Reminders of Blanchie have been born every year since her death. The very next year the Lord sent a pair of sparrows. They decided that the hanging pot of geraniums on our back-upper deck was the perfect spot for a nest. Every bird for miles around must have known that I was a softy. They had no fear that I would harm them. So for the month of June, Patrick, Christina and I all had wonderful fun first checking the tiny blue and white eggs for changes, and then seeing the brand-new hatchlings. It was all too soon when they reached the fledgling stage and started standing on the edge of the nest. The sight of those five tiny little birds was awe-inspiring. They were so helpless, but then I thought of the great Creator and how He loves all His creatures so much, and I knew that He in His greatness would care for them. How wonderful God is that He can make the entire universe, but at the same time still love each tiny creature.

The very same year we had a pair of cardinals nest in a mountain laurel bush in full view of the sliding doors of our family room. We could peer into the nest to see the tiny babies with just a touch of red on their mainly nut brown bodies. How I wished that baby birds could always surround us.

Just this last year at the pond, we had two nesting pairs of Canadian Geese. One set had eight babies and the other set had six. Al and I walked over every day in the early morning to see all the new babies. We watched them take their first steps into the water, and their first circuit around the pond. I brought my camera and captured many photos of our lovely spring babies. Several were made into oil paintings as a lovely tribute to new life.

Rainbows—Old Testament joys that filled my life with wonder and delight were around every corner, especially just after my awakening. They popped out of everywhere—in the sky after rain, on the walls as a reflection of crystal, projected onto furniture as a double reflection of light from a window onto glass, and reflected to the wood. The magical color spectrum so utterly beautiful became a constant. Each one reminded me of God and of His continuous presence. Many spoke of sunshine and happiness after difficult, deep trials, as a promise of the love of God that surrounded my every move.

One bright morning at around 8:10 a.m., as the sun entered the windows of the upper hallway in my home, the rays caught the crystal chandelier in our dining room and the whole room filled with rainbows. Kaleidoscopes of rainbows by the hundreds projected onto the blue-flowered wallpaper—twinkling as the branches of a tree partially blocking the sun swayed in the wind.

"When a ray of light strikes a crystal, it gives a new quality to the crystal. And when God's infinitely disinterested love plays upon a human

soul, the same kind of thing takes place. And that is the life called sanctifying grace. The soul of man, left to its own natural level, is a potentially lucid crystal left in darkness. It is perfect in its own nature, but it lacks something that it can only receive from outside and above itself. But when light shines in it, it becomes in a manner transformed into light and seems to lose its nature in the splendor of a higher nature, the nature of the light that is in it. So that natural goodness of man, his capacity for love which must always be in some sense selfish if it remains in the natural order, becomes transfigured and transformed when the Love of God shines on it."

— THOMAS MERTON

The most magnificent, glorious rainbow I have ever seen was on view from our office windows on the eighth floor at about 4:45 p.m. one fall afternoon. At least five miles across and a mile high, the entire horseshoe shaped rainbow was visible. And for the first time I could ever recall I could clearly see the golden, filtered sunlight as it hit the ground on both sides of the rainbow. The yellow sunlight reminded me of all those leprechaun stories—little green men chasing rainbows looking for the pot of gold at the base. It was now apparent how that legend sprung up. This rainbow produced a golden pool of light at both of its bases. The colors were intense, almost cartoon-like, and outrageous—in the whole spectrum you associate with rainbows—green, yellow, orange, red, blue, and purple. The purple was on both sides of the rainbow. Purple is symbolic of the highest spiritual plane and also is associated with kingship. This rainbow was surely a gift from God. And it occurred just as I was reading an e-mail on Mother Theresa. Surely, it stood as a sign of her soul's now stunning eternal beauty—a spectacular, perfect rainbow of God's amazing love, grace, and light living in the eternal plane forever. Wow!

"I set my bow in the clouds to serve as a sign of the covenant between me and the earth. When I bring clouds over the earth, and the bow appears in the clouds, I will recall the covenant I have made between me and you and all living beings."

— GENESIS 9:13–15

On October 22, 2002, after a difficult evening of teaching my CCD class of eighth graders, I returned home to a list of chores. After an evening of work around the house, I climbed into bed hoping for a quick descent into sleep. Unfortunately, my wish was not to be realized that night. Instead I felt like I spent my mostly unsuccessful sleeping hours fighting a pack of dark swirling energy spirits, which disturbed me all night long. Possibly they were reflecting the darkness of doubt that some of my students had recently developed.

In the early morning hour of 5:30 a.m., I dragged myself out of my side of the bed and headed toward the bathroom. As I passed my bureau my eyes opened wide because the wooden front of its walnut surface and my bedroom wall behind the bureau were covered with brilliant, vivid rainbows somehow made from the light of the early morning sun. As I looked around, I couldn't tell exactly why all these rainbows were showing up in the spots they appeared since there weren't any crystals or mirrors in the sun's path. Then I thought back to the spiritual struggle just last night, and God's gift became perfectly, colorfully clear. I knew that God was sending me rainbows just as He had done for Noah. A symbol to remind me that storms of all sorts eventually pass, allowing for clearer, brighter air, and fresh breezes to blow in change.

These rainbows came in a variety of forms. One morning after a particularly difficult night full of spiritual trials, I was driving to the office. At the end of my street I looked up and the sight that met my eyes stopped my breath. There was a massive cloud arrow and at the end of the pointed arrowhead was a beautiful rainbow. It was a vivid conformation that God would always point out the goodness in my every difficulty. The meaning of all the parts of my journey would someday be a beautiful rainbow for the entire world to behold.

> *"When one is looking for something and sees no sign that it is where he is searching, he will keep on looking there only with painful reluctance. If, however, he begins to find traces of it, then he will hunt gladly, gaily, and in earnest."*
>
> — MEISTER ECKHART

⚜

As I looked out my bedroom window before getting out of bed one morning, I saw the sun as it filtered through my almost sheer flowery curtains. The rays as they came through the fabric formed a golden blazing cross. As I looked at the beautiful sight, my mind contemplated how the sun was reflecting the intersection of the vertical and horizontal threads woven through the fabric, and then I made the connection that the cross is a symbol of the intersection of the natural and supernatural planes.

It struck me that Jesus as the Son or "Sun" is the way through to the Father. Jesus is the intersection of the two planes. Nailed to the cross, He visually and powerfully shows that following Him will naturally lead to the vertical crossbar, which is really the highest supernatural plane. The "cross" gift seemed to bring this inspiration. As I meditated on it, I realized in sharp contrast that if a cross is turned upside down, the plane is reflective of the lowest supernatural plane—the hellish region that cults of devil worshippers use as their ultimate symbol.

Crosses seemed to appear at every corner. Natural and man-made objects that I had never before seen as "crosses" suddenly popped out at me. In one early morning meditation a cross appeared. It was a silver cross, and it was high overhead in the air over one of the local churches. The cross was set against a stormy sky. The clouds rolling behind the cross were steel-gray and near enough to touch it. A major storm was brewing. The deep meaning of the meditation touched me: No matter what stormy testing period came onto the horizon, hang onto the cross.

> *"He who has God thus, in reality, has gotten God divinely; to him God is apparent in all things. Everything smacks to him of God; everywhere God's image stares him in the face. God is gleaming in him all the time. The vision of his God is ever present to his mind."*
> — MEISTER ECKHART

All seasons harmonized in their expression of God's presence. One winter morning the moon was full and visible even at 6:00 a.m. As I intently gazed upon the lovely sight, I noticed that on this day there were rays coming off the moon. They extended out into the early morning sky in the perfect shape of a cross.

My own visions of the cross are a natural for bringing us to the next blessings chapter on the second Person of the Holy Trinity: Jesus. Jesus is the central figure in every Christian's spiritual journey. He is our fearless leader, and we follow Him. The truth that He spoke here on earth 2000 years ago is still the truth now.

From my earliest memories, I have always thought of Jesus as a close friend. In my heart I could always feel His close and loving presence. Feelings of deep love spring into my heart at the mention of His name. I consider Him to be my true friend and confidant. Many, many were the times I poured my troubled heart out to Him, and even before the events of February 2002, He would pour comfort into my soul—perhaps not in a mystical way as He would after February 2002, but as a friend would.

Nothing separates us from Jesus if we love Him—not time, not distance, not doubt. His loving, gentle, tender, caring and compassionate spirit is always near. He is ever there when we need Him, pulling out the figurative kitchen chair for a long chat whenever, wherever. Much later as a grown women as I read His words secondhand through the gospels, I would realize that Jesus also carried a strong, fearless side. But for me He has never shown that side—because He is my dear older brother.

"Here I am, Lord' song by Dan Schutte

I, the Lord of sea and sky, I have heard my people cry.
All who dwell in dark and sin my hand will save.
I who made the stars of night, I will make their darkness bright.
Who will bear my light to them? Whom shall I send?

Here I am, Lord. Is it I, Lord?
I have heard you calling in the night.
I will go Lord, if you lead me.
I will hold your people in my heart.

I, the Lord of snow and rain, I have borne my people's pain.
I have wept for love of them. They turn away.
I will break their hearts of stone, give them hearts for love alone.
I will speak my word to them. Whom shall I send?

Here I am, Lord. Is it I, Lord?
I have heard you calling in the night.
I will go Lord, if you lead me.
I will hold your people in my heart.

I, the Lord of wind and flame, I will tend the poor and lame.
I will set a feast for them. My hand will save.
Finest bread I will provide till their hearts be satisfied.
I will give my life to them. Whom shall I send?

Here I am, Lord. Is it I, Lord?
I have heard you calling in the night.
I will go Lord, if you lead me.
will hold your people in my heart.

13

THE SECOND PERSON

JESUS

Big Brother and Friend
King Eternal
Gift of Souls
Secrets Revealed
Calvary Reflection
Prince To Dispel the Darkness
Musical Touches
Bread of Life
Brotherly Advice

"Behold, I call you friends. Jesus, as the son of God, is the first Other in the universe; he is the prism of all difference. He is the secret anam cara of every individual. In friendship with him, we enter the tender beauty and affection of the Trinity. In the embrace of this eternal friendship, we dare to be free."

– JOHN O'DONOHUE

"He is the image of the invisible God."

– COLOSSIANS 1:15, CLOUD 6

"In the beginning was the Word, and the Word was with God, and the Word was God. He was in the beginning with God. All things came to be through him, and without him nothing came to be. What came to be through him was life, and this life was the light of the human race; the light shines in the darkness and the darkness has not overcome it."

– JOHN 1:1–5

"To me, if you live deeply the teaching of Jesus, everything you say and do in your daily life will be deeply spiritual."

— THICH NHAT HANH

"Most often, though not always, the Christian mystic identifies the personal and intimate Lover of the soul, of whose elusive presence he is so sharply aware, with the person of Christ; the unknowable and transcendent Godhead, the Undifferentiated One in Whom the Trinity of Persons is resumed."

— ST. JOHN OF THE CROSS

Jesus is not just some historical figure that we read about in a book. I am convinced that He is real, and He is present. A particular experience validated this for me. I was sitting at my desk processing data into the company invoice system. As I typed away, I suddenly felt an awareness of a living presence at my side. Jesus, my dearest friend, was near.

So strong and compelling was the awareness that I stopped typing and closed my mind to stimuli coming from the physical dimension in order to listen instead to Him who was calling to me from the eternal dimension— from inside my heart and mind. With His faintest asking, I rose from my seat, closing out of the program I was working on, and grabbed my purse. Luckily it was close to my lunch hour, but of course He already knew this. I could feel my left hand gripped by an unseen hand. With His invisible hand in mine, together we walked to the elevator banks. And then Jesus sent a telepathic picture into my mind's eye: A multi-story building sitting on a busy city block and a close up of a door. Just above the door a view of a larger than life statue of the crucified Savior appeared, and then I knew where we were going. As soon as the vision passed, Jesus and I exited the elevator banks and passed through the revolving security doors. Out onto the street, we walked at a very fast clip to the North Quincy subway station.

As we were standing on the platform waiting for the train, my memory ventured back to the first time the Lord had put His hand in mine. It had been in mid-January 2002, just before my awakening, and I was sitting in a wooden pew on the right-hand side of the aisle in St. Paul's upper church listening to a Sunday sermon by Father Raffey. As I listened intently, my attention was drawn to my palms, which were beginning to throb. Sharp pain penetrated the center part of my palm. I tried flexing my hands and rubbing them, but the sensation remained. Eventually the pain turned into a strange void feeling in the center. They did not look any different than normal, but somehow I could feel wind passing through them—spiritual stigmata. During that Mass Jesus' hands had been inside mine.

Now my hand was awakened again with the feeling of deep emptiness right about where the nail had been driven into His hands as portrayed by numerous crucifixes I had seen. I was lost in my spirit with the Lord and barely noticed the speeding commuter train as it entered the station but did not stop. Standing in the yellow warning zone on the platform, normally I would have been frightened of falling onto the tracks. But more spiritually than physically present, in a semi-trance-like state, with my Protector by my side, I was unafraid. My spirit legs were walking. My physical legs were just there for show.

> The Lord is my shepherd
> I shall not be in want.
> He makes me lie down in green pastures.
> And leads me beside still waters.
> He revives my soul
> And guides me along right pathways for his Name's sake.
> Though I walk through the valley of the shadow of death,
> I shall fear no evil;
> For you are with me;
> Your rod and your staff, they comfort me.
> You spread a table before me in the presence of those who trouble me;
> You have anointed me with oil,
> And my cup is running over.
> Surely your goodness and mercy shall follow me all the days of my life,
> And I will dwell in the house of the LORD forever. (Psalm 23)

When the Red Line North Quincy T-train stopped, Jesus and I stepped over the void between the platform and the train. We chose a seat on the left-hand side of the train so that we could enjoy the beautiful view of the ocean and Boston skyline on the way to Downtown Crossing. After passing through JFK/UMass, Andrews, Broadway, and South Station, we arrived at the Downtown subway stop, where we stepped off onto the platform only to come face-to-face with a man who was physically deformed and mentally retarded. My heart filled with compassion, and my first thought was, "How I wish I could help him."

Because I was so aware of Jesus by my side, and hoped that the Savior would somehow help him, I started my approach. But when I got near enough to touch him, he jumped away telling me to leave him alone, and to get away from him. I had frightened him without meaning to. He must have had some experience or maybe many that made him give strangers a wide berth. I couldn't blame him, but I had only wanted to help.

"We are fools on Christ's account, but you are wise in Christ; we are weak, but you are strong." – 1 Corinthians 4:9–10

Saddened somewhat, we continued walking up the subway steps into the street behind Macy's, near Sheehan's Church Goods. Turning left and making headway down Arch Street, we passed many downtown office workers on their lunch breaks. No one smiled. I pulled open the heavy metal and glass doors for us both and walked into the entrance. Pausing a moment to dip my forefinger into the font of holy water in the center of the foyer, we then proceeded through the doors into the Arch Street Chapel. There are two churches at Arch Street. The upper one is ornately beautiful with a representation of many heavenly scenes in back of the altar all worked into mosaic tile. The lower church is also quite lovely with recessed statues and banked intention candle stands.

We padded down the left-hand side of the church where the confessionals were located. Kneeling in a pew offering an Act of Contrition, I pulled to my memory all my recent sins. Then another listing sprang into my head of all the additional questions that I really wanted to ask about my spiritual journey. With sudden insight I realized the Lord had inspired coming here and going into a confessional because it was a perfect place to ask someone face-to-face anonymous questions without having to read their eyes or expression. Having read my mind, and wanting very much to ease my heart of all its inner turmoil, much like a treasured older brother, He was giving me His sage advice. He had known what would be best for my soul and my spiritual well being.

I rose from my pew after the heavy velvet curtain swirled back into place from the person exiting the confessional. As I rose and entered the confessional, I felt the Savior also enter and stand just behind me—slightly to the right. He was there with me giving me His support and love. He knew that alone I would have probably not have been courageous enough to ask what I desperately sought to know. Instead I might have chosen to look my questions up online, but with the Lord's strength penetrating my very soul, I was determined to try. Perhaps, also, now that I was awakened, confession would help me turn over a fresh slate, and my old sin patterns would be buried forever. I started with the rote part of confession when the inner window slid open to expose the tiny open holes so that sound could pass to the priest's ears, and the priest on the other side warmly welcomed me.

"Bless me Father, for I have sinned, it has been three months since my last confession, and these are my sins." I then listed all the sins that I could think of and asked for forgiveness. They were all of the minor venial type. Although, unfortunately I had committed some major mortal types (hence the very difficult period after my awakening), I had always believed that dying with those on my soul was extremely perilous, and I always went to confession afterward. However, the roots of my sins had remained, and sometimes I had stumbled back into them again.

After I paused, signaling that I was finished, the priest asked me if I was truly sorry for my sins and then asked me to say a good Act of Contrition. After I finished, he began saying absolution. Jesus, just behind my right shoulder blade, sent me a gentle reminder that what I was really here for was not yet finished. He reached his hand into my spirit. My neck and upper right shoulder began to tingle and vibrate; His hand produced a warm, comforting heat, and then He enveloped my spirit with His own until I was acutely aware of only His strong presence in the small, enclosed space of the confessional. So strong was the feeling of His love and so steadying that I found myself wanting to lean back to put my head against His strong chest.

Another communication came through—urgency. I was going to lose my chance if I didn't speak up. The kindly voice of the priest was just about done with his part, giving me the penance that I would need to say as soon as I left the confessional, when I interrupted him: "Father, there is sometime that I really need to ask you. Do you mind?" Then, as if an opening had broken through the Hoover dam, the emotions that I had been holding back came out in a great and overwhelming flood, and I poured out my great need to talk about all the strange spiritual things that had been happening to me since my awakening. I even felt at ease enough to relate some of the incidents where the devil had seemed present to me. The stories poured out, and as my words relieved the pressure that had been building, I felt better.

After I had finished, I tentatively asked if anyone else ever mentioned problems related to spiritual oppression with the enemy. After all, I reasoned, if this was common, surely a priest here in such a large church in a major city would hear about this at least once in a while. His response was not quite what I hoped for. He rarely heard about the devil in the confessional. *Oh dear*, I thought. *So I am a spiritual freak.* Asking Jesus for just a little more of His strength, I further ventured to ask if there was anything that could be done if one was plagued by demons. His gentle and non-judgmental voice flittered through the plastic holes with pure comfort. *God bless his soul forever,* I thought. *He is not going to judge me.*

Instead of casting judgment, he seemed eager to answer my questions just as Jesus would want every priest to answer. "Holy Communion and confession help because then you receive God's grace. I highly recommend holy water, prayer, and intimately listening to God." I noticed that in no way did he deny the devil's existence, nor downplay my ability to feel him.

To tell the truth, I had expected him to allay my fears by telling me that I was imagining everything. When he did not, I again realized that I might have to accept that my spiritual incidents may be something I would have to learn to live with—maybe forever.

I was later grateful that I did not share St. Teresa of Avila's experience. I don't know that I could have born it. Even though I had been wicked, the Lord is very merciful:

> *"But when the poor soul, harassed by the same fear, goes to the confessor as to a judge, and he condemns her, she cannot fail to be upset and tortured by what he says—and only a person who has passed through such a trial will know how great it is. For this is another of the great trials suffered by these souls, especially if they have been wicked."*
>
> – ST. TERESA OF AVILA

While he still lent his ear, I asked him about a spiritual state called "ecstasy" that I had read about during compulsive online searches amongst various Catholic Web sites. He said, "It is a strong prayer state entered by a person that God, Himself, gave as a gift. In this state the person is no longer really on earth, but in heaven. It is a beautiful feeling and can be associated with levitation, trance, visions, and flight of spirit." Then he cautioned me: "One must never ask for this state because it would be presumptuous and only God can know who should receive this gift." Somehow the mention of the word "presumptuous" brought that poor man on the subway to mind. Then I realized that I had been presumptuous. Only God held all the answers.

"Yes, you are right. To act without authorization is presumptuous." I resolved never to ask God for it.

As I left the confessional, I realized that I had received a great gift of grace from Jesus, and also from Jesus' "human agent." Enormous burdens of fear and isolation dropped from my spirit. There were people who could listen to my story and not condemn me, and perhaps even understand. I was filled with fresh hope. I exited the confession and chose a lonely pew to say my penance. Dropping to my knees, I absorbed the tranquil sanctuary atmosphere. Minutes later, the priest came out of the confessional and strode toward the altar; and then as if he had changed his mind, he made an about-face heading to the back of the church where I knelt in prayer. As he walked by, his eyes met mine, and I could see that he somehow knew I had just been with him in the confessional. Instead of an expression of disgust, which I would have expected, his eyes held my gaze and mirrored something that he had already achieved—holiness.

As Jesus and I left the Arch Street Chapel to head back to the subway at Downtown Crossing, I noticed that my whole being was drenched in the most intoxicating feeling of peace. It was well beyond my usual mindset of hectic thoughts; I felt like I was in a different world. My spirit was as placid as a mountain lake with a perfect mirror surface that only reflected the beauty that surrounded it.

Its Our Confession
Sung by the Daughters of St. Paul

It's our confession Lord that we are weak, so very weak, but you are strong.
And even though we've nothing Lord to lay at your feet, we come to your feet
And say help us along.

A broken heart and a contrite spirit you have yet to deny.
Your heart of mercy beats with love's strong courage.
Let the river flow, by your spirit now Lord we cry.

Let your mercies fall from Heaven
Sweet mercies fall from Heaven.
New Mercys for today
Shower them down Lord as we pray.

"Sometimes, of course, when we enter into God's presence we will find ourselves speechless. We will be ready to speak to him to hear what he has to say to us. Usually he will respond in quiet inspirations. Stay quiet in his presence if words fail you. He will see you there, and bless your silence. And perhaps he will reach down and take you by the hand, walking with you, chatting with you, leading you gently through the garden of his love. Whatever happens is a great grace."

— ST. FRANCIS DE SALE

"Whence it comes to pass that each man, being derived from a condemned stock, is first of all born of Adam, evil and carnal, and becomes good and spiritual only afterwards, when he is grafted into Christ by regeneration: so was it in the human race as a whole. When these two cities began to run their course by a series of deaths and births, the citizen of this world was the first-born, and after him the stranger in this world, the citizen of the city of God, predestinated by grace, elected by grace, by grace a stranger below, and by grace a citizen above. By grace—for so far as regards himself he is sprung from the same mass, all of which is condemned in its origin."

— ST. AUGUSTINE

As the bitter cold of February melted into March of 2002, I was often to feel Jesus walking beside me holding my hand just as He had done when we traveled together to Arch Street. He always took my right hand, and I knew this was because He sits always at the Father's right hand and only his left hand is always open. His presence was invisible, yet my spirit could sense His. My hand would never fail to ache in a stigmata response. He became my constant companion. I had so often lifted my eyes to His image at St. Paul's, but now that my faith had born beautiful fruit, I could sense and feel His very close and very real living presence. I had become one of the present day witnesses to His two-thousand-year-old resurrection. Jesus was no mere image on my church walls; Jesus is alive and well!

This was perhaps one of the most wonderful spiritual gifts that I was ever privileged to receive. What could be better than walking beside the risen Savior—feeling His close presence, sharing everyday life with Him? In human understanding, He reminded me of a wonderful and beloved friend who had made a long journey just to be with you. And words were unnecessary, just like human friends who know each other very well. I had only to be open to Him to enjoy His wonderful companionship.

In response to this experience, I would later read all of St. Teresa of Avila's *Interior Castle*. In her book St. Teresa specifically mentions this gift saying, "Sometimes it is the weakest whom God leads by this road; and so there is no ground here either for approval or for condemnation." But, oh how wonderful it is to be weak so that we can feel our Lord's close presence. Everyone should pray to be made spiritually weak so that Jesus will come to assist her. St. Theresa had much to say on this spiritual gift. I took it that this particular one was a fairly well-known and common possibility for a contemplative or a Christian mystic:

"It may happen that, while the soul is not in the least expecting Him to be about to grant it this favour, which it has never thought it can possibly deserve, it is conscious that Jesus Christ Our Lord is near to it, though it cannot see Him either with the eyes of the body or with those of the soul. This (I do not know why) is called an intellectual vision.

"She was conscious that He was walking at her right hand, but this consciousness arose, not from those senses which tell us that another person is near us, but in another and a subtler way which is indescribable. It is quite as unmistakable, however, and produces a feeling of equal certainty, or even greater. Anyone who has it must know it does not in reality come from him, but is a gift from the hand of God.

"Yet this brings a special knowledge of God, and from this constant companionship is born a most tender love toward His Majesty, and yearnings, even deeper than those already described, to give oneself wholly up to His service, and a great purity of conscience; for the Presence which the soul has at its side makes it sensitive to everything.

"The soul experiences a vivid and almost constant love for Him Whom it sees or knows to be at its side."

"The breadth and depth of prayer is shown to us from the Scriptures. Throughout the Bible story the heroes of faith have a communion with God that is intimate and real. In the book of Genesis, prayer is likened to walking with God. Both Noah and Enoch and Adam were said to have 'walked with God.'"

— DWIGHT LONGENECKER

"Then there is a quietud sabrosa, a tranquility full of savor and rest and unction in which, although there is nothing to feel and satisfy either the senses or the imagination or the intellect, the will rests in a deep, luminous and absorbing experience of love. This love is like the shining cloud that enveloped the Apostles on Thabor so that they exclaimed: 'Lord, it is good for us to be here!' And from the depths of this cloud come touches of reassurance, the voice of God speaking without words, uttering His own Word. For you recognize, at least in some obscure fashion, that this beautiful, deep, meaningful tranquility that floods your whole being with it truth and its substantial peace has something to do with the Mission of the Second Person in your soul, is an accompaniment and sign of that mission."

— THOMAS MERTON

Centering prayer equipped me to meet my Savior on many occasions. On one such summer morning, a vivid image visited me of myself holding Jesus' hand. He asked me if I was ready to enter the room with Him. I was eager to follow Him but still slightly hesitant. After I walked with Jesus into the room, though, I discovered that it was pitch-black, and I soon lost sight, sound, and touch of Him. I was smothered in the blackness and groped to find the exit door, which during that session I could not find.

I believe I received this meditation for two reasons. Certainly one was to inspire me to always stay close to Jesus' side or risk finding myself lost in total blackness. St. Theresa of Lisieux relates that for her it was common to sometimes feel this thick darkness on the spiritual journey, even in the midst of occasional wonderful joy and holy lights. The other meaning is that although Jesus would remain at my side always, I would no longer be able to feel Him in this same way again—this gift neared its end. I was now growing much stronger as well as maturing spiritually and would not have as much need of it. When I realized this, I was bereaved for a time until I came to understand that I would feel Him in many other new ways.

"During those very joyful days of the Easter Season, Jesus made me feel

that there were really souls who have no faith, and who, through the abuse of grace, lost this precious treasure, the source of the only real and pure joys. He permitted my soul to be invaded by the thickest darkness, and that the thought of heaven, up until then so sweet to me, be no longer anything but the cause of struggle and torment. This trial was not to last a few days or a few weeks, it was not be extinguished until the hour set by God Himself and this hour has not yet come."

— ST. THERESA OF LISIEUX

"To those temperaments in which consciousness of the Absolute took the form of a sense of divine companionship, and for whom the objective idea 'God' had become the central fact of life, it seems as though that God, having shown Himself, has now deliberately withdrawn His Presence, never perhaps to manifest Himself again."

— ST. JOHN OF THE CROSS

There are many types of mysticism, but one of the more common varieties, especially for a Christian mystic, is something called a "spiritual betrothal," which eventually leads to spiritual marriage. In essence, and after a long road walked together, the Lord's spirit merges with our soul. Many of these passages with Jesus relate to my spiritual betrothal with the Lord. Truly in February and March of 2002, that was the meaning behind Jesus' close presence. It was so that I could get to know Him intimately before the consummation of our souls—when He was eventually to dwell fully inside my heart. Just as in a betrothal or engagement, the lovers walk side-by-side discussing the important things and falling deeply in love. So it is in spiritual betrothal. Jesus is our spiritual beloved.

The book of Genesis gives the very best meaning of the word "marriage" in chapter two:

"This one, at last is bone of my bones and flesh of my flesh. This one shall be called 'woman' for out of her man this one has been taken. That is why a man leaves his father and mother and clings to his wife and the two of them become one body."

— GENESIS 2:23–24

Since the Bible is all about the spirit, God is talking about the body as the spirit body. In other words, in the sacrament of marriage, He is joining two people's spirit bodies. Their two spirits become one. That is why divorce is so hard and painful, because man is trying to separate what he has no real way of doing—disengaging joined spirits. Try asking some divorce lawyer to do that! Somehow, marriage has become interpreted simply as two people having sex. Sex is not marriage, only a perk of marriage given to increase the spiritual love and bond of the married couple. A spiritual marriage is absolutely devoid of any sexual connotations physically. The Lord's spirit is given and totally merges with the soul's spirit and the two spirits become one. Here are some beautiful quotes on spiritual marriage. And truly, because the Lord never has a bad day, He makes the perfect spiritual spouse:

> *"His Majesty, Who will know quite well if this is the case, is pleased with the soul, so He grants her this mercy, desiring that she shall get to know Him better, and that, as we may say, they shall meet together and He shall unite her with Himself."*
>
> — ST. TERESA OF AVILA

> *"But the Spouse, being Who He is, leaves her, after that one visit, worthier to join hands (as people say) with Him; and the soul becomes so fired with love that for her part she does her utmost not to thwart this Divine betrothal."*
>
> — ST. TERESA OF AVILA

> *"Where can I go from Your Spirit? Or where can I flee from Your presence? If I ascend to heaven, You are there; if I make my bed in hell, behold, You are there. If I take the wings of the morning, and dwell in the uttermost parts of the sea, even there your hand shall lead me, and your right hand shall hold me."*
>
> — PSALM 139:7–10

On July 8th, the evening view of the sun mimicked a newly minted gold coin in the sky. There was a huge Canadian fire, and the smoke rose into the painted sky with far-reaching effect. As I looked up and viewed its beautiful golden color, I reflected on the sun, and on Jesus, the Son. Today God's Son looked pure gold. From long ago, I heard the words echoing from a long-buried memory. Our opening prayer of every ESP class had been: "May the long-time sun shine upon you. All love surround you and the pure light within you, guide your way home." Surely, these words can only be describing the Lord. (You will hear all about this long ago fateful class in the angel/spirit chapter.)

> Jesus, what a beautiful name
> Son of God, Son of Man
> Lamb that was slain
> Joy & Peace, Strength & Hope
> Grace that blows all fear away

Jesus, what a beautiful name

Jesus, what a beautiful name
Truth revealed, my future sealed
Healed my pain
Love & Freedom, Life & Warmth
Grace that blows all fear away
Jesus, what a beautiful name

(Words and music by Tanya Riches, 1995)

❧

Just as the Father had sent His comfort in the form of a deep and loving meditation, when I received my thirty-third rejection letter from publishing houses for *Pandora's Story* in late July, Jesus also sent His comfort on a different day for the same reason. I felt the need to keep talking to the Lord in my mind using constant prayer; my spirit had been particularly troubled. All the rejection letters coming in had really been painful to bear. Honestly, not because I had dreams of being a superstar author, but because God had given me the words to put into the book and as such were sacred and I believed to be shared with the world. One publisher, which had seemed just the right fit for the book, still had not responded. When the evening mail came in with a rejection letter from that particular publisher, I felt like a knife punctured my soul.

I am sure that Jesus understood my pain and sympathized with it, because in the same batch of mail, as if as a counter against the pain, another packet came that same evening. Always when life seems too painful, Jesus will send you a gift to bring joy to your heart even in the depths of despair. That something was a letter to me from the Holy Face Society. The Holy Face Society promotes the veneration of the Holy Shroud of Turin. Believed to be the burial cloths wrapped around the crucified Savior as He was laid in the tomb, the Shroud of Turin shows clearly the face of Jesus and his wounded body. Special blessings are received from this devotion. In fact, after I experienced the Beatific Vision of the Lord, a 16" x 20" picture of the Lord's face as portrayed on the shroud had just been hung in the lower church at St. Paul's during the week. Let me confirm for you again that this is His true human face.

They sent me a thank-you note for my gift of $50. Included was a clear picture depicting Jesus from the Shroud of Turin. On the back of the picture the following prayer was inscribed: "He shall receive blessings from the Lord and reward from the God who saves him. Such are the men who see Him. Seek the Face of the God of Jacob. Most Holy Face of Jesus, I adore You and love you. Imprint Your Face on my heart and make me a saint."

I loved the saying, and it made me realize that Jesus was telling me that I would be one of His saints. He was consoling me for my loss regarding the book.

"Thank you for your kind donation that will help save so many souls, may God reward you for all Eternity. Now is the time when we should be fearless in our God given Catholic Faith. We need the special protection of the Holy Face of Jesus. This image of His Holy Face acts as a shield, which our Heavenly Father has given us for the days of trials. It gives us confidence and encourages us to persevere.

"Remember that those who are mindful of what God has done and who place themselves and their homes under the protection of the Holy Face of Jesus, are promised to receive the Grace and strength to overcome all adversities. Let us undertake to place this image of the Holy Face on the doors of our homes and offices. In this way, we will proclaim our love and confidence in God." – The thank-you note received from The Holy Face Society

Six months after receiving this note, an office co-worker stopped by my desk and happened to notice my Holy Face picture of Jesus where it hung from the side of my office cubicle. She had been having a difficult time at work lately, and I was worried about her. When she asked about the picture, I felt sure that somewhere inside her was a need to have a copy of His picture.

As I was dressing the next morning, I looked at the Holy Face picture I kept by my bedside and, remembering that my co-worker could use inspiration, I went into my closet and pulled out my packet that contained all the medals and documents regarding the Holy Face and the Holy Shroud of Turin. Removing one picture, pamphlet, metal, and prayer card, I placed them in an envelope with her name on it and took them to work with me. I knew they would help her, for the Face as revealed by the ancient shroud is powerful.

Holy Face Association; The Devotion as revealed to Sister Maria Pierina: "The devil, maddened, fell upon this soul to frighten it and prevent the distribution of the medals: He threw her down in the corridor and down the steps: He tore the images and pictures of the Holy Face, but she bore everything. She tolerated and sacrificed all in order that thus the Holy Face may be honored."

At a beautiful Mass in late July in the upper church at St. Paul's, I could see energy swirling above the cream colored columns that supported the high ceiling of the church. Jesus' face in the stained glass window was turned. His turned face was superimposed on the regular direction of his face. He was looking at me again, and I told Him how much I loved Him.

"Right well hast thou said, for the love of JESUS. For in the love of JESUS; there shall be thine help. Love is such a power, that it maketh all things common. Love therefore JESUS; and all thing that He hath, it is thine. He by His Godhead is maker and giver of time. He by His manhood is the very keeper of time. And He by His Godhead and His manhood together, is the truest Doomsman, and the asker of account o dispensing of time." – The Cloud of the Unknowing

⚜

In the late evening of July 27, 2002, I experienced one of my most incredible, memorable mystical experiences, one that I will treasure and reflect upon until my last inhaled breathe. It was another one of the many examples of how God—the Father, Son, and Holy Spirit—can bestow eternal understanding through spiritual experience. I was lying in my bed with my Bible and cross on my chest. I had just turned out my bedside lamp and was praying several prayers of thanksgiving for the day as was my usual custom, when the now familiar feeling of a spiritual descent wrapped around my body and soaked into my spirit like a loving but fiery brand. I became a glove for the Holy Spirit's hand. I continued praying more deeply as my whole body began at first to tingle and then to burn—the feeling of burning so strong, I was sure blisters were going to sprout on my skin

I didn't know at first that it was Jesus' Holy Spirit. So many spiritual encounters were occurring, and my mind and understanding were darkened. As was usual with all these nighttime spiritual experiences, all logical thought seemed to be blocked and automatically suspended. Only afterward, in the morning when my mind cleared, would I begin to comprehend the gift of grace that Jesus had sent. These kinds of spiritual encounters with God are at first very frightening, because there is no way of knowing and interpreting them until afterward. But then when understanding dawns, they live in your memory as absolutely magical and enchanting.

As I lay there in prayer, trying hard to keep my mind centered on the Lord, almost against my will, I felt the urge to lift my arms and hands until they were even with my shoulders, like arms inside my own were lifting mine from the inside. But the arms were longer than mine. There was energy emitting beyond my fingers. My palms began feeling uncomfortable, just as I had noticed on several other occasions when the risen Lord had been very present to my awareness. But instead of a void feeling, now there seemed to be

203

something solid embedded into something else and a pulling feeling in my hands and wrists. An image of a nailed object came to mind. As I was noticing these strange sensations in my arms and hands, a new one began under my left breast. No pain or pressure came from this one, but a flowing sensation. There was an impression of a spiritual substance flowing freely down my skin, over my ribcage and my left hipbone. Somehow I could feel a gaping opening from which a stream poured out. Spiritually scanning my lower body for any other strange sensations, I noticed that between my legs, on top of my own genitals, I could feel something that my own body does not have—male genitals. This latest sensation produced shock and embarrassment, until the next feeling where my whole spirit seemed to shift overrode it. With a dual awareness of still being in my bed, I also simultaneously realized I was hanging. There was a hard surface against the center of my back, and then immense pulling and tension in my upper body, which now felt heavy. I was not lying on the ground, but suspended above the earth. Swirling angry spiritual energy surrounded me, other people could be sensed, their voices unclear and bended like a record played on the wrong speed, shouting, cursing. Weeping?

The next morning when I awoke, and instantly remembered the entire spiritual episode, it all suddenly came together and made sense. I realized with astonishment and utter amazement that through His Holy Spirit I had experienced, on a spiritual level, Jesus as He had hung on his cross 2,000 years ago at the very moment when He had died for me and for all people. Jesus had been superimposed on my own spirit, like a double image photo—one where the film didn't advance and a new photo was superimposed on the old one. The wound from the sword had just been inflicted and what I had felt pouring out was His blood and water, both. His blood is symbolic of His Mercy. It was His mercy that was pouring over my spirit. He had died so that my own sins could be forgiven. His nudity had been evident also. My own felt shock and embarrassment echoed His own utter humiliation. Such an intimate part of his crucifixion had been given. It seemed that whatever could have been seen and recorded from that historical event, I could feel.

That day I went to work but was only partly there, because my mind dwelled over and over on the grace given. My heart, already very in love, was swollen with even more love, compassion, and empathy because Jesus had given me total understanding of His experience. I had received a small amount of the pain, but a huge serving of perception at the love in the Savior's heart that knew no bounds. It is true, I believe, that every Christian must at some point in her life come to an understanding of why and at what cost Jesus loved us. He did this for me by allowing me the privilege of hanging with him for the twenty or so minutes that the experience lasted.

"Have you forgotten that when we became Christians and were baptized to become one with Christ Jesus, we died with him? For we died and were buried with Christ by baptism. And just as Christ was raised from the dead by the glorious power of the Father, now we also may live new lives. Since we have been united with him in his death, we will also be raised as he was. Our old sinful selves were crucified with Christ so that sin might lose its power in our lives. We are no longer slaves to sin. For when we died with Christ we were set free from the power of sin. And since we died with Christ, we know we will also share his new life."

— ROMANS 6:3–8

After that experience, I became particularly devoted to praying the Stations of the Cross during the Lenten season. Every Friday during Lent St. Paul's holds this devotion, which is sung and prayed as we make a circuit around the inside of the upper church. Stopping at each station we sing a song and pray a special prayer of empathy at the all sculptured pictures. Beginning with Jesus' being condemned to death unfairly, to His pain at His three falls, the sorrow of His own mother's grief, humiliation at His being stripped naked, and excruciating agony at the penetration of the nails in His wrists and feet, the Eternal King accepts all. Threaded through His agony is also His passion, love, and gratitude for the compassion of Veronica and the other women, and the help extended from Simon of Cyrene. Perhaps since He already knew the outcome, He was also thankful to Joseph of Arimathea for the gift of His freshly hewn tomb.

I know that I feel such joy every Friday after I walk the way of the cross with the Lord and the other members of St. Paul's. The music and the prayers never fail to inspire a remembrance of my astounding mystical experience of being with Jesus on His cross.

"Just as the Lamb had to be killed to be raised upon the throne of glory, so the path of glory leads through suffering and the cross for everyone chosen to attend the marriage supper of the Lamb. All who want to be married to the Lamb must allow themselves to be fastened to the cross with him. Everyone marked by the blood of the Lamb is called to this, and that means all the baptized. But not everyone understands the call and follows it. There is a call to following more closely that resounds more urgently in the soul and demands a clear answer."

— EDITH STEIN

Many months later I was given a meditation in which I was at the foot of the cross of the Lord. Surrounding this meditation was the question often asked in the media at the time: "Why can't women become Catholic priests?" The meditation led me backwards from the cross through the streets to Jesus' trial. During the Meditation, the Lord asked me to notice something. "Who were His persecutors? Were they men or women?" Then I returned to the moment when Abraham sacrificed a ram instead of his son, and then several scenes from the Old Testament featuring the theme of sacrifice. Again, I was asked to notice who was doing the sacrificing. I replied to the Lord, "Men on both counts. The women were not involved in either animal sacrifice or Your death, my Lord." Then the Lord reminded me that the Mass is an eternal sacrifice of His holy body enacted at His own request. The inference given to me was that since women had never been called to offer sacrifice, and were not directly involved in His crucifixion; they were never called to be priests—since the eternal sacrifice was the principal job of every Catholic priest. Instead, He told me, I should long for the highest calling: to be a prophet.

"I Give You My Heart"
Words and Music by Reuben Morgan.

This is my desire to honour you.
Lord with all my heart I worship you.
All I have within me I give you praise
All that I adore is in you.

Lord I give you my heart; I give you my soul.
I live for you alone.
Every breath that I take, every moment I'm awake.
Lord have your way in me.

"The Crucified Himself comforted her by saying that He was giving her all the pains and trials which He had suffered in His Passion, so that she should have them for her own to offer to His Father."

— ST. TERESA OF AVILA

Speaking about Mary Magdelene: "So she could reach Him for love of whom her soul was already wounded and enkindled."

— ST. TERESA OF AVILA

"The Confucians believed that a society governed by a just and "human-hearted" prince would once again bring out the concealed goodness in the subjects. Men would once again be themselves, and would gradually recover the ability to act virtuously, kindly, and mercifully."

— THOMAS MERTON

❧

On October 9, 2002, as I was driving in my car on an errand, I had my *Godspell* CD playing. There is a song on that CD called "By My Side." In that song Mary Magdalene asks Jesus to take her hand because "it is cold, and needs warmth." At that exact part of the song, I felt my hand grasped. Jesus' Holy Spirit, I thought. The Spirit held my right hand, and the feeling of warmth, love, fire was strong in that hand only. At that same moment, my nose was filled with the aroma of Chrism—the Holy Spirit's special signal that He is near. Now with me as the driver, here He was sitting in my passenger seat, our hands clasped over my five-speed stick shift. The grace, or gift, eventually ended when I reached my destination, but it was a wonderful feeling—a dream come true.

Months later in February of 2003, I was once again listening to my *Godspell* CD when the same song began playing. Again the Lord came to my side and used the song to signal His very close presence. In the part of the song when the singer puts a pebble in her shoe and walks the path with the Lord, I felt a sharp twinge in my instep just as if there really was a stone in my shoe, and I was taking a walk and feeling this discomfort, but accepting it with pleasure.

Music has often played into my spiritual encounters. Once a song was playing that talked of smoke, and as I was listening to it the car suddenly filled with the scent of smoke. Another time a song was playing from my *Godspell* CD and it was repeating a gospel passage. The words are Jesus' own. He was advising others to make sure that they take the plank out of their own eye before trying to remove the speck from someone else's. As I was listening to this part, Jesus reached over and touched the corner of my right eye, signaling to me that He was removing a speck from it.

These four examples came from a single CD. But countless were the times when I was listening to music and God the Father, Son, the Holy Spirit or even the Virgin Mother signaled their close presence using the words of the song and my awakened spiritual sense to touch me and send me a message. Sometimes Jesus did this in such a way that it was extremely funny, and He and I would share a private laugh across spiritual dimensions—my dearest closest friend from the eternal world.

By My Side (Godspell)
Lyrics by Jay Humburger and Music by Peggy Gordon

Where are you going? Where are you going?
Will you take me with you?
For my hand is cold and needs warmth.

Where are you going?

"Far beyond where the horizon lies, where the horizon lies and the land sinks into mel-
low blueness,
Oh, please take me with you.
Let me skip the road with you, I can dare myself, I can dare myself.
I'll put a pebble in my shoe and watch me walk, I can walk and walk.
I shall call the pebble dare. We will walk together about walking
Dare shall be carried, and when we both have had enough, I will take him from my shoe,
singing, "Meet your new road." Then I'll take your hand finally glad that you are here by
my side.
By my side, by my side, by my side."

"The spiritual senses are an analogy of the material ones; sight, hearing, smell, touch, and taste. In bodily things, taste and touch are the most intimate because an object of the senses is present directly when we taste or touch it. It is less directly present when we see it, hear it, or smell it. Touch is experienced when an object of sense is present to our bodies. God is present in the inmost depths of our souls, and if he makes his presence felt there, the most appropriate analogy of it is taste—the most intimate and direct of all the experiences of the senses. Here taste is not a sensible reality, but a spiritual experience."
– Fr. Thomas Keating

Understanding surfaced in the spring of 2003 about something I have noticed in Mass since I was a little girl. During Sunday Mass, as I listen to the sermon, I can sometimes withdraw into myself and the physical world becomes less present. If I happen to be looking at the priest standing at the altar of a church or a lector speaking at the podium, I can see a radiant light surrounding them. The sun radiates behind them—a gentle golden-white glow. Although I have noticed this phenomenon since my childhood, I have never attached any special significance to it. Today, in sudden insight, it hit me and I realized that this was really Jesus' radiant light present because the person was in the altar, the place closest to heaven in every church. At a later Mass I discovered another reason why I love lecturing and giving out the Holy Eucharist: I have a wonderful feeling of belonging at the altar near Jesus in heaven.

Withdrawing slightly from physical reality allows the Lord's light to be revealed. Drawing inward to experiment with different objects, I noticed that His light is present in all His creation—from the curvy seashells to the intricacies of pinecones. Man-made items also shine this way, but the light is much fainter. But the most brilliant light comes from watching a priest on fire with love for Jesus during a sermon.

April 7, 2003.

It was a Tuesday during lunch hour, and I retreated to my car for a moment of meditation at Wollaston Beach in Quincy as waves of passion washed over me. They felt just like regular human passion. So powerful were the waves that I spent that meditation trying to discern the Spirit's meaning, hoping to understand the spiritual significance of this powerful, wonderful feeling that I have always associated with sexual passion. Throughout the rest of the week, the feeling came over me again and again. I was mystified until I finally made the connection days later, on Sunday. The day was Passion Sunday, and it was now two years since I had sang my a cappella solo Mass for Jesus. Here the Lord's Spirit was reminding me all along of my passion for Him and His special passion for all people.

From that meditation, I learned something else that truly changed my out-look—something that we can all rejoice over. Jesus was telling me that this feeling was the very same one that I would feel throughout all eternity, not just in occasional lovemaking, but forever. It was the exquisite sensation of in-tense love, and God existed in the feeling. What two people can have together here on earth for only moments is only a small foretaste of the way heaven will feel always for all eternity.

> *"And, because the receptive passion of the understanding can receive intelligence only in a detached and passive way (and this is impossible without its having been purged), therefore until this happens the soul feels the touch of intelligence less frequently than that of the passion of love. For it is not necessary to this end that the will should be so com-pletely purged with respect to the passions, since these very passions help it to feel impassioned love."*
>
> – ST. JOHN OF THE CROSS

A new insight about Holy Communion was delivered just after Easter. When we eat the body and blood of Jesus, as He asked us to do in memory of Him, then we get tiny elements of His actual spirit in the physical bread. It oc-curred to me that when we eat anything, along with physical consumption we also eat the spirit of the thing. I believe this is why Jesus asked this, so that we may grow holier each time we receive His body and blood in Holy Mass. The more we receive this gift from Jesus, the better. Since Jesus is the Word made flesh, eating the bread at communion is like eating God's wisdom.

All the senses are involved in the Mass. In the body and blood of Christ we can taste, see, and touch the Lord. The music and readings are for hearing. The beauty of the interior of churches with their stained glass windows, their many statues, their rich gold communion cups, and banked floral arrangements are for our eyes. The incense of Chrism and flowers add fragrance to the air for a wonderful aroma. We touch each other when we greet each other and shake hands at the Sign of Peace.

The House of the Great King, Simply Worship

Here in this house of the great king.
We come together now to worship him.
This house is built on Christ our rock.
Cannot be shaken, cannot be shaken.

God is awesome in this place.
We sense his presence as we sing his praise.
There is power here for miracles.
Set the captives free. Make the broken whole.

"Melchizedek, king of Salem, brought out bread and wine, and being a priest of God Most High he blessed Abram with these words: 'Blessed be Abram by God Most High, Creator of heaven and earth; And blessed be God Most High, delivered your foes into your hand.'"

– GENESIS 14:18–20

(Note: Salem is traditionally identified with Jerusalem. Shalom, meaning peace, may have originated from Salem. Jerusalem means city of peace.)

"In the reserved sacrament (Jesus) is to be adored because He is substantially present there through that conversion of bread and wine which, as the Council of Trent tells us, is most aptly named transubstantiation (Eucharisticum Mysteriu,m, 3f). The unique and indivisible existence of Christ the Lord whereby he lives in the glory of heaven is not multi-

plied by the Sacrament but rendered present in every place where the
Eucharistic Sacrifice is celebrated."

— POPE PAUL VI

On Divine Mercy Sunday, which takes place the Sunday after Easter, I received a special gift of insight. I had been meditating on the passion and death of Jesus, and what was still unclear was why the Lord had to descend to hell just after His physical death. Suddenly, the answer appeared. Jesus, in the act of being crucified, collected all the sins of the entire human race—past, present, and future. In fact, the sins of all mankind were so heavy that they weighed Him down to the lowest spiritual plane. They brought Him to hell for the purpose of depositing the sins of all mankind where they belonged— in the flaming soil of hell. He buried the sins there and broke the chains of death, thereby saving mankind from eternal damnation. Then being much, much lighter, He rose back to earth and set the final touches on the Father's plan for man's salvation through His apostles and His teachings. With that done, He rose to sit at the right hand of the Father, light as air, finished and complete with His mission.

"I will not easily forget how I felt that day. First, there was his sweet, strong, gentle, clean urge in me which said: 'Go to Mass! God to Mass!' It was something quite new and strange, this voice that seemed to prompt me, this firm, growing interior conviction of what I needed to do."

— THOMAS MERTON

"For the monks of old, the secret of success in the practice was to keep the name of Jesus always in mind. The name of Jesus brings the energy of God, namely the Holy Spirit, into your own being."

— THICH NHAT HANH

By February 2003 I was so saturated by my new supernatural knowledge and understanding of the gospels and Jesus' messages that I became "evangelical," for lack of a better word. Every life experience struck me as relating to a particular incident in the gospels, and I freely related it to anyone who would listen. I understood on a totally new level why people would choose to be missionaries and brave any savage people to bring this message to a part of the world still in darkness. People everywhere needed this knowledge, this understanding, and it was utter joy to speak of the Savior. It brought incredible happiness.

"Zeal for souls is the effect and the proof of true love for God. If we really love God, we cannot but be consumed with desire for saving souls, the greatest and dearest interest of Jesus."

— MOTHER TERESA

"A woman in this state will be distressed at being prevented from doing this by the obstacle of sex and very envious of those who are free to cry aloud and proclaim abroad Who is this great God of Hosts."

— ST. TERESA OF AVILA

"The joy of the soul is so exceedingly great that it would like, not to rejoice in God in solitude, but to tell its joy to all, so that they may help it to praise Our Lord, to which end it directs its whole activity."

— ST. TERESA OF AVILA

One night I was hosting a dinner party for some friends and one of the men related how two of his painting contractors had recently left the United States to go to Romania to preach the gospel. Hearing this story brought a wave of envy to my heart, because I felt that I had a similar calling. How wonderful to be able to just pack up, go, and preach the Gospel. Unfortunately, a mother with two school-aged children can rarely pull up stakes, uproot children, and go bring her vision of the gospel message to the masses. So I had to content myself with flowering in the soil where I was planted.

Then I had another inspiration that made me see that my life had purpose and meaning even without my becoming a missionary. In fact, everyone's does, and now I also know that the most important thing that you will ever do may be something that you don't even notice at the time of your action. In the gospels there is a story of a poor widow who puts her two pennies into the temple collection. Upon noticing her and her gift, Jesus takes His disciples aside and tells them that she has put in far more than any of the others, even though some were putting in large sums. Those two pennies that she offered would cause her to go without—to sacrifice—while none of the other givers would eat less, go naked, or in any other way feel any pinch.

After I sat and reflected on the story I was moved to think of how great an impact she had on Christians as a living model for giving over the last 2,000 years or so. Her offering of love had been noticed and remarked on by the Savior. Just imagine, this one act was her single great work that would be the shining moment of her life, remembered forever—very likely the reason she was born—and she didn't even know that her giving had been noticed. She had no idea, during her lifetime, of the great impact that she would have over the next twenty centuries and beyond, or that her gift would make such a lasting impression on all of us who would read the gospels and try to follow her example. Just goes to show that none of us knows when we will do something that will have been the most significant thing we will ever do.

> *"Finally, I realized that love includes every vocation, that love is all things, that love is eternal reaching down through the ages and stretching to the uttermost parts of the earth."*
>
> — ST. THERESE OF LISIEUX

Over a year after my awakening, after dealing with all the negative publicity and comments aimed against the Catholic Church, and having become a fighter for my faith tradition, one Sunday morning before Mass I had a wonderful, invigorating meditation. I couldn't enter into contemplation because there was so much going on in my mental TV screen that I simply had to watch. There was a television camera crew driving up to St. Paul's, and they were asking for my opinion about why I go to Mass. So I told them, probably not like anyone else had ever dared, not about the physical structure or about the people who attend, but about all the supernatural effects happening at every Mass. First I told them to "look up and view the church steeple. Notice that we need to walk up into the church; our bodies are physically rising to meet God. Upon seeing its spot in the sky, every Catholic should rise supernaturally to place their hearts with God in heaven. Step through the door," I urged, then continued, "Notice by the scent that greets you in the entrance that the Holy Spirit is ushering you in Holy Mass. Bless yourself liberally with the holy water. This jolts your slumbering personal demons from your spirit as you walk up the aisle. Don't forget to bless yourself after you leave. After all, do you really want them back?" I query. "Enter the pew, kneel, and open your heart to God. Tell Him how happy you are to be before Him. Listen to the wisdom, God's wisdom, in the readings and the gospel. Enjoy and savor the rich banquet of words, letting them drench your spirit. Hear the beauty of the angels joining in to sing the parts of the Mass. Don't they sing the high notes so lovely? Watch the Holy Spirit move into the host and wine to make the ordinary bread and wine into Jesus' true and living spirit, given as the greatest gift to make us much holier."

This was the extent of the Meditation, but it was awesome—so uplifting. It made me feel wonderful. How I would love to show everyone how wonderful Mass is looked at with different eyes, ears, noses, tongues, lips, and hands. When we shake hands with everyone we reach out and connect as God—as one body.

That morning at Mass, I listened intently. The first reading seemed to echo my morning Meditation in a beautiful way, and I was filled with joy to be in the Lord's House.

"For those blessed souls who have entered into the unity of life in God, everything is one: rest and activity, looking and acting, silence and speaking, listening and communicating, surrender in loving acceptance and an outpouring of love in grateful songs of praise. As long as we are still on the way and farther away from the goal, the more intensely we are still subject to temporal laws, and are instructed to actualize in ourselves, one after another and all the members complementing each other mutually, the divine life in all its fullness. We need hours for listening silently and allowing the Word of God to act on us until it moves us to bear fruit in an offering of praise and an offering of action. We need to have traditional forms and to participate in public and prescribed worship services so that our interior life will remain vital and on the right track, and so that it will find appropriate expression. There must be special places on earth for the solemn praise of God, places where this praise is formed into the greatest perfection of which humankind is capable. From such places it can ascend to heaven for the whole church and have an influence on the church's members; it can awaken the interior life in them and make them zealous for external unanimity. But it must be enlivened from within by this means: that here, too, room must be made for silent recollection. Otherwise, it will degenerate into a rigid and lifeless lip service. And protection from such dangers is provided by those homes for the interior life where souls stand before the face of God in solitude and silence in order to be quickening love in the heart of the church."

— SISTER MIRIAM OF LITTLE ST. THERESA

Jesus, just before His Passion, tells His apostles that He is going to send them an Advocate who will bring them news of Him and disclose eternal things to them. Caring, loving Brother and Friend that Jesus is, He knew that they would be lost without Him. The next section is about this Advocate— His Royal Highness, the Holy Spirit. He is full of surprises and unexpectedly pops in to visit all of Jesus' friends and siblings. He brings us to perfection, whispers eternal truths into our inner ears, and gives us news of both the Father and the Son. He brings us to holiness and heals our broken spirits with operations not listed in any medical textbooks because they are mysterious, supernatural, and divine.

"I have much more to tell you, but you cannot bear it now. But when he comes, the Spirit of truth, he will guide you to all trust. He will not speak on his own, but he will speak what he hears, and will declare to you the things that are coming. He will glorify me, because he will take from what is mine and declare it to you."

— JOHN 16:12—14

14

THE THIRD PERSON

THE HOLY SPIRIT

Spark That Ignites Divine Delight
Ghostly Friend
Spirit Witness
Healer Divine
Invisible Teacher Of The Supernatural
Holy Fragrance of God

Photo taken on Easter Sunday 2002 in the lower church at St. Paul's

"What is faith all about? I see it as an opening, a window, a door on an entirely different world than the world of secular reality. The faith we need now most of all is faith in the Holy Spirit. This is very important in a time of such enormous change, a time in which none of us is wise enough to know what the right decisions are. This is a need for a special kind of faith in that Spirit."

— FATHER THEODORE HESBURGH

"The Advocate. If you love me, you will keep my commandments. And I will ask the Father, and he will give you another Advocate to be with you always, the Spirit of truth, which the world cannot accept, because it neither sees nor knows it. But you know it, because it remains with you, and will be in you. I will not leave you orphans; I will come to you. In a little while the world will no longer see me, but you will see me, because I live and you will live."

— JOHN 14:15–19

"The Kingdom of God is available here and now. The energy of the Holy Spirit is the energy that helps us touch the Kingdom of God."

— THICH NHAT HANH

Good Friday 2002 had arrived (happily, it is a company paid holiday!). I know it is supposed to be a somber day, but this year I couldn't help but dance around the house, singing a joyful noise, if a bit prematurely: "Jesus Christ has risen today. Ah-h-h … la … luia."

I attended the Passion service at 3:30 p.m. at St. Paul's and thanked the Lord for the ultimate gift of Himself that He gave to each of us. But overriding the solemnness of the day for me was the huge, almost here, Holiday of Easter—a day of such eternal joy and rejoicing—a day of celebrating the wondrous truth of Jesus' resurrection. This year, emerging from my forty days and nights of spiritual trials and difficulties, I wanted to arise reborn, transformed, new as the Savior had done.

The third draft of *Pandora's Story* was done! All during Lent 2002 up to Holy Week, I had continued working on *Pandora's Story*—writing and refining the book. On Holy Thursday, I read and edited the last page of my third draft, and I knew it was complete. I felt incredible relief at finishing the book, a testament of my coming through many difficult spiritual trials that were given during the season of Lent. I loved the book and clung to hopes of publishing it, immense relief rushed through my veins when I finished editing the last page. With grand aspirations, I looked forward to passing back through the spiritual door into normalcy again. I had guessed that all the "special spiritual effects" from the Lord were tied to the book. (This, of course, was not to prove true.)

The Easter celebration for my entire family took place at my house that year. Brimming with excitement; I could just tell that this Easter was going to be amazing. On Holy Saturday, filled with Easter jubilation, I cleaned the house singing as I vacuumed, cooked, decorated, and filled Easter baskets and eggs. All the windows were decorated with posters of Jesus rising to the Father with a few Easter bunnies and colored eggs thrown in for fun. Multi-colored displays of pansies sat in freshly turned over earth in both our front and backyard.

It was a beautiful Easter on April 7, 2002, with unseasonably warm temperatures. Marshmallow clouds set against a robin-egg blue hue sky raced each other to get across the sky first. When the children woke up bright and early, I made Sam and I a cup of coffee, pulled bags from the cabinet for the children to use for collecting the hidden Easter eggs, and yelled up the stairs, "OK, kids, on the count of three, come down and start looking for eggs the Easter bunny has hidden." They both raced down the stairs at breakneck speed, in stiff competition to find the most eggs. They loved the assorted candies and little wrapped presents in their baskets, and their mouths were immediately full of gummy bears, peanut butter cups, and chocolate kisses. I had to cut all the fun and games short because I was singing at the Easter Mass with the Carraways and needed to get to the church early to warm up.

The Mass was inspiring and the joy of singing for God on such a day filled all my dark shadows with light. By the end of the Mass, I was overflowing with God's love. Afterwards Sam had a picture taken of our family in front of the altar, which was festively decorated and heavenly scented with Easter lilies. We all headed home to a wonderful family fun-filled Easter day. My nieces and nephews raced in the grass looking for eggs. My siblings, mother, and stepdad hung out in the house eating seven-layer dip, lamp chops, mashed potatoes, and spring garden salad while sipping wine between mouthfuls. Afterward there was our traditional "bunny cake." This is my sister, Caroline's, specialty. She forms the face and bowtie out of vanilla cake and decorates half with white frosting and colored coconut for the adults, and the other half with no coconut and rainbow-hued candy pieces for the kids. The day passed quickly, as great ones always do, and eventually everyone headed home to the Cape happy and full.

Within a couple of days, Sam brought home the Easter pictures taken that day. Christina, Patrick, and I sat down on our olive green family room sofa ready to leaf through them. I paused momentarily as a bird flying by caught my eye, taking in the beautiful view of our back deck through the double set of sliding glass door windows. The room was comfortable with a small wood burning stove, maple paneled ceiling, and green and gray Berber rug. My kids practically lived in this room. Christina and I opened the photo packages and turned over all the pictures together.

They all came out really nice. I smiled as I looked at the ones of Patrick and Christina stuffing candy in their mouths, and the nieces and nephews turning cartwheels on the lawn. When we came to the picture taken of our family after the Easter Sunday Mass, I paused. Something in the picture stopped me. I looked at it for a moment trying to figure out what was holding my attention, and then I saw it. In the upper left-hand corner of the picture was an opaque white dove shape—a spirit-like dove hovered above and to the left of Sam.

The spirit dove was flying toward the altar and the cross of Jesus, its wings more diffused and fuzzy than the lower body. As I examined the picture, it hit me full force, with utter conviction. This was a picture of the Holy Spirit. God had actually given me a visible sign of Himself to keep forever—the eternal Dove of Peace, the Love of the Father, and the Son, and the Breath of God as well as His finger. A picture that I would treasure forever because it showed visible, tangible proof of the Holy Spirit! Here was God's Spirit giving me yet another sign that I and even my whole family was part of His family.

As I looked closely studying it, I noticed many things. For one, the Holy Family is in the background looking over all our shoulders. The Virgin Mother is on the right side of the picture, her body turned toward Jesus. The Savior is hanging on His cross above the tabernacle with the Holy Spirit in the air on the left-hand side—several crosses are scattered throughout the picture along with many other symbols of Easter, including lilies, corsages, and candles. My physical family is captured in the foreground in a beautiful family portrait, with everyone smiling, and the joy is evident on my face. But perhaps for the first time ever my entire immediate families—both natural and supernatural—were all visible in one glimpse.

> *"I have told you this while I am with you. The Advocate, the Holy Spirit that the Father will send in my name—he will teach you everything and remind you of all that (I) told you. Peace I leave with you; my peace I give to you. Not as the world gives do I give it to you."*
>
> — JOHN 14:25–27

> *"After Jesus was baptized, he came up from the water and behold, the heavens were opened (for him), and he saw the Spirit of God descending like a dove (and) coming upon him."*
>
> — MATTHEW 3:16

From the Angelfire Web site; Animal and bird totems: "Birds are symbolic of unity, freedom, community. The Dove, in particular is noted for feminine energies of peace, maternity, prophecy, and promise of future."

"Then he sent out a dove, to see if the waters had lessened on the earth.
But the dove could find no place to alight and perch, and it returned
to him in the ark, for there was water all over the earth. Putting out
his hand, he caught the dove and drew it back to him inside the ark.
He waited seven days more and again sent the dove out from the ark.
In the evening the dove came back to him, and there in its bill was a
plucked-off olive leave! So Noah knew that the waters had lessened on
the earth. He waited still another seven days and then released the dove
once more; and this time it did not come back."

— GENESIS 8:8–12

Jubilation like a thousand-person choir singing Alleluia filled my heart, and it was so strong that my body needed to express it as the full knowledge that this was the Spirit's picture sunk in. For the next thirty minutes I danced and leaped all around our house, and then, because I still needed to express my awe and delight, I ran down the street jumping, shouting, and laughing with my daughter, who had joined me just for the fun of it. My neighbors must have raised their eyebrows, but I was beyond elation over God's amazing gift.

After I calmed down just a bit, I decided that such an amazing picture should be given to everyone I knew. So I examined the negative, and reflected on the same image, only in black this time. "How wonderful," I thought. "I will be able to make copies to give everyone!" After making the copies, I composed a letter to send with the picture to my mom, aunt, brothers, and sisters. I couldn't wait to hear their reactions.

My mom and Aunt Bernie, who are also strong Catholics, had the faith to believe that the picture showed the Holy Spirit. But unfortunately, all six of my brothers and sisters were either lapsed Catholics, had switched religions, or had given up any belief in God altogether, and none had the necessary spiritual ability to see it for what it was—a tremendous gift from the hand of God!

Oh, I knew just how Jesus must have felt when His family rejected him. My own family's disappointing response to the photo, however, did not stop me from showing it to everyone I knew. I am sad to say that most had the same response as my family. One of my co-workers openly asked how I could believe that this was a picture of the Holy Spirit; I mean, what have I ever done to deserve such a gift? The truth is that God sends amazing gifts all the time to everyone, but most are oblivious to His wonderful generosity. Some people looked at the picture and could not quite believe, but thought it too strange a coincidence to totally deny its validity. After all, the picture was taken on Easter Sunday morning in a church! Inside their hearts something held them back from total disbelief, but their faith was not quite strong enough to totally overcome it. Of course, I did realize that no one had been living in my head, nor read any part of *Pandora's Story*, nor lived through my overwhelming Lenten mystical experiences. So in a very real way, this book is in response to so many people's disbelief about the "Holy Spirit Picture."

"Jesus was rejected in his home town of Nazareth. His former neighbors, scandalized at his new ministry, asked one another: 'Where did this man get all this? Is not this the carpenter, the son of Mary?' Mark (Mark 6:2–3) continues: 'He could do no mighty work there … And he marveled because of their unbelief.'"

With a mind to convince at least some of my family on the validity of the photo, a couple of days later I went to a local Hingham camera shop to ask an expert what he thought. His professional opinion was that when the flash went off, it reflected against something and that produced the image. However, I knew that his professional explanation was incorrect. In the lower church at St. Paul's there are no windows, nor lighting on the back wall of the altar. All lighting is recessed, and it is overhead. All the statues are lit from within their alcoves and the statues block these lights. No other families were having pictures taken at the altar. Even on a major religious holiday, picture taking is rare in a Catholic church.

Also, the shadows on the picture are going toward the right and the back, which leads to the obvious conclusion that the strongest light was coming from the windows and lights in the congregational part of the lower church at St. Paul's. If I went with the possibility that the film was flawed, why then were none of the other twenty-three pictures on that roll flawed? Also, the dove's placement is perfectly laid out against the background. It is not flying in front of us or near the lower half of the picture, but way up high. It is flying in the air as if it had just left the statue of the Sacred Heart of Jesus (just out of the picture on the left). This is perfectly in tune with the gospels, which read that Jesus sends us the Advocate. The Holy Spirit exists as the love between the Father and the Son, and Jesus can send this love to anyone at any time. Usually, though, the love cannot be seen, although sometimes it can be. For example, in the gospel scenes depicting Jesus' baptism, St. John the Baptist sees a dove descend onto Jesus. Also, there are several stories of saints that mention a dove descending on them that could be seen by others.

"Sometimes an apparent sign from heaven clinched the matter; a dove alighting on the head of presbyter Fabian in 236 was taken as proof that the Holy Spirit had chosen him to become bishop of Rome."

– BRIAN MOYNAHAN

"Our God does to the soul in this state so that it may know itself to be His. He gives it something of His own, which is what His Son has in this life."

— ST. TERESA OF AVILA

I was never to really convince my siblings that the picture was real and valid. In fact, after that Easter they continually razed me on my strong beliefs. This has continued to this day. I had risen to a new life, but my family, still in the exact same place, would constantly try from this day forward to bring me back down to earth. However, I know that I never want to go back to the way life used to be. Once you experience a much better way, why would you ever want to return to the "old you"?

During the pre-awakening, a particular song struck me that would again resonate truths in my recent spiritual experience. "Be Not Afraid" would hold three prophesies in it for me. Here is where the final verse comes true:

Blessed are your poor,
For the kingdom shall be theirs.
Blest are you that weep and morn,
For one day you shall laugh.
And if wicked tongues insult and hate you
All because of me, blessed, blessed are you!

Be not afraid, I go before you always.
Come follow me,
And I will give you rest.

The following is the journal entry I recorded on the day that Blanchie died a year later that illustrates this point:

"I drove down to my sister's house at the Cape. All my brothers, sisters, and family were there. Everyone was in a jolly mood, and of course, they were having a lot of fun giving me grief over my strong faith in the Lord. They just don't get it. I did not, surprisingly, feel at all upset, but only had some great laughs. I am getting past that point where what others say against my faith bothers me."

Or perhaps I was drawing strength and comfort from St. Teresa words of advice to newly awakened souls, which she gave to her nuns, telling them not to let what others say bother them—but to keep following the Lord.

"How holy she's getting!" they exclaim or "She's only going to these extremes to deceive the world and to make other people look sinful."

"Then people whom she had thought her friends abandon her and it is they who say the worst things of all and express the deepest regret that (as they put it) she is 'going to perdition' and 'obviously being deluded.'"

"The worst of it is, these things are not soon over—they last all one's life long. People warn each other to be careful not to have anything to do with persons like oneself."

"The soul is fortified rather than daunted by censure, for experience has shown how great are the benefits it can bring, and it seems to the soul that its persecutors are not offending God, but that His Majesty is permitting this for its great advantage."

Now that I have confirmed for you that I actually did receive the Holy Spirit, the Advocate, let us now proceed to explain all about how He is sent to change, transform, enlighten, heal, and teach. Ah, those mystical memories...

My first real visit from the Holy Spirit—or the Holy Ghost, which is His more old-fashioned name, and to my mind the more accurate way to think of Him—was in March, the evening of March 4, 2002, to be precise. Around 7:30 p.m., as I was finishing up the dinner dishes at the kitchen sink, an uncomfortable pins and needles sensation prickled my skin. Then I felt a sharp stab directly into my back between my shoulder blades of what felt like a large hypodermic needle. I turned to look over my shoulder to see if anyone was behind me. Then I ran into the bathroom, removed my shirt, and scanned the surface of my flesh for the reddening patch of a bee sting. Nothing.

Void of a purely physical explanation, the stab had apparently been spiritual. In fact, the injection must have been of spiritual fire, because immediately after I returned to the kitchen to begin putting away the dishes, I could feel my spirit blaze up into a bonfire—the heat was intense and powerful, like someone had just struck a match, touched my spirit, and set it on fire. So overpowering was the feeling that I became terrified that I was going to spontaneously combust. Once I had read about just such a thing happening in Ripley's Believe It or Not. There the person caught on fire and was consumed to ashes within minutes.

> "*The Christian Pentecost—Fifty days after the Christian Passover (Christ's death and resurrection) the Christian Pentecost occurred in the Upper Room. Led by Mary, the apostles and disciples, numbering 120 people, had completed nine days of prayer for the coming of the Spirit. The Upper Room become like a new Sinai. Once again the mighty breath of God and the fire of his presence swept through the communion*

*of believers. The Holy Spirit confirmed them as the Christian commu-
nity and manifested the Church, The Spirit filled them with enthusiasm,
a term that means 'The God within.'"*

— ACTS 2:1–4

*"The Jewish Pentecost—In Jewish liturgy, Pentecost was the feast that
celebrated the giving of the covenant at Sinai. It recalled both God's
covenant with Israel as well as the giving of the Ten Commandments. A
mighty wind and fire swept the slopes of Sinai evoking the awesomeness
of the occasion. The wind represented the breath of God as the source of
all life. The fire symbolized God's glory that manifested his presence to
his people. The Jewish Pentecost took place fifty days after Passover."*

— ACTS 2:1–4

*"When sitting quieting meditating in the chapel, he suddenly had an
intensive experience of heat and burning that was so real 'as if it were
being done by physical fire,' just as 'when a finger is placed in the fire.'"*

— RICHARD ROLLE, THE FIRE OF LOVE

"Like the phoenix, the soul catches fire and springs into new life."

— ST. TERESA OF AVILA

*"John answered them all, saying, "I am baptizing you with water, but
one mightier than I is coming. I am not worthy to loosen the thongs of
his sandals. He will baptize you with the Holy Spirit and fire."*

— LUKE:3:16

Rushing up to my bedroom, I grabbed my rosary beads, got down on my
knees, and prayed fervently a rapid but heartfelt rosary. My hands felt like
flesh-covered fireballs. They were so intensely heated that I was afraid they
would spout fire. By the last decade of the rosary, the sensation subsided.

*"While the soul is in this condition, and interiorly burning, it often hap-
pens that a mere fleeting thought of some kind (there is no way of telling
whence it comes, or how) or some remark which the soul hears about
death's long tarrying, deals it, as it were, a blow, or, as one might say,
wounds it with an arrow of fire."*

— ST. TERESA OF AVILA

*"Divine light and knowledge, so delectably and delicately that it aids
the will to conceive a marvelous fervour, and, without any action of its*

own, there burns in it this Divine fire of love, in living flames, so that it now appears to the soul a living fire by reason of the living understanding which is given to it. It is of this that David speaks in a Psalm, saying: 'My heart grew hot within me, and, as I meditated, a certain fire was enkindled.'"

– ST. JOHN OF THE CROSS

"The Hymns of Divine Love are powerful poems celebrating the contemplation of God as a vision and experience of indwelling, as a 'light and fire' that ultimately are the gift of divine outpouring rather than the result of sustained mental prayer."

– SYMEON

❦

July 2, 2002.

I was awakened late into the night, sometime after midnight, with the sensation of cramping in my lower abdomen. As I lay staring up at the darkened ceiling, I could feel a presence, another being or a spirit, which seemed to be hovering over my lower body. I began to pray, frightened, blind, and unable to guess the reason for the visit. Then something spiritual was probing and starting to penetrate the area just under my tailbone. Whatever it was that was pushed in was after a short time pulled out. It felt like a spiritual vacuum drawing something out of my spirit. Physically, waste exits this area, and later I would wonder if possibly the spirit was drawing out spiritual poison from my soul or unblocking a part of it that was plugged. Almost immediately, I again felt the same sensation. Something was being thrust into the lower end of my body cavity, not physically but spiritually. And again there was a strong pulling sensation, and there was awareness that something was being pulled or drawn out.

After my initial terror receded, and I worked backward through my layers of fear to acceptance, my curiosity got the better of me, and I just lay quietly observing the Spirit. Each thrust went higher up into my body cavity. The first one was right around the base of my spine, and then progressively the thrusts went up to where my uterus would be, then my intestines, my stomach, and my rib cage. It was like I was being spiritually purged with some kind of a spiritual lance or sword that was pushed into my soul and when it withdrew it felt a little like my bowels came with it.

For several hours, this pushing/pulling spiritual sensation repeated as I lay in my bed. Oddly, even though I might have expected such a secret spiritual operation to be extremely painful as well as frightening and otherworldly, there was only a little pain involved; instead I sensed only pressure/tightness. Overwhelmingly, though, over the course of the experience I had quite a wonderful feeling of contentment and even bliss, leaning almost to the edge of ecstasy—a beautiful loving feeling, bountiful and full of goodness. It was like I was being wounded by God's love. When I had this inspiration, I was filled with peace and love for God. The Spirit seemed to be aiding a purging of negativity or spiritual toxin from my soul and providing not pain but a delightful feeling of caring and loving. Yet my understanding was darkened and I knew not who was responsible for the experience. The next morning, thinking back on the experience, my understanding suddenly lit up with a brilliant light, and I knew then that the spirit had been holy. The Holy Spirit had come to touch and heal my spirit.

St. Teresa of Avila 's book *Interior Castles* mentions this particular spiritual blessing and also very accurately describes it:

"I cannot say; I know that this distress seems to penetrate to its very bowels; and that, when He that has wounded it draws out the arrow, the bowels seem to come with it, so deeply does it feel this love. I have been wondering if my God could be described as the fire in a lighted brazier, from which some spark will fly out and touch the soul, in such a way that it will be able to feel the burning heat of the fire; but, as the fire is not hot enough to burn it up, and the experience is very delectable."

"Here all the senses and faculties are active, and there is no absorption; they are on the alert to discover what can be happening, and, so far as I can see, they cause no disturbance, and can neither increase this delectable pain nor remove it. Anyone to whom Our Lord has granted this favour will recognize the fact on reading this; he must give Him most heartfelt thanks and must not fear that it may be deception; let his chief fear be rather lest he show ingratitude for so great a favour, and let him endeavor to serve God and to grow better all his life long and he will see the result of this and find himself receiving more and more."

"Note especially the emphasis of Meng Tzu on the 'night wind,' which is here rendered 'night spirit,' the merciful, secret, and mysterious influence of unconscious nature which, according to him, as long as it is not tampered with, heals and revives man's good tendencies, his 'right mind.'"

– THOMAS MERTON

"Our unconscious contains all the emotional trauma of a lifetime (that we have repressed) as well as enormous levels of energy and creativity. Every significant event of our life history is recorded in our bodies and

nervous system. The undigested emotional material of a lifetime must be moved out in order for the free flow of grace and the natural and spiritual energies in the unconscious to manifest themselves."

— THOMAS KEATING

"Indeed, the word of God is living and effective, sharper than any two-edged sword, penetrating even between soul and spirit."

— HEBREWS 4:12

"Beatrij's experiences are much less visual. But tactile sensations play an important part, as when she feels God's presence passing through her whole body. The sword pierces her soul with the fire of his love, as with the point of a sword."

— URSULA KING

I, as a newly awakened Christian soul, was in need of a great amount of healing, which of course God knew about. So wonderful a Father and Brother are they that they sent their helper, the Advocate, to heal me. He heals totally through love. From July 2002 on, He visited almost every night to bring about healing almost as soon as I lay down to sleep. The supernatural is much more able to be felt when the distractions of the physical world and the day are finished, and sleep is the only thing left on the agenda.

A comparison might be helpful. If my soul had once been a graceful dove able to soar the distance from earth to heaven and back with no effort, then when I began to sin, chains were thrown over my once light soul, weighing it down. More sin produced more chains (picture Jacob Marley from *A Christmas Carole*). After a while the chains, in order to be carried, had to be wrapped and tightened, and finally, they were too heavy to carry while flying. I became earthbound. More sin added more chains, until the beautiful shape and contours of my soul were damaged and disfigured. My beautiful wings were squeezed and crushed against my body until finally they shriveled from disuse, and I could no longer fly to heaven. God feels sorry for us, because even with all His wonderful laws, we still manage to find ourselves in lots of trouble. That was the state of my soul before my awakening: sick, gasping, barely able to even look toward the Beloved.

In addition to healing, often the Holy Spirit might bear witness, bring news, and teach about the Father or His Son. Either is possible since the Holy

Spirit is the love that is between them, and the force that purifies and wipes away the darkness from the human soul to make it divine.

> *"It is needful for the enamored soul, in order to attain to its desired end, to do likewise, going forth at night, when all the domestics in its house are sleeping and at rest—that is, when the low operations, passions, and desires of the soul (who are the people of the household) are, because it is night, sleeping and at rest."*
>
> — ST. JOHN OF THE CROSS

> *"Thus it would be met that their operations and motions should be put to sleep in this night, to the end that they may not hinder the soul from attaining the supernatural blessings of the union of love of God."*
>
> — ST. JOHN OF THE CROSS

It was thundering in the early evening of July 9th, so I was unable to go out into the garden and pick the fresh peas that I was so looking forward to eating. Instead, I read the *Fruits and the Gifts of the Spirit* by Thomas Keating. What a beautiful book! Toward the end of the book I dozed off only to be awakened by Sam and the children as they drove up the driveway in our silver minivan on the way home from Fire Island. I noticed that my body still had the tinkling, snug, deep heated feeling of being in union with God.

Later that same night after everyone else was in bed I took out my cross and my Bible and read. I finished the final pages of Keating's book, when I suddenly felt the Holy Spirit descend and impart on me a similar spiritual experience to the one I remembered from one week ago—another deep soul wounding/spiritual cleansing. I was laying on my back with my cross on my abdomen and my hands clutching my Bible, which was just below on my lower stomach. Under my back beneath the sheets were the seven stones that the Father had inspired me to pick up over Fourth of July weekend, and the piece of hematite nestled in its totem pole—obtained during my shopping trip in Canada shortly after my awakening—hung from my throat. I kept thinking of the Father and the Son, and how I wanted to give all my love to God—to give Him all I am and hold nothing back.

This time the spiritual sword went much further up into my body; in fact, I could feel it penetrate my spirit all the way from the base of my spine through to the top of my head. Perhaps rather than a sword it was more like the light saber that Luke Skywalker had used as a Jedi Knight. I pictured it cauterizing all the black sins on my soul. As the Holy Spirit worked up my entire spirit body, beginning with the base of my spine, a memory surfaced from my long-ago ESP class about Chakras, and as the Holy Spirit worked on my soul

I mentally recalled there were different Chakras at different points on a soul. As I rewrote this section later, after some research to refresh my memory, I filled them in where they are in a human body. This spiritual encounter and healing truly reflected this ancient knowledge about Chakras. There are, of course, seven of them on the body.

From the base of my spine (root Chakra), the sword penetrated to the center of my abdomen (orange Chakra). It penetrated and then it was pulled out again. There was a sensation of pulling out whatever was blocking my soul or sucking out of spirit—ridding it of darkness or sin. Next, the spiritual lance went up into my solar plexus region and the area of the lungs. Because the entire spiritual process became more understandable, the longer it went on, by the time the Spirit got to my heart Chakra, I was able to relax and spiritually observe. At the same time I filled my mind with constant prayers until my spirit began to repeat the prayers so that I could hear them but did not actually have to say them in my mind—sort of like a prayer computer program.

Finally, passing through the throat, brow, and crown Chakras, the spiritual sword finished its work. It had passed through all my Chakras, opening everything up, unblocking, and unplugging my entire spiritual body. All the while during this spiritual operation there was a feeling of being suspended in a gentle flowing stream that cleansed my body. The stream flowed from my head to my feet, and as I was rid of negative issues/emotions they washed away from my bowels and under my legs.

At the same time as the sword was working its magic there was also a feeling of pressure and massage on my bowels, stomach, chest, neck, throat/mouth, nasal passages, eyes, ears, the third eye, and the top of my head. I remember that my eyes were pushed into their sockets and held during this part. From time to time the Holy Spirit paused in His work and allowed me to rest, but not for long. After a particular spirit body part was healed, sometimes there was a burning or numbing sensation afterward. Sometimes there was pain, especially toward the end; I tried to welcome it.

The Holy Spirit seemed to read my mind as He did his work. Whenever a sensation became too painful or too overwhelming, and I had this thought, the Spirit eased up a bit. He was going with my ability to endure the purging/healing, which just goes to show how loving and merciful God really is. Purgatory is quite different from hell, because although there is fire in both places, in purgatory the pace of purging will go only on the individual's pain tolerance level. In hell, it is all consuming and never-ending.

The process during this night lasted about two hours. After the cleansing of my spirit, the sensations described became less distinct. They were of general body burning, numbness, gentle touches, and probes.

Take My Life
Song by Scott Underwood

Holiness, Holiness is what I long for.
Holiness is what I need.
Holiness, holiness
Is what you want from me.
Faithfulness, faithfulness is what I long for.
Faithfulness is what I need.
Faithfulness, faithfulness
Is what you want from me.

So take my heart, and form it. Take my mind; transform it. Take my will; conform it to yours, to yours, O Lord!

"Say to those whose hearts are frightened: Be strong, fear not! Here is your God. He comes with vindication, with divine recompense. He comes to save you. Then will the eyes of the blind be opened, the ears of the deaf be cleared, then will the lame leap like a stag. The tongue of the mute will sing." – Isaiah 4:35–36

"Just once, let the love of God take entire and absolute possession of your heart; let it become to your heart like a second nature." – Mother Teresa

The Chakras; From the Web site of the Brofman Foundation for the Advancement of Healing

"Crown Chakra: Top of Head, Violet, Brain, nervous system, shows relationship with God the father. Sense: Empathy, unity, experiencing another person's experience as if you were inside them, being them. Element: Inner Light. Metaphysically, this is considered the most subtle element of which the entire physical universe is created."

"Brow Chakra: Third Eye, Center of forehead, Midnight Blue, forehead and temples, Sense: ESP, inner senses corresponding to the outer senses, which together is considered spirit-to spirit communication. These include, clairvoyance (inner sense of vision), clairaudience (inner sense of hearing), and clairsentience (inner sense of touch). Spirituality, subconscious."

"Throat Chakra: Base of Throat, Sky Blue, throat and neck, arms and hands. Sense of Hearing, Consciousness: The aspects of expressing and receiving, artistic expression, listening to one's intuition. This is the first level of consciousness in which one perceives directly another level of Intelligence, and experiences one's interaction with this other Intelligence."

"Heart Chakra: Center of Chest, Emerald Green, heart and circulatory systems and the lungs and chest. Sense: The sense of touch from inside the body. Perceptions of love, relationships with people."

"Solar Plexus Chakra: Yellow, muscular system, the skin, stomach, liver, eyes. Sense: Eyesight. Consciousness: Perceptions concerned with power, control, freedom, ease of being, and mental activity."

"Orange Chakra: Center of the Abdomen—Reproductive system, sexual organs. Consciousness—associated with food and sex. Pleasurable, having children, willingness to feel emotion."

"Root Chakra: Red Perineum, base of the spine, Skeleton system, Sense-smell, survival, passion, vitality, instinct, security, trust, relationship with money, home, job, connection with Mother Earth."

There was a sense of closeness to death, and at one point I remember crying because I didn't want to leave the children; then I remembered with incredible joy their birth and the love I have for them. I told the Holy Spirit that it would be all right if He took me and I passed out of this life, but I would rather stay and complete my mission of motherhood, the earthly part of my spiritual journey and His vision for me. After several minutes of feeling that my soul was going to leave my body, the feeling passed. Then other touches happened. I drifted in and out of awareness.

Next, I recalled a vivid internal vision of myself pushing up through a cocoon-type egg. When I emerged I was different. For one thing, in my vision I had wings. The wings were wet and wrinkled against my back, and I was very tired. Even though I knew that God was above me, I could not summon the courage or energy to look up. I lay on top of the cocoon spent and needing rest. All the while during my vision my body was leaden, and I knew I couldn't move even if I had wanted to. Sometimes it felt like I would stop breathing. Twice I drifted into union and felt all the beauty of God and heaven touch me. After the purification was over, I lay on my side and envisioned wings stiffening and drying on my back. I drifted to sleep. My spiritual wings, which have so long ago been crushed, broken, and forgotten, had been reformed. Now I could return to heaven at will. (This is what the act of contemplation is all about!)

August 28, 2002

This particular date brought about another Spirit visit to perform another spiritual operation on my soul. It was a very strong one—especially in my lower body—and it lasted two hours. The Spirit brought burning, tingling, numbing to the point of pain in my lower body on that night.

According to St. John of Cross' *Dark Night of the Soul*, which I had by this point read and highlighted many sections, I judged myself to be somewhere in the Dark Night of the Spirit. Only for me it was not only one night, but many different nights.

> *"So great are the weakness and imperfection of the soul that the hand of God, so soft and gentle, is felt to be so heavy and oppressive, though merely touching it, and that, too, most mercifully; for He touches the soul, not to chastise it, but to load it with His graces."*
>
> — ST. JOHN OF THE CROSS

> *"No less wonderful are the effects of the powerful Divine illumination, which from time to time enfolds the soul in the splendours of glory. When the effects of the light that wounds and yet illumines are combined with those of the enkindlement that melts the soul with its heat, the delights experienced are so great as to be ineffable."*
>
> — ST. JOHN OF THE CROSS

> *"As we are saying, then, this little butterfly has not died, full of joy at having found rest, and within her lives Christ."*
>
> — ST. TERESA OF AVILA

> *"God implants Himself in the interior of that soul in such a way that, when it returns to itself, it cannot possibly doubt that God has been in it and it has been in God. A certainty remains in the soul, which can be put there only by God."*
>
> — ST. TERESA OF AVILA

> *"Human beings were created for intimacy with the Holy as well as intimacy with the human."*
>
> — JERRY D. KEENEY

Throughout the fall of 2002, I added in a special supplemental lesson each week for my CCD class (I will relate some stories on my CCD classes and other charity experiences in a coming chapter), which covered my various learning about God the Father, Jesus, and the Holy Spirit. For Jesus I planned to talk about His Holy Face and the Shroud of Turin. For the Holy Spirit, I anticipated showing my Holy Spirit picture to my class and sharing some of my experiences of Him. Not the mystical ones, of course; I considered those too spiritually advanced for them yet. I had copies of the photo made—one for each student. In the evening before the CCD class where I was to pass out the picture of the Holy Spirit, I was in my car thinking about the wonderful surprise I had in store for my students—my special picture of the Holy Spirit. As I neared St. Paul's, on the way home the interior of my car suddenly had the very distinct aroma of Easter lilies. Their fragrance was so beautiful, and it surrounded me in a cloud so that my spirit became intoxicated with it. I knew that the special scent was from the Advocate. On the night of class I passed out one picture to each of my students to show them that every once in a while God does become visible. They were really blown away.

Later that same evening, as I was thinking of how well it had all gone, I took another look at my picture and realized exactly why the Holy Spirit had sent that particular aromatic gift. In the background of the picture my family had our backs to a very large collection of Easter lilies, which were on display for the rest of the Easter season. The Holy Spirit was applauding my giving the picture to my students in His own special, creative, and unique way.

Although the author of the Cloud of the Unknowing is not really impressed by "the scent of strange perfumes, the hearing of sweet sounds," it is nevertheless wonderful when you are the recipient of these kinds of divine gifts. They make you feel so special.

⚜

Just as Jesus does, the Holy Spirit loves to send quick messages to my mind through inspirations. I have become a big fan of this genuine type of spiritual gift. Sometimes they came just in time to explain something puzzling in the gospels, for instance. Or they might be sent to strengthen, bring new hope on an old problem, help you get over an old hurt, or just put a smile on your face. Many times they inspired a fictional scene in which I saved a small part of the planet or a friend—making me feel exactly like a spiritual superhero. There really is no telling what type of inspirational gifts the Holy Spirit might send—but I can guarantee that they will all be astonishing.

One day in the summer of 2002, I felt an inspiration to send an e-mail to a friend. The e-mail was frankly written to display the hurt I felt over what had happened between us in the past, and I felt totally justified, but I still hated to send it since I knew that he would hate reading it. But I needed to get it off my chest. When I hesitated sending it after it was written, I felt the Holy Spirit just under the seat of my pants. He was pushing me upward, urging the message to go ahead and click the send button. So I did.

For the next four days not getting a response I felt saddened and a little lost. I thought a lot about what St. John of the Cross says in a passage of *The Dark Night of the Soul* that speaks to the part of the journey were the soul feels alone and friendless, and I wondered if I wasn't going through the same thing. Lately it seemed that I had lost all my friends; only God felt close. I had noticed, though, that my recent meditations seemed to be focused on freeing up the bonds of hurt and frustration from my past that have been holding me back on my spiritual journey. I think the Holy Spirit was giving me a crash course in assertiveness training.

Maybe it was because I was the oldest girl in a large family, or maybe it was because I have always been very compassionate and empathetic, or maybe it was growing up female. Perhaps it was all three things, but I have never been confident or assertive. I spent all my life bearing the brunt of other's stress, anger, or greed. I never stuck up for myself, and I always backed down from a fight. I played the part of a little brown mouse, running back into my hole whenever anything confrontational surfaced.

I simply gave in.

My whole life, starting from babyhood, had been spent letting other people step on me to allow them to grab the largest piece of cake, my boyfriend, or a higher opinion of himself or herself. Sometimes the Spirit of Truth illuminates these dark, hidden corners of your soul and forces you to take a good look at them—bringing them to light. He forces you to deal with your long-buried issues. This part of the journey is very uncomfortable. In addition, my soul seemed to be constantly releasing pent up emotions through the form of spiritual energy. The energy release could feel like pinpricks, twinges, or sometimes like pressure on my brain causing it to shift from one side to the other inside my skull.

The next day, my girlfriend Paula sent me an e-mail that I'm sure was inspired by His Holy Highness. It was about two angels who stay at a rich man's house. In the rich man's house, the older angel works on fixing up a hole in the man's house even though the couple had not been very hospitable. In the poor but nice people's house, the older angel kills the couple's cow. The younger angel is confused by the act and asks what the older angel is doing. Then the older one says to the younger one that all is not what it seems. He plugged up the hole so the rich couple would not find the gold hidden in the cellar and gave the cow to the angel of death instead of the wife.

That e-mail really spoke to me. I wondered if the story was sent to illustrate that the same principal was true in my own life. All the bad things that were happening were on a broader level good things; I must trust and be patient. Sometimes it is incredibly hard to trust and be patient when the stress of life builds up; its tough advice to take. The car breaks down; one of the children's teachers calls to you about an issue that is news to you; the boss is suddenly taken ill and will be out for six weeks and you need to step into his shoes. All these things feel awful at the time but signal changes that are either coming or that you need to bring about.

The following day, I received a call from my friend. We ended up having a long conversation, clearing the air of a lot of tenseness and misunderstanding. After I hung up the phone, I grabbed my car keys and drove to the beach to take a long walk and unwind. It had been a very "heavy" conversation. As I got to the beach, I walked and watched a man using the wind currents to fly his hang glider. He looked so content sailing in the air above the ground that I wished I could somehow fly with him. With sudden insight, with my eyes still focused on the rainbow hue of the glider wings, I remembered that two hang gliders had been featured prominently in the oil painting I had given my friend just the year before for Christmas. With dawning understanding, I knew that the two of us were now free from all the past pain. We would both be able to fly above it now. Thanks to a little help from my Holy Friend.

❦

The Holy Spirit has a wonderful sense of fun. One night as I sat watching a movie, I was laughing because the movie was very comical. In between belly laughs, I felt the Holy Spirit well up inside me, and I could feel loving, gentle, caressing touches on the inside. He was signaling me from inside my heart that He was enjoying my laughter. This reminded me of the witty side of God after I had another humorous incident the following spring when I requesting a blessing upon some metals and crosses at Arch Street. This time it was Jesus' Spirit who laughed with me. One of the metals was of St. Lucy, the patron saint of the blind. It was for my sister Caroline's friend who had just become blind during an operation to fix a deviated septum. And the other was of the Immaculate Mother, for my sister, who has always had a deep love for Mary. At the church office I found a priest and asked him to bless the metals. He did so but in so perfunctorily a manner, that it was like he was not blessing them at all. Inwardly I laughed at the scene. Inside my head, I asked Jesus, who I could sense right at my side, to bless them again properly, which, of course, He did. Then the Lord and I both had a good inward laugh over the priest's quick sign of the cross and five seconds of mumbled blessing. Jesus did not seem upset at all at his holy-less blessing. Jesus must have known what issues and concerns were playing in his head that had made this priest so very distracted.

235

"God is extremely down to earth and has a certain humor and play-fulness, qualities that Jesus manifests in the Gospels, especially in the parables."

— THOMAS KEATING

In September 2002 the Holy Spirit delivered an amazing spiritual gift—one that would always be a cherished memory of my spiritual journey. As I was lying on my side of the bed with the lights turned off, trying to sleep, I felt spiritual energy swirling, not from around me or over me or even underneath me, but for the first time *within* me. What started out as a tiny point of energy grew and grew until it was full human size. The Holy Spirit had made the trip from heaven this time from inside of my heart rather than from somewhere outside my spirit. The path had been cleared. My highway to heaven was now open. The Holy Spirit helped me unblock my very own "narrow way"—a direct path—to the Father, Son, and the Holy Spirit. My conscious awareness could now descend into heaven through my own heart.

As the Holy Spirit flew into my awareness from the deep place in my heart that is heaven, He brought me a gift. At first it was just a gentle waft such as one might notice as they were walking by a rose garden, although I could distinctly tell that the fragrance was not from the surrounding area, but from inside. The smell stopped at the bridge of my nose and did not get released into the room. Every time I breathed in I smelled it, not at the outer edge of my nose, but deep inside under the bridge. From gentle waft the scent intensified to a heady aroma. But when He was fully with me, my whole spirit was doused with holy fragrance so strong that it was a little alarming in its intensity, but its scent was intoxicating. The Holy Spirit had come from heaven bringing the perfume of His home with Him. My spirit seemed to be absolutely saturated, and it was a very strange sensation to have it poured into my soul. Somehow, though, it was such an incredible gift that my amazement and awe were much bigger than my fear. I wondered if this fragrance would be the only thing that I would ever be able to smell again; so overpowering was it that surely, I thought, no other scent would ever be strong enough to surmount it. Then I wondered if others could smell it on me.

The Holy Spirit perfumed my spirit that day, making it smell Holy, dousing it with his essence—which is love. Love has a holy aroma. An insight and connection would soon reveal Jesus behind this particular gift. It was straight from the Gospel of Matthew:

*"A woman came up to him with an alabaster jar of costly perfumed oil
and poured it on his head while he was reclining at table."*

— MATTHEW 26:7

Surely, our Lord had smelled the perfume just as intensely when it had
been poured over His holy head. Jesus had immediately understood the significance of the gift and thanked the woman for her good deed—telling her
that whenever this story was told, her memory would be honored.

The scent was familiar. I had smelled it in church on any number of occasions, and I have come to love it as something wonderful in and of itself.
The fragrance of heaven is Holy Chrism. Rubbed into the doorways of every Catholic Church, Holy Chrism is as a sign of the presence of the Holy
Spirit. It is used at baptisms and confirmations, because He is invoked in
particular ways on these occasions. The bishop, at the Chrism Mass held in
Boston's Cathedral of the Holy Cross, blends the holy essence every year on
the Wednesday—just before Good Friday. Holy Chrism is partly composed of
the essence of the type of wood that was used for the cross of the Savior. The
very next Sunday, as I was walking into St. Paul's, the smell of Holy Chrism
surrounded me. It was exactly like the Holy Spirit was welcoming me to the
church and cementing the connection between Himself and St. Paul's, and St.
Paul's and heaven. How beautiful.

*"The fragrance it experiences, we might say, is as if in those interior
depths there were a brazier on which were cast sweet perfumes; the light
cannot be seen, nor the place where it dwells, but the fragrant smoke
and the heat penetrate the entire soul, and very often, as I have said,
the effects extend even to the body. People who have not experienced it
must realize that it does in very truth happen; its occurrence is capable
of being perceived, and the soul becomes aware of it more clearly than
these words of mine can express it."*

— ST. TERESA OF AVILA

*"It is true that God gave to these people the inward grace symbolized by
the outward circumstances. He communicated the interior perfume of
his presence to Mary of Bethany and the interior touch of divine union
to John."*

— FR. THOMAS KEATING

The sweet presence of the Holy Spirit visited me often. On a fall day in
October, as the leaves shed their green and embraced warmer hues of or-

anges and reds, I felt my Comforter travel up my legs and into my torso. His fire/light presence had become familiar. This morning, though, as the Spirit traveled up, the fire feeling disappeared and for the first time I felt numbness. Losing any ability to feel physical sensation in those body parts, it seemed as if my body was disappearing. By His inspiration I knew that He was showing me how unimportant the body really is.

"Notice," He said, "that your essence is in your spirit, and that you will still feel just like you without your body."

After the Spirit of the Father had totally filled me up, I experienced a rush of submersion in His spirit, which I had come to think of as union with Him. This deep feeling of immersion, vibration, warmth, and of being held in an enclosed way were easily recognizable as coming from God, the Father's Spirit. For the next two weeks I spent every morning in deep meditation. Every day there was a feeling of the fire of Love working its way gradually up through my body until the top of my head was covered in the heat of the Spirit. Sometimes the rush feeling came at the same time and sometimes it did not.

> "I confess, then, though I say it in my foolishness, that the Word has visited me, and even very often. But, though He has frequently entered into my soul. I have never at any time been sensible of the precise moment of His coming. I have felt that He was present."
>
> — ST. BERNARD

> "Man says, It is indeed thy Beloved who visits thee; but He comes in an invisible shape, He comes disguised, He comes incomprehensibly. He comes to touch thee, not to be seen of thee: to arouse thee, not to be comprehended of thee. He comes not to give Himself wholly, but to be tasted by thee: not to fulfil thy desire, but to lead upwards thy affection. He gives a foretaste of His delights, brings not the plenitude of a perfect satisfaction: and the earnest of thy betrothal consists chiefly in this."
>
> — EVELYN UNDERHILL

> "The Spirit says to us: 'You will never find happiness in any of your instinctual needs. They are only created things, and created things are designed to be stepping-stones to God, and not substitutes for God.' The Spirit presents us with the true source of happiness, which is the experience of God as intimate and always present."
>
> — THOMAS KEATING

I later discovered a charismatic gifts Web site with a test I could take to discover what special supernatural gifts the Holy Spirit had sent me, in addition to the divine gifts and all the blessings I had been receiving. How exciting! I couldn't wait to find out the answer. After I had answered all the questions, I clicked the "submit" button and was given a response. I had the charismatic gift of faith as my number one gift (of course, I already knew this one), with the ability to heal through prayer as the second. Below is my score for my top five gifts:

Faith: 20 Points—A gift whereby the Spirit provides Christians with extraordinary confidence in God's promises, power, and presence so that they can take heroic stands for the future of God's work in the church.

Music: 19 Points—A gift whereby the Spirit enables certain Christians to praise God through various forms of music and enhance the worship experience of the local congregation.

Intercession: 19 Points—A gift whereby the Spirit enables certain Christians to pray for extended periods of time with great positive effect for the building of the Kingdom.

Healing: 19 Points—A gift whereby the Spirit employs certain Christians to restore health to the sick.

Giving: 18 Points—A gift whereby the Spirit enables certain Christians to offer material blessings for the work of the church with exceptional willingness, cheerfulness, and liberality.

(From the Spiritual Gifts Profile sheet www.cforc.com/sgifts.cgi. Try it yourself when you have a moment.)

"Spiritual gifts are given to benefit the realm of the spirit of man, the realm of an individual's relationship to God. We have all been treated to the painful experience of listening to a Christian sing without exercising any spiritual gift. We find our hearts left cold and unmoved by a technically excellent performance, but without spiritual power. Supernatural gifts are not just the possession of the apostles in the Bible. Other non-apostles also were given supernatural gifts by the Spirit." – The Holy Spirit and Spiritual Gifts; From the Web site: new-life.net/sprtgift

He might send you, as a member of the Body of Christ, His church, any one of the listing below—you might be surprised. They differ from my original seven spiritual gifts, and are not the type covered in the blessing section. They reflect a whole new type of gift, which might also be called a spiritual " job." From Romans, 1 Corinthians, Exodus, 2 Chronicles, and Judges:

"Prophecy, Service, Teaching, Exhortation, Giving, Leadership, Mercy."
— Romans 12: 3–8

1 Corinthians 12:7-11, 27-30 adds: "Wisdom, Knowledge, Faith, Healing, Miracles, Discerning of Spirits, Tongues, Interpretation of Tongues, Apostle, Helps, Administration."

Ephesians 4:11,12 adds: "Evangelist, Pastor-teacher."

Other possible spiritual gifts (different locations in Bible) are: Celibacy (1 Cor. 7:7), Hospitality (1 Peter 4:9,10), Voluntary Poverty (1 Cor. 13:3), Martyrdom (1 Cor.13:3), Craftsmanship (Exodus 35:30-36:2), Music (1 Chron. 16:41,42:2Chron, 5:12,13: 34:12), and Physical Strength (Judges 14:5,6).

One can't help but appreciate St. Paul's wonderful comparison in 1 Corinthians and Romans of one body consisting of many different parts to illustrate how each person is uniquely gifted according to calling.

> *"Now you are Christ's body, and individually parts of it. Some people God has designated in the church to be, first, apostles; second, prophets; third, teachers; then, mighty deeds; then gifts of healing, assistance, administration, and varieties of tongues. Are all apostles? Are all prophets? Are all teachers? Do all work mighty deeds? Do all have the gifts of healing? Do all speak in tongues? Do all interpret? Strive eagerly for the greatest spiritual gifts."*
>
> — 1 CORINTHIANS 12:27–31

> *"For by the grace given to me I tell everyone among you not to think of himself more highly than one ought to think, but to think soberly, each according to the measure of faith that God has apportioned. For as in one body we have many parts, and all the parts do not have the same function, so we though many, are one body in Christ and individually parts of one another. Since we have gifts that differ according to the grace given to us, let us exercise them; if prophecy, in proportion to the faith; if ministry, in ministering; if one is a teacher, in teaching; if one exhorts, in exhortation; if one contributes, in generosity; if one is over others, with diligence; if one does acts of mercy, with cheerfulness."*
>
> — ROMANS12:3–8

Saturday night, January 11, 2003, in the darkness of the early morning hours, I woke up to a sharp pain in my solar plexus, like a big knot. Afraid I was going to be sick, I dashed to the bathroom and massaged the area between my ribs trying to ease the pain and tightness. After a few minutes, sure that I was going to be OK, I snuggled back under my comforter. The knot must have been a spiritual wakeup call, because shortly after I got back into bed, I felt the Spirit descend and begin working on my soul in a similar way to the experiences I had in July and August. Again I felt the sensations of a thrust into my lower backside area and up into my chest cavity. Repeatedly this happened. As the spiritual sensation exited, it was replaced with a strong pulling sensation. I remembered this same experience from July, but in comparison, this time the sensation was much stronger and seemed to actually penetrate my heart. The next day, I felt physical discomfort at the point in my chest, very near to the right-hand side of my heart where the penetration had ended. I was utterly exhausted.

For many weeks after the experience and even from time to time to the present day, I can still feel discomfort in this exact spot, and I have wondered about it. The continual ongoing spiritual injury seemed to reflect the cliché of my having a "bleeding heart," or a heart continually pouring love into the world. Was the continual feeling a spiritual awareness that I would never have a "closed heart" again, and that I would truly emphasize with all people in spiritual pain and bleed spiritually to bring this love into the world?

"On August 5, 1918, Padre Pio received the transverberation, which, according to St. John of the Cross, is 'the soul being inflamed with the love of God which is interiorly attacked by a Seraph, who pierces it through with a fiery dart. This leaves the soul wounded, which causes it to suffer from the overflowing of divine love.'"

"Then will He sometimes peradventure send out a beam of ghostly light, piercing this cloud of unknowing that is betwixt thee and Him; and shew thee some of His privity, the which man may not, nor cannot speak. Then shalt thou feel thine affection inflamed with the fire of His love, far more than I can tell thee, or may or will at this time. For of that work, that falleth to only God, dare I not take upon me to speak with my blabbering fleshly tongue: and shortly to say, although I durst I would do not. But of that work that falleth to man when he feeleth him stirred and helped by grace, list me well tell thee: for therein is the less peril of the two." – The Cloud of the Unknowing

"As in earnest of that need, sometimes He will enflame the body of devout servants of His here in this life: not once or twice, but peradventure right oft and as Him liketh, with full wonderful sweetness and comforts." – The Cloud of the Unknowing

Valentine's Day 2003 I awoke to the intense feeling of fire centered on my legs. Accompanying this was strong pressure on both sides of my skull and around my eyes. So strong was the pressure that I felt myself lose normal consciousness, instead forced into an altered conscious state that was so alien that I very quickly became frightened—nearly panicking. The strong feeling of pulling and movement caused me to open my eyes and try to ground myself to my surroundings. As I opened them, they seemed to crackle and spark. The very air seem blue, the light in the hallway radiated blue light rays instead of the normal golden/white ones. From underneath my sheets and up and over the top of my blankets, my bed suddenly felt like it had transformed into a babbling brook running through, over, and around a bed of smooth-edged stones. For a time I seemed to merge into any stream I had ever admired, the one along the Kacamangus Highway in New Hampshire, or the tiny trivets of water emerging from rock in countless spots in the White Mountains. The stream flowed into my left shoulder, gushed through my chest, and washed out through the bottom of my feet.

I was sure that I was going to be washed away into another dimension by the sheer force of the living spiritual water that was flowing over and through me. Perhaps, I was being carried to the distant shore of death by the strong current. The feeling of being somewhere else was strong and overpowering. I prayed the Jesus prayer over and over, telling God that I knew that I was His and that I knew that I couldn't choose my time to die. "It's up to you, Lord," I confirmed aloud, but part of my mind rebelled thinking of my children left to grow up in their father's care.

Mentally, I was not prepared to die. I wondered if anyone who is not utterly incapacitated or in a horrible life situation is ever really ready. I very much hoped that God prepared every heart before death. Some time later I realized that this trial was one I had been given because I was afraid of dying. It shook me up mentally and battered my preconceived notions about what happens when a soul dies. I found myself dwelling on my eventual death, and what that experience would be like. I wanted it to be peaceful, gentle, and not scary, not overpowering or alien.

> *"When God finds a soul awash with a living faith he pours into it the fullness of his grace. It flows like a torrent, spreading themselves wherever there is an opening."*
>
> — BROTHER LAWRENCE

"The Lord answered Moses, 'Go over there in front of the people, along with some of the elders of Israel, holding in your hand, as you go, the staff with which you struck the river. I will be standing there in front of you on the rock in Horeb. Strike the rock, and the water will flow from it for the people to drink.'"

— EXODUS 17:5–6

"It is as if a mighty river were running through the soul and from time to time bringing these favors with it."

— ST. TERESA OF AVILA

Sweet Mercies
Song by David Ruis

It's our confession Lord that we are weak, so very weak, but you are strong.
And though we've nothing, Lord, to lay at your feet, we come to your feet and say,
"Help us along."
A broken heart and a contrite spirit you have yet to deny.
Your heart of mercy beats with love's strong current;
Let the river flow by your spirit now, Lord, we cry.

Let your mercies fall from heaven, sweet mercies flow from heaven;
New mercies for today, oh, shower them down, Lord as we pray.

A broken heart and a contrite spirit you have yet to deny.
Your heart of mercy beats with love's strong current;
Let the river flow by your spirit now, Lord, we cry.

Let your mercies fall from heaven, sweet mercies flow from heaven;
New mercies for today, oh, shower them down, Lord as we pray.

Eventually I drifted back to sleep, but the next day I was barely able to function. The night had left me low, sad, and even depressed. St. Teresa of Avila would have understood this. In one of her passages from *Interior Castle* she writes: "For betrothal with the King of Heaven I must warn you that there is more need of courage than you imagine, because our nature is very timid and lowly for so great an undertaking, and I am certain that, unless God granted us strength, it would be impossible."

Several days later, after I had mentally recovered and bounced back somewhat, I was able to revisit the experience. The beauty of it emerged to be examined once I stepped back from it. I realized that the experience was akin to being submerged in a great body of water, below the surface. The Spirit of Jesus is this living water, and I had been transformed for a short time into His fluid, living energy. That is why my eyes saw blue when I looked out. But this living body of water was not water in the sense of a wet liquid, but spiritual water—pure energy, with a flow and current to it. I was later to recall many passages about Jesus and His living water to validate it, one taken from John chapter four:

Jesus answered and said to her, "If you know the gift of God and who is saying to you, 'Give me a drink,' you would have asked him and he would have given you living water. (The woman) said to him, 'Sir, you do not even have a bucket and the cistern is deep; where then can you get this living water? Are you greater than our father Jacob, who gave us this cistern and drank from it himself with his children and his flocks?' Jesus answered and said to her, 'Everyone who drinks this water will be thirsty again; but whoever drinks the water I shall give will never thirst; the water I shall give will become in him a spring of water welling up to eternal life.' The woman said to him, 'Sir, give me this water, so that I may not be thirsty or have to keep coming here to draw water" (John 4:9-15).'"

"Let anyone who thirsts come to me and drink. Whoever believes in me, as scripture says: "Rivers of living water will flow from within him." He said this in reference to the Spirit that those who came to believe in him were to receive. There was, of course, no Spirit yet, because Jesus had not yet been glorified." – John 7:38–39

Triple Trinity Treat Day—I dubbed the day this name because it was 3/3/03—three times the number three. I lived this day high above the ground full of joy and enlightenment. The Lord had been close and revealed Himself through many loving touches and also twice through music. He tapped my watch from the supernatural dimension to draw my attention to the clock face. It read 3:13 p.m. on 3/3/03. I think God, the Holy Spirit, is amused that I was going around the office telling a few friends that it was Triple Trinity Treat Day. Later, I would relate this wonderful revelation to my CCD students.

"The Holy Spirit nudges us to perceive that what we hear refers to our personal situation and is meant to be a challenge and an encouragement to us." – Thomas Keating

On 3/7/03 I received another special, fun inspiration. I have a cherry pie candle on my office desk that a co-worker made for me as part of a small side business she runs out of her home. Just above the candle, taped to the side of my cubicle, is a picture of Jesus' Holy Face taken from a display of the Shroud of Turin. The candle is in a pie plate, and in the center is red cherry-scented gel. The "pie" is topped with tan wax molded into a lattice shape. I have noticed that often when I feel the Lord's presence at my desk, the cherry scent seems to permeate from the candle, wafting into the air. It is like someone has lit one of the wicks, releasing the fragrance. The Holy Spirit is always depicted as fire. Perhaps His nearness ignites the wicks spiritually.

> *"When our whole being is rooted in God, we see him in everything and everything in him. This is not the fruit of one experience, but the full development of the spiritual senses."*
>
> — FR. THOMAS KEATING

I awoke from a dream in late July 2003 that envisioned one of my brothers trying to harm me in some way. A spirit (not the Holy Spirit) was above me and then dove into my soul. I could feel him from the inside probing in my head and searching my mind. I could feel pressure inside and around my head. I fought to stay conscious and to keep my fear in check. Fear is the one thing you can never give way to—as I have already mentioned. I prayed intensely—the Our Father, Hail Mary, and the Jesus prayer. Whereas I used to find the Jesus prayer to be the most comforting, lately it had been the Our Father. In fact, Jesus seemed very far away at that moment. But believe me, I was not above calling out to the Heavenly Father and my Spiritual Mother in my time of stress.

After an intense spiritual struggle, which lasted about an hour, I received a gift—a beautiful feeling of expansion, light, warmth, love, and protection, which filled my chest and then like rays on the sun radiated out. *Why*, I realized, *it is just like part of the song that we sang all the time in the spring at church*: "Come Holy Ghost, Creator Blessed and in thy heart take up thy rest. Come with thy grace and heavenly aid to fill the heart which thou has made." The Spirit of God rose from His place inside my heart to look out and stare down the enemy. The sense of another presence ended abruptly. With the warmth of God's love filling me, I was able to fall back asleep like a child wrapped in a blanket, nestled against a father's strong chest.

Later I would know just which one of my brothers had caused the experience. It was one of my younger brothers who had strongly questioned my faith and had vocalized the need to understand it on a new level; perhaps his spirit was trying to find the answer that night by trying to see me from the inside out.

"It seems that Our Lord wants everyone to realize that such a person's soul is now His and no one must touch it. People are welcome to attack her body, her honour, and her possessions, for any of these attacks will be to His Majesty's honour. But her soul they may not attack, for unless, with most blameworthy presumption, it tears itself away from its Spouse, He will protect it from the whole world, and indeed from all hell."

— ST. TERESA OF AVILA

Come, Holy Ghost
Music by Louis Lambillotte

Come, Holy Ghost, Creator blest,
And in our hearts take up thy rest;
Come with thy grace and heavenly aid to fill the hearts which thou hast made;
To fill the hearts which thou hast made.

O Comforter, to thee we cry,
Thou heavenly gift of God most hight,
Thou font of life and fire of love, and sweet anointing from above;
And sweet anointing from above.

Praise be to thee, Father and Son,
And Holy spirit with them one;
And may the Son on us bestow the gifts that from the Spirit flow;
The gifts from the Spirit flow.

"Now the Spirit is not brought into intimate association with the soul by local approximation. How indeed could there be a corporeal approach to the incorporeal? This association results from the withdrawal of the passions, which, coming afterwards gradually on the soul from its friendship to the flesh, have alienated it from its close relationship with God. Only then after a man is purified from the shame whose stain he took through his wickedness, and has come back again to his natural beauty, and as it were cleaning the Royal Image and restoring its ancient form, only thus is it possible for him to draw near to the Paraclete."

— ST. BASIL THE GREAT

"And He, like the sun, will by the aid of thy purified eye show thee in Himself the image of the invisible, and in the blessed spectacle of the image thou shall behold the unspeakable beauty of the archetype. Through

His aid hearts are lifted up, the weak are held by the hand, and they who are advancing are brought to perfection. Shining upon those that are cleansed from every spot, He makes them spiritual by fellowship with Himself. Just as when a sunbeam falls on bright and transparent bodies, they themselves become brilliant too, and shed forth a fresh brightness from themselves, so souls wherein the Spirit dwells, illuminated by the Spirit, themselves become spiritual, and send forth their grace to others."

— ST. BASIL THE GREAT

Monday night, Sept. 22, 2003.

A spirit came to rest upon me as soon as I lay down to sleep. There was a heavy weight on my lower legs, and the spirit crept up and settled upon my lower body. I could clearly feel the readjusting of the blankets as they were moved and rearranged several times. The Spirit was making Himself comfortable in preparation to taking up His rest, and that is what He did all that night—rest on me. I also filled with fire once or twice. But I was only mildly disturbed and prayed the Jesus prayer, a couple of Our Fathers, Hail Marys, and Glory bes.

When I woke up the next morning, I showered, ate breakfast, and readied myself for reading at Mass by reviewing the Bible passage I was scheduled to deliver to the congregation. Then the reason for the Holy Spirit's visit became crystal clear. From the Book of Numbers, the passage was about the seventy elders who were scheduled to receive a portion of God's spirit that had been given to Moses and which God wanted to reallocate over the whole group. "As the spirit came to rest on them, they prophesied." (See Numbers 11:24–30.) A couple of the elders had not been at the gathering when the others had received the Spirit—or felt the Spirit come to rest on them. When one of Moses' aides did not think they should get God's gift, Moses set him straight saying that he wished that all humans were God's prophets and that all people would be given the gift of God's Spirit.

My beloved Spirit of God seemed to be emphasizing this particular reading with His presence that night. "Thank you, God, for all your gifts. If only I was always so sure that I could stop being afraid. Sometimes they do make me fearful. I wish my human thoughts and awareness were more able to cope with the incredible awesomeness of you I experience so often. If only I had not read so often in the past how wary one must be of the enemy's deceptions and snares from St. Teresa of Avila, St. John of the Cross, and St. Loyola to name just a few. But even if the enemy is always there to trip us, I truly trust that You will arrive shortly to protect me. Amen." I prayed with heartfelt love the next morning.

> *"If you are reproached for the name of Christ, you are blessed, because the spirit of glory and of God rests upon you."*
>
> — 1 PETER 4:17

> *"The spirit of the Lord came upon Jephthah."*
>
> — JUDGES 11:29

> *"Now there was a man in Jerusalem whose name was Simeon. This man was righteous and devout, awaiting the consolation of Israel, and the holy Spirit was upon him. It had been revealed to him by the holy spirit that he should not see death before he had seen the Messiah of the Lord."*
>
> — LUKE 2:25–26

> *"The Spirit of the Lord will rest on all who live in this way and persevere in it to the end. He will permanently dwell in them. They will be the Father's children who do his work. For the Spirit scrutinizes everything, even the depths of God."*
>
> — 1 CORINTHIANS 2:10

One Saturday in November I went to confession and that night the Holy Spirit came to me and swept into me, and I felt the feeling of fire over and over. The feeling was burning hot, but not at all painful. I remember distinctly the Spirit reached over and touched my cheek as I prayed. It occurred to me two days later that the Spirit was doing a cleansing to finish up the act of reconciliation done by Father during confession. It also reminded me of the Exodus reading. God appeared as cloud during the day and as fire during the night, just as he had for the Hebrews.

Before going to bed, I looked out my bedroom window and observed the perfect full moon that was a glorious pumpkin orange. It reflected to my eyes the Holy Spirit's nighttime visit and His feeling of fire.

"The Lord preceded them, in the daytime by means of a column of cloud to show them the way, and at night by means of a column of fire to give them light. They could travel both day and night. Neither the column or cloud by day nor the column of fire by night ever left its place in front of the people." – Exodus 13:21–22

❦

Now it is almost time to enter into the blessings given by the Virgin Mother. There you will hear Her message, which is just as current now as ever. But before you turn the page, I would like to leave you with one more reflection and give you my counsel and advice.

Coming back from seeing Sister Margretta (you will meet her in the saints chapter), I sat on the train after our session. I had related my life to her during the last two spiritually turbulent months, and as my eyes remained fixed on the scenery passing outside of the subway window, I noticed a clear reflection of the window on the other side of the train. On the smooth face of the glass, I could see what was happening on the other side of the train without even looking there. It struck me forcibly that here was a good example of the supernatural. First, it reflects the other side, where most people would never even notice the reflection of the other window or even care if someone else pointed it out to them. Second, if they did notice it, they would ignore it. Third, very few people would let it actually enter into their consciousness and notice the images passing by on the window. Yet the window is there for all to see.

For myself, I noticed the window reflection, and I noticed that the reflection was clearer when you are going through tunnels and under things (just like God is often clearer when you are going through dark and difficult times). When the train passed under the light, the reflection all but disappeared (in the good, sunny spots of life, if one is not careful, then reflecting on God and thinking on Him can disappear). The reflection came and went but was never really gone—just like God. Perhaps the next time you are on a subway train you will notice this and your mind will lead you in your own special way to a new understanding of the supernatural side or the eternal dimension.

> *"Look at this window: it is nothing but a hole in the wall, but because of it the whole room is full of light. So when the faculties are empty, the heart is full of light. Being full of light it becomes an influence by which others are secretly transformed."*
>
> — CONFUCIUS

Many of you may be wondering why did I get the supernatural gift of mysticism? Why me? What makes me so special? The truth is that everyone is special. God loves ordinary people. Please don't be too worried if God has not called you to mysticism. That is, if you are otherwise living by the Ten Commandments and Jesus' own additional summarizing one that you should love your neighbor as yourself. (If you are not doing this, get worried!) God has countless ways of using His children in the world; most do not require a personal revelation of God. As you have just read in the last four chapters, my experiences came directly from God and reflect the mission that He gave me to explain to you about all His spiritual gifts. Believe me that He loves you absolutely and just as fully in whatever He has called you.

There may be an additional reason for my revelation, and it is this: God sensed my great need for Him and my loneliness. I believe that to comfort and console me, God came to put His loving arms around me. If you are like me, a little lost and lonely in this world, then pray to Him and ask Him for what your heart needs. According to St. Teresa, "It is to the weakest that His Divine Majesty gives favours."

> "God made me always desire what He wanted to give me. God's gifts came invariably through the agency of my own longing."
> — ST. THERESE OF LISIEUX

"Not everyone who God uses as an instrument must be prepared in this way. People may also be instruments of God without their knowledge and even against their will, possibly even people whom neither externally nor interiorly belong to the church. They would then be used like the hammer or chisel of the artist, or like a knife with which the vine-dresser prunes the vines. For those who belong to the church, outer membership can also temporally precede interior, in fact can be materially significant for it (as when someone without faith is baptized and then comes to faith through the public life in the church). But it finally comes down to the interior life; formation moves from the inner to the outer. The deeper a soul is bound to God, the more completely surrendered to grace, the stronger will be its influence on the form of the church. Conversely, the more an era is engulfed in the night of sin and estrangement from God the more it needs souls united to God. And God does not permit a deficiency. The greatest figures of prophecy and sanctity step forth out of the darkest night. But for the most part the formative stream of the mystical life remains invisible." – Ursula King.

Take heart if your marriage is less than ideal and especially if religion is the cause of strife in your marriage. Or if your spouse criticizes you for raising your children in the faith, take heart. For God always strengthens, supports, and helps parents of either gender in their mission if you ask and pray.

"God bursts into the life of a woman in this situation with the message of his love for her. It is not that he does not love her husband, neighbors and friends, but there are times when God seems to hone in on certain individuals to reassure them strongly and deeply that he cares about them. Both the teaching of the Bible and actual experience suggest that God often directs his love most to those who find themselves at a disadvantage." – excerpt from Michael Fanstone's Raising Kids Christian When Your Husband Doesn't Believe

"In reality it is necessary in every state of life for our help to come from God."

"The Holy Spirit is not a vague, ethereal shadow, nor an impersonal force. He is a person equal in every way with God the Father and God the Son. A primary role of the Holy Spirit is that He bears 'witness' of Jesus Christ" (John 15:26, 16:14). He tells people's hearts about the truth of Jesus Christ. The Holy Spirit also acts as a Christian's teacher (1Cor. 2:9–14). He reveals God's will and God's truth to a Christian. Jesus told his disciples: "The Helper, the Holy Spirit, whom the Father will send in my name, He will teach you all things, and bring to your remembrance all that I said to you."

— JOHN 14:26

"When in inner union he is beyond the world of the body, then the third world, the world of the spirit is found, where the power of the All is, and man has all: for he is one with the ONE."

— Upanishads (Hindu)

15

THE VIRGIN MOTHER, MARY

Beautiful, Loving Mother
Holy Inspiration
Delicate Fragrance of God
Gentlest Touch
Ave Maria Reverence
Window to God
Blue Mantle Surrounding

My soul rejoices in the Lord
My soul proclaims the greatness of the Lord
And my spirit rejoices in God, my salvation.
For he has shown me such favor—me, his lowly handmaiden.
Now all generations will call me blessed, because the mighty one has done
great things for me.
His name is holy, His mercy lasts for generation after generation for those
who revere Him.
The Magnificat

"THE BLESSED MOTHER has said: 'Tell everyone that it is you who are divided on earth. The Moslems and the Orthodox for the same reason as Catholics, are equal before my Son and me. You are all my children. Certainly all religions are not equal. All men are equal before God.' It does not suffice to belong to the Catholic Church to be saved. It is necessary to respect and obey the Commandments of God in following one's conscience. Those who are not Catholics are no less creatures made in the image of God and destined ultimately to live in the house of God our Father. Salvation is available to everyone without exception. My Son Jesus redeemed all people." – Message from Jelena (locutionist) from the book The Visions of the Children: The Apparitions of the Blessed Mother at Medjugorje, Janice T. Connell

Above my head were the soaring rafters, around me statues of saints and martyrs almost too numerous to count, and in front of me the breathtaking altar surely a true vision of heaven. As I walked up the center aisle, I glanced admiringly from side to side, taking in the inspired masterpieces, then turned left and walked up to the side altar totally dedicated to the Blessed Mother of the Lord Jesus at Mission Church in Roxbury, MA. Kneeling in front of her statue, I prayed a Hail Mary and a personal prayer. The urgent calling and need stilled for a few moments.

Last year a co-worker had told me all about Mission Church then took me to a midday Mass. A minor Basilica, but a huge Catholic Church just the same, located in Roxbury just outside of Boston, the entire focus of Mission Church is devotion to the Blessed Mother. Numerous miracles had occurred after a visit and the Holy Water in each of the fonts was seeped in holiness and blessings from her and her Royal Court in heaven—which included the saints and angels, as well as the prayers of the pilgrims who pray here. The entire church seemed to vibrate with eternal peace—exactly what I needed to regain my own inner peace and strength.

Just days back home from that fateful family ski trip in Canada and my awakening (it was February 22, 2002), I obeyed her calling, a voice that requested that all my crosses be blessed—including my rosary beads, two new crosses, and my new crystal crucifix. Somehow I was led to Mission Church over any other church. This call had emerged from an interior vision. In the vision all the articles were submerged in a baptismal font of Holy Water. The Blessed Mother had sent this message; of this, I was positive. I could feel her pulling me closer, putting her motherly arms around me offering me her special protection.

Before I left home for work that morning, after the vision had cleared from my mind, I packed my items into a cream canvas bag and placed them in my car. At twelve noon, I promptly left my desk and headed to Mission Church. After I took a quick trip around the interior of the church to admire all the lovely statues during my visit, and spoke my prayers in the front of the Virgin's statue, I chose a pew near the front of the church and began to pray a rosary. The Blessed Mother had asked us all to pray at least one rosary per day while meditating on one of the holy mysteries. Praying a rosary felt infinitely right at Mission Church, and I wanted to give Mother some prayers before I asked Her for Her shelter.

"The rosary is the chain that binds generations to Eternal Life." – The Visions of the Children: The Apparitions of the Blessed Mother at Medjugorje; comment made by the Blessed Virgin and relayed to Vicka (one of the seven visionaries) -Janice T. Connell

As I prayed, I kept a sharp eye out for any priest who could bless the objects I had brought. During my second decade, I noticed a young priest who appeared in his thirties casually walking around the side of the church, so I got up and walked up to him. I asked him if he would mind blessing some items for me, and of course, he said he would not. I turned my back to him and pulled out all my assorted items from around my neck and even inside my bra. My face was beet red, and he must have thought me very odd, even a nut. I tried to smile, but I could not mask my embarrassment. Yet my task was absolutely necessary, so with resolve I handed the items over. He may not have understood, but then he was not living in the dark nights of my soul. Taking the items, he reverently made the sign of the cross over them with his free hand and said a vocal blessing. As he finished, his kindly eyes met mine without any judgment, and he gently placed all the items back in my open palms. A huge burden seemed to lift from my shoulders.

Upon an impulse, instead of returning to the pew and finishing up the last three decades of my rosary immediately, I went to the small side office located on the lower level of the church and paid for a Mass intention for myself and my family to keep us all safe from the evil one. The elderly receptionist behind the open glass window, who took the piece of paper on which I had written the actual intention, gave me quite a look when she read the intention. I didn't blame her because I would have looked at someone else just the same way if I hadn't just lived through my recent experiences. Both incidents squashed my pride, and I gained some ground in humility. I comforted myself with that thought. It helped to know that even if I saw these people again, they probably would never remember me.

Entering back into the main part of the basilica, I strolled around the perimeter, lighting candles and saying prayers. I stopped at the marble oval font filled with holy water in the center back of the church and slowly lowered all my items into the holy water. Letting the excess drain from the items, but leaving them to dry on their own, I made my way back to a pew. Then I knelt down to finish the last three decades of my rosary. As my knees touched the pew pad, I felt the oddest sensation of a spirit coming up and slipping under my coat. My coat actually billowed out with the presence just like someone had turned on a small fan in the floor pointing it up under my coat. I felt the sensation of wind, although obviously there was no wind. I could only imagine that this particular spirit was usually part of the group that lived in Mission Church. Perhaps it was an angel sent by the Virgin to guard me as a shield; everyone in heaven must know my troubles. I didn't mind too much;

after all, any angel that lived here was a good one.

Yet another thought crossed my mind. Maybe this spirit was really uncomfortable in the atmosphere and needed a place to hide from the beauty of the church. Just in case, I took my coat off and shook it out. I looked at my watch—12:45 p.m.—definitely time to head back to the office. Giving the magnificent church and the Blessed Mother a final farewell, I exited and walked back to my car.

Even with the strange looks I had received, I felt better somehow; some of my inner resilience had returned—there was great comfort here for me. Three more times during that Lent I returned for comfort, prayer, and peace—once with a friend, once just to pray, and one time to take my crystal angel in and expose her to the atmosphere in the church. I knew that it would transform the man-made crystal object into a holy one. As I took her out of her blue velvet box and exposed her to the candle-lit, incense filled atmosphere, a beautiful rainbow light immediately shot through her—Jesus and His Mother had blessed her.

> *"The soul of man, left to its own natural level, is a potentially lucid crystal left in darkness. It is perfect in its own nature, but it lacks something that it can only receive from outside and above itself. But when the light shines in it, it becomes in a manner transformed into light and seems to lose its nature in the splendor of a higher nature, the nature of the light that is in it."*
>
> — THOMAS MERTON

On Wednesday, July 10, 2002, again on my lunch hour, I took the subway to Boston for a quick trip to Sheehan's Church Goods to buy metals for my sister, Caroline and her blind friend. The next day I went back to Mission Church to have the rosary beads and metals dipped into the Holy Water for Caroline and her friend. While in the car on the way home from the church, just before the exit to 93 South, I was listening to a song called "Suzanne" on my Joan Baez CD. The song "Suzanne" has a part where Joan sings about the seaweed and garbage at Our Lady of the Harbor. When the words "Our Lady of the Harbor" were mentioned, I felt the most incredibly gentle spirit touch I have ever felt. It was the Blessed Virgin telling me that she was near. Often God had communicated through words that were being sung on the radio or through my collection of CDs, but this was the first time that the Blessed Mother had communicated directly to me. My heart overflowed with joy that she was with me. She had signaled her presence by the song.

As I was walking to the copier in the office only a day or two later, the air suddenly became perfumed with the smell of Chrism, and I breathed in the most wonderful waft of church incense. It was the exact same fragrance of both St. Paul's and Mission Church. In my mind's eye I saw the Virgin Mary. She was with me at the office. She had sent me the fragrance to signal her protecting presence. That day she became a comforting mother to me. The feeling she invoked reflected a gentle breeze over a placid lake, so slight but ever so refreshing.

During one of my purification sessions with the Holy Spirit, I remember praying to the Virgin. The fire of God's love was awfully hot that night, so I prayed to her and immediately she sent me a cooling breeze, which made the heat bearable—just as if she were gentle sea breeze refreshing me as I was baking in the sun on a hot summer's day.

In early September, one of the other mothers in St. Paul's gave me a book that recounted the Virgin Mother's visits to Medjugorje. My friend and her family had made a pilgrimage there, and upon returning she had been so inspired by the visit and the peace that she had felt that she bought books on the apparition and freely handed them out along with a set of rosary beads to many of the members of St. Paul's Parish. One night when we were both teaching CCD classes, she asked me if I would like one. I eagerly accepted it.

Reading the book had an enormous effect on me. One of the first messages that sunk in from the book was her message to fast. So strong was the encouragement from the Blessed Mother to fast that I decided to try it for a day. On the way home from work I went to the Hingham Fruit Center, bought pita bread, took it home, and said a rosary over it. When I sat down to eat it, I was starving, but I was able to truly reflect on the bread as I chewed each morsel. It reminded me of the act of taking Holy Eucharist, the host, and how eating the host brings Jesus inside us. After that experimental day, I began to fast on Wednesday and Fridays eating only bread and drinking only water. I kept the practice up for a year and a half until I was then inspired to return to my normal diet. I gained a lot of spiritual ground over that time, and I certainly hope that I helped a few poor souls in purgatory along the way. Fasting is becoming a lost spiritual device, which is sad because it can help remove our passions and powerful impulses.

Here is some inspiration from various spiritual sources on fasting. The Virgin recommends a food-type fast, but fasting is not just for eliminating waste from the body, but all aspects of life. Wherever there is an uncontrollable impulse, fasting works by starving it until it is controllable and even dispensable. Many of the references are interwoven with prayer. That is because fasting and prayer go hand and hand. You must ask God for help during fasting for spiritual benefit.

"Q. - Jelena, all creation honors God. Human beings alone among His creatures have freedom to choose God or ignore Him. Does Our Lady speak about that?"

"Answer - Yes. The only way to recognize God in the world is through the heart. A heart filled with love recognizes God in everything. That is why the Blessed Mother asks us to pray, fast, and do penance. In that way we can know God. When we know God we have life and we are one with all life." – Visions of the Children, The Apparitions of the Blessed Mother at Medjugorje by Janice T. Connell

"Fasting is the most powerful spiritual discipline of all the Christian disciplines. Through fasting and prayer, the Holy Spirit can transform your life. Fasting and prayer can also work on a much grander scale. According to Scripture, personal experience and observation, I am convinced that when God's people fast with a proper Biblical motive-seeking God's face not His Hand—with a broken and repentant, and contrite spirit—God will hear from heaven and heal our lives, our churches, our communities, our nation and world. Fasting and prayer can bring about revival—a change in the direction of our nation, the nations of earth and the fulfillment of the Great Commission. The awesome power can be released through you as you fast through the enabling of the Holy Spirit. A renewed closeness with God and a greater sensitivity of spiritual things are usually the results of a fast." – "Your Personal Guide to Fasting and Prayer" on www.billbright.com

> "'You must fast,' said Confucius. 'Do you know what I mean by fasting?
> It is not easy. But easy ways do not come from God.'"
> – THOMAS MERTON

"The story of the Woodcarver: Khing, the master carver, made a bell stand of precious wood. When it was finished, all who saw it were astounded. They said it must be the work of spirits. The Prince of Lu said to the master carver: "What is your secret?" Khing replied: "I am only a workman: I have no secret. There is only this: When I began to think about the work you commanded I guarded my spirit, did not expend it on trifles that were not to the point. I fasted in order to set my heart at rest. After three days of fasting, I had forgotten gain and success. After five days I had forgotten praise or criticism. After seven days I had forgotten my body with all its limbs. By this time all thought of your Highness and of the court had faded away. All that might distract me from the work had vanished. I was collected in the single thought of the bell stand. Then I went to the forest to see the trees in their own natural state. When the right tree appeared before my eyes, the bell stand also appeared in it, clearly, beyond doubt. All I had to do was to put forth my hand and begin. If I had not met this particular tree there would have been no bell stand at all. What happened? My own collected thought encountered the hidden potential in the wood; From this live encounter came the work which you ascribe to the spirits." - Confucius

> *"Then as before, I lay prostrate before the Lord for forty days and forty nights without eating or drinking, because of all the sin you had committed in the sight of the Lord and the evil you had done to provoke him. For I dreaded the fierce anger of the Lord against you."*
> — DEUTERONOMY 9:18–19

Of the references I read, the ones that disturbed me most spoke of purgatory—a place I was raised believing that I would definitely see before heaven. They were chilling because they matched my own Lenten experiences. Based on my own awareness, I knew them to be real. This understanding led me to being deeply concerned for my own family, who still had a long way to go as they laughed at everything I had to say. The book on the apparitions of the Blessed Mother shared amazing things about purgatory and how to live the Christian life in general. The quotes from the book are included here because the Blessed Mother, as our spiritual mother, has asked us all to pray for the souls that are there. Understanding purgatory is very important. If these sections disturb you also, pray for direction. There is always a reason for that uneasy feeling.

Taken from Visions of the Children, The Apparitions of the Blessed Mother at Medjugorje, by Janice T. Connell:

The Visionary, Vicka – The Blessed Mother says: "All my children think that Jesus and I are far away from them, but dear children, we are always right beside you. We never leave you, not even for a moment. If you open your hearts, you will be able to recognize us with your hearts and you will know how much we love you."

Q. Have you experienced this, Vicka?

A. Yes. Through prayer. Just by obeying the Blessed Mother, I have learned that all of us on this earth live our whole life right before the face of God our Father, surrounded by all the angels and saints. I have discovered, through prayer, that everything that comes upon my path each day comes from God. He allows it. Often He wills it. My only choice is to accept what comes upon my path with love and trust in God as my Father, or to rebel.

The Visionary, Mirjana –

Q. What should believers do, Mirjana?

A. First of all, the Blessed Mother says those who know are particularly requested by her to pray fervently, intensely, and frequently for those who do not believe. She is pleading with her faithful children who know about God, who know about her presence here in Medjugorje, to pray. And she will pray with us for all the unbelievers on the planet, especially our own loved ones.

Q. How do we choose Jesus or His mother, Mary, Mirjana? Do you know?

A. Well, the Blessed Mother say that to choose Jesus, we must be like him.

Q. Otherwise we won't be able to find Him to choose Him, will we?

A. Many people call themselves believers. They speak the right words, they do the right things, but they lead pagan lives. A real Christian is Christified.

Q. What does that mean?

A. A true Christian is like Jesus.

Q. Did you experience heaven with your heart, or did you really see it with your eyes?

A. I saw heaven with my eyes.

Q. What did you see?

A. Heaven was like a video unfolding before my eyes. I saw happy, healthy people, both men and women. The grass was of a beauty I can't describe. The flowers were so beautiful I can't describe them.

Q. Have you ever truly seen purgatory?

A. Yes, I saw one place. Many people were there. They were suffering immensely.

Q. What kind of suffering?

A. Physical suffering.

Q. What kind of people were there?

A. They were normal people, all kinds. There was much physical suffering. I could see the people shivering, thrashing, and writhing in pain. Nothing can live in the sight of God but pure love, God's justice cleanses. That's why we have purgatory.

Q. Why did the Blessed Mother want you to see purgatory?

A. She said so many people who die are quite abandoned by their loved ones. They cannot help themselves in purgatory. They are totally dependent on the prayers and sacrifices of the generous people on earth who remember them. Our Blessed Mother hopes her own children will help the souls in purgatory by prayer and fasting and various penances for the poor souls to make restitution for them.

Q. Mirjana, why do people on earth have to make restitution for people who have died?

A. Because those who have died no longer have free will as they had on earth. On July 24, 1982 the Blessed Mother said: "We go to heaven in full conscience: that which we have now. At the moment of death, we are conscious of the separation of the body and soul. It is false to teach people that we are reborn many times and that we pass to different bodies. One is born only once. The body, drawn from the earth, decomposes after death. It never comes back to life again. Man receives a transfigured body. Whoever has done very much evil during his life can go straight to heaven if he confesses, is truly sorry for what he has done, and receives Communion at the end of his life."

Q. Mirjana, how do the prayers of those who are still on earth and the penances help those who have died?

A. The Blessed Mother explained that the prayers and the penance of those on the earth soften hearts of stone, melt hearts of stone. When the hearts of stone of God's children are melted, great love is possible even on this earth.

Q. Mirjana, is it true or do you know whether the poor souls in purgatory can see us on the earth?

A. They can see their loved ones during those moments when we pray for them by name.

The visionary, Marja – Marja has said that a soul at death is given the "light" to see its whole life, from the moment it is breathed out of the Heart of God into its mother's womb until the moment when its freedom of choice is ended at biological death. Marji says that in such a "light," a soul can see the fruit of every choice and decision the soul has ever made. She says at that moment, the soul knows where it belongs. The soul happily enters heaven if its choices have been totally compatible with God's will.

The visionary, Vicka – The soul, however, gratefully accepts purgatory, a place of some sort of reparation. Here a soul must wait until someone else among the people still on earth corrects, through God's graciousness, all the deliberate violations that soul has caused to God's loving plan for the universe and His beloved children who interacted, in His plan, with that soul. Vicka has said that the Blessed Mother often visits the souls in purgatory to comfort them. She says they are absolutely helpless to help themselves. Vicka said that the Blessed Mother revealed to her great numbers of souls "from religious on earth who just now do not believe there is a purgatory. These souls are quite abandoned by their families and their churches.

"No one prays for them. They need prayers and penance so that they too can go to heaven. Please ask my faithful children to pray much for my beloved ones in purgatory who have no one to pray for them. The Blessed Mother asks all families to pray for their own dead by name.

"In purgatory there are different levels: the lowest is close to hell and the highest gradually draws near to heaven. It is not on All Souls Day, but at Christmas, that the greatest number of souls leave purgatory. There are, in purgatory, souls who pray ardently to God, but for whom no relative or friend prays on earth. God allows them to benefit from the prayers of other people. It happens that God permits them to manifest themselves in different ways to their relatives or friends on earth in order to remind people of the existence of purgatory and to solicit their prayers to come close to God, Who is just, but total goodness.

"The majority of people go to purgatory. Many go to hell. A small number go directly to heaven."

> *"Those who lie in purgatory suffer great misgivings as to whether they will ever go forth from it and whether their pains will ever be over."*
> – ST. JOHN OF THE CROSS

Dressing for work one Friday, I felt so close to the Blessed Mother after fasting and reading about Medjugorje that I decided to wear a blue dress in her honor, along with my blue topaz earrings. Later that afternoon, as I was walking through the office corridor, I breathed in and smelled the distinctive aroma of a rose garden in the early morning sunshine. The pungent smell of the damp, peat earth mingled with the sweet perfume of dozens of roses surrounded me in a spiritual fragrance cloud, and I knew that the Blessed Mother was close to my side and that she was sending me her distinctive spiritual calling card—the smell of roses. I was filled with joy.

❧

In October I awoke from a dream, a dream where I was assigned to take care of two babies not my own. The babies were needy and wanted lots of comfort. After I awoke, I remembered with affection nursing my own two babies. That thought led me to thinking how the Blessed Mother must have felt nursing Jesus. It must have given her great joy and bliss. My own feelings of utter love overwhelmed me as I pictured the infant Jesus. There was a longing in me to experience the feeling of nourishing Jesus in this special way.

I felt the Spirit enter with His usual feeling of love and fire. Then to my utter amazement, I felt something that I would have believed impossible. It was the feeling of nursing a baby; only this feeling penetrated me from inside my body—like I was nursing a baby from inside my soul. It felt indescribably wonderful, intimate, and intensely pleasurable. I wouldn't know how to explain it to anyone, but the feeling was beautiful. I wished it could go on forever.

❧

For the Christmas Eve Mass that year, I was scheduled to sing the "Ave Maria." I had wanted to sing the song especially for my beloved deceased dad, who loved the song "Ave Maria" so much, as well as in honor of our Blessed Mother. So I volunteered to sing it as one of the Communion songs. Not being the most confident soloist, I rehearsed non-stop during the Advent season. I knew that the children's Mass on Christmas Eve would be totally packed at St. Paul's.

The spiritual vibration in St. Paul's Church that builds throughout the advent season climaxes on Christmas Eve. It is like the entire structure is holding its breath, waiting for the wonder that will unfold, the joy that will abound in everyone's heart for this one magical evening and the following morning. The floorboards seem to pulsate with the joy of the heavenly choir, waiting only for the first opening bars of the entrance song to burst forth with unrestrained elation at the incredible gift of God's Son—magically reborn in all hearts to experience for a day the fullness of joy.

My eyes scrolled down from my lofty perch high up in the rafters to the festival sight of the massed poinsettias in burgundy, cotton candy pink, and pure snow white spilling down from the altar. The twinkling Christmas lights on the Jesse Tree and the polished golden glint of the tabernacle where our Lord resides always flashed blazing radiance. A Eucharistic minister had just stepped up to the choir loft to administer communion, and now my moment had arrived. I said a silent prayer to God and to my deceased dad. Then I inched toward the microphone; I was so nervous and my legs were shaking so badly that I thought I would faint.

Then an amazing thing happened. When the first notes were sounded on the piano, I felt a surge of spiritual energy—a supernatural filling of grace—enter my body, and I knew then that I was getting a little help from the Lord or perhaps, Mary, His mother. "Ave Maria" is a song of adoration for the Blessed Mother. I didn't have but a second to hope that He sent down one of his finest from the heavenly choir to help me sing the song as it should be sung. So I opened myself up and let the Spirit come through and bring His gift to the congregation.

The song flowed from my spirit just like honey from a beehive—slow, smooth, even, intoxicatingly sweet, and golden. So easily and perfectly did it come that I was filled with amazement. I looked down at the congregation to find several people looking directly at me. I didn't avoid their eyes; instead, I exchanged eye contact. Their wide-eyed amazement, even at the distance of a hundred feet or more, was all the praise I would ever need. They had given me their own sense of awe.

When I had sung the last note, I was exhilarated and treasured with joy the perfect moment. My heart was soaring in the rainbow clouds of heaven, attuned to the pleasure of all the saints and angels. Just like the little drummer boy of that wonderful Christmas TV movie, I had given everyone the gift of my voice, laid at the Lord's feet the only treasure I had to give. Somewhere in my heart I could hear my dad clapping from his own spot in the heavenly choir, and the other members of the choir clapped a silent clap. The song was by far the most magical memory of that Christmas holiday. By far outweighing the every-year pleasure of a Christmas morning spent watching my children's happiness blossom as they unwrapped their many brightly colored packages.

"Ave Maria"
Ave Maria, gratiaplena,
Maria, gratiaplena, Maria gratiaplena
Ave, Ave dominus, dominus tecum,
Benedicta tu in mulieribus
Et benedicttus,
Ed benedicttus, fructus ventris
Tui, Jesus
Ave Maria

(Hail Mary, full of grace,
The Lord is with you.

Oh how blest are you among all earth's women.
And how blest is the fruit of your womb, Jesus.)

St. Mary's in Scituate, Massachusetts, a beautiful parish near the ocean, was having Ivan, one of the Medjugorje visionaries, lead the church in the Joyful, Sorrowful, and Glorious Mysteries on January 8, 2003, and speak on his experiences of the Virgin Mother. Even now Ivan transcends into a strong prayer state called "ecstasy" every evening at the same time of the day as he visits with the Virgin Mary. He has done this since the early 1980s.

Excited about the possibilities of seeing one of the visionaries in person, I planned on attending the session. When I was at my office desk just before lunchtime, a strong urge sprouted deep inside me. The need and feeling became so intense that I had to obey it. The inspiration directed me to the Glastonbury Abbey bookstore in Hingham. I had been promising myself several books on the Virgin Mary, a miraculous medal, and a rosary bracelet, and now it appeared that I needed to have them with me when I went St. Mary's tonight. I pulled my purse from my desk drawer and headed back to Hingham to do a little shopping.

I made my way down 3A South to the Abbey and spent twenty minutes in the small, packed bookstore feeling totally at home surrounded by all the wonderful spiritual books and religious items. In enjoyment I grazed the selection of rosary bracelets, silver and gold medallions, scapulars, prayer cards, and books specifically on the Mother of God. Choosing the items that really "called" me or drew me, I purchased them and headed back to the office. Back on 3A going north, as my thoughts centered on the Blessed Mother, suddenly the interior of my car was filled with the aroma of roses. It couldn't have been clearer to me that her presence was with me in the car. Oh, how happy I was that she was there.

That evening I went to the Mass at St. Mary's and enjoyed it. Together with the other thousand or so people, I prayed the Joyful, Sorrowful, and Glorious Mysteries. With intent focus, I watched Ivan and the area in the altar that drew his concentration, but I could not see Her image. Several people afterward told me that they could see something, but for me there was no supernatural vision. I kept all the items I had brought with me in my hands and pockets, certain that Mother had wanted me to bring the items so that she could bless them in a special way that night at St. Mary's. I wondered why I did not experience the level of joy and elation that I frequently experienced at St. Paul's or when I was praying with God alone.

Sister Margretta later told me at one of our sessions that for some people the group experience helps them to find God through what others around them are feeling. But for some, like me, being in a large crowd doesn't work as well. For those individuals, seeking God alone, on a beach, or in a darkened room at night is more helpful. It is important to recognize what works for you as an individual.

All spring of 2003, I had been working on doing the First Saturday Devotions to the Blessed Virgin Mother. This required confession, Mass, communion, a rosary, and prayers every first Saturday of five consecutive months. By May 4, 2003, I had finished my devotion to the Blessed Virgin Mother. Now I would always be under her protection for the rest of my life. Since the last Saturday just happened to fall on the Saturday of all the First Communion Masses of the second graders at St. Paul's, I decided to offer a special gift for all of the first communion classes as a spiritual gift for Mother. An appropriate thank-you would be to make colored chocolate rose-shaped lollipops for the thirty-six communion students at the three o'clock Mass in her honor.

For the two weeks prior to the Masses I melted chocolate morsels in a rainbow of colors—blue, purple, red, yellow, white, and pink, and ladled the melted chocolate into rose-shaped lollipop molds. I wrapped each one up in colorful springtime plastic wrap and tied it with ribbon. The children may not have understood the message of the gift, but I knew that Mary did. Mary is the Queen of Roses, and she often announces her presence by their intoxicating fragrance (as she had proved to me through my many fragrant spiritual experiences). May is her month, and the month of May is known for flowers. In addition, the chocolate represented the spiritual sweetness of life. That Saturday, carrying a large armful of rainbow-colored chocolate roses, I went up to the CCD teachers who led the classes. With surprise they accepted the roses for their students. I smiled as I left. My Saturday Devotions were now complete, and I could go home happy.

June 9th brought a small miracle from our Blessed Lady. The weekend before I had lost the tiny crucifix on the silver rosary bracelet I had blessed by the Blessed Mother at St. Mary's during the visionary visit. It had become dislodged while I was washing the windows during spring cleaning. Sometime before lunch I was telling a co-worker who had recently lost her best friend that according to the visionaries at Medjugorje, Mother had said that when you pray for someone and call them by name, they can see you and be comforted by you. About one half hour later, my husband called to tell me that he had found my tiny crucifix on the driveway. How amazing, I thought, that just as I was mentioning her to someone else, Mother inspired my husband to look down and see my half-inch crucifix, then had him call me to tell me that he had found it.

Several days later a co-worker and I had made plans to visit Milton Hospital. The Blessed Mother's image had miraculously appeared overnight on one of the third story windows. In her honor, I was wearing a blue dress with a pattern of roses in varying hues of cerulean. The day seemed to drag on forever due to my anticipation, for the story was in the news and was being hotly debated everywhere as to whether or not the image had anything to do with the real Virgin. I had no doubts because as I was walking about on the ninth floor of the office at approximately 10:50 a.m., I again experienced a spiritual fragrance cloud of that loveliest of smells—a garden full of roses in June—the Blessed Mother's calling card. I acknowledged her loving presence and sent her a prayer. She was with me in a deep way that day because of the special occasion. I was sure that she yearned to validate the experience for me. For the past month, since my Saturday Devotions, she had been with me constantly at the office, in my home, my car, and my thoughts.

When we arrived at the Milton Hospital parking lot a little after five o'clock, there was already a crowd. The hospital banned visitors before five, so the people had been waiting and milling around. It was a balmy day, but not too warm, and the sun was just beginning to sink below the tree line as we arrived, which made the image easy to see since the glare of the summer sun was now gone. We all walked over to the side of the hospital where the image had appeared. From the first moment I saw her image, as I turned the corner of the parking lot going around the brick sides of the building, I was struck by how clear it was. Kevin (my co-worker) and I walked up to see the window a little closer, and I took a whole range of pictures from near to far, from the right side to the left side, and straight in front. Everyone was gazing at the astonishing sight. I noticed many people talking amongst themselves. Some had strong faith and were praying rosaries to the Blessed Mother. Others were pondering out loud the scientific probabilities, and still others were openly skeptical that moisture trapped between two plates of glass could ever be considered miraculous—even if it was interesting. The conversations reminded me vividly of my own discussion with my family and co-workers regarding my Holy Spirit picture, and all the debate that it had sparked. One's faith was very clear in the ability to believe when a special sign is sent. That had been clear then and it was also playing out in the Milton Hospital parking lot where we all were assembled.

As I looked at the unique sight, I noticed something about the window that was probably not commonly noticed. Her pose closely resembled the Madonna Statue in the lower church in Saint Paul's. (The statue is in my Holy Spirit picture.) Since we had the statue in our church, certainly there were many similar statues in other Catholic churches in the area. How very interesting and telling that this should be so. She resembled her own very popular image openly displayed in countless churches. Turn back to the Holy Spirit picture and compare it to the Window of the Virgin. You will able to see almost the exact image in both places.

I believe that God, the great artist, painted the window for all to view—an amazing picture of the Virgin Mother. In addition, the window is situated three stories up and in three windows—the magical, mystical number of three that represents the Trinity.

> *"Mary, who is empty of all egotism, free from all sin, was as pure as the glass of a very clean window that has no other function than to admit the light of the sun."*
>
> — THOMAS MERTON

Photo taken at Milton at Hospital of the Virgin Mother
Window Image - 2003

Sunday, May 23, 2004.

I was taking a walk at World's End in Hingham with my Bichon Frise, Al. It was a gorgeous day, warm and sunny with a slight breeze on top of Planter's Hill. From Planter's Hill there is a wonderful panoramic view of the Boston Skyline, Hingham Harbor, and Hull. Looking out toward the sandy strip of beach at Hull, Al and I sat on a bench at the top and enjoyed the gorgeous view. There was a mist over the water and in the far distance someone was playing "Amazing Grace" on the bagpipes as a seagull flew overhead. The sound flowed through the air, bringing joy with it. My heart sang with the notes, and I thanked God for the precious moment. Even Al was behaving remarkably well for the wild puppy that he usually is.

We were walking back toward the gate at the main entrance to go home after enjoying the peace and quiet, the multi-colored wildflowers, the rich lime green of the newly sprouted maple leaves, and I was in a beautiful mood inspired by it all and thanking God for providing such a perfect day. When on the graveled road, I noticed a couple of women walking purposely forward with a long cardboard box between them. There were a couple of flower arrangements visible on top, but whatever was in the box was hidden. As I took in their attire—long black capes with hoods and black shoes—I recognized them as New Age witches. Both were middle-aged with dyed brown hair and plain features. Nearing them, I caught myself staring as I tried to meet their eyes. They had stopped talking, and one kept her eyes focused on the ground. The other, probably the head witch, looked straight ahead with her head held high. Obviously, they were not into making any friendly contact. The sun was still shining, and the spring day was still beautiful, but I felt a shadow creep over my soul, as if a sinister aspect had just entered the day. My soul was immediately troubled.

I forced out memories of the last time I had had an experience with a witch. It had been over twenty years ago, but she was still so vivid in my mind's eye. At least she had proclaimed to be a "white witch." And she had also been friendly and bubbly. (See the angel chapter for more on that story.) These two looked like her polar opposite. They definitely weren't "white" ones, but I knew also that I shouldn't judge them.

Getting back to my car, I loaded Al in and, as I turned to get into the driver's seat, I spotted two men and a boy dressed in formal dress. The boy was in a long-hooded cloak. As I passed the main entrance to World's End, I noticed a parked limo and a man in a tux looking anxiously at the road. Limos and tuxes always make me think of weddings, so I ventured to ask the security guard if there was going to be a wedding there that day. She said, "Yes, but the bride is very late."

I prayed then that she had changed her mind. What an awful way to get married—by witches, no family, no God, no beautiful nuptial Mass, no music, no words of wisdom from Father, no inspiring readings from St. Paul on love, and no true joining of spirits from the Eternal Father. Surely, that wedding saddened the Blessed Mother. I hadn't noticed any mother of the bride that day—probably because no mother would enjoy that kind of a wedding. What a terrible start on what might very well be a very rocky road (marriage is not easy, even among believers!).

Later that day at the Marian celebration at St. Paul's, I couldn't stop thinking of that sorry event—a wedding of witches at World's End. As we prayed the rosary and carried the statue of the Blessed Virgin around a half mile square of the old graceful colonial houses that sat back from the tree-lined streets of Hingham around St. Paul's, I dedicated my rosary to that poor misguided couple. Even several days later I couldn't shake the sadness my soul felt at the thought of that union.

> *"Hidden from the entire world, the heavenly Jerusalem had descended to earth. From this first joining in betrothal, there had to be born all the living building blocks to be used from the mighty structure: each individual soul awakened to life through grace. The Bridal Mother was to become the mother of all the redeemed. Like a spore from which new cells stream continually, she was to build up the living city of God. This hidden mystery was revealed to St. John as he stood beneath the cross with the Virgin Mother and was given over to her as her son. It was then that the church came into existence visibly; her hour had come, but not yet her perfection. She lives, she is wedded to the Lamb, but the hour of the solemn marriage supper will only arrive when the dragon has been completely conquered and the redeemed have fought their battle to the end."*
>
> — EDITH STEIN

The next two chapters involve my stories of prayer and charity. They are under the Blessed Mother's mantle because of her close association with both. She very much hopes to inspire you to take up these two wonderful practices. In closing, I want to quote a well-known song about the Virgin Mother and Thomas Merton's wonderful advice given for keeping the Sabbath holy. The Blessed Mother would love everyone to follow his simple advice:

Possibilities for awaking your creative freedom (contemplation)

1. Move into the country or to a small town where you can have more time to think.
2. Use the early morning hours, when no one else is awake.
3. Use Sunday, as a day set apart by nature and tradition, as a holy day.

No matter where one seeks the light of contemplation one commits one's self by that very fact to a certain spiritual discipline. This is just as true outside the cloister as in it. Perhaps indeed some of the difficulties of people in the world exact from them greater sacrifice than they would find in a cloister. Mere conformism and lip service is not enough. It is not sufficient to "be a good Catholic." One must penetrate the inner meaning of the life in Christ and see the full significance of its demands. One must carryout the obligations not simply as a matter of form, but with a real, personal decision to offer the good one does to God, in and through Christ.

Carey Landry, OCP Publications

Hail Mary: Gentle Woman

Hail Mary, full of grace, the Lord is with you;
Blessed are you among women and
Blest is the fruit of your womb, Jesus

Gentle woman, quiet light,
Morning star, so strong and bright,
Gentle Mother, peaceful dove,
Teach us wisdom, teach us love.

You were chosen by The Father;
You were chosen for the Son;
You were chosen from all women,
And for woman, shining one.

16

PRAYER & CHARITY

Gift That Leads to All Things
Gift That Purifies and Enlightens
The Soul Becomes Brighter and Brighter
Miracles Happen
Prayer Leads To Rosaries
Rosaries To Meditation
Meditation To Comtemplation
Well-Spring Of A Happy Heart
Joy Overflowing Into The World

Prayer

I asked God for strength, that I might achieve ... I was made weak that I might learn humbly to obey.
I asked for health, that I might do greater things ... I was given infirmity, that I might do better things.
I asked for riches, that I might be happy ... I was given poverty, that I might be wise.
I asked for power, that I might have the praise of men ... I was given weakness, that I might feel the need of God.
I asked for all things, that I might enjoy life ... I was given life, that I might enjoy all things.
I got nothing that I asked for, but everything I had hoped for. Almost despite myself, my unspoken prayers were answered. I am among all men, most richly blessed! – Anonymous

"*The door by which it first enters the castle is prayer and Meditation.*"
— ST. TERESA OF AVILA

"*A short time ago, I was told by a very learned man that souls without prayer are like people whose bodies or limbs are paralyzed: they possess feet and hands, but they cannot control them."*

— ST. TERESA OF AVILA

"Let us say no more, then, of these paralyzed souls, who, unless the Lord Himself comes and commands them to rise, are like the man who has lain beside the pool for thirty years: they are unfortunate creatures and live in great peril. Let us rather think of certain other souls, who do eventually enter the castle."

— ST. TERESA OF AVILA

"Prayer is looking up into the face of the Eternal. We can do this only when the spirit is awake in its innermost depths, freed from all earthly occupations and pleasures that benumb it. Being awake in body does not guarantee this consciousness, nor does rest required by nature interfere. 'To meditate on the Law of the Lord,' this can be a form of prayer when we take prayer in its usual broad sense. But if we think of 'watching in prayer' as being immersed in God, which is characteristic of contemplation, then meditation on the Law is only a means to contemplation."

— SISTER MIRIAM OF LITTLE ST. THERESA

Even though you have seen throughout the other chapters that prayer is a big part of my life for many reasons, I couldn't resist adding in a few stories that provide evidence of the power of prayer in many circumstances, both dire and frivolous. God listens to all requests, and with faith all things consistent with His will are possible.

On the evening of September 13, 2002, my daughter came into my bedroom when I was on my knees just about to begin my evening rosary.

"Can you please ask Jesus not to send any rain tomorrow when you pray your rosary, Mommy? Showing in the rain would be awful."

She was worried because all day long soaking rain was being predicted for the next day—the day of one of her many summer horse shows. I asked her if she would like to ask Jesus with me, and she said that she would stay for ten prayers. So together we bowed our heads over our rosary beads and said the Hail Marys together. Then as abruptly as she came, she left and closed the door behind her. Since she had asked with such faith in her heart, after she left I said a prayer to Jesus for His help. I asked Him to please see what He could do to hold back the rain. Even though I could think of many other more pressing matters to pray for, I asked the Lord to grant her wish to strengthen her faith. The most touching part of her asking me was that she intuitively seemed to know that I can ask Jesus for a small favor, and He would fulfill it.

The next day was overcast and windy as an unsettled weather pattern loomed in the distance. As I watched Christina on Tanner, a 16½ hand, dark bay gelding—one of the tamer, older horses in the stable—circling the ring in her walk/trot class looking anxious to do well, I continually prayed to Jesus to hold off the rain. And He did. Through all the classes on equitation, senior walk/trot, and costume, the rain held off. At about noon we walked over to the concession stand and ordered grilled burgers and watched the rapidly advancing cloud mass pass over our heads, only to be followed by many darker grey ones. All the while the sky looked ready to burst. At one point we had mist, but no rain. It was only after Christina had exited her last class of the day, and began un-tacking her horse prior to leading him into the horse trailer headed back to the barn, that the sky couldn't hold back another moment. The drops suddenly cascaded down in sheets. Perfect timing. I thanked dearest Jesus. The benefits of faith are many.

> *"When these are the results of all the experiences and favours that come to the soul in prayer, it need not be afraid, but may rest confidently in the mercy of the Lord, Who is faithful."*
>
> — ST. TERESA OF AVILA

During the day as I watched all the children showing their horses, I thought back to the very first time that I had been inspired to pray a rosary. It had been last year when one of my friends, Jake, mentioned his friend's son had died on September 11, 2001, in one of the Twin Towers. The father fell into despair and Jake had been extremely worried and overcome with guilt. The father had once asked Jake if he could give his son a job in Boston, which Jake had not done. He now felt somewhat responsible for the son's death, because the son could have been safe in Boston instead of working in New York City.

His sorrow and remorse touched me, and I decided that I would pray a rosary every night for forty days for Jake, his friend, and his friend's son. Every night I went up to my bedroom early—skipping TV or reading—to pray for them. Somewhere I recently read that if you do something for forty days, it will become a habit. Forty days cements the new habit into the pattern of your life. Perhaps this is why Lent is forty days long.

I found truth in that saying, because ever since those forty days, I have said at least one rosary every night. I pray for my family, my circle of friends, any recently deceased, my parish family, the souls in purgatory, and any special requests from others. And now I wouldn't be able to sleep without praying one.

At some point afterward, inspired, I typed up a sheet with a grid of rows and all the names of all the people in my circle who needed prayers. And then, so that everyone would get a rosary in turn, I placed a checkmark near each name after the respective rosary was prayed for them. The following night I would move to the next person on the listing.

Praying rosaries are a spiritual form of charity. All rosaries are given to the Blessed Mother so that through her intercession our prayers will be put into action with whatever that person or family might need help with on the eternal level. Praying rosaries is a labor of total love and trust in God to help the person/persons with special heavenly graces that only God can deliver. I only ask for the person, but God, the incredibly loving Divine Being that He is, spouts miracles. I have lost count long ago of the everyday blessings and miracles that have resulted from these rosaries. Suffice it to say that I don't know how I ever survived before. Life has become so much better by just adding this one devotion to my daily life.

The best part is that no one knows how to attribute the changes. They will never know why their lives suddenly got easier, or how they finally found an answer to a major problem, or healing from an injury. When I pray for someone, just like a secret agent for God, I call upon Him to make those around me happier, healthier, and also eventually to help them achieve a beautiful eternal life.

> *"Perchance whole nights—in prayer, penances are its pleasures; fasts its joys; and its consolations are to make use of the sacraments and to oc-cupy itself in Divine things."*
>
> – ST. JOHN OF THE CROSS

From praying that one rosary a night beginning in December 2001, I have found such spiritual benefit from this practice that I was inspired to con-tinuously add more prayers to my daily prayer routine. Currently my prayers go as follows: early morning informal prayer to God, Meditation from one publication on the readings for the day, one from a spiritual master, and a thirty-minute Meditation/contemplation session. Throughout the day: seven Our Fathers, seven Hail Marys, and seven Glory Bes to the Father, Son, and Holy Spirit. Scattered prayers for people in need or in praise of a beautiful day, for example. Evening: one rosary, one Divine Chapel, one reading from a spiritual master, one reading from the Old Testament and one from the New Testament, informal prayer of thank-you for the day. During this period in my journey, every prayer I read from my prayer books seemed utterly inspired, and if it was praise, I had the ability to feel the same heartfelt emotion as the person who originally wrote the prayer—to understand totally the expression of their joy translated into words.

Three or four times a week, I take long walks and enjoy a lovely, lively prayer discussion with the Lord. Friends and co-workers have often asked if I like walking alone all the time, but I tell them that I like that time to clear my head. The truth is that I need my conversations with God much more than idle chitchat. He is my very best friend and the only one I can count on absolutely. I have often wondered if others have these conversations with God. It's so hard to tell. Certainly, though, popular music does include many references to God and Jesus. And "stars" upon receiving an Emmy do thank God quite profusely. Whenever I hear that I always hope that they are not just giving lip service to the Lord.

By November of 2002, I had developed a beautiful new awareness through prayer—the ability to see God in everyone I came in contact with. Kindness shone brightly in such interactions, and the darkness that might have been hidden in the heart of that person was obliterated by the light and goodness that I could feel coming out from deep within them. This discovery was so beautiful that my heart filled to bursting with thankfulness to the Lord.

> *"Wherever people are praying in the world, there the Holy Spirit is, the living breath of prayer."*
>
> — POPE JOHN PAUL II

One Saturday night I received a desperate call from Jack Carraway asking for prayers for CJ, his stepson. CJ had recently been diagnosed with a serious, fast-moving bone cancer. At the time of the call, the doctors gave the family very little hope that CJ would live for even a few more months. Pam and Jack, in utter helplessness, called everyone they knew to pray for their son.

Perhaps because I could now see this wonderful light shining from all people, the next day after I had sang a solo Mass in the lower church at St. Paul's, I felt brave enough to ask the congregation to please pray for Pam's CJ. Unfortunately, I broke down in tears in the middle of making the announcement in front of the whole church, because I was so sad for Pam and Jack. So no one understood my message. Afterward, several members of the church were moved to come up and ask what was wrong, and I explained that I had wanted everyone to pray for CJ because he would die without their fervent prayers. After I told them why, they were more than happy to pray for him.

Feeling humiliated for the better part of the next several days because of my tears, I realized later when I was praying about the incident that sometimes the Spirit inspires tears to connect the speaker to others. Later that week, I called Jack Carraway to ask how things were going, and he told me that they were still waiting for all four of their other sons' test results to see if they could be possible bone marrow donors. CJ's chances were much greater if they found a match. Shortly after that phone call, I knelt down to pray a rosary for the Carraways. While I was in the middle of praying the rosary less than twenty minutes later, I received another call from Jack. They had found a match for CJ's bone marrow transplant. CJ would now have a chance to go into remission.

That night, God, having answered our prayers directly, made me realize that through prayer, even the seemingly impossible would happen if you asked and truly believed and had faith in Jesus. God wanted me to make the connection; He wanted me to remember and reflect on when Jack's call had come—during prayer—so that I would always know that He was listening and was ready to help.

"We know that God does not listen to sinners, but if one is devout and does his will, he listens to him."

— JOHN 9:31

"I was very much impressed to see that someone who was young and beautiful could with such simplicity make prayer the real and serious and principal reason for going to church. She was clearly kneeling that way because she meant it, not in order to show off, and she was praying with an absorption which, though not the deep recollection of a saint, was serious enough to show that she was not thinking at all about the other people who were there."

— THOMAS MERTON

"It is absurd to think that we can enter Heaven without first entering our own souls. For that reason we must perforce pray, lest we enter continually into temptation."

— ST. TERESA OF AVILA

In March 2003, my life was bursting at the seams with a mountain of charity projects. Most revolved around Easter projects I was doing with my CCD class. Needless to say, I was exhausted—so much so that by the end of the day I could barely walk upstairs to drag myself into bed. Invariably, because I was so tired, workdays were difficult. For me, tired days bring sad thoughts and a feeling of emptiness. Though, in retrospect this might actually be a good thing because being more empty means God can fill me with more of His love through prayer.

On one particularly draining day, I experienced a trial regarding my own brothers and sisters who no longer practiced the Catholic faith. That was the day I had read an inspirational passage from the Medjurgorje book *Visions of the Children.* The selection talked about who would end up in purgatory and hell. After reading that section, I had an overwhelming feeling of sadness for them and cried for most of the rest of that day. What Mary tells the children in the book is that many people choose hell and that the vast majority go to purgatory where they are cleansed. Only the smallest numbers go directly to heaven.

I felt incredibly sad for all the souls who have not taken Jesus' words to heart. My heart felt like lead, causing me to walk extremely slowly as I carried out my daily tasks. How dependent those souls are on the love and prayers of the people who loved them on earth. The passage seemed to speak about my own family, and I suffered painfully that day that they all might end up in purgatory or worse hell, and there was nothing I could do for them. Scary thoughts assaulted me all day long. I prayed and as always the Lord sent me some much-needed peace.

> *"When it sees God being offended, it becomes greatly distressed. Although its greatest grief is over the loss of Christian souls, many of whom, it fears are condemned."*
>
> — ST. TERESA OF AVILA

> *"One of the first signs of a saint may well be the fact that other people do not know what to make of him. In fact, they are not sure whether he is crazy or only proud; but it must at least be pride to be haunted by some individual ideal, which nobody but God really comprehends."*
>
> — THOMAS MERTON

❧

Prayer works in all kinds of circumstances, and although I haven't recorded them all here, I have seen countless miracles from my prayers. I pray especially intensely for serious illness for anyone who asks, as I did for CJ, and the Lord has always heard my plea. In fact, there have been no recent illness situations that I can remember that I have prayed over that did not take a turn for the better. Sometimes a situation looked impossible, but I always trusted that something could be done, and then seemingly by "magic," the situation would get resolved or eased—usually within a short period of time.

I admit to sometimes asking the Lord for help on less important matters just as I had for my daughter. He is so understanding and wonderful that He cares even about our little daily battles. The following incident occurred in September 2003.

We had decided to have our driveway repaved and had hired a contractor.

Both Sam and I were out when he arrived to do the driveway, so the contractor just did things his own way, instead of applying what Sam had requested him to do. I came home first, walked all around the perimeter of the driveway admiring the work until I got just past the garage and noticed that the backside of the garage had not been done. Then I went up to the contractor, who was in his mid-forties, wiry, and moving extremely quickly while throwing assorted tools into his truck. I pointed the situation out to him. The contractor decided, however, that since his truck had left, I would have to have my husband call him to arrange to finish the job on another occasion. He was not about to take my word for it. I was a little upset because once a contractor leaves the job with most of the work done, it might be a long time before you can get him to come back and finish it. So I prayed to the Lord.

As if by magic, within moments, just as the contractor was getting ready to leave in his other truck, Sam pulled into the yard. The two had a quick conversation, and the contractor immediately called back his truck from the other site and finished our job. Amazing. I had been looking forward so much to having the driveway done, and I had told the Lord so that I don't think He wanted me to be disappointed. How loving He is!

> "This means, in practice, that there is only one vocation. Whether you teach or live in the cloister or nurse the sick, whether you are in religion or out of it, married or single, no matter who you are or what you are, you are called to the summit of perfection: you are called to a deep interior life perhaps even to mystical prayer, and to pass the fruits of your contemplation on to others."
>
> — THOMAS MERTON

> "Prayer is the doorway through which God's greatest gifts enter the soul. If this door is kept shut, I do not see how God can bestow these gifts. Therefore when God plants in our soul, a desire to pray, as unprepared as we might be, it is among the greatest of gifts. Besides, God does not wait for the next life to reward our love, but begins to enrich us even here. It is the devil who makes us think that the lives and actions of the saints are to be admired but not imitated. If we do not limit our spiritual goals, we can with great confidence, little by little, reach those heights that by the grace of God many saints have reached. If you have not yet begun to meditate, I implore you by the love of our Lord not to deprive yourself of so great a good. Anyone who perseveres in seeking God's friendship is amply rewarded."
>
> — ST. TERESA OF AVILA

❦

February 7, 2004–2:00 a.m.

Sam woke up screaming in his sleep, which he has occasionally done for as long as I have known him. This time instead of waking him up so that he would stop screaming, I put my hand on his shoulder and prayed an Our Father. It worked. He immediately stopped screaming. Prayer effectively drives out whatever makes him scream like that in his sleep.

❦

Charity, the fruit born from a prayerful, joyful heart, will begin to flow like a stream into your life as soon as you add time to pray into your life. Prayer always flows into charity.

Charity

"I ask you to love me with the same love with which I love you. But for me you cannot do this, for I loved you without being loved. Whatever love you have for me you owe me, so you love me not gratuitously but out of duty, while I love you not out of duty but gratuitously. So you cannot give me the kind of love I ask of you. This is why I have put you among your neighbors: So that you can do for them what you cannot do for me—that is, love them without any concern for thanks and without looking for any profit for yourself. And whatever you do for them I consider done for me." – St. Catherine of Sienna

> "It is also strongly desirous of serving Him ... and how great is the extent of its obligations."
>
> — ST. TERESA OF AVILA

> "These souls have a marked detachment from everything and a desire to be always either alone or busy with something that is to some soul's advantage."
>
> — ST. TERESA OF AVILA

By early September 2002, my heart—now to a great extent healed and continuously receiving such a super abundance of joy and love through prayer from God—felt an overwhelming need to give of myself beyond my family. So, shortly after I began my twice–a-week bread and water fast, inspired by the book on Medjugorje, I decided to enter into charity work, knowing that charity is any act of kindness born out of love for all fellow human beings. I wanted the charity work to be beyond the scope of parent/teacher associations, coaching my children's basketball games, or writing checks to various wonderful charitable organizations. I wanted to find a way of physically helping the poor, preferably mothers and their children. It didn't take me long to find a place in Boston that really spoke to my deep longing—Rosie's Place.

> *"People need joy quite as much as clothing."*
> — MARGARET COLLIER GRAHAM

> *"The Fruits (of the spirit, joy is one) are the first indication of our transformation in Christ."*
> — THOMAS KEATING

> *"Joy is the serious business of Heaven."*
> — C.S. LEWIS

I signed up for a volunteer orientation session and on the way there I turned on the radio, and Whitney Houston's song entitled "The Greatest Love of All" played in the background. Of course, the lyrics reminded me of God, because He is the greatest love of all. I spent the drive to Rosie's Place singing the song to Him, praising Him, and telling Him that I believe with all my heart that He is the greatest. When I arrived at Rosie's, I parked the car in the tiny front lot in the only space left. Rosie's' Place is housed in a simple square brick building, which from the outside looked no different from any older office building or a small apartment complex. Driving past it on the way to Commonwealth Avenue, for instance, one would never guess that it is a shelter for homeless women.

With anxious steps, I approached the front door and rang the bell. Within a minute someone opened the door and invited me into the front lobby. On the left there were about fifteen or twenty women idly standing and sitting. They seemed to be just hanging out, biding their time, waiting. On the right there was a busy, middle-aged receptionist. She was in the process of helping three people at once. Eventually, after I had patiently waited in line for a while, I introduced myself and told her that I had parked in the lot. She handed me the sign-in sheet and asked me to fill in the line detailing my vehicle information.

With that done, I looked around at the beige walls that appeared freshly painted. Simple furniture was scattered around the waiting area, the kind typical of an office. Chairs along the left wall were filled with occupants. Rosie's Place seemed a pleasant oasis for poor women who were waiting for something good to happen to them. That was my first impression.

Since I had come for the orientation meeting, which was to be held in a conference room off the main receiving area, and it was due to start in another fifteen minutes, I wandered over to a bulletin board and read the various notices pinned to it.

On the front page of a local Boston newspaper, there was an article on Rosie's Place, which I took the time to read. The written praise for this privately funded shelter was truly inspiring. In the first paragraph, the writer mentioned that Rosie's had an official song—kind of like a theme for these women. The song: "The Greatest Love of All," the very same song I had just heard played on the radio driving in. Most people might say this was coincidence, but I knew otherwise. It was a sign from the Lord. He was confirming for me that He had work for me to do here and that I would learn new things through my service.

The Greatest Love of All
by Whitney Houston

I believe the children are our future
Teach them well and let them lead the way
Show them all the beauty they possess inside
Give them a sense of pride to make it easier
Let the children laughter remind us how we used to be
Everybody searching for a hero
People need someone to look up to
I never found anyone who fulfilled my needs
A lonely place to be
So I learned to depend on me

I decided long ago, never to walk in anyone's shadows
If I fail, if I succeed
At least I'll live, as I believe
No matter what they take from me
They can't take away my dignity.
Because the greatest love of all
Is happening to me
I found the greatest love all
Inside of me
The greatest love of all
Is easy to achieve
Learning to love yourself
It is the greatest love all

And if by chance, that special place
That you've been dreaming of
Leads you to a lonely place
Find your strength in love.

The next morning I woke up restless, unsettled, as unhappy thoughts accompanied painful spiritual stings and pricks. I recognized the negative vibes and knew immediately that they were from the devil. I thought back to my orientation from Rosie's Place and realized that instead of the joy that I had felt and was still feeling after the uplifting afternoon orientation, he wanted to replace it with other feelings—despair, anger, foulness, and unhappiness. He was obviously trying his best, or worst in his case, to hinder my newfound charity work at Rosie's Place. I ignored his negative spiritual energy that hovered around me all morning as I got up from bed, showered, ate a bowl of cereal and milk, drove up 3A to the office, and answered e-mail and collated invoices.

Around noontime I got up from my desk and walked over to two of my office coworkers, Kevin and Greg, to share with them my uplifting orientation experience at Rosie's Place.

As I related the story, I felt myself begin to cry with the beauty of the memory. The orientation had been so inspiring, so beautiful. I had sat surrounded by other volunteers listening to the coordinator, watching a video, and hearing the questions from the others on working at Rosie's Place, and all the while I had felt surrounded by a cloud of such love that I held back my tears of joy for most of the session, not daring to say a word lest I break down. After the meeting, we were taken on a tour of the shower room, laundry room, food storage area, the back room where boxes of new and used clothing were stored, and finally the dining room. There was a large school catering group serving dinner that night, and they were playing karaoke music to entertain the ladies at Rosie's Place. The atmosphere was festive, reminiscent of the Christmas season even though it was late summer. The students all had on matching green shirts, and expressions of joy and happiness adorned their bright faces.

Finding an echo of Mother Theresa's great love of helping women from the poorest parts of Boston, I fell in love with Rosie's Place that first day. According to Mother Theresa, "Vast regions of the world are covered by spiritual deserts," but it immediately became apparent to me that Rosie's Place was not one of them. As I talked to my co-workers, explaining the joy that filled my heart, I was again surrounded by a cloud of happiness. During that afternoon, as I returned to my accounting spreadsheets, my mind returned again and again to Rosie's Place.

The next day I signed up to volunteer at Rosie's place for two shifts a month in the dining room. It seemed a perfect fit for me, having grown up in a large family where I often helped with meals. Perhaps my memories were partly the reason I was filled with exhilaration at the challenge of serving 150 women lunch or dinner. Or maybe it was the other delightful people that also worked at Rosie's either as employees or volunteers. Either way, I only knew that I loved it. Certainly the "ladies" who considered it their second home, or maybe their only home, also had plenty of character and personality. It didn't take me long to fall in love with many of them. As I assembled countless sandwiches, cleared tables, and washed hundreds of dishes, I could feel the beauty of Mother Theresa's loving spirit as she guided me in loving the "poorest of the poor" in the Boston area.

Not Too Far From Here
Sung by the Daughters of St. Paul

Somebody's down to their last dime.
Somebody's running out of time, not too far from here.
Somebody's got nowhere else to go.
Somebody needs a little hope, not too far from here.

And I may not know their name, but I'm praying just the same
That you'll use me Lord to wipe away the tears.
Cause somebody's crying not too far from Here.

Somebody's troubled and confused.
Somebody's got nothing left to lose, not too far from here.
Somebody's learned how not to trust.
Somebody's dying for love, not too far from here.

It may be a stranger's face, but I'm praying for your grace
To move in me and take away the fear
Cause somebody's hurting not too far from here.

Help me Lord not to turn away from pain.
Help me not to rest until they all believe.
Give me your strength and compassion when somebody
Finds the road of life too steep.

"We all long for heaven where God is, but we have it in our power to be in heaven with Him right now—to be happy with Him at this very moment. Being happy with Him now means loving like He loves, helping

like He helps, giving as He gives, serving as He serves, rescuing as He rescues, being with Him twenty-four hours a day—touching Him in His distressing disguise."

— MOTHER TERESA

From personal letter from Father Walter J. Burghardt, S.J–"A word about Christmas. It is at once an enduring reality and an ongoing challenge. The reality is God giving to humankind, to each of us, God's own son in our flesh, born as we are, living our life, dying our death. The challenge was briefly and pungently expressed in the First Letter of John: 'Beloved, if God so loved us, we ought also to love one another ... If we love one another, God dwells in us, and His love is perfected in us' (4:11-12). Whenever we embrace the outcast, feed the hungry, house the homeless, cloth the naked; it is then that we love as Jesus loved."

C.S. Lewis divides human love into four categories—following the Greek tradition: "Storge, affection between members of a family; Philia, friendship; Eros, romantic love between people 'in love'; Agape, the love one has toward God and one's neighbor." Agape is the best because it is the kind God has for us and is good in all circumstances. Agape is all giving, not getting.

"For the author of the Cloud of the unknowing, energy is the mark of true affection."

September 20, 2002.

After working my first dinner shift at Rosie's, as I was driving home in our silver van I noticed something was prodding, pinching, and pricking my spirit. The spirit swirled around me, trying all different sides of my body. I could feel it almost breathing down my neck. It seemed that I had inadvertently picked up a spiritual hitchhiker—allowed entry to some malicious spirit that hovered around Rosie's Place and now it was driving home with me in the minivan. Its despondency and misery was extremely palatable even though it had passed from this life into the eternal one—communicating its anger and distress, which death had not taken away. Having not achieved lasting peace, it seemed to be communicating its eternal unhappiness to me. I pictured it in my mind's eye.

Rosie's Place is located in a depressed area of Boston, very near the old Boston City Hospital, an area not without all the usual inner-city problems of drug trafficking, prostitution, rape, and gang warfare. I could only think that this spirit had, maybe quite recently, died a violent painful death after having lived in a miserable life situation. Instead of fear, my heart was wretched with compassion for this unhappy ex-person. When I got home I knew I had the luxury of being able to pray a rosary for that unhappy soul, and ask the Virgin Mother to ease the burdens it now carried into the afterlife. Prayer is the only thing that helps departed souls who find themselves on the other side in a realm far from heaven—almost hell.

After I lay in bed that night to go to sleep, utterly spent with my feet aching, but my heart full of love and joy at the gift of my new charity work, I felt the Holy Spirit enter from around my feet traveling up my whole body. As I lay there, the Spirit filled me up with a very large dose of His living water. His grace was a strong spiritual current that suffused my spirit with heavenly gifts and aid. He just kept filling my spirit until I was overflowing with His strength and love. How beautiful, gentle, and loving the Spirit of God is.

"When you go out for your task, spread all around you the joy of belonging to God, of living with God, of being His own." – Mother Teresa

"A joyful heart is the normal result of a heart burning with love." – Mother Teresa

"The spirituality of the second stage of life calls us to transcend the self in order to enter into the mystical meaning of the Oneness of all life. Clearly, the spirituality of the second stage of life fits us for the next. Eternity begins to feel more like home. We venture to focus on the life to come, we begin to slow down enough to savour this one, we undertake to enter the centre of ourselves where life is really whole, we reach out to the whole human race and in the reaching find the meaning this is Mystery and the Mystery that is God around us, beside us, in front of us, behind us and within us." – Joan Chittiser, OSB

My feelings of caring and love and being able to serve dinner to the many women who came every night to Rosie's moved me to tears on many occasions. Such powerful feelings of empathy and compassion emerged that my eyes were constantly flooded, my feelings finding release through my eyes. The eyes are often said to be the window of the soul. I believe this is so, and my soul flowed freely into the atmosphere at Rosie's. The work of preparing dinner and carrying plates to the tables and waiting on the women was, in essence, my love in action.

(Gift of Tears) "When we are baptized, we often find ourselves crying tears of joy. No one will ever prove from the divine Scriptures that any person was ever cleansed without tears and constant compunction. No one ever became holy or received the Holy Spirit, or had the vision of God experienced His dwelling within himself, or ever had Him dwelling in his heart, without previous repentance and compunction and con-

stant tears ever flowing as from a fountain. Such tears flood and wash out the house of the soul: they moisten and refresh the soul that has been possessed and inflamed by the unapproachable fire."

— ST. SYMEON, THE NEW THEOLOGIAN

"It practices the charity of God, since it is not now moved by the pleasure of attraction and sweetness, which it finds in its work, but only by God. It likewise practices here the virtue of fortitude, because, in these difficulties and insipidities, which it finds in its work, it brings strength out of weakness and thus becomes strong. All the virtues, in short—the theological and also the cardinal and moral—both in body and in spirit, are practiced by the soul in these times of aridity."

— ST. JOHN OF THE CROSS

"I try to remember, too, that possibly the greatest service I will give to the Church is not that which I give when my life is filled with joy and enthusiasm—the greatest service I will give to the mystical body of Christ will be in those moments when I will be making up for what is lacking in the members of that body."

— STEPHEN TUMILTY

Through Rosie's Place I came to an understanding of what it is to hunger on a deep level. Twice a month, always Wednesday lunch and Friday dinner shifts, I had contact with women who hungered in many different ways. Since these were also my fasting days, days where I survived on just bread and water, I could deeply relate to their physical hunger. Many were the days when weakness hit me, causing me to sway on my feet due to my own physical hunger, after helping to prepare, serve, and then clean up the dining room at Rosie's Place. My physical hunger bonded me to all the women.

But hungers of other kinds surfaced. I often observed women fighting over some small sample bottle of a well-known brand of shampoo. As I watched them argue over who should get the bottle, I pondered over what kind of hunger would make them care so much about a tiny bottle of shampoo that only contained enough shampoo to wash their hair twice. Was it really a hunger for being just being physically clean, or were they really wishing to be pure again on a spiritual level? Was that shampoo bottle somehow a symbol of cleanliness?

Some needs and hungers were easy to fix. One woman had arrived at Rosie's Place with one shoe on and one shoe off, but it was easy to help her.

I went into the back storeroom that held all the items that people had donated—clothing, shoes, and household items and found a pair of new sneakers in her size. God had inspired someone to send in those sneakers because He knew that she would need them.

I vividly remember one evening when one of the ladies was so sick that I had to hold her up until the EMTs arrived. She was a big-boned black woman, and she was swaying in her chair, nearly ready to collapse just after she had started eating her dinner. I later wondered if she had really been sick or if she was just hungry for human touch, for human caring, for someone to notice that she was alive.

The Indian woman seated across from her ate her dinner ravenously. When she had finished, seeing that the woman I was holding up wasn't going to finish her dinner, she asked to finish the other woman's meal. Across my mind flashed images of bacteria and viruses that I had seen on TV shows in the past, and thinking about the woman I was holding and her sickness, I cautioned the Indian woman across the table. But I also didn't stop her. Quickly she reached over and grabbed the plate. A couple of bites later all the food was gone.

At Rosie's miracles happen everyday, and sometimes they resemble the gospel miracles. One day as we waited for a group of volunteer caterers to arrive with the dinner for the evening, I asked another volunteer, Ruthie, (the dining room shift coordinator) if they ever had a problem with not having enough for dinner, either because the caterers never show up, or they brought too little food. Ruthie told me that no matter what conditions occur, the food always is enough to feel the ladies who show up. She told me that once in a while she can't understand how the food feeds everyone, and has thought that they would run out, but just like the multiplication of the loaves, the food stretches to feed every hungry woman and child.

In addition to volunteering at Rosie's Place, I decided to teach my son, Patrick's, eighth grade CCD class. My quiet, sweet dark-haired thirteen-year-old son was a very good sport; although he did tell me a number of times how embarrassing it was to have such a religious mother. No longer being at all self-conscious of my love for God, I found that I was ready to begin sharing and teaching. God confirmed that sentiment when Sister Kathy once called me a true witness. I liked to think that I am a witness to the power of God to transform and mold an old sinner into something more acceptable to God.

> *"Buddhism has a remedy to counterbalance whatever negativity you created. Here are some of the suggested ones. Serving the poor and needy, visiting people in the hospital, saving the lives of animals, making offerings to monasteries or other religious organizations, reciting passages from traditional dharma tests, drawing holy images."*
> — JONATHAN LANDAW AND STEPHAN BODIAN

> *"Let us have charity and humility. Let us give alms because these cleanse our souls from the stains of sin. Men lose all the material things they leave behind them in this world, but they carry with them the reward of their charity and the alms they give."*
> — ST. FRANCIS OF ASSISI

Here all my newfound knowledge of God overflowed in joyful and creative ways, because I truly believed that God was anything but boring. In fact, He is magical. Every lesson inspired a creative burst, which I believed that my thirteen-year-olds enjoyed. Of all the charity I was doing, this was my favorite kind. And from every class, I also learned a new nugget of wisdom, which was such a gift.

I tried other charity work, including: mailings for the Diabetes and Heart Association, clean-up at the diabetes's walk, and making blankets for the Binky Patrol. I became open to any possible volunteer opportunity, and I was delighted to help in whatever way I could. I felt a great need to give out alms to every charity that asked. My heart was delighted every time I sent out a check. I sent out dozens, and I was rewarded with lovely thank-you notes ...along with more envelopes asking for additional donations within a month. So after about a year, I unfortunately had to slow down my donations, since I ran into quite a bit of debt, which took me several years to pay off.

Also, I sponsored a child named Yenny Perdoma, a Honduran girl, through Children, Inc. I wrote her a letter and she wrote back a beautiful note of gratitude. My heart swelled with love for this faraway little girl of eleven, the new daughter of my heart.

> *"God has implanted in the heart of man a love of virtue and a love of happiness; consequently, God, because of His wisdom, must by rewarding virtue establish perfect harmony between these two tendencies."*
> — CATHOLIC ONLINE ENCYCLOPEDIA

The more charity I gave, the more my mind dwelled on a very creative plane, and I dreamed up a game craft fair for my CCD class as a fund-raising project. How much fun it would be, I thought, to put together a craft fair that would reflect Jesus, be innovative, and offer loads of fun. We could make a seven-room prayer maze based on Saint Teresa's Interior Castle book, a game of the narrow/wide gate into heaven, the Sea of Galilee teaming with foam fish—some with coins in their mouths, find the jewels of the kingdom hidden in a kiddy pool of foam peanuts, and a game with many vines leading into the tree of life—Jesus.

The children could paint wooden crosses and decorate them with jewels and flowers as a way to represent that the cross symbolizes heaven and is the way to heaven. Other projects could include making foam pictures of Noah's Ark and planting seeds for faith in decorated clay pots. We could sell frozen cookie dough with cross cookie cutters, holy spring water, and small loaves of bread shaped like crosses saying that Jesus is the bread of life.

The ideas continued in a steady influx. We could build a cardboard castle to signify the living mystical castle that Jesus is building with His Church. I pictured it having many rows of cardboard bricks to show the passing of the years. On the lowest row would be Jesus, the next row the apostles, and as the rows climbed upward, the names of all the martyrs and the saints. Toward the top would be people like the children's great-grandparents, grandparents, parents, and at the top the children themselves. We could put famous saints in their own brick-sized spaces. The children could even choose names of their own future children to illustrate that the church will go on long after we are gone from the earth.

Alas, unfortunately, the other teachers and my students thought the whole idea would require too much effort, and I knew that unless their hearts were in the project, it would not go well. I was disappointed, but I kept an open mind, knowing that whatever we ended up accomplishing would be what God had in mind.

Looking back after all the projects we completed, we all felt immensely proud. Although we had not gone forward with the craft/game fair idea, we brought joy to many people, and all the children had fun—I made sure of that. In a beautifully simple way, the service based pay-it-forward program worked out perfectly. We were able to do seven charitable works that Lent, which brought Easter sunshine to all our recipients.

I started the ball rolling by making fifteen phone calls and came up with some wonderful projects—projects that combined service but were also amusing and would bring joy to the recipients, just as I had asked the Holy Spirit for in prayer. I committed myself to funding all the projects as a gift of charity. First, our class of twelve thirteen-year-olds (sometimes I called them my apostles, jokingly of course) cooked a lunch for the 120 women at Rosie's' Place. I brought in all the ingredients to our classroom. We had fun opening giant cans of tuna fish and mixing it with mayonnaise, celery, and relish. Next we made a Sunshine Salad with romaine and spinach leaves mixed with mandarin orange segments, red onion rings, and sliced water chestnuts. I had baked in advance 130 egg-shaped cookies, and the children had a blast decorating them with colored frosting, sprinkles, and candy toppings. The next morning I finished assembling the luncheon and drove it to Rosie's Place and helped to serve it to the ladies. They loved it.

Next I went shopping for all sorts of candy and little toys. The following week we assembled Easter baskets and an Easter egg hunt for the moms and their kids at the Mary Martha Learning Center. The Mary Martha Learning Center is a home for teenaged, homeless mothers in Hingham. The following weeks we did creative projects for some of the Hingham elderly and poor. At the Cohasset Knoll, we brought ice cream and fixing for sundaes. In addition, the students helped the seniors to paint wooden lighthouses and tiny birdhouses. We decorated boxes for Easter delivery from the Hingham Food Pantry. After that we constructed centerpieces, cards, and party favors for the Hingham Elder Center for their spring luncheon. For the Queen Anne's Nursing Home residents, we decorated cookies, make hand-molded rainbow-colored chocolate candy, and dipped strawberries in milk chocolate to pass out on trays. Finally, we went to the Cardinal Cushing School in Hanover, Massachusetts, to help a group of students paint clay pots, fill them with soil, and plant flower seeds in them to add a little color to their dormitory rooms.

During that wonderful yet busy spring, I felt like God had appointed me to His Easter/Spring/Sunshine Committee. As we made, decorated, molded, painted, assembled, drew, baked, and stuffed, I hoped that we sent others a message of the joy that Easter and spring should be in all our hearts, minds, and lives. Many people wondered where I found all the energy to carry out all these projects with my students, along with working full-time and pursing an MBA degree, but I had a wonderful secret that I totally was willing to share: God.

When God asks for work, He always provides the means and the energy required to carry the task to fruition. And when weariness set in, my meditations deepened whenever I grew tired. He would compensate me in this refreshing way. Believe me, there is nothing more energizing that taking a dip in the cool, eternal spring water of the Holy Spirit who is the source of living water.

"Many people associate renunciation with giving up material pos-sessions and involvements and pursing a life of detachment and withdrawal. But true renunciation is an internal (rather than an ex-ternal) movement or gesture—though it can certainly express itself in action. You adopt the radical view that you can achieve lasting peace and happiness only by clearing your mind and heart of negative be-liefs and emotions, penetrating to the truth of reality, opening yourself to your inherent wakefulness and joy, and experiencing what Buddha called the "sure heart's release."

– Jonathan Landaw and Stephan Bodian

"When we love God's will we find Him and own His joy in all things. It is the easiest thing in the world to possess this life and this joy; all you have to do is believe and love."

– THOMAS MERTON

"According to Saint Bernard of Clairvaux, it is the comparatively weak soul that arrives at contemplation but does not overflow with a love that must communicate what it knows of God to other men. For all the great Christian mystics without exception, St. Bernard, St. Gregory, St. Theresa, St. John of the Cross, Blessed John Ruysbroeck, St. Bonaventure, the peak of the mystical life is a marriage of the soul with God which gives the saints a miraculous power, a smooth and tireless energy in working for God and for souls, which bears fruit in the sanctity of thousands and changes the course of religious and even secu-lar history."

Teaching another CCD class in the fall of 2003, my exhaustion compelled me to ask the Lord for energy before I even stepped foot into the classroom. He sent it along with a great upsurge in joy that lasted until the next morning. That night at class, I suspected that the Lord had inspired people to say nice things. Sister Kathy remarked that Ben thought I was a wonderful teacher be-cause of my enthusiasm. Also, a parish lady commented on my lector ability, saying that she could clearly hear the love I have for the Lord come into my voice, allowing the Lord to use me to love and talk to His people.

Upon reading the next CCD class agenda, I was at sea as to how to make the class entertaining for the kids ... until the morning of the class. During my dawn meditation, I felt beautiful spiritual touches on my hand and my face. My skull felt like hands surrounded it, and then I perceived a slight shift inside my head and a little pressure. The Spirit must have been giving me in-spiration because then a great idea for a relay race between the boys and the girls using the Ten Commandments suddenly appeared in my mind. *That will be perfect,* I thought.

> *"May the God of hope fill you with all joy and peace in believing, so that you may abound in hope by the power of the Holy Spirit."*
> — ROMANS 15:13

⚜

April 16–April 20, 2003. Holy week and Easter Sunday.

Interestingly enough, although I went to Mass every day, no special insights, spirit/angel encounters, or other events occurred. It was almost like I needed to be solidly and firmly present in the natural (as opposed to the supernatural) plane during this week.

It was a happy, holy week filled with anticipation for the Easter celebration I had planned with my family. But other than a few deep meditations, nothing unusual happened. I think a busy, somewhat stressing time eliminates the possibility of the supernatural side of things for me. I spent all week thinking and planning my family party, which went well with three Easter egg hunts, five appetizers, three main courses, and a whole heavenly court of dessert (rainbow cakes, angel petit fours, cross cake, peeps, and chocolate roses).

Lent and Easter of 2004 was vastly different. After we returned from our February ski vacation, Sam had a series of incidents, which led to his being incapacitated for the next two months. My husband was diagnosed with a bulging disk in his lower back, putting him on bed rest. One of the first problems that arose was his mood change. Sam had never been really been an easygoing man, but during this period of time, he seemed to change into an "ogre." Whenever I came home he became very demanding—yelling for his breakfast, his newspaper, to help him put on his socks, and so on. Feeling the immense burden of carrying him, I became very stressed and exhausted and not my patient usually kind self. I thought I would crack under the strain. I often found myself in tears and feelings of deep depression surfaced. Eventually we would realize that his personality change was due to his pain medication, which caused an addiction issue.

There are always gifts given even in the worst circumstances. As we worked through the months of Sam's injury, I began coming to understand on a new and deeper level all five of the sorrowful mysteries of Jesus' suffering and crucifixion. In the Garden on Gethsemane, our Lord fought incredibly as mankind's sins, pains, and feelings almost overcame Him. The load of our sins came onto Him. Just like Jesus when He asked the Father to take the cup away if possible, I wanted in the worst way to leave the situation. I wanted to leave

293

and begin a new life without Sam who had always been a strain to live with but now was impossible. I didn't though; I ended up crying everyday because of the awful stress instead.

> *"It is easy to smile at people outside your own home. It is so easy to take care of the people that you don't know well. It is difficult to be thoughtful and kind and to smile and be loving to your own in the house day after day, especially when we are tired and in a bad temper or bad mood. We all have these moments and that is the time that Christ comes to us in a distressing disguise."*
>
> – MOTHER THERESA

Everything during those months hit me hard. It seemed as though the devil was inspiring others to say very unsympathetic things, rubbing my faith into the salt of my wounds. They accused me of not caring enough about Sam's pain, telling me that I wasn't sympathetic. A couple of friends just before Easter day berated me loudly on my lack of understanding and empathy. This seemed so unfair. I felt like I was being attacked from all directions, scourged, slapped across the face, and mocked. "Couldn't anyone else realize how incredibly hard I was working and that I was almost at the cracking point?" I asked myself.

I felt like I was carrying the heavy cross with our Lord—the cross of family life and being a mother and a good person who accepts insult without saying too much. The cross, which is handed to us, is the cross that is rounded to our particular shoulders, and being a true Christian means carrying it just as Jesus did. In my mind's eye I often pictured all sorts of good people carrying crosses for many different reasons—broken marriages, sickness, natural disaster, war—people willing to carry the brokenness of their immediate world and the greater world at large. Simple, good people do this very laborious, difficult job, which this world doesn't reward. But thankfully Jesus does.

To top it all off, one evening my sister called. She mentioned that my brother and his wife had decided to have their son, Fletcher, baptized, and they needed a place to have the party afterward. Even with all the stress I was under from Sam's injury, I decided to offer our home for the baptism. I thought, well, how hard could it be to host a family party?

At the time I was in a prayer group with Father Raffey and the baptismal minister and his wife. In the booklet we had been using for our discussion sections, there was a section called "Living Your Faith." That week printed in that section was the suggestion to schedule a baptism. How appropriate, since I had just been asked to have Fletcher's baptism. The Lord seemed to be confirming that I should take on this additional responsibility, that there was a reason why Fletcher should be baptized at St. Paul's. I am now sure that it was because the Lord wanted to answer our prayers, and that He wanted to claim Fletcher for His own. Fletcher, you see, had been born with several physical ailments that were causing him to not gain weight or thrive. During the coming summer, he would be healed of all his ailments.

The week after I had volunteered to host the baptism, I found out that my sister-in-law planned to invite fifty people, but I didn't say anything. It would be more work than I had planned, but I felt ready to handle it. Going into high gear, I purchased decorations for a rainbow and Noah's Ark theme to signify the baptism. I pictured that beautiful rainbow promise that the Lord had sent to Noah. At the time of that great flood, it was almost like God was baptizing the earth. All the beautiful rainbow gifts reminded me of my own spiritual journey. I planned the menu and made yellow-colored chocolate crosses as favors, ordered balloons, and did all the sundry things necessary for a party.

Perhaps it was because I needed a helping hand, but the Lord sent a tremendous gift—a miracle. Exactly one week before the baptism, Sam woke up and his back was spontaneously healed. The pain had completely gone—disappeared without a trace. The difficult Lenten period was over. I praised the Lord highly, thanking Him very gratefully for an end to Sam's pain, and told Sam to do the same. Sam, however, only believed that the medical profession had been responsible for his recovery and never acknowledged or thanked God who had healed him so miraculously.

During the following week, with renewed vigor and hope, I set about decorating the house and the yard—hanging crepe paper, putting up posters, arranging the house to accommodate the fifty people expected, and working outdoors making the yard colorful with the vivid hues and happy faces of a hundred pansies. During the week the Lord sent lots of rain and perfect flower forming weather. The day before was busy but great. I finished planting the flowers, cooked two types of lasagnas, baked rainbow cookies, and tied up all the candy crosses on the stairway in a cascade. In the morning I went to Mass, made fruit salad, and did the final prep work. It began raining around 11:00 a.m. At 2:00, I went to the church with Patrick and waited. Father was there, but there were traffic delays for both the north and southbound routes, and every family member was delayed by one half hour.

Luckily for my brother, I knew Father well enough to delay the baptism until everyone arrived, and he was kind enough to allow it. Patrick, my son, enjoyed the delay. My very musical son decided that this was the perfect time to try out the organ in the choir loft since the church was empty. From high in the choir loft, I could hear his crashing notes on the organ that seemed to emphasize the rain and wind outside. (My son is a wonderful drummer who also loves to play the keyboard and is open to trying all instruments. One day it hit me that God had sent me a modern version of the Little Drummer Boy from that wonderful Christmas special. The Lord, I am sure, had noticed that that TV show, since my own babyhood, had always touched my heart.

Every time I watched it, I cried in utter joy. He sent me the perfect son for my heart's yearning.)

Eventually, everyone did arrive and the baptism started at 2:30 p.m. I did a couple of impromptu readings at Father's prompting and helped sing appropriate songs for the occasion with Father. We were the only ones to open the missellettes and do so. Shining and full of spring warmth, the sun peeked out from behind the clouds by the time we left the church. The rest of the party couldn't have been better.

Later, as I reflected on the day, a couple of spiritual things struck me this time from the Joyful Mysteries. First, all the people had to experience the upset before the joy (they all got stuck in traffic and a few got lost) just as in the Joyful Mysteries where Mary and Joseph find the child, Jesus, in the temple after three days of searching. Second, Father reiterated what everyone's Christian responsibilities were since Fletcher was being baptized in the church or "presented" as in the fourth Joyful Mystery. He reminded everyone that this life of Christianity is one of carrying crosses—it is not easy street. "All the family members are called to help bring up Fletcher in the faith," he counseled. As I heard his words, I fervently prayed that they all had ears to hear—that they too would pick up and begin to carry their own faith in their hearts again.

On June 30, 2004, I gave a presentation on the International and Indian Child Labor Law and the giant problem of child labor in India to my Babson MBA class as a final project for Business Law. I admit that I offered the very grim statistics to them "straight up" without any whitewashing. The use of child labor in India is appalling; and that was my point. My fellow classmates, seventeen men, six of them from India, and the woman lawyer teacher, had quite a reaction to it. The speech startled them, and after I was done, they all started talking at once in an agitated buzz. The presentation stirred up a wave of controversy and questions, even though there was supposed to be no talking between individual presentations. I knew it was because God was really giving the speech through me, and He was present and touched their hearts, awakening their awareness of the issue.

It was my hope that the Indian students in the class would become part of the solution for their people. In response to my presentation one of the students mentioned that he is supporting three children going to school (how wonderful). One of the other students, Ram, later sent me an e-mail giving me his opinion on the difficulties surrounding child labor in India. Because some of the students were upset, the teacher had all the Indian students stay after class for a few moments while I made a quick getaway. I think that she wanted to make sure that they did not corner me. I had the most beautiful feeling of joy from the presentation and for a week straight thought with wonder at the power of it.

When I went to class on the last night, three of the Indian students were waiting for me after the break wanting to know if I hated their people. I told them, "far from it," that I really loved their people who I had read so much about through Mother Theresa's books. I also told them that the people called "untouchables" were the cement on which their society has stood for centuries and what incredible strength and acceptance had been bred into them for millennium. "India, in my opinion," I told them, "has great need of their unique strength. They should be willing to help those children get an education to release their great human spirit potential to the world. The world is going to need all the strength it can get."

I left them uplifted and smiling, friends who now understood a little more than they had before about India's poorest children, and also about the human spirit. I wondered after I left for home if God was going to work through one of them as a part of the solution to the child labor issues in India. I won't be a bit surprised if this was the case.

> *"It is better to make mistakes in kindness than to work miracles with unkindness. It is very important to be kind to ourselves and control ourselves by keeping our balance. If we want to live in peace and harmony with each other we must pay attention to our tongue."*
>
> — MOTHER TERESA

Sometimes paying attention to our tongue by speaking out can produce good results. That speech was for you, dear Mother Teresa.

Speaking of saints, let's now move on to the next chapter. How I will love to be in their number when they all come marching in ...

SAINTS

Living and Eternally Living
Another Kind of Help
Footsteps In The Path of Life To Follow
Leading Onward To Eternity

"*If you are humble nothing will touch you. If you are a saint, thank God. If you are a sinner, do not remain so.*"

— MOTHER TERESA

(Personally, this is my favorite quote. I adore Mother Teresa)

"*We cannot decide to become saints without a great effort of renunciation, of resisting temptations, of combat, or persecution, and of all sorts of sacrifices. It is not possible to love God except at one's own expense.*"

— MOTHER TERESA

According to Mother Teresa, the following listing offers good practice towards humility. Humility is necessary for sainthood:

- "To speak as little as possible of one's self.
- Mind one's own business.
- Do not to want to manage other people's affairs.
- Avoid curiosity.
- Accept contradictions and correction cheerfully.
- Pass over the mistakes of others.
- Accept insults, injuries, being slighted, forgotten, and disliked.
- Be kind and gentle even under provocation."

*"If we consider what a large number of people God can draw to Himself
through the agency of a single soul, the thought of the thousands converted by the martyrs gives us great cause for praising God."*

— ST. TERESA OF AVILA

*"For each Mass we hear with devotion, Our Lords sends a saint to com-
fort us at death."*

— ST. GERTRUDE THE GREAT

*"For the city of the saints is above, although here below it begets citizens,
in whom it sojourns till the time of its reign arrives."*

— ST. AUGUSTINE

*"It is a wonderful experience to discover a new saint. For God is greatly
magnified and marvelous in each one of His saints: differently in each
individual one. There are no two saints alike: but all of them are like
God, like Him in a different and special way. In fact, if Adam had never
fallen, the whole human race would have been a series of magnificently
different and splendid images of God, each one of all the millions of men
showing forth His glories and perfections in an astonishing new way,
and each one shining with his own particular sanctity, a sanctity destined for him from all eternity as the most complete and unimaginable
supernatural perfection of his human personality."*

— THOMAS MERTON

The good news is (trumpet blast please): My dad has made it into heaven
and is now one of God's elect—-a saint. How do I know this? Read on.

I loved my dad very much. Unfortunately he passed away when he was only
sixty-seven. I was thirty-three at the time. Looking back now, I know that
God was very good to Dad and to our family. He gave him an easy, peaceful
death. At that time since I was suffering so much myself, though, I would not
have been capable of viewing his passing as beautiful. But now as I look back
on the memory of his death, it has been transformed into one of the most
loving scenes of my life.

Looking into his loving eyes before he drew his final breath, I could see all
the special events in my own life reflected in his. One of those events that I
relived as I sat by his bedside holding his hand in the emergency room of the
Cape Cod Hospital surrounded by my mother, my brothers, and my sisters
was my tenth birthday. The years rolled back in my mind to that special day
and the memory of my own young self and my loving father. Dad had made
that birthday very special for me. Even though he had seven children, Dad

had always managed to make me feel special and loved amidst the crowd of my siblings.

⁂

It was August 1969, and a couple of my friends, my two brothers, and two sisters were gathered around our family's picnic table on our deck under the pine trees in Norfolk, MA. (My second to youngest brother was one and was probably napping, and my last brother was due to arrive in October.) Our heads were adorned with party hats, and we filled the air with joyful sounds as we blew our pink paper horns. My brothers looked funny in their pink cone-shaped hats, but I knew I shouldn't laugh lest they end up leaving the table, which would make Mother mad at me. Mother brought my birthday cake to the table—vanilla cake with vanilla frosting on top. There were ten lit candles on top.

"Okay, everyone, let's sing happy birthday to Irene."

Happy Birthday to you.
Happy Birthday to you.
Happy Birthday dear Irene,
Happy Birthday to you

My lovely brothers added a verse:

How old are you?
How old are you?
You look like a monkey,
And you smell like one too.

I made a wish, and blew out the candles. We ate cake, and I opened the presents from my two friends. Mom's presents were a T-shirt and a horse statue. After I was done, we kids ran around the yard playing tag and hide-and-seek—darting in and out of the hundreds of pine trees that sat on what should have been a spacious lawn. Since Dad hated the idea being a slave to a lawn mower for six months out of the year, he had nurtured a beautiful pine forest in its place. Fallen pine needles and peat-like dirt cushioned the ground. We laughed and yelled as we raced around our yard. At 5:30 p.m. Dad arrived home. He parked his car under our combination deck/carport, and as soon as he got out of the car, he came looking for me.

"Irene? Irene?"

I heard him calling my name and I raced around the house to find him.

"Hi, Daddy. Did you remember that today's my birthday?" I asked.

"How could I forget, my doll?" He opened the car trunk and pulled out two bags.

"I haven't wrapped them yet, but I'll bet you don't care."

Of course I didn't care! I opened the first bag and found a bike basket, horn, and handlebar streamers to go on the bike that I had received last Christmas. In the second bag, there was a drawing pad, a wooden box holding fifty colored pencils, an eraser, and a blending stick.

"I thought you might enjoy these items for your bike and since you are always using my drafting pencils, I thought that maybe it was time to get you a set of your own. Do you like them?" Dad asked.

"I love them, Daddy! Thank you." I threw my arms around him, and he hugged me tight.

My brothers and sisters gathered round. "What did you get? What did you get?" Peter, my older brother, tried to grab the pencil box away from me, but I held on tight. I wasn't going to let anything happen to my special gifts from Daddy.

We all walked inside, and I showed Mother what Dad had given me. She didn't say anything but just smiled at my dad.

"Daddy, this is my best birthday ever," I told him. It was a memory I would forever cherish.

⁂

My eyes, closed in memory, opened again to look upon my dad lying in the bed of the tiny room where we all gathered. As my eyes scanned his dear face etched with lines showing his age, I was so grateful that he was not in any pain. The emergency room nurse had reassured us that he was not suffering. Diabetes, poor circulation, and congestive heart failure had ruined his health, and his heart was failing and his body shutting down. His body seemed to be only holding on to soak up the love from his family before his spirit took the final step of separating and flying free. We all took turns holding his hand and saying a few final words. I half listened to what everyone else had to say, but my mind continuously returned to the past.

What a warm, laughing, gentle man he was with his black hair that never went totally gray and beautiful bright blue eyes that he passed on only to his youngest son, Mark. His hair was tousled and needed a combing. It usually stuck straight up from his head in unruly curls, and today was no exception. His light-blue eyes were closed, but I had only to close my eyes to see them laughing, his smile lines extending halfway down his face. He had loved to laugh so much, especially at his own jokes on Confucius. We would all miss his numerous Confucius sayings, most of which had never been real sayings by Confucius. Words of wisdom thought up on the spur-of-the-moment, they were related to us, and anyone else listening, mostly to be funny. "Confucius says man who don't enjoy a drink now and then don't enjoy anything," was one that came to mind.

Never unkind, I couldn't recall a single time when he had laughed at anyone else except himself. He was a dreamer, an innovator, a gifted photographer, an artist, and a creative thinker. Self-employed as an architect, he did his best to support his wife and seven children; his love of flourish, ornamentation, grandeur, and style was evident in all his work. A mini masterpiece in itself, his signature was always one inch high and two inches long with much embellishment of circles and twirls. He had worked for himself in his own office, which was probably a good thing because he loved to sing all day long with the radio tuned to an oldie's classic station. The solitude of his one-man office seemed to suit him because at heart he was a deep thinker who loved to ponder the profound meanings of the universe. Just like me. But when the clock stuck 5:00 p.m. he would always come home to be with his family.

Although we were not wealthy, we were never in want. Dad used to love to tell us children that we were all his masterpieces and that he was the richest man alive. A true family man who loved to be surrounded with all his children, we never lacked toys or games, because Dad never totally grew up and applauded a house filled with hundreds of playthings.

Our basement had been filled with his projects when I was a little girl. One table was set up with a piece of brown parchment paper printed with a design. Every once in a while I would see him meticulously gluing toothpicks onto the pattern. I don't remember what it was supposed to be, only that when assembled it would stand three feet tall. I am not sure that he ever finished it. In other small rooms in the basement, there was a dark room and a mini-office with a drafting table.

In the furthest depths of the basement, Dad had set up on a ten foot by ten foot table an extensive model town. Double train tracks ran around a square-cut hole in the middle of the table for the train operator of the day. The trains were supposed to be for my brothers, Peter and Michael, but Dad was never very far away when they were running it. Hundreds of hours went into making the town and laying the tracks, and all the little buildings had electrical parts that did various things. There was a crane for picking up mini logs from the freight train and a holding pen with cattle. When the train stopped, the cattle loaded into one of the cars. Some of the buildings lit up as the train passed by, and there were several crossings where the gate dropped, stopping trains on the other track. Once in a while us girls would come down and watch the trains as they chugged around the track, enjoying the lights, sounds, and the clever close-to-real-life effects of it all. But when it came to our favorite pastimes, we preferred the outdoors and all our creatures.

Other siblings relating this or that past event interrupted my memories from time to time. But my eyes stayed on Dad. His lips were not totally still, but he could not form any words. I was sure, when looking at him, that he was trying to tell us how much he loved us all and wanted to say good-bye. He didn't need really to say anything, because I could tell that he loved me, as I am sure all my family could. As the hour drew to a close, somehow I could sense Dad's spirit was ready to say farewell and move on. His grip on my hand was near the strength of a young man trying to crush my hand in his own. It was obvious that he had held onto life until we were all assembled in the hospital room. I believe that for especially good people, the Angel of Death grants us one last wish before we go. I am sure that Dad's wish was to see all of his family together one last time.

Just before he went, I bent down and told him that I loved him, and when he crossed over, he should think of the most beautiful place he could imagine and then go there. I promised him that someday he would see us all again. (Note: This was a promise I made to him on his deathbed, and the Lord heard it. Dear Family, this book, and all the faith poured into it, is yet another tactic in my long strategy toward fulfilling my promise to Dad and God.) As soon as I said that, my younger brother Michael, who had heard what I said to Dad, told me that that was not true and that I shouldn't have said that to Dad. At the time I let him yell. I guessed that maybe his grief was taking him away from God and not toward him. There was nothing to say that would not have caused an ugly scene at Dad's deathbed and that would have been very wrong. So I let it go knowing that someday our own eventual deaths would prove him wrong.

I didn't really have any worries about my dad's chances of getting into heaven. Intuitively I knew that he had had his own set of mystic experiences in the last few years of his life. His testimony to the experiences and to the Lord had been to erect a six foot high plain wooden cross in the dead center of the backyard of our family home in East Sandwich, Massachusetts several years before he died. He was given plenty of harassment about the cross, even from Mom, but he flatly refused to take it down. So stubborn was he on the subject of the backyard cross that it seemed like his final mission and statement in his life. When I saw it on the next visit, I admired his handiwork and certainly did not add my voice to the others who were pleading with him to take it down. In my spirit I understood what he was trying to say to the family and the world in his own way.

My mother, after losing such a wonderful man, was very distraught for years after his death. In fact, she cried for two years but eventually recovered enough to find another great guy. His name is Ron, and in time they decided to be married. They exchanged wedding vows on a beautiful winter's day in a small chapel in West Barnstable. Dad, when he had been alive, Mom, as well as all us children had been to this chapel for many Sunday Masses over the years. A very small chapel, seating only about seventy-five people, its homey interior of unfinished wooden planks was comfortable and provided the perfect setting. The wedding group, so small and intimate, chatted away before the ceremony just as if it was any family function. It was not a formal, stiff wedding, nor had Mom wanted it to be. Mom had wanted her second wedding to be intimate so only her children, their families, her three sisters with spouses, and her mother were there. We were all laughing before the service, talking, and walking around in the pews. We were all so happy for Mom. Even Father Callahan chatted away with the bride and groom in the center aisle before the organist struck the first chord on the traditional wedding march song.

I was seated in a pew with Sam and my children on the right-hand side of the church, only four or five rows from the front. The sun was shining into the chapel's colorful, sparkling, stained glass windows giving a luster to the dark oak pews, which gleamed with fresh stain and polish. Finally, the service began. About ten minutes into the service I felt an arm circle from my right side, go around my back, and touch my left arm. I thought it was Sam, at first, but when I looked over at him, he was sitting with both hands folded on his lap. I quickly looked behind me, but my Aunt Bernie and Uncle Eddie sat quietly looking at my mom and Ron. I knew then that Dad was with us at Mom's wedding. He was communicating his close presence and attendance at her second wedding, giving me a hug to tell me that he was there, happy for Mom, and sending his blessing. He obviously approved of her choice.

> *"The light was on. Suddenly it seemed to me that Father, who had now been dead more than a year, was there with me. The sense of his presence was as vivid and as real and as startling as if he had touched my arm or spoken to me. The whole thing passed in a flash."*
>
> – THOMAS MERTON

His gesture confirmed that he was glad that she had finally been able to move on with her life. That she needed to continue to live her life to the fullest possible. Just as Dad would have if he had been the one who had lived and Mom died. His being with me on that day was a special gift. Dad loved all his children equally, and I am sure that he went up to everyone in the church and touched them all, but I guess the others couldn't feel him. His loving touch communicated his utter joy and happiness. Since joy and happiness emulate only from heaven, I knew without a shadow of a doubt that he had made it and was now in the presence of the Almighty eternally. In my mind's eye I could envision him having all sorts of wonderful conversations with his deceased family members, great architects of the Renaissance, and of course, Confucius.

Later at the reception in the Daniel Webster Inn amidst polished silverware and sparkling champagne filled flutes, I told all my brothers and sisters that Dad had put his arm around me in the church, and then I asked them if they had felt him too. They laughed if off. About a half an hour later, though, my brother Michael's daughter, Ashley, who was only eleven at the time, told her father that Granddad had just put his arm around her—right there at the reception. What was interesting was that Ashley had definitely not heard my comment to my sisters and brothers since she had not been in the room at the same time. Of course, Michael did not believe her and told her that she was just imagining things. "Granddad is dead and can't come back, although he always loved you very much."

It was a shame that Michael hid from her the truth about what she felt ...

"If you know how to touch your ancestors in the ultimate dimension, they will always be there with you. If you touch your own hand, face, or hair and look very deeply, you can see that they are there in you smiling. The ultimate dimension is a state of coolness, peace, and joy. It is not a state to be attained after you 'die.' You can touch the ultimate dimension right now by breathing, walking, and drinking your tea in mindfulness. Everything and everyone is dwelling in nirvana, in the Kingdom of God." – Thich Nhat Hanh

> "When the soul leaves the body, it is no longer under the burden and control of space and time. The soul is free; distance and separation hinder it no more. The dead are our nearest neighbors; they are all around us. Meister Eckhart was once asked, 'Where does the soul of a person go when the person dies?' He said, no place. Where else would the soul be going? Where else is the eternal world? It can be nowhere other than here."
>
> – JOHN O'DONOHUE

"This suggests that the dead are here with us, in the air that we are mov-

ing through all the time. The only difference between us and the dead is that they are now in an invisible form. You cannot see them with the human eye. But you can sense the presence of those you love who have died. With the refinement of your soul, you can sense them. You feel that they are near."

– JOHN O'DONOHUE

"My father used to tell us a story about a neighbor who was very friendly with the local priest. There is a whole mythology in Ireland about druids and priests having special power. But this man and the priest used to go for long walks. One day the man said to the priest, Where are the dead? The priest told him not to ask him questions like that. But the man persisted, and finally, the priest said, I will show you; but you are never to tell anyone. Needless to say, the man did not keep his word. The priest raised his right and; the man looked out under the raised right hand and saw the souls of the departed everywhere all around as thick as the dew on blades of grass. Often our loneliness and isolation are the result of a failure of spiritual imagination. We forget that there is no such thing as empty space. All space is full of presence, particularly the presence of those who are now in eternal, invisible form." – John O'Donohue

Ever wonder if the course of your whole life would be changed if you had only taken someone's advice—perhaps even a stranger's advice? Well I have often wondered this because of the encounter you are about to read. I now know that from a lovely stranger's mouth I could have taken a totally different course to find God—a different route, a much easier way—instead of the route that had gotten me into such trouble. But as Pat Kendall, my ESP teacher, had observed, I would never choose the easy, fast route rather the long, circular, twisting, turning route around.

In fact, you will probably wonder why I did not chose this course all along because by now you might understand as I do that I belonged to God. Why not formalize the relationship? Sometimes I wonder if this option would have been better all along. Certainly it would have been faster, but then I would have missed being a mother—a role that I cherish so much.

It was a spectacular summer day on Cape Cod. Warm, but still invigorating air, and sunshine filtered through branches of the scrub pine trees over my family home. I had just gotten up and enjoyed a hearty breakfast with my mother. I was about to begin doing all the fun things you do on the Cape in the summer when you are twenty-one years old with no responsibilities—preparing a picnic lunch on the beach, swimming, picking blueberries from the many bushes on the street, and then going shopping at the Cape Cod Mall. When the doorbell rang at 10:00 a.m., I went from our cozy wood-paneled kitchen into the long hallway that was really a display area for my dad's oil painting collection. My bare feet sunk into the wine-red oriental carpet on the way to the front door. I couldn't imagine who might be calling on us. We weren't expecting any company.

As I pulled open the door, my eyes met the kindly eyes and gentle smiles of two nuns—one an older nun, about fifty; the other a very young nun, no older than twenty. They were dressed in black habits, their faces shining out of the white-framed black kerchief-veils that hid their hair. Under their habits peeked out the ugliest black work boots I had ever seen on a woman's feet. I looked quickly away, slightly embarrassed at their footwear. Their arms both held several Bibles each; in fact, the purpose of their visit was to sell Bibles door-to-door.

As soon as I opened the door, they introduced themselves as Daughters of St. Paul and asked me if I would like to buy a Bible. I paused for one moment before retreating inside to ask my mother if we should buy another Bible, and in that moment I studied the younger nun—I could hardly take me eyes off her face and the way she glowed. Radiantly shining in her face was the joy that she had obviously found in her vocation. Somehow the dress and boots made her even more beautiful. As if her beauty could never be dimmed, no matter what she wore. It was very clear that she had found her calling in Jesus.

She looked so beautiful in her joy that I felt a new stirring inside myself, one that I had never considered before. *Perhaps I should join her; perhaps God was calling me too*, I thought. Realizing that I was bordering on being rude staring at them, I forced myself to look away and go inside to ask my mom. "Let me ask my mother. Just wait here a moment," I said.

I left the door open and found my mother and asked her to come to the door with me. "Mom, these nuns would like to sell us a Bible." Mother took one look at them and dismissed them as salespeople she didn't want to bother with. "Hi, I am sorry, but I already have a Bible, which is a family heirloom, and don't need another."

They smiled. Their disappointment was well hidden. I could see that they were ready to go. "Wait." I said. I wanted to know about the younger one. So I looked directly at her and asked: "Excuse me, but what is your name?"

"Theresa," she replied.

"You look so young. How old are you? When did you decide to join the convent?" I asked.

"I joined when I was seventeen and am now nineteen years old," she told me.

"Are you happy? I mean, was joining the convent the right choice for you?"

This was a pretty dumb question, since obviously it was the perfect choice for her. What I guess I really wanted to know was if it would be the right choice for me, also. She answered my inquiry with a gentle, soothing voice that was as lovely as the gentle breeze through a stand of marsh grass. There was happiness, excitement, and conviction there. Intuitively, she seemed to understand that I was really asking for myself.

"Absolutely. You should join us. You could be just as happy." She handed me some literature on the Bibles and their order. On it was listed the convent they both belonged to. It was located in the Midwest. My heart sank. I didn't think that I could go so far away from home. I would miss my brothers and sisters too much.

Interestingly, about four years ago, I again discovered the Daughters of St. Paul. Theirs is an order promoting the gospels and the Lord through the media—books, educational materials, and music. Every year since I have rediscovered them, I have gone to their concerts held in the Greater Boston Area, and I have bought most of their recordings on CD, which I play often in my car. Their voices blend just like an angelic choir. If I had joined them when I was young, I could have sung with them. They would have been the perfect order to join; Jesus would never have steered me wrong.

For the rest of the summer and into the fall, during the ESP class and beyond, those nuns were never far from my mind. I especially wondered about that beautiful, young nun. I'm sure that she was happy, but how I would have loved to know her better. God gave me a choice that day, but I decided against it. But, as you know by my story, I was eventually to find the Lord; that joy has not been denied me. But, boy, it was a long, hard road. I was eventually to meet several other nuns—both living and eternally living that would mold and shape my life into a more divinely configured shape. They were St. Teresa of Avila and Sister Margretta of Arch Street Chapel in Boston. Both were a tremendous blessing in my life.

"This seems to me to be the condition of a soul which, though not in a bad state, is so completely absorbed in things of the world and so deeply immersed, as I have said, in possessions or honours or business, that, although as a matter of fact it would like to gaze at the castle and enjoy its beauty, it is prevented from doing so, and seems quite unable to free itself from all these impediments. Everyone, however, who wishes to enter the second Mansions, will be well advised, as far as his state of life permits, to try to put aside all unnecessary affairs and business." – John O'Donohue

"He knows better than we what is good for us and which of us truly love Him." – John O'Donohue

In April 2002 with Lent just over, our family took a trip to Washington, D.C., during the children's spring vacation. When we returned, I was inspired to begin in earnest to research all the Catholic doctrine I could get my hands on as I had mentioned previously. I needed to find some answers, and a sudden insight urged me to begin looking closely at the writings of my own church and the lives and stories of the saints. Almost the very first book I hit upon on my quest was St. Teresa of Avila's book *Interior Castles*. It was in that book that I received my first clues and inklings as to what direction my life had taken, and I was profoundly affected by it. Shockingly as I read her book, I recognized many of the mystical gifts that she had undertaken to explain to her nuns in *Interior Castles* were exactly the same gifts that God bestowed on me. Imagine reading a book written by a sixteenth century Roman Catholic nun who was also a great mystic and being able to totally relate to her experiences because they paralleled your own. Not every one, of course, and I have had some unique ones she did not mention, but near enough to realize that God was molding me in a similar way as St. Teresa, a mystical way. The book blew my mind, but somehow it healed it, made sense of what before had been incomprehensible.

Everything—the awakening, the spiritual trials—made sense as I would never have believed possible. There was a mirror in her book that accurately reflected my own journey. When I noticed the amazing similarities, I questioned God. I couldn't understand why God was giving me this type of journey. I was sure that only nuns were called to the mystical path. This was a misconception of mine that would be dispelled forever. God leads a person any way He pleases. It doesn't matter what walk of life we are in. That is why you have read so many references to *Interior Castles* here in this book, because I owe my own understanding and even sanity to her great insight into mysticism—specifically the mysticism of the Catholic faith.

Throughout the ages, St. Teresa has profoundly affected many people who were going to be given a mystical spiritual journey. Both when she was alive, and when she passed into heaven. Edith Stein, a Jewish convert who lived through World War II, is another woman who has no doubt profoundly thanked St. Teresa of Avila for her work:

> *"Less well know perhaps is the German Carmelite nun Edith Stein (1891–1942), a Roman Catholic convert from Judaism. Born into a wealthy Jewish family, she became an atheist when still very young, studied philosophy and was so gifted that the philosopher Edmund*

> *Hussert invited her to become his assistant in his work on phenomenology. She obtained a doctorate in philosophy and was later introduced to Roman Catholicism. It was particularly her profound encounter with Teresa of Avila's autobiography at a friend's house that led to her conversion in 1921."*
>
> — URSULA KING

Interior Castle is all about the infinite possibilities and varieties of divine gifts or spiritual blessing. My journey as well reflects His divine gifts. I can personally attest that God is infinitely creative in giving them, and perfect in his timing for each individual. Many reflect Heavenly favors. In *Interior Castle* St. Teresa envisioned the soul as a seven-room castle—with many side doors leading to an infinite variety of special places. Each room contained specific gifts. She believed that mystical experiences were within the reach of all her daughters. But also that any favors God gives are granted not because those who receive them are holier than those who do not, but in order that His greatness may be made known.

"To some extent it is possible for us to enjoy Heaven upon earth." – St. Teresa of Avila

"How shall I ever be able to tell you of the riches and the treasures and the delights which are to be found in the fifth Mansions?" – St. Teresa of Avila

I believe that I am one of her spiritual daughters. St. Teresa of Avila founded the Carmelite Order of nuns. Once in 2004, after doing a faith-sharing, someone approached me after the group was dispersing and told me that I have a Carmelite spirituality. If someone tells you that you have a "Carmelite" spirituality, they are noticing that your faith is based on a more mystical plane than other spiritualities. There are many families of different spiritualities.

> *"His Majesty knows that if, as I say, our actions and our words are one, the Lord will unfailingly fulfill our petitions, give us His kingdom and help us by means of supernatural gifts, such as the Prayer of Quiet, perfect contemplation and all the other favours which the Lord bestows on our trifling efforts."*
>
> — ST. TERESA OF AVILA

> *"During the later part of his life, Pascal had the awareness of an unmerited union with God. He describes a direct "seeing" with the eyes of faith, an intensive mystical experience, culminating in a continuous sense of God's presence. The grace of faith alone gives the required insight to read the signs of the hidden God in both nature and scripture. 'All things speak of God to those who know him, and because they reveal*

Him to all those who love him, these same things hide Him from those who do not know Him."

— URSULA KING

By May of 2002, after understanding finally dawned with the knowledge that I was being formed into a mystic, I realized I lacked something quite common in fifteenth and sixteenth century Europe, but now in this present time had become uncommon—a spiritual director. No aspiring Catholic on a quest for God in the fifteenth and sixteenth centuries would have been without one.

Psychologists, I was quick to learn, had no advice to offer me. I needed someone more up-to-date on the spiritual battlefield that my life now was. I needed a person who God had similarly called. I needed a nun who was also a spiritual director. But how did one locate a spiritual director? Were there any such people in the present-day world of stockbrokers, real estate brokers, accountants, and nuclear scientists? Well, ask and you shall receive; seek and you shall find; knock and the door shall be opened onto you.

I opened the main door to the Arch Street Church in early June 2002, guided to go there on my quest. Upon entering into the foyer with its double staircases leading the to upper level church and its simple marble font of holy water, I noticed a wooden table with ordinary church bulletins of the kind that you will find in any entrance to any Catholic church. I picked one up and began looking at it randomly. On the front cover I noticed that a Sr. Margretta was the director of Spiritual Direction. Upon seeing her name, I received a deep conviction within my heart that she might be the one to help me. I could hire her as my own spiritual director. I sent a quick prayer to the Lord, thanking Him for his love and guidance.

So I set up the first appointment for a month later and met with Sister Margretta. She was a willowy, soft-spoken woman of great gentleness, her eyes doe-like, her mouth small, and her cheekbones sharp in a face framed by hair cut short and left in its natural salt-and-pepper hues. She wore a very conservative blouse and skirt, which could pass for street clothing. I liked and trusted her instinctively. Our entire first meeting in late July 2002 was spent with her listening as I poured out five months of frightening yet awesome, powerful yet mysterious supernatural experiences. Her brow furrowed when she heard about the seven days of births, but she said nothing. She let me just talk and did not once tell me or even suggest that I was crazy. I felt profound relief. Here was someone to talk to who could really understand, as my sisters Caroline and Anne and my psychologist had not. She had never heard of my particular spiritual awakening scenario but was very open-minded, willing to believe that the Lord might give any number of spiritual gifts or graces. There was no containing God to a particular formula or pattern. I was "unique," she said.

In that session she mentioned a couple of significant things. One was that I should use caution. My sister, Caroline, had also suggested the same thing, but for different reasons. Sister Margretta counseled that when something feels bad/wrong/uncomfortable, use Jesus' name and a crucifix to ward it off. Jesus' name, a crucifix, and holy water are the best defenses against the evil one. I couldn't tell if she was speaking from actual experience, but the advice matched exactly what Father and the priest in the confession had said, so I accepted it. She also said: "Never invite it in," meaning if I could sense a spirit, just use the name of Jesus and pray.

She also told me that she thought that my true vocation was as a mother, and that I must focus on my children and loving Jesus with all my heart—that I should do nothing that would conflict with my vocation as a mother. She said this in response to my feeling that maybe I should go away for a time to be alone and sort through everything. She told me to give less and less attention to the unusual occurrences. Look only toward Jesus. She also said that she thought that the ESP class had been a mistake because it had opened me up to spirits. She mentioned St. Ignatius Loyola's book on *Spiritual Exercises,* which might guide me on how to live with my newfound awakened spirituality. I did read it and found many wonderful insights there, all of which helped me understand how to deal with the profound changes my spirituality was undergoing.

She told me she was glad that I had done so much research, that she felt it was very helpful that I was looking for my own answers. Next, we talked about some of the spirits in St. John's "Dark Night of the Soul." Certain that I had not yet met the entire lineup, I was sure that I had encountered the dark spirits of fornication, blasphemy, and nitpicking. The first one was the worst though. I could barely let my mind venture back to those three awful nights in February 2002 before the first birth. The spirit of blasphemy had only had a small effect on me, which I felt only twice. Intuitively, I understood that this was because I seldom truly blasphemed or sworn—never my thing. Nit picking was also a pain in the neck, but not to be as feared as some of the others. After I left her, I went to confession in the lower church and also lit a couple of candles positioned around the perimeter at the back of the church. I felt like I had released a huge burden.

After I exited the front doors of the chapel, I took a long walk around the Boston Public Garden enjoying the beautiful day and thinking through our conversation. I had taken a half-day off from work knowing that our first session might be for me highly emotional and that I may not be able to return to the office and go on in my usual professional manner. I bought myself a bagel and iced coffee, and I crocheted on a park bench in the shade of the Boston Common, watching as people sauntered by, usually in a hurry. Then I went into a bookstore and bought two books on St. Teresa of Avila, a saint whom I felt very close to. I no longer hungered for my past fare in books—mystery, romance, and fantasy. Instead, my soul was being fed hearty sustenance with spiritual/Catholic books, and their appeal was more delicious than chocolate cake.

After our first hour meeting, we met regularly for about three years every other month. She was such an expert on spirituality, and I was so grateful to her for helping me shift through all the spiritual energy, feelings, and ghosts I seemed to be dealing with. Never once did she condemn me but only offered gentle guidance, wonderful listening skills, and direction on how to negotiate and counter the spiritual warriors of the netherworld. I will always be profoundly grateful that God placed me in her hands—one of His present-day living saints.

"That was the second thing I should have done: I should have sought constant and complete spiritual direction. Six weeks of instructions, after all, were not much." – Thomas Merton

> "At all times in the history of Christian perfection, there has been a dearth of persons qualified to guide souls to the highest states of prayer: The Interior Castle will both serve as an aid to those there are and to a great extent supply the need for more."
>
> – ST. TERESA OF AVILA

At every Sunday Mass I began to experience incredible peace and joy. My heart overflowed with love to the point of tears at seeing all the familiar faces of the congregation. A transition took place, and I began to think of them all as my heavenly brothers and sisters, and to really believe that we would all be together forever.

> "But that cry, 'Creo en Dios!' It was loud, and bright, and sudden and glad and triumphant: it was a good big shout, that came from all those Cuban children, a joyous affirmation of faith. Then, as sudden as the shout and as definite, and a thousand times more bright, there formed in my mind an awareness, an understanding, a realization of what had just taken place on the altar, at the Consecration: a realization of God made present by the words of Consecration in a way that made Him belong to me. But what a thing it was, this awareness: it was so intan-

gible, and yet it struck me like a thunderclap. It was a light that was so
bright that it had no relation to any visible light and so profound and so
intimate that it seemed like a neutralization of every lesser experience."

— THOMAS MERTON

Experiences of the saints, who now surrounded me, were another everyday experience. I would feel them touching me and guiding me in many different ways. I had many vivid experiences of them. One I particularly remember took place during an evening prayer group during Lent 2003. Our group of six was discussing Bible passages and their meanings. During the entire session, as I listened to the other group members, I could feel presences all around me touching my face, arms, hands, and my legs. Gathered with us were many saints present invisibly in that small room listening in on our conversation. By their touches I could tell if they agreed or disagreed with what was being said—St. Teresa of Avila and Thomas Merton both had strong opinions. My spirit was so saturated with their books and sayings that they were like my nearest and dearest friends. I wanted to share my awareness of them with the other members of the group, but such a long explanation would have been necessary that I decided not to.

"Sometimes, again, the companionship is that of a saint and this is also
a great help to us."

— ST. TERESA OF AVILA

"This is a question which the soul cannot answer, nor can it understand
how it knows what it does; it is perfectly certain, however, that it is right.
When it is a saint, and no words are spoken, the soul is able to feel that
the Lord is sending him to be a help and a companion to it; and this
more remarkable."

— ST. TERESA OF AVILA

In the Spring of 2002 I bought a copy of Joan Baez's Greatest Hits on CD and fell in love with the song called "Blessed." As I listened to the words, "Blessed are the one-way ticket holders on a one way street," the lyrics really spoke to me. They reminded me of what it takes to be a saint or a martyr. The saints lived their lives on a one-way street to God. For them there were no side streets, and no turning back from God, only the direct route to Him. Once they took God into their hearts, they traveled forward to what God would have them become. Oh how I yearned to be like them!

In September 2002, laying on my flowered sofa in my small sunny guest room, reading the story of St. Gertrude, I felt the gentlest touch of a hand pressing the skin over my heart—like a hand was placed over my heart. St.

Gertrude was present with me in the supernatural dimension as I read about her story, and she had wanted me to understand that she was with me. She is particularly associated with the devotion of Jesus' Sacred Heart.

> *"Some are of the opinion that heaven is everywhere, as God is every-*
> *where. According to this view the blessed can move about freely in every*
> *part of the universe, and still remain with God and see everywhere.*
> *Everywhere, too, they remain with Christ (in His sacred Humanity) and*
> *with the saints and the angels. For, according to the advocates of this*
> *opinion, the spatial distances of this world must no longer impede the*
> *mutual intercourse of the blessed."*
>
> — FROM THE CATHOLIC ONLINE ENCYCLOPEDIA

November 19, 2002.

I was reading about the Greek Orthodox Church and their many saints. From the few times I have attended an Orthodox Mass, I had noticed how very much they revere their saints and mention them particularly throughout Mass and their talks. Very highly exalted, many Eastern Orthodox saints achieved the highest perfection by monitoring all their thoughts and stopping or defusing negative thoughts as soon as they are noticed. I thought how interesting it sounded, so I decided to try to see if I could eliminate negative thoughts before they overwhelmed me and became constant noise in my brain.

Over the next few months, I tried to notice when a thought just popped into my head. Sometimes I noticed that they immediately caused me a great deal of distress. According to the Greek Orthodox Church, this happens because a thought can be fed through from the other side—the dark side—purposely to upset a soul for no other reason than just to disturb or keep the person's thoughts from God or loving their neighbor. So when a new and disturbing thought surfaced and seemed to come out of midair, I tried to let it go before it made me angry or upset.

This is the art of "Nepsis" or "Logismoi," which the Greek fathers teach. I found it a wonderful help as well as necessary as I drew closer to becoming God's own, because the enemy was constantly battling me and would try anything to upset me. This could be a good practice for all religions, teaching people how to attribute a bad thought to its real source, and remove it from the mind before it becomes an action.

> *"Nepsis is a Greek word which means to be watchful, alert, vigilant,*
> *and to basically keep a look out. Attention must be so united to prayer*

*as the body is to the soul. Attention must go forward and observe the
enemies like a scout, and it must engage in combat with sin, and resist
the bad thoughts that come to the soul. St. Symeon, the New Theologian,
regarded the struggle of Nepsis thusly. 'Our whole soul should have at
every moment a clear eye, able to watch and notice the thoughts entering our heart from the evil one and repel them. The heart must always
burn with faith, humility and love. Do not fear the conflict, and do not
flee from it; where there is no struggle, there is no virture. With Nepsis
and watchfulness, comes a charismatic gift, discernment.'"*
– FROM THE CHARISMATIC ORTHODOX CHURCH WEB SITE

I received a valuable insight in November 2002 on death and the griev-
ing process. When someone close to you dies or is sick, God gives us grief
intentionally. Grief is useful because it causes you to pray to help the person,
and also to seek God for an answer. God can also use grief to teach people
to learn to trust in God—to leave your problems in His beautiful hands. The
sick, dying person desperately needs the spiritual help to cross in a more
beautiful place, so instinctively we are instructed to help the person through
the vehicle of grief.

We are taught in the Catholic faith that most people who die pass over into
purgatory, not reaching perfection in this life; they must purify to come face-
to-face with God. The soul must be released from all its sins and passions.
Sins and passions act as darkness and even tight straps that stop a soul from
making progress toward God. Purgatory is God's answer to releasing these
tight, constricting bindings, to release and free the soul from all that weighed
it down on earth. Please know, however, that purgatory can be done on earth
while the body is still alive. This is exactly what all the saints experienced on
earth, so when they died they could simply pass right through purgatory.

Speaking of a great aid for purgatory ...

Divine Mercy Sunday. Baltimore, April 27, 2003.

While we were on a family vacation in Baltimore, Maryland, I got up early
and left everyone else still asleep in their hotel beds. Then I walked about ½
mile to the Catholic Church nearest to the hotel and went to 9:00 a.m. Mass.
The inside of the church was painted a simple white, but there were wonderful stained glass windows, which were shone to beautiful advantage against
the walls. They sparkled with a jewel-like beauty as the sun rose in the sky.
What a wonderful gift it is to be able to attend Mass on a Sunday practically
anywhere you might go on vacation. What joy it is to see the beautifully appointed churches, to hear a different priest's sermon, and to join the voice of

the congregation as they sing. On that particular Sunday I was in for a real treat. The vocalist was a black male Washington, D.C. opera singer. His voice was so strong, so pure, and he sang so passionately that my heart swelled with happiness—totally enjoying this blessing.

This year was to be the first one ever for the Devotion of Divine Mercy. The presiding priest announced it at the beginning of Mass and took a moment to explain that Divine Mercy Sunday was a fairly new devotion, which Jesus had given Sister Faustina—probably when she was in the state of ecstasy. The devotion is for all sinners and it allows a special grace of mercy from Jesus directly. It is a tremendous blessing for all the dying because it ensures that our Lord stands by the person and helps them at the time of death. I admit that I love this devotion and say the prayer every night on my rosary beads. It is one of my favorites and never takes more than five minutes a night.

There were prayer cards left at the back of the church, so upon leaving, I took one. After reading the prayer card, I make the connection that the pastel painting I had done of Jesus for Easter Sunday that past year was really Jesus in His image as Divine Mercy as He was shown to Saint Faustina.

One week before Easter I had been attending Mass at St. John the Baptist in Quincy. While kneeling in front of the blessed family statues, I noticed a small pile of mini posters proclaiming the words on the Divine Mercy prayer card: "Jesus, I trust in You." I picked one up and took it home to draw it into a pastel portrait. What an amazing coincidence.

Perhaps I relate so well to Saint Faustina and love the devotion so much because she and I are spiritual sisters in that we have both had many spiritual trials.

> "Sister Faustina began to have a number of religious experiences far from what one might consider the norm. These visions lasted throughout her entire life. From trials of spiritual darkness, to the manifestations of Christ, she was seemingly caught in a battle of good and evil, her soul the arena."
>
> – ON SISTER MARY FAUSTINA FROM THE MEDJUGORJE WEB SITE

Here is the Divine Mercy Chaplet:

Say one Our Father, One Hail Mary, and the Act of Contrition then take your rosary beads in hand and pray:

"Eternal Father I offer you the body, blood, soul, and divinity of your dearly beloved son, our Lord Jesus Christ, in atonement of our sins and those of the whole wide world." (one time)

Then: "For the sake of His sorrowful passion, have mercy on us and on the whole wide world." (10 times)

Then repeat this sequence for a total of five times.

Conclude with: "Holy God, Holy Mighty One, Holy Immortal One, have mercy on us and on the whole world." (3 times)

You will receive anything you ask if it is also God's will if you pray this chaplet at 3:00 p.m. on Good Friday. The nine-day novena of Divine Mercy extends from Good Friday to the next Saturday night and the following day is Divine Mercy Sunday.

> *"The first step toward holiness is the will to attain it. With a will that is whole we love God, we opt for Him, we run toward Him, we reach Him, we possess Him."*
>
> — MOTHER TERESA

> *"Jesus wants to possess your heart completely. He wants you to be a great saint. The good God never asks the impossible."*
>
> — SAINT THERESE OF LISIEUX

> *"We should hide our good works from the eyes of others and even from ourselves, so that the "left hand knows not what the right hand does." From that moment on, I have felt a daring confidence that I shall become a saint. I do not trust to my own merits for I have none, I trust in him who is virtue and holiness itself. It is he alone who, pleased with my poor efforts, will raise me to himself and by clothing me with his merits, make me a saint."*
>
> — SAINT THERESE OF LISIEUX

> "Oh, when the Saints Come Marching In
> Oh, when the Saints Come Marching In,
> How I'll love to be with that number,
> When the Saints Come Marching In."

INTRODUCTION

TO

THE ANGELS/SPIRITS AND DEMONS SECTIONS

WHEN YOU EXPERIENCE a spiritual, mystic adventure, I guarantee that you will meet countless spirits. Many come bearing wonderful truths—gifts that help you gain understanding of the eternal dimension. Almost like I was the baby Sleeping Beauty and the fairies were bestowing spiritual presents at my birth. These are the sweet, amazing stories. But as in any other area of life, the good and the bad come hand-in-hand. Sometimes in the dead of night, there would be an endless lineup of specters that could have been cast as extras in Charles Dickens's *A Christmas Carol*.

"Ebenezer, you had it easy—one night and three ghosts. A mystic should have it so good."

To tell you the truth, during a number of other periods in my life before my awakening, both types of spirits have visited me. In the angel and demon sections I recount stories from my early twenties. The supernatural side sometimes appeared at key periods or "forks in the road" of my life to steer me in the right direction. Before we enter into this rather spooky spiritual territory, let us have a little visit with St. Loyola and his Spiritual Rules. They help in determining which are the good spirits and which are bad. I hope you will see, though, that even the bad experiences reap good fruit in my life. Just remember what happened after the spirits visited good old Ebenezer.

St. Ignatius of Loyola; Spiritual Exercises - "First Rule: In the persons who go from mortal sin to mortal sin, the enemy is commonly used to propose to them apparent pleasures, making them imagine sensual delights and pleasures in order to hold them more and make them grow in their vices and sins. In these persons the good spirit uses the opposite method, pricking them and biting their consciences through the process of reason.

"Second Rule: In the persons who are going on intensely cleansing their sins and rising from good to better in the service of God our Lord, it is the method contrary to that in the first Rule, for then it is the way of the evil spirit to bite, sadden and put obstacles, disquieting with false reasons, that one may not go on: and it is proper to the good to give courage and strength, consolations, tears, inspirations, and quiet, easing, and putting away all obstacles, that one may go on in well doing.

"The fourth rule: Spiritual Desolation: I call desolation all the contrary of the third rule, such as darkness of soul, disturbance in it, movement to things low and earthly, the unquiet of different agitations and temptations, moving to want of confidence, without hope, without love, when one finds oneself all lazy, tepid, sad, and as if separated from his Creator and Lord. Because, as consolation is contrary to desolation, in the same way the thoughts which come from consolation are contrary to the thoughts which come from desolation.

"The fifth rule: In time of desolation never to make a change; but to be firm and constant in the resolutions and determination in which one was the day preceding such desolation, or in the determination in which he was in the preceding consolation. Because, as in consolation it is rather the good spirit who guides and counsels us, so in desolation it is the bad, with whose counsels we cannot take a course to decide rightly.

"The seventh rule: In those who go on from good to better, the good Angel touches such a soul sweetly, lightly and gently, like a drop of water which enters into a sponge; and the evil touches it sharply and with noise and disquiet, as when the drop of water falls on the stone."

From the notes on perceiving and understanding scruples and persuasions of our enemy:

"The fourth rule: The enemy looks much if a soul is gross or delicate, and if it is delicate, he tries to make it more delicate in the extreme, to disturb and embarrass it more. For instance, if he sees that a soul does not consent to either mortal sin or venial or any appearance of deliberate sin, then the enemy, when he cannot make it fall into a thing that appears sin, aims at making it make out sin where there is not sin, as in a word or very small thought.

"The fifth rule: The soul which desires to benefit itself in the spiritual like, ought always to proceed the contrary way to what the enemy proceeds; that is today, if the enemy wants to make the soul gross, let it aim at making itself delicate. Likewise, if the enemy tries to draw it out to extreme fineness, let the soul try to establish itself in the mean, in order to quiet itself in everything."

18

ANGELS AND SPIRITS

Divine Messengers
Eternal Helpers
Guardians and Friends
Spiritual Aid Beyond All Description

"In the year 500, in the seventh month, on the fourteenth day of the month in the life of Enoch. In that Parable I saw how a mighty quaking made the heaven of heavens to quake, and the host of the Most High, and the angels, a thousand thousands and ten thousand times ten thousand, were disquieted with a great disquiet. And the Head of Days sat on the throne of His glory, and the angels and the righteous stood around Him."

— BOOK OF ENOCH, CHAPTER 60

"And He will summon all the host of the heavens, and all the holy ones above, and the host of God, the Cherubic, Seraphin and Ophannin, and all the angels of power, and all the angels of principalities, and the Elect One, and the other powers on the earth (and) over the water."

— CHAPTER 61

"The almighty God, who can do absolutely anything on earth, or direct his angels to fulfill his will, chooses instead to accomplish many of his plans by using frail and vulnerable humans who love him. This is astounding!"

— MICHAEL FANSTONE

When I was twenty-two, I had the opportunity to take an ESP class offered at a local community college. Those three letters combined drew me in like a

magnet: ESP. Deciding almost immediately that it was a prospect too enticing to pass up, I wasted no time in sending in my application and check. The
write-up on the class promised it would shed light on what the "beyond" held.
So I followed my yearning, and my adventure began in September 1981. The
things I would learn in that class were exciting, spiritual, but also haunting ...
and ultimately terrifying.

"It's funny and sort of weird to be back in a classroom at Cape Cod
Community College," I said to myself as I stepped foot in the familiar building in search of my classroom. Instead of the usual typing and shorthand
classes, I was taking one on the great unknown, the cosmos. My excitement
and hopes were high that I would find some clues on my quest in search of
the Divine one. The suburban campus, set in a woodsy environment with its
cement and brick buildings circled by a perimeter road, brought back many
memories. Reminiscences floated in and out of my mind, recollecting memories of my classes in shorthand, typing, economics, personal development,
psychology, backpacking, tennis, and English—taken and "aced" in most
cases—on my way to my associate's degree in executive secretarial science
and my graduation in 1979.

Pulling down the lever, I opened the door into the classroom. My eyes met
many other sets of eyes. "Wow," I thought, "a lot of people are interested in
this subject." Taking a seat at the large, round boardroom-sized table, I waited
impatiently for the beginning of the class. At precisely 7:00 p.m., Pat Kendall,
who had been sitting quieting flipping through some assorted notes, got up
and went to the head of the table. Of medium height, with brown frizzy hair,
sparkling green eyes, and hands in constant motion, she had a rounded, ma-
tronly shape, which made her seem very approachable—your generic motherly type.

As soon as she faced the room her lively, bubbly personality overflowed
into the space like a fire hydrant exploding on the street. The quiet was replaced and filled by her effervescent laughter, which rang out with her very
first sentence—loud and joyful. It was one of her great charms, and it enhanced her mesmerizing presence. Glowing with inner radiance, she had an
enormous, winning smile, which never left her face. Perky, lively, and happy
despite, as we would later learn, a very difficult, sometimes broken marriage
situation, she almost immediately displayed the silly, giddy side of her persona. By the end of the first class, though, I could also sense her inner essence
was fathoms deep, and that it was simmering like a smoking cauldron of a
thick, rich soup just below the surface.

"Hi, class. How wonderful to see you all here. I am Pat Kendall, and will be leading you into a place of discovery into your inner depths and other psychic phenomena. I am what can be called a 'white witch.' We white witches use white light to surround other people and bring about healing and new dimensions," she proclaimed. "White light," she went on, "brings healing, joy, and pleasure to life. In case you don't know what white light is," she continued, "it is Jesus' or God's pure goodness or essence. And it's really great stuff. For instance, if you want to keep a loved one from harm, you can visualize them surrounded by a bright white halo around their entire body. It protects them from physical or spiritual harm, and its use delivers all sorts of everyday helps such as finding a parking space in a difficult place, running into friends who will be happy to see you, and bringing humor into everyday life."

From this first opening statement, it was immediately obvious to me as well as to all the other students that she had spent a good portion of her life questing into spiritual matters and was now a long way down the road of her spiritual journey. She seemed to have achieved inner peace, experienced the spirit world, and accepted what "normal" people never will. Her manner was matter-of-fact and reflected this. Then she prayed an opening meditation that was to become the standard for every other class: "May the long time sun shine upon you. All love surround you, and the pure light within you guide your way home."

The fifteen other people sharing the class with me all looked like your average next door neighbors kind of people. We had a young couple living together, students, a lesbian couple, several homemakers, a couple of "career" women, and a few professional men. As I looked around the room that first night, I asked myself, "What are these other people looking for? Do they want to delve deeper into spirituality, religion, and ESP? Or were they just bored with their lives and looking for an adventure? What has led these people here?" I wondered.

Then I asked myself the same question. "Why am I here?" I knew I found the subject interesting, but more than that I had this pressing need to push outward beyond the borders of what everyone else considers acceptable, normal. As they say in the TV show *Star Trek*: "To boldly go where no man has ever gone." Of course, I knew that many people, since time began, have made this particular trek. I more or less wanted to follow in their footsteps. The galaxies and the unknown outer space were interesting, but my interest focused on our minds, our inner space. Acquiring this knowledge was far nearer and dearer to my heart and, I felt, more needed. I hoped it would help me in my search to find God. Although at the time I didn't understand this, something from deep inside my hidden self was beginning to take shape, emerge, straining for my attention.

The class was stiff at first. People definitely needed time to warm up to each other. But with Pat's leadership, we were soon on our way. One of the first demonstrations, which Pat conducted on the first night, was fascinating. She looked around the room and chose the two biggest men.

"Henry, Steve, come up and I will show you that the eyes are truly the windows of the soul. The soul is your strength, and anyone can weaken your personal strength by knowing this. Henry, I want you to lift your arms up until they are the level of your shoulders, and then I am going to try and pull them down with my arms."

Pat took her two arms and pulled for all she was worth downward but really couldn't budge Henry's arms. She looked at the group. "Henry is pretty strong now, but we will see in a minute if he is still as strong. All I have to do is look into Henry's eyes, and when we have eye contact I will raise my eyes above his head. I will visualize his spirit above his body rather than in it." Pat looked directly at Henry, and Henry looked and smiled back. Pat lifted her eyes to a spot just about a foot over Henry's head, and then she pulled down on his arms. They fell limply to his sides.

She demonstrated the same principle with the slightly stronger Steve. It still worked. She asked us to try this principle out on as many people in the room as it will take to convince us that using this technique weakens people. It worked every time. I loved it. I resolved to practice this the very next time I was in a bar and had a few macho men around.

Pat took us through all sorts of great spiritual/paranormal stuff. We had lectures and discussions on such interesting things as past life regressions, jewelry readings, affirmations, tarot cards, crystal balls, color and crystal healing, religious discussions (mostly eastern-based), natural healing, out-of-body experiences, levitation, and the astral plan. We all began dream logs to write down our dreams right after we had them so that we could look for life patterns and issues and resolve them. That first class we talked about white light, its power, and specific uses. And we practiced visualizing it around other people.

I must admit that from the very first night, she opened my mind and showed me possibilities beyond my ordinary existence, beyond this physical place. I began to live for her class—to be in her presence and to absorb the electrifying experiences sure to follow.

If we had had the Internet back then, and I had read the following passage, I would have realized I was getting off track, but I was just a kid and had to make a few mistakes.

"It is clear, however, that mysticism is not the same as magic, clairvoyance, parapsychology, occultism, nor does it consist in a preoccupation with sensory images, visions, or special revelations. Nearly all Christian mystical writers relegate these phenomena to the periphery. Nearly all Christian mystics avoid the occult arts entirely. Briefly and generally stated, mystical theology or Christian mysticism seeks to describe an experience, direct, nonabstract, unMeditated, loving knowing of God, a knowing or seeing so direct as to be called union with God." – On the World Wide Web; Definitions of Mysticism

No doubt C.S. Lewis would have understood my fascination with the occult because apparently he had the very same attraction to the paranormal, magic, and spiritualists. What he eventually found out, I would soon learn:

> *"I don't have the same excuse, I am afraid. I wasn't looking for Joy, but I was looking for God as I could find him in any way that I could. I was more curious than anything. The Lord was to show me that my curiosity would land me in trouble, and soon I would run back to the church full speed ahead."*
>
> – C.S. LEWIS

The following quote offers a warning when interfering with the supernatural spiritual realm: "When one starts out talking to angels, you end up talking to demons."

⚜

Pat was great at using games, awareness exercises, ritual Meditation, mandalas, and psychological logs to broaden our understanding of our minds, bodies, and our souls. She explained about the Chakras, or power centers, in our body; what colors they are; and what the colors mean. Handing us long lists of books to read to increase our understanding, I found all my waking hours immersed in: Monroe's *Out of Body*, Powell's *Why Am I*, Assagolie's *The Act of Will*, Moody's *At the Hour of Death*, and Dr. Thelma Moss' *The Probability of the Impossible*.

Looking back, it was lucky for all of us that she was a practitioner of good or white magic. How easy it is for people looking for answers to fall under the tutelage of a person who does not uphold goodness and "whiteness." Pat was a wonderful person who absolutely believed and practiced only the good side—never the dark side. She did not, however, deny the power or the attraction of the evil one or his followers.

Throughout all our classes, we were fully aware that she keenly observed each of us as a person. Special insight would come to her regarding who we were. And beginning at about our fifth or sixth week, she began to let us know what the insight was. Each person got a different insight, and none were really negative. They were issues she could see that might hold us back in our spiritual development. For example, Betsy, who was one of our lesbian couple, got the insight that she let others into her heart too easily. She should be aware of safeguarding her heart for a longer period of time before making a new friend. That way she wouldn't get hurt as easily as she had in the past.

Pat's personal insight for me was rather unique. She told me that I would always choose the longest route to get anywhere rather than the shortest, most direct way. She told me that I liked to enjoy the scenery too much. She also told me that I had a very old soul—ancient by classmate standards—that had been reincarnated many times. She told me that all humans on the earth plane now are a mix of brand new souls, fairly new souls, old souls, and ancient souls. I was in the ancient category. She didn't say anymore about the oldness of anyone else's soul, or mine, but I was left to wonder about it. God's name for me of Pandora is a true reflection of her observation. She could see something very ancient in me, even though I was captive in my twenty-two-year-old body.

One other person about fifteen years later would also tell me that he knew I had a very old soul. He was a philosophy teacher I had when I went back to pursue my second degree in accounting at Northeastern University. He wasn't nearly as sure as Pat was about the paranormal, nor was he absolutely positive about the existence of God, but he could see something about me that Pat had also seen.

Where had I been in the past, and doing what? What had I learned in past lives that I could use in this life? I must admit that the whole idea fascinated me. We even did a past life regression, which was immensely fun. We visualized balloons lifting our spirit up, up into a different time. In this exercise, we first entered into a meditation state, then were directed to let our balloon fly free of the earth, sensing by our instinct how long to stay up in the air. In whatever timeframe felt right we were told to bring our balloon back to the ground. When your balloon landed you knew that you were in a past life. When mine landed I ended up in England in the year 1759 (two hundred years before my real birthday). I was the wife of a sea captain with five children. My husband was on an ocean voyage at the time of the visit, so I never got to meet him, unfortunately.

So the fall class progressed loaded with new, exciting worlds to explore. It was right before Christmastime in 1981 after a party for our ESP group that

I had my first experience with a spirit. Our ESP group had grown very close over the weeks, and we had shared many interesting and unnerving experiences together. We were bonded. So when Pat suggested the idea of getting together for a holiday party, we all readily agreed. We were having fun together, why not?

Pat arranged the place for the party—oddly enough it took place at a children's preschool in Yarmouthport, MA. One of her close girlfriends had offered the large room as a good place to hold a gathering. We were all assigned tasks, mine being to bake brownies and cookies. The lesbian girls were to bring in room decorations. The young couple was to bring in soda and salty munchies. Others were designated other tasks.

We all arrived around 7:00 p.m., and together we decorated the room so that it was festive for the party. We hung red and green streamers, arranged a table with a pretty paper Christmas tablecloth, and loaded all the food on the table. Five or six others put up a small Christmas tree. One of the guys even placed tiny red foil gift boxes under it. Everyone was happy, in a festive mood. For the first hour we ate and talked. We knew enough about each other's lives to care about how everyone was doing.

There were a couple of announcements to the group. The lesbian girls had moved into their own apartment and made a statement about their "coupleness." After that, the young couple who was living together announced that they were engaged. They planned to marry having a small, informal ceremony in about two months—since the girlfriend was pregnant.

Steve, a guy who I knew better than the rest of the group since I worked for his dad, did a really sweet thing. He hand-crafted snowmen as Christmas ornaments for each person. No bigger than three inches high, it was formed from pieces of wood—three small circles, the bottom one the largest, the middle one slightly smaller, and the smallest one on top. Steve crafted tiny top hats made of black felt; a single strand of thread inserted through the hat allowed the snowman to be hung from a Christmas tree. The face was adorable with small black dot eyes, a red slash line for a mouth, and a sliver of wood painted orange and glued onto the face for a nose. He finished them off with a black felt scarf and tiny arms made of minute twigs. I have hung this memento of that night on my own Christmas tree every year since. It never fails to bring back a flood of memories. Steve was a very sweet guy—extremely thoughtful and caring. His last name is Sweetman—a coincidence? No, because there are no coincidences. All things happen for a reason. If something strikes you as odd, it is meant to be of special significance to you, as I learned from Pat.

We finally gathered together for the "class" part of the evening. We all took seats wherever we could find them. Some of the groups were assembled in small chairs roughly facing the front of the room. Pat took a seat facing the group. I took a seat on a pile of gym mats conveniently placed along the front left wall to clear space in the classroom. It was a comfortable perch on which to sit. Though I was a little removed from the group, I could see everyone else perfectly.

Pat introduced the idea for the night. Whoever wanted to could get up and talk to the group about an experience they had that they felt was significant. It could be any type of experience. After calling forth everyone's attention, together we recited our opening Meditation and a prayer. She then invited any spirits who would like to be present to assemble around the group to guide us.

"I invoke and invite only the highest spirits whose sole purpose is to bring good into the universe. Please come and aid us in our quest for truth on this special night. Everyone close your eyes and visualize a bright white halo, which will surround the entire building. None of the dark spirits are welcome or invited."

Although the evil dark spirits were told to leave, I later found out that they hovered only just beyond the edge of the white light. They were watching closely from a distance. They would wait for the group to leave the building and then they would look for an opportunity to take their revenge.

One thing I learned was that they hate to be left out of a party where alcohol is being served. This is their usual medium to join in and have a little fun. How? You guessed it. They are given free rein to your souls when you become intoxicated. It's no wonder why drinking was not considered a good idea for any Christian according to St. Paul.

A couple of members got up to talk to the group. They talked about odd things that had lately occurred to them. We all listened attentively. The next to get up was Sally, one half of the lesbian couple. Sally started relating her experiences of how difficult it was for people to accept her.

While listening intently, I suddenly felt my conscious self retreat. It was a feeling of being pulled inside, like what happens sometimes when you are looking in a direction and then you realize that although your eyes may be open and looking at something, you have just been a million miles away inside yourself and blind to a great extent of the view in front of you. My whole body relaxed and for the first time in my life I entered into a deep state of trance. There is really no other good way to describe it. I was aware of what was said, but I had entered into the state not of my own accord. My eyes remained open and I could see, but I no longer had control of my body. A spirit had entered, and needing my physical form for its own purpose, it felt free to use it.

A higher, supposedly good spirit attending our gathering decided to give Sally a Christmas healing—a present of sorts. The spirit had obviously checked out the other members of the room but had decided that I was the best choice. Pat was to tell me afterwards that the spirit chose me because I am a natural spirit medium. Spirits can easily induce trance in me and can work through me. I experienced a numbing, vibrating sensation in my back. It felt like someone had placed a store-bought hand massager on the spot below my right shoulder and turned it on low. The spirit lifted me so that I stood up and then guided me gently to walk and stand directly behind Sally who was sitting about ten steps away.

I stood behind Sally for a moment or two, confused, asking myself what I was doing here. The spirit quieted my mind, and then it raised my left arm. Its energy lifted my arm from below and kept lifting until my hand was just over Sally's left shoulder. Then it very gently lowered my hand until it rested on Sally's shoulder.

Sally had an immediate reaction to the spirit's touch. She began crying almost hysterically. The rest of the group watched this spectacle quietly. I now think that they didn't fully understand what was going on. It was Pat who reassured the group that a spirit was giving a healing to Sally. I was merely its instrument. Sally brought herself under control and finished her thoughts. My hand stayed on her shoulder for five minutes.

Just as the spirit was about to leave me, I heard in my mind the following communication mind-to-mind, spirit-to-spirit: "Hi, Pandora. How are you doing? You know you are going to write a great book someday." Then with that weird message the spirit left me. But I heard the message ringing over and over again in my head. What could it possibly mean? My name was Irene, not Pandora. How could the spirit possibly call me by the wrong name? I thought about the part of the message that I would someday write a book. Cool, I thought. I would love to write a great book someday—a thrilling murder mystery or perhaps another amazing immortal romance novel like *Gone with the Wind*. That would be great.

Little did I know what the prophecy would lead to.

After the spirit left, my hand was allowed to drop, and I came out of my trance. I was deeply embarrassed. I didn't know what had come over me, or what everyone in the room must be thinking of me. I very quickly returned to my seat and tried to make myself as unnoticeable as possible. Violent spasms shook through me; my teeth chattered. I endured the spasms for about five minutes, before I looked over at Pat. "Pat, why am I shaking like this?" I asked her.

She said that the spirit had given me a healing at the same time as Sally. The spasms were my body's way of getting rid of the emotional waste from my past. Finally, after about an hour, the trembles subsided.

During the other members' sharing, I was only able to half listen. That strange name the spirit had called me keep repeating itself in my mind. In fact, the only uplifting part of the message had been about writing a great book. That part was a small crumb to hold onto. As soon as my mind got a rest from the spirit message, then my thoughts turned to what Pat had said—that I was a spirit medium.

Does this mean, I wondered, *that I am condemned to working in some trashy fortuneteller's parlor in some equally sleazy part of a major city?* My imagination took the reins and painted the picture ...A darkened room separated from the entrance by a fall of fake crystal beads strung from the ceiling. The kind of place where the walls were draped in a heavy maroon or black velvet, cave-like, with the only light coming from a small table draped in heavy black material—a lone crystal ball centered in the middle. I, the woman behind the ball, would be dressed in some sort of long-sleeved, multi-colored caftan, and I would be bidding the next guest or victim into my lair offering to share knowledge about the "other side." The victims, saddened by a recent loss perhaps, would ask me to contact their dead "Aunt Millie" to see if she had made a successful crossover.

No way. I stopped my thoughts, not wanting to pursue this train any further. Even if I had this talent, I knew that I wanted no part of all those charlatans. I was going to have a normal life, kids, a house nestled behind a white-picket fence, summers on Cape Cod. I was definitely not going to live a life devoted to helping other people contact the spirits of the dead. It wasn't going to happen. I could just imagine what my family would say when people asked whatever happened to Irene ... They would ignore the question, avoid eye contact, their embarrassment acute, and I wouldn't blame them. Good girls from Catholic families don't do that kind of thing—let the gypsies tell the fortunes and help the newly bereaved. The world didn't need this gift of mine; it was much better off without it.

The party lasted about another hour or two, but the group was not in the same kind of a mood after Sally's healing. We were all thoughtful and ready to go home. As you can imagine, I was exhausted, overwhelmed and real fear was creeping in. If a spirit could enter me when it decided, how could I learn to block it and decide whether or not I wanted its presence? I was fascinated but also repelled. I needed to go home and do some thinking. I left the group with a word of thanks; some of us hugged. I went to my car and got in. I was still surrounded by God's white light, but unfortunately the white light only surrounded me with a margin of about three feet. After that darkness prevailed in the night.

How do I tell you this in a way that you would believe me?

As I drove home that night, several of the hovering spirits—not the good ones, believe me—followed me home. I guess the dark side noticed this talent of mine and wanted to use me also. They were to hover around me for weeks waiting for their chance. They entered my dreams. They peeped in on me when I bathed. When I didn't consciously surround myself with white light, they waited to get in.

I began to live in deep mortal fear for my very soul. I found it absolutely terrifying to think that a spirit could possess me when I let my guard down, had too much to drink, or took drugs (which very thankfully I had never been into). Luckily, I had never stopped going to Mass. I went every Sunday. Something in me knew that one way to keep my soul safe was to go into a church and pray. Church became my sanctuary in my desperate need. Evil spirits cannot stand churches, and I needed all those evil spirits to get the message. Whenever I felt tired or weak, I would go to a church and sit in a pew and just rest. Going to church was my protection. As long as I could walk into a church, I felt that either no spirits inhabited me—or only very good ones. Spirits, who are in heaven with God, are only going to do good through you. When I was not in a church, I prayed constantly to be kept from harm.

It's really no wonder that I have become such a devout Catholic, or that my faith in God is unshakeable and absolute. I had all the proof, and then some, that I would ever need. After all, if demons and good spirits exist, then so does God. God must have been watching over me and helping me to understand how to fight the evil ones and how to protect myself. I am sure that He knew that in the not too distant future I was to be tested by the most evil one of all. Since He knew that I wanted Him to have my soul instead of the other guys, He gave me the strength I needed in my upcoming battle. A battle that would forever change me ...

Sorry, readers, but the rest of this particular story picks up in the demon section. It fits well as you will see. But because this is the angel chapter, we will move on instead to an angel story that brought two hearts together—a story of love and supernatural guidance.

I met my husband, Sam, in a very unique way. Possibly you will think as you read my story that God would appropriately enough send an angel to me to announce such a major thing as an arranged marriage. And of course you would be right, because He did.

In the spring of 1983, I felt the need to fly from the nest of my close family to strike out on my own. I felt strong enough now to live alone after such awful experiences of two years ago. So I found a job through a search agency located in Boston. With a source of income figured out, the next item on my to-do list was to find a new place to live. Wanting to be where the action was, I decided to find an apartment in or very near to the city. So I prayed to the Lord. I prayed for a good, cheap, but safe apartment to live in. And the Lord heard my prayer and promptly answered it. I found my perfect starter apartment in one weekend of looking, an all-time record in Boston. Ask anyone who has ever tried it before. And it was a great place too. Only two rooms, true, and with psychedelic carpet in the bathroom—no less but safe, clean, and only $265 a month—utilities included. Boy, did God provide that day. It was just north of Boston, in the town of Malden

When you pray for something to happen, it always does. Prayer works for everyone. It really is a shame that other people don't believe this. They are missing out on a really good thing. By the way, prayer does not work for anything that is against God's will. Take it from me. And yes, unfortunately, to my shame there would come many a time when I would have loved to pray for something not very nice. In general, though, I have always prayed devoutly telling the Lord about my day, thanking Him for the flowers, asking for forgiveness when I felt I have not done my best or lost my cool, or just to touch base. I made it a strict point when I went to bed to thank Him for the gift of the day, even if it had been a terrible day.

There was one more thing I asked for, one more thing that would make a new life a little nicer: a boyfriend. You see, I was lonely. For the past two years I had severely limited my visits to bars, nightclubs, and the like. I had one recent relationship, but that had ended up being a nightmare. So, I hadn't been in the market for a date, lately. But I figured I would try the whole singles thing again with my new apartment, new job, and my new life. I'll bet you all know how it is; I just hated to spend every Saturday night alone.

One beautiful Saturday morning in April of 1983, I had worked out an arrangement with a co-worker to share a ride (and the cost) to the Cape. I planned on spending the weekend with my family. Because I hate to be late and traffic is always an issue, I took an extra early bus to the downtown area of Boston that day, so I had about an hour to kill before meeting my friend. Having decided that today was as good a day as any to start hiking the Freedom Trail, I walked from the bus station in Haymarket and up Congress Street. Standing in front of the Old State House building, I clearly heard a voice from somewhere surrounding me emerge from out of midair. The voice was speaking to me. The disembodied voice said: "Today you will meet a man who will play an important part in your life." That was it. No other direction or any clue about what this new man might look like; just that he would be important. Looking back on Cupid's message now, twenty-one years of marriage later, I agree that Sam would be important. However, it is always good to bear in mind that important does not necessarily mean easy or peaceful, or a bed of roses.

I heard the message, and I accepted it. "Okay," I said back, "just point me in the right direction." No further words were exchanged, since apparently I was already going in the right direction. I walked up to the corner of the intersection of Court and Tremont Street and turned left, marveling at how different the city was on a Saturday morning than on a weekday. The place was dead.

Something unique about the Freedom Trail is that there are a couple of historic graveyards. I have always found graveyards very interesting, since I have quite an imagination and love to contemplate other people's struggles, loves, children, wealth, and illnesses.

But that's another story. The first graveyard I came to on the left was the King's Chapel Burial Ground where such Boston greats as John Winthrop (Governor of Massachusetts), Mary Chilton (passenger on the Mayflower), and her husband, John Winslow were buried. I stopped for a good look, but the place held no real attraction for me, so I left after only two or three minutes.

I strolled leisurely back to Tremont Street and walked about 500 yards up to the Granary graveyard on right-hand side of the street. Here Mother Goose (or rather the woman who wrote Mother Goose) was buried, along with many monuments to our countries' great statesmen and freedom fighters (John Hancock, Samuel Adams, and Paul Revere). Many of the victims from the Boston Massacre were also buried here. In the center there is a large stone engraved with the word "Franklin" on it. I was standing in front of this tall stone for a moment or two to shift the heavy load of my overnight case to a different shoulder—I always pack too much—when a man who was standing on the other side of the stone came over to talk to me.

He was about medium height—5'9" with medium brown hair that was mostly hidden under a very worn burgundy and gold ski hat. His face was pleasant, with deeply etched smile lines radiating from his green eyes—eyes that looked at me and then away from me. I took this to mean that he was shy, but since he seemed friendly and wanted to talk, I saw no harm in a conversation. After all, it was midday on a bright crisp Saturday. The sun was shining. What could happen? I remembered the voice. If I am to meet that important person, then I must remain open to everyone.

He opened the conversation with "Are you a tourist here?"

I thought about this statement for a moment. You see, he had a very distinctive southern accent. I thought it odd that he was asking me if I was a tourist when I have the ultimate Boston accent. Then I remembered that I hadn't opened my mouth and spoken, so how could he know? Also, he could clearly see my overnight bag. Perhaps he was asking because he, himself, was a tourist. Being the nice well-bred New England girl that I am, I gave him a polite answer: "No I am not a tourist here. Are you?"

"No, I live in the city."

So we began talking, and we liked each other. He did seem a little too old for me, but what the hay, you have to start someplace. Apparently, he was also lonely, because it didn't take him more than two minutes to ask me out to dinner. Now girls, I know what you are thinking, and I was thinking the very same thing. Never accept a date with a total stranger to dinner, right? Suggest lunch instead.

So I countered with the suggestion of lunch—any day, right here in downtown Boston. He told me that since he worked in Cambridge across the river that lunch in the downtown district would not give us more than a quick bite together before he had to run back to the office. He suggested dinner again. I agreed reluctantly and gave him my work number. I looked at my watch and saw that I was almost late to meet my co-worker. With a quick good-bye, I turned to leave. But just before I hurried away, I remembered that I didn't even know his name. "By the way, I am Irene Bilodeau." I held out my hand, and he put his in mine and told me:

"Nice talking to you. I'm Sam Manian."

Almost running, I hurried down toward Post Office Square. It was only after I was dropped off at my parent's house on the Cape later that evening that I had time to remember that the voice had said that I was to meet someone important this day. Well the day was almost over, and the only new person I had met was Sam. Was he it, or did I miss out on meeting the right person? I would wonder that many times over the course of our marriage.

Sam called on Monday of the next week and asked me out for the coming Thursday night. I said okay, but I insisted on meeting him in the city. We agreed to meet in front of Samuel Adam's statue, in front of Fanueil Hall. We had a lot of laughs that night and that was just the beginning. We dated for a year and a half before Sam proposed marriage, again in the same graveyard. Pretty romantic, huh? Actually, Sam was an awesome date. We did all sorts of fun things together, romantic trips, weekend getaways, and dinner out twice a week. He was generous, buying me all sorts of presents. The only downfall was that he just was never the type that I could *really* talk to.

Early on in the relationship, I met and begin dating another man at the same time as Sam—a sweet Irish, Catholic guy. His name was Bobby. When Bobby found out that I was dating another man, he asked me to end it. So the following weekend I told Sam that I was breaking up with him, that I had met another guy. Sam told me that not only were we not breaking up, but that I was going to go back and tell the other man good-bye. Sam persuaded me that we had a future together. I had my doubts, you see, because I felt that maybe he wouldn't want children because he was nineteen years older than I was. He insisted, upon being asked, that he did want children.

I stuck with the relationship even though we didn't have a lot of common interests or discussions into deep subjects, or from Sam's point of view, I wasn't a sports fanatic. Perhaps, the real reason that we were never able to see eye-to-eye was because Sam, deep down, didn't believe in God. Still, there was something charming about him, and on top of that I could never forget that voice. So I stayed with the relationship and accepted the marriage proposal.

We arranged a yearlong engagement and were married in September 1985 in Sandwich, MA. The nuptial Mass was beautiful and memorable with both Father and the reverend from Sam's protestant Armenian church in attendance to give words of wisdom. Warm and in the 90s, it flew by all too fast as we took pictures in the garden at the Daniel Webster Inn with the family and dined on chicken cordon blue while drinking champagne in the glass conservatory filled with full-sized potted trees on the floor and blooms on every table. During the engagement, I learned that Sam had never been baptized. I was rather astonished by this fact since he told me he went to church as a boy as well as going occasionally to an Armenian church in Belmont. As a Catholic I believed that you needed to be baptized to go to heaven, and I didn't want Sam to spend eternity in Limbo because of this oversight, so I talked him into being baptized. After all, if you want to marry someone, you hope that you will be able to see him or her for all eternity, not just in this life.

On the day before we were to be married, at the rehearsal dinner, my family found out just how old Sam really was. They were shocked. My mother asked me if I wanted to call the whole thing off. I reassured her that I did not want to. I was in love, or at least had talked myself into believing I was. But more importantly, I believed the words of the angel that Sam would be very important in my life. God, through the angel, had arranged the marriage; of that I was sure. Now I just needed to find out why.

> *"Maybe there are few people in your church who have a harder time than you do. Christian wives whose husbands do not share their faith can find life very strained. While other people's problems often come and go, wives in this situation have a continuing struggle. Life for them is highly demanding and often painful."*
>
> — MICHAEL FANSTONE

That was my last encounter with any spirits that I was aware of until the Palm Sunday Mass in 2001. Just after the awakening in 2002, over twenty years later, I had a number of experiences that have struck me as coming from the angels or good spirits. As I have mentioned before, it can be very hard to discern if they were good or bad, angel, Holy Spirit, or demon.

Over the April 10–15, 2002 school vacation, just after the fateful Lent, our family took a trip to Washington, D.C. It had been a wonderful trip as we saw all the sights—the White House, the Mint, the House of Representatives, the Supreme Court, the Vietnam Memorial, and other popular tourist attractions. God had decided that I also needed a vacation from the spiritual, so I hadn't felt anything in the night, which was the first time of peace since my awakening.

That is, until the last night, when I felt a descent upon me. But unlike any of the previous times, I could sense that this spirit simply wanted to be with me. I was lying on my side, and the presence wrapped its spirit arms around me and cradled me. It hugged me like a friend who was trying to comfort me, or a lover who was spent. *What a very comfortable, loving feeling this one has,* I thought just before I fell asleep.

Throughout the night the spirit kept his arms and body at my back and around me just as if he was my defender and comforter. When I awoke in the early morning, I noticed that the spirit had not left my side the whole night long: *Must be my guardian angel.*

From the Bible, passages on Angels: They sit down (Judges 6:11), They look like women and have wind in their wings (Zechariah 5:9). They look like men: and eat (Genesis 18:2) They are spirits (Psalms 104:4: Hebrews 1:7) They are like fire: Psalms (104:4)'

⚜

On August 8, 2002, my forty-third birthday, after I turned out the lights, I felt angels, working on my soul. They seemed to be healing my soul after a particularly difficult conversation with a friend. The conversation was so heated and unhappy that it probably had done major damage to my spirit.

As I was lying on my side retired for the night, I felt the first touches at the base of my spine, then many on my hands and arms. The areas went numb—first feeling tingly and then heated. After that my legs experienced the same touches, numbing, and heating. I lay with my side touching my Bible and crucifix and in my mind said: "I love you, Jesus, please be near me," because I was ever aware of the possibility of trickery from the other side. But when I awoke the next morning, I realized that I felt immeasurably lighter, that many of the negative thoughts from the painful conversation were gone.

"For this ladder of contemplation, which, as we have said, comes down from God, is prefigured by that ladder which Jacob saw as he slept, whereon angels were ascending and descending, from God to man, and from man to God, Who Himself was leaning upon the end of the ladder. All this, says Divine Scripture, took place by night, when Jacob slept, in order to express how secret is this road and ascent to God, and how different from that of man's knowledge." – St. John of the Cross

"He makes his angels winds and his ministers a fiery flame."
                                        – HEBREWS 1:7

"Now, recognizing what is expected of me, and not unmindful of my promise, and relying, too, on the same succor, I will endeavor to treat of the origin, and progress, and deserved destinies of the two cities (the earthly and the heavenly, to wit), which, as we said, are in this present world commingled, and as it were entangled together. And, first, I will explain how the foundations of these two cities were originally laid, in the difference that arose among the angels." – St. Augustine

> *"The classical Buddhist texts describe what happened next with barely contained excitement. The accounts say that the world held its breath as the moment that would transform history approached. Siddhartha sat under the Tree of Enlightenment, and the spirits of the air rejoiced."*
> –JONATHAN LANDAW AND STEPHAN BODIAN

⚜

Ring. Tingle. Gong.

From the depths of my dream state, I awoke on Ash Wednesday 2003 to the chiming of the bells at the abbey. As I slowly opened my eyes and lifted my head to look at the clock, I remembered that today I didn't have to go into work. As a special anniversary present to the Lord, on this day one year after my awakening, I had signed up to spend a special day at Glastonbury Abbey—a day of peace, prayer, meditation, discussions about religious topics, and Holy Mass. I wanted to make a wonderful beginning to the forty days of Lent by honoring Ash Wednesday as a special day that marked the beginning of the season. Very much in my mind was the Lent of last year, which had changed me forever. I wanted to give this day of prayer as a beautiful thank-you to the Lord. What a memorable day it would turn out to be, full of beauty and surprises.

The abbey is situated in Hingham, a couple of miles from Nantasket Beach in Hull, and only two miles from my home. From our back deck, I can hear the bells calling the monks five times a day to chapel and worship—Vigils, Lauds, Mass, Vespers, and Compline. Six main buildings at the abbey house the monks and overnight retreatants. Amidst the lush grass, surrounded and closely bordered by pine and maple stands offering welcome shade, there is a feeling of sanctuary, a spiritual feeling of entering into a protected en-

337

closed space as soon as you drive up the long driveway toward the chapel and bookstore.

In addition to this day at the abbey, I had planned several charity projects with the Lord of my heart in mind so that I could give back to the Lord for all His wonderful graces over the past year: The CCD charity projects (in the Charity Chapter), singing in Mass, a renewal program of spiritual healing with a small group from the church, an extra Mass a week, Stations of the Cross, and Soup and Bread on Fridays, plus my Wednesday and Friday bread and water fast. Any extra time was spent reading the Bible. For Easter Sunday, I planned a family party that I was really looking forward to a great deal. One of the ways I prepared for the party was to draw several portraits in oil pastel of the Savior to put up for Easter that I couldn't wait to show my family. (One was the Divine Mercy Vision of the Savior by Sister Faustina.)

The day at the Abbey started out with Mass at 9:30 a.m. where the entire congregation received ashes. Ashes are symbolic of dust, and we hear when we receive them that we are really dust and to dust we shall all return. Then from 11:00 to 12:00, all the retreatants gathered at the retreat house, which is actually a fairly new and lovely building nestled in a pine tree setting. The building has an open architectural design with lots of glass, and as we entered the front doors, the enticing smell of fresh brewed coffee and warm-from-the-oven muffins greeted us—drawing us in to refresh our bodies and our souls. Feeling utterly blissful, and so looking forward to having the day to just listen and be still, I hung up my coat and wandered over to the display. Since I had given up sweets for Lent, I passed up the muffins regrettably and helped myself to a cup of Earl Grey tea. I took a moment to savor its full aroma before taking a sip. I wanted to relish every second of this day.

Since Father Tom had finished setting up and appeared ready to begin, I pulled up a chair and brought it into the semi-circle setup of standard banquet chairs in the second row toward the left of the large central meeting space. I settled myself in my seat and waited for a moment for the others to do the same while he waited patiently. On the board were the words: "Demons" and then "Pride, Lust, Anger, Greed, Sloth, Envy, and Gluttony." After reading the last word, I was glad I had restrained myself from taking that muffin.

Father Tom smiled warmly as we quieted. About 5'9" with light blond hair, sparkling eyes, and dressed in a floor length black robe tightly cinched around his rounded waistline, he looked ready to give us words of wisdom on how to deal with all these pests we call demons, and the great effect they all had on our lives. I must admit that I was waiting in great anticipation to hear what he would say about them, and how to engage them in battle. As you have read in the awakening and lent chapters, and will read in the demon chapter, I had plenty of these awful entities around that I needed to get rid of.

Before beginning his talk, he took ten minutes to guide us into a relaxing meditation. From his spot in front of the group, he turned on a tape recorder playing a continuous selection of ethereal melodies. As soon as I closed my eyes and felt the opening stanzas of the music enter into my spirit, I felt the tension fall away from my body and soul as if Father had taken a pair of scissors and cut away the layers of fear and stress that the last year had wrought on my being. Then his soothing voice took us to a place inside ourselves. He told us to find a place where we could experience God.

Within a couple of seconds, I saw my favorite stretch of Nantasket Beach— soft white sand, deep teal ocean with gentle rolling waves continuously breaking on the shore where seagulls jockeyed for sea clams, crabs, and mussels. After we had found our spot, his voice then guided us to envision Jesus walking up to us, sitting down next to us, and beginning a conversation. When he said this, instantaneously, I could feel Jesus' close presence by my right hand side. Going deeper into my mind, I could see Him clearly. His white robes were gathered around His legs as he sat cross-legged on the beach with me. His leg was against mine on the sand. There was no one else at the beach with us, and it was extremely peaceful. Jesus looked deeply into my eyes, showing me that He was ready to listen to whatever I had to say as soon as Father said: "Tell Jesus whatever you would like. He is ready to listen to whatever you have to say."

My heart opened up, and I told the Lord in an instant exactly what I was feeling. I was so overwhelmed by His answer to my heart that my soul flooded with joy and love that burst the tightly held dam on my emotions, and I spent the rest of the ten-minute meditation sobbing. Just before the Meditation, Father Tom had read from a passage in Hosea, and it had been the very same passage read at last Saturday night's Mass.

> I will espouse you to me forever
> I will espouse you in right and in justice in love and in mercy
> I will espouse you in fidelity and you shall know the Lord.
> (Hosea 2:21–22)

To hear the reading twice meant that the Lord wanted me to hear it, recognize it had a special meaning for me, and remember it always. Written in the first person, the passage spoke to me directly, telling me that Jesus was espousing Himself to me spiritually. This was the message that I had longed to hear since I had read from St. Teresa of Avila that such a gift was possible, and on that beach in my meditation, Jesus confirmed this message to my soul.

Father Tom gently asked us to return to the room, and very reluctantly I opened my eyes from that deeply wonderful and profoundly altering meditation. But before I did, I heard Jesus promise that soon He would be the spouse of my soul.

Coming back from that heavenly spot deep inside myself, I focused my attention back on Father Tom. Next, he was going to give us the talk on our personal demons and how they interfere in our lives. I hoped to learn how to neutralize my own.

As I sat in my seat, now ready for Father to begin, it occurred to me that the Lord was working through Father for my personal benefit. Even though there were thirty other people there, it felt like the talk was just for me. Jesus, who had been walking beside me for the entire year, and intimately knew exactly what would strengthen me, had inspired Father with a talk that would give me a few tools and a prospective that I had not considered.

The following is a listing of the seven deadly sins from the Internet:

"Pride is excessive belief in one's own abilities that interferes with the individual's recognition of the grace of God. It has been called the sin from which all others arise. Pride is also known as Vanity.

Envy is the desire for others' traits, status, abilities, or situation.

Gluttony is an inordinate desire to consume more than what one requires.

Lust is an inordinate craving for the pleasures of the body.

Anger is manifested in the individual who spurns love and opts instead for fury. It is also known as Wrath.

Greed is the desire for material wealth or gain, ignoring the realm of the spiritual.

Sloth is the avoidance of physical or spiritual work."

As serious as this subject may have sounded—and also remember it was Ash Wednesday, a solemn day of reflection and fasting in the Catholic Church—I can tell you that I have never laughed so hard or been so amused by any speaker that I can ever recall. All the other thirty-odd people there felt exactly the same way. Father Tom has an incredible gift to make even the scariest, most difficult topic into a humorous subject. Not only was what he said funny, but his body language was hilarious. If ever a monk could be called merry, it was Father Tom. Privately, as I listened to him I nicknamed him the Merry Monk of Glastonbury Abbey.

He took the subject of each demon, wrestled it to the floor, stomped on it, and then showed us its vastly deflated persona—a mere shadow of its former self, which could then be rolled up just like a punctured balloon and thrown in the trash. I remember him telling us all how he just loved to get really mad, how it felt so good to let off all that steam into the room, but how he had learned over time to control that impulse. He frankly admitted that he hadn't totally licked the gluttony demon yet, but he was working on it with a new exercise routine. Lust had never given him much of a problem. However, every once in a while he wondered what his children would have been like.

Pride was the worst of them all, he told us. Many of the new monks as they first arrived at the abbey had had to really work hard to defeat pride. He was everywhere and in everything. Lurking even in the corners of the abbey, always ready to steal hard-won humility, pride was a very ugly monster, and constant surveillance was necessary to keep him from finding a home in our souls. He summed them all up, and all their various tricks, and how to guard against them. By the time he finished I was prepared to give him a bear hug and a hearty round of applause. In that short talk he gave me fresh and new courage to face the haunting specters that visited me nightly in my bedroom. He had beaten his own demons, or most of them, and hope surged in my heart that I would too.

At noon, Father wrapped up his talk, and we all got up and began our walk back to the chapel for a short noon midday prayer. As I walked silently across the parking lot and over the grass to the chapel, I was lost in recollections of the beautiful morning. My heart was full. Hope and joy—as if they were Christmas presents wrapped in boxes—lay open in my heart and, expanding like a cloud, seemed to materialize and walk with me through the doors of the chapel. I scanned the simple, homey space and chose the furthest spot from the rest of the group on the left side of the church so that I could be surrounded by silence. In contrast to most Catholic churches, the altar at the abbey was in the middle of the space with pews on all the sides. Jesus was suspended from a cross, which hung from the ceiling in the center of the chapel.

As soon as I sat down in a pew, I was almost immediately joined by a young man of about thirty years old. A little disappointed to have such a close neighbor, I quickly hid my disappointment and glanced at him with a friendly smile, not meeting his eyes because I wanted to remain alone and not strike up a conversation. I noticed, though, that he was dressed in a brown and blue plaid flannel work shirt, tan khakis, and a clean pair of orange-tan work boots. I guessed him to be a carpenter by trade. He was very ordinary looking of about average height with dark brown hair. I didn't recognize him as part of our group, and he certainly was not one of the monks. I wondered if he came here often on his lunch break everyday to share in the song and prayers of the abbey. If he did, he would not be like any other carpenter I had ever met. They seemed to love to sit in a public place as they ate their sandwiches. To gawk at the passersby and whistle at the attractive young women who were on their way to shopping expeditions.

Having taken a quick glance at him, I turned away to watch the monks filing into the chapel in their long black robes, including Father Tom, of course. But as the service was about to begin, I noticed that I had taken the only booklet left and now there was none for the young man beside me. I looked to my right, but the other people on that side had taken all the other prayer books. There were none to his left either. Since I couldn't imagine that he had memorized the prayers, I decided to do the nice thing and offer to share mine with him.

As I turned toward him, with a gesture offering to share my booklet with him, my eyes met his and then in answer and understanding, he turned toward me and smiled back. At the instant our eyes met, I received a jolting shock. A lightening bolt of recognition pulsed through my soul. From his very ordinary human face, like an open door looking directly into heaven, his eyes and smile transcended this time and dimension. His face and smile reflected not his own personality, but the Lord of heaven. His smile was the means of transmission. His message was clear and simple. Jesus' eyes and smile peered from His face in a radiant supernatural message. The smile that I could see was mesmerizing, radiant, and indescribably beautiful. In that smile I could see the joy and happiness of my hoped for final destination: heaven. All the love that the Lord had for me was radiating from this man's smile.

From that eternal glimpse, I painfully wretched my eyes away and turned my attention back to the service. As my eyes focused on the monk at the podium, they instead wanted to return again to the face of this total stranger to confirm and see that beauty again. With an iron will, I controlled myself, keeping my attention firmly where it belonged. I tried to tell myself I was being silly and that my imagination was running away with me, but my heart was not buying it because it knew the truth.

I kept my eyes down as we recited all the answering prayers together, our fingers touched as we turned the pages of the missellette together. How intimate we were being, I thought. After about five minutes, I couldn't help myself. I looked into his eyes again, and the heavens opened, and Jesus was smiling at me again. Then I knew with utter certainty that this man was not a man at all, but an angel sent by the Lord with a message. And it was a beautiful one. His face carried it. He sat beside me and at the same time, as always, in front of the Lord of the heavens, his face mirrored Jesus' message. It was bizarre, but through this angel at my side, Jesus was with me at this service at the abbey. I wanted to shout to the congregation and the monks: "There is an angel at the abbey! There is an angel in the abbey church. Look into his eyes and you can see heaven." But, of course, I did not. No words were spoken, and no one else around us guessed, nor apparently could they see anything out of the ordinary happening in the chapel. But from the depths of my being,

I knew that we had a real live angel sitting among us appearing as a human being.

Then another understanding dawned, and Jesus told me in my heart that every smile of every human being is really a reflection of His love if only we have our eyes opened to see.

> *"The face is the mirror of the mind, and eyes without speaking confess the secrets of the heart."*
>
> — SAINT JEROME

> *"We will never know how much good just a simple smile can do. We tell people how kind, forgiving, and understanding God is—are we the living proof? Can they really see this kindness, this forgiveness, this understanding, alive in us?"*
>
> — MOTHER TERESA

> *"If in the after-death state you encounter apparitional beings. Some may appear as beneficent angels, gods, or goddesses. Others may appear as frightening demons, ghosts, or wrathful deities. Embrace them all with a heart overflowing with love and compassion."*
>
> — JOEL; THROUGH DEATH'S GATE: A GUIDE TO SELFLESS DYING

The noontime service was short, only about twenty minutes, so almost as soon as it had started it was over. I got up and walked to the front of the chapel. The rest of the retreat was going to resume shortly at the conference center, and I needed to get back. The angel also got up at the same time and stayed by my side. I smiled at him as we exited the hallway and entered the bookstore to say good-bye. This time as the heavens opened, I shared his smile with a new understanding. The smile warmed my heart instantly. Here was an eternal friend and, perhaps, he was also my guardian angel. I was never to know.

I didn't speak to him; what could I have possibly asked him that he could answer in that quick walk though the bookstore? I only knew that it was a magical moment for me, and that words were out of place. Even if I could formulate a question, I wouldn't have wanted to spoil the perfect moment. And my heart was so full that utterances would have stumbled out of my mouth.

After we stepped out of the bookstore and into the bright sunshine, I began speed-walking across the parking lot to get to the conference center, which was about a ¼ mile away. At the end of the pavement, I glanced back for one last look, knowing that it was probably the last time I would ever see him. He had stopped at the entrance to the bookstore and was just standing there. He had been watching me as I walked away with his arms folded across his chest like he had nowhere else to go. He must have needed everyone else to leave before he did. After all, a good angel is a messenger from God and is sent with a mission. When the mission is completed, the angel departs.

I turned away, giving him privacy to leave as he wished. I never did see him actually leave. As I kept walking towards the conference center, I was in mild shock. I had witnessed something I never thought I'd actually see in my life: an angel. One of God's own messengers—an angel sent from God in physical form just for me.

> *"A spirit from God always acknowledges that Jesus is the Christ who came to the world to die for our sins and redeem us from Satan's bondage. An Angel of God will always glorify God. Holy angels do not draw attention to themselves. They work quietly, most often behind the scenes, then when the work is done, they leave."*
>
> — ANGEL WEB SITE

"They feed us: 1Kings 19:5, They deliver us: Acts 5:17:21, They give us warning of impending danger: Genesis 19:15, They guard and protect us: Psalm 91:11-12 Psalm 34:7, They go ahead to prepare our way: Exodus 33:2."

"Angels are always in a hurry, they can't be traced, they travel light, they have a tendency to vanish once their mission is accomplished. They travel at inconceivable speeds, they don't talk much."

> *"I believe we have all seen angels; however, I don't think we are aware of it. Scripture tells us to 'Be not forgetful to entertain strangers, for thereby some have entertained angels unawares.'"*
>
> — HEBREWS 13:2

Back at the conference center, lunch was being served. Due to the excitement, I hadn't realized it, but now my stomach lurched with hunger pangs. I helped myself to a generous serving of cheese tortellini soup with a tomato basil base, two thick slices of homemade wheat bread smeared with a thick coating of butter, and a steaming cup of herbal tea from the table where lunch had been laid out. I ate silently. I tried to read some material that Father Tom had laid out earlier, but instead I reflected on the encounter with the angel.

The author of Hebrews says that you will meet them unawares, which probably means that the angel will look just like everyone else—not out of the ordinary. In fact, without the clue of his smile, I would never have known who he was. I was convinced of it; the encounter had been a gift directly from Jesus in heaven. Just then I saw the man in my mind's eye again and remembered how he was dressed—as a present-day carpenter about to return to work, but who had wanted to praise God during his lunch hour. In a moment it hit me—Jesus had been a carpenter in long-ago Nazareth. Jesus must have told him exactly what to wear. Why, he had "Jesus" written all over him

"For, when the light of God illumines an angel, it enlightens him and enkindles him in love, since, being pure spirit, he is prepared for that infusion. But, when it illumines man, who is impure and weak, it illumines him, as has been said above, according to his nature. It plunges him into darkness and causes him affliction and distress, as does the sun to the eye that is weak; it enkindles him with passionate yet afflictive love, until he be spiritualized and refined by this same fire of love."

– St. John of the Cross

After I finished the simply wonderful Lenten lunch, with the best bread I have ever eaten and made right there at the abbey, I felt so overwhelmed with emotion that, although the sky weighed heavily with dark clouds, I decided to grab my umbrella and go for a walk to the ocean, which was about two miles away. Both the clouds and ocean reflected the event of Ash Wednesday perfectly. They were both an ash gray.

At 2:30 p.m., I returned to the conference center after my long walk to finish up my day at the abbey with the rest of the retreatants to join in a group focused art project. Since I love doing any form of art, I couldn't wait to get started, sure that it would be especially wonderful. Father Tom brought us to a small conference room in the lower level of the building. On one side of the room on banquet tables, he had laid out dozens of sheets of stickers, some glue sticks, old magazines, markers, and cardboard boxes which had yet to be folded and assembled.

He started up the session explaining that this afternoon we were going to decorate boxes. "On the outside of the box we are going to use stickers, old magazine clippings, and drawings of things that you show to the world, and on the inside of the box, where others can't see, put pictures of the things that only God knows, your relationship with Him and your own inner journey." He handed us all a sheet of paper saying, "Here is a listing of questions to ask yourself before you start." Then he said something I shall never forget: "Don't forget to put the name that God has given you on the inside of the box. You know, the one that God calls you. Everyone has a new name from God, as you know. Put that inside in the top cover. No one else needs to know it."

Outside:

Who are you to the world? Job? Church? Family. Example for others (be humble)

What aspects of yourself do you present to others?

What do people see when they look at you?

Which one of your characteristics do people wish they had?

What do you like about yourself?

What do you like to do? (Garden, listen to music, dance, exercise, hike)

What makes you happy? Sad? Upset?

What or who are the things that give you support?

How do you pray? Are you disciplined in your prayer life?

Inside:
What is the name which God calls you by?
(just leave a space for it—don't write it down)
What and who don't you show to the world?
What are your fears?
What are your inner most thoughts? Desires? Hopes?
What are your scar-pains not healed, you still live with?
What lies at the center of your soul?
What goals haven't you attained?
What is your relationship with God?
How do you pray?
How would you describe your spirituality?

I guess that Father Tom knew for certain that God always renames His close followers. I vividly remembered God giving me my new name "Pandora" on Christmas Eve 2001. As I have mentioned before, the name "Pandora" is a Greek name that means all gifts. Imagine God giving you a name signifying "all gifts" on Christmas Eve. A time when all Christians and many non-Christians are getting ready to exchange millions and millions of gifts around the world! Also, Christmas time 2001 was when I had just finished the first draft of my original book *Pandora's Story*.

Then what Father said hit me in another different way. I was holding a box in my hands that was really and truly "Pandora's Box." I sat there shell-shocked as the final incredible gift of that day was given. I had to stifle my gasps of laughter, sure that no one would understand. But it suddenly struck me as funny. "God, dearest, what a joker You are! First You gave me that incredible meditation in which You told me soul-to-soul that You loved me, then You had Father Tom give that wonderful demon eradicating talk because You know that I have been having a lot of trouble with them. Then You sent Your angel to smile down your love, and now You have Father Tom think of this wonderful art project that will reflect my name and mission. In fact, when I open this Pandora's Box, what will be revealed will be my own inner journey. I am to reveal my inner journey to the world, right? And somehow what will be revealed will become a gift to the world?"

No sooner did I finish my conversation with God when it also struck me that when God had begun opening my "box" or starting my inner journey, all the bad gifts had been thrown out. That had been the true meaning of my awakening week.

"Okay, I believe. I am so sorry if I have ever, ever doubted you."

I went to work with a vengeance. When it was done, I sat back with satisfaction. My little cardboard box had pictures of women representing my two sisters, music notes, pictures of animals and flowers, and babies on it. On the inside I wrote out the names of the spiritual gifts that I had been given—faith, selfless love, charity, empathy, trust, patience, and perseverance. I added all sorts of frills and pretty stickers to embellish them, although they certainly didn't need any being so beautiful just as they were. Then I closed the lid and reopened it—my way of symbolically letting these gifts out into the world. My mission became to give the world a view of the inside of my box. Perhaps by doing so, I will somehow be able to give the world a dose of fresh hope.

At 4:15 p.m. I took my daughter, Christina, to the Ash Wednesday service at St. Paul's. I had already received ashes, but she really wanted to go because all her friends were getting them, and she didn't want to be left out. I was very happy to grant her wish and get my second round of ashes for the day.

After my visit to the abbey, Lent progressed with many more angel and spirit visitations. None were physical, however. But they each had some thing slightly different about them—something that distinguished them from one another. Somehow, I could tell that they were all not only different angels, but even different levels of angels. I believe that they came to strengthen me and help transform my soul. Jesus had also received their angelic ministering at two times during His recorded life—at the beginning of his mission in the desert for forty days and in the Garden of Gethsemane.

"To strengthen him an angel from Heaven appeared to him." – Luke 22:39

Friday, March 21, 2003.

I had fasted and gone to Rosie's Place. That night as I lay in bed, I felt the presence of an angel. This time when the angelic being descended, I could feel that his aura was not calm at all, but instead of rolling energy, his spirit emitted sparks. Mentally, I saw him looking just like a sparkler firecracker that some one had just lit with a match. Sparks were shedding from his spirit and little tiny bits were falling onto my own spirit—burning and exploding as they hit my spiritual skin. I was in a very trusting mood that night and fell asleep with the spirit working on my soul. I couldn't even begin to guess what operation he had come to perform on my spirit. I just prayed the Jesus prayer until I fell asleep.

The next night, a spirit that was again noticeable by the sparks I could feel coming from his aura, awakened me in the middle of the night. Perhaps because it was in the middle of the night, I was startled by the spirit and much more fearful than the previous night. But in any case, I prayed the Jesus prayer, and my anxiety of what was happening decreased. I laid my Bible and cross on my chest and patiently prayed and "observed" the spirit. By observed I mean I remained aware of the touches I felt and where on my body I could feel them.

Tonight I noticed that this particular angel seemed to be somehow stretching my soul. I could feel pressure and pulling on both sides of a particular area of my body as the spirit traveled up. About an hour passed as the spirit worked on. Then I had a very strong awareness and an intense feeling of heat centered in my chest. The heat radiated and pulsated like it was filling my heart with love and warmth. In fact, I felt like my heart was being enlarged. The thought reminded me of the Christmas special *How the Grinch Stole Christmas* because in that holiday TV special, the Grinch's heart actually blew up and expanded as he finally was given ability to give and receive love.

I think that sometimes as you grow spiritually, your spirit needs to be expanded to allow you to be able to receive the love of God and dispense it to everyone you encounter—like a human love channel. Throughout that long, mystical, restless night, I felt several periods of superheating through my soul.

> "No, but the wisdom of God, by whom all things were made, was there, and wisdom insinuates itself into holy souls, and makes them the friends of God and His prophets, and noiselessly informs them of His works. They are taught also by the angels of God, who always behold the face of the Father, and announce His will to whom it befits."
>
> — ST. AUGUSTINE

> "It is clear that dilation or enlargement of the soul takes place, as if the water proceeding from the spring had not means of running away, but the fountain had a device ensuring that, the more freely the water flowed, the larger became the basin. So it is in this kind of prayer, and God works many more wonders in the soul, thus fitting and gradually disposing it to retain all that He gives it."
>
> — ST. TERESA OF AVILA

> "So a man must be penetrated with the divine presence, and be shaped through and through with the shape of the God he loves."
>
> — FREDERICK BAUERSCHMIDT

◦⚜◦

At my co-worker, Helena, mom's memorial Mass in April, I had the most fantastic spiritual feeling. I was sitting in a pew far from the altar at St. Mary's Church in West Quincy, as I hadn't wanted to disturb Helena's large, extended family, but I wanted to share in her grief. But far from feeling sad during the Mass, instead I felt the descent of hundreds of delicate spirits that I experienced as a cloud of fairy-sized, miniature angels from heaven. The angels flickered and touched my soul like butterflies. All during the Mass, they fluttered over and around me brushing their silken, gossamer wings against my skin. A flood of joy filled my soul as I realized that the angels were sending me a sign that Helena's mom had been one of the fortunate ones that had gone on straight to heaven. Her memorial Mass and her family had drawn her back to the natural world, and she had brought all her little angels with her.

Later I confided my revelation to Helena that her mom was definitely in heaven and to rejoice for her. Her answering smile showed many things—her faith, her love of her mom, and her ability to grasp things beyond this physical realm.

> *"For often, in the midst of these times of aridity and hardship, God communicates to the soul, when it is least expecting it, the purest spiritual sweetness and love, together with a spiritual knowledge which is sometimes very delicate, each manifestation of which is of greater benefit and worth than those which the soul enjoyed aforetime; although in its beginnings the soul thinks that this is not so, for the spiritual influence now granted to it is very delicate and cannot be perceived by sense."*
>
> – ST. JOHN OF THE CROSS

Sunday, May 12, 2003; Mother's Day.

I awoke to bright sunshine and the same light, tender butterfly kisses I had felt at Helena's mom's memorial Mass. There was also a wonderful sweet feeling of passion from the Spirit of Love. It was Mother's Day, and the angels seemed to be giving me this gift as a celebration of my motherhood.

"The body experiences the greatest delight and the soul is conscious of a deep satisfaction. So glad is it merely to find itself near the fountain that, even before it has begun to drink, it has had its fill. Persons in this state prefer the body to remain motionless, for otherwise their peace would be destroyed: for this reason they dare not stir." – St. Teresa of Avila; The Way of Perfection

> *"St. Bernard gives in one of his sermons a simple, ingenuous and obviously personal account of such 'privy touchings,' such convincing but elusive contacts of the soul with the Absolute."*
>
> – EVELYN UNDERHILL

> *"Rolle—To follow his description of the stages of love and union, after the first stage of heat and burning, the stage of fire, there is a second stage of great joy in spirit brought about by heavenly song and intoxication, followed by a third stage of great sweetness, which he compares with divine drunkenness."*
>
> — URSULA KING

❧

June opened the door to a unique angel experience which must have come from one of God's nature or gardening angels. As I lay on my side, I felt the spiritual touch of an angel. This one was very gentle. I could feel him reach into my soul at about my stomach area and give a gentle tug. Then I felt long, thin strands of a spiritual fiber being pulled out. It felt exactly like someone was pulling out a very long taproot from deep in my spirit from inside one of my legs. It must have been the root of a sin that my soul had had in possession for a good long time because I could feel the long strand loosening from way down in my lower legs. My past sins must have had roots that implanted themselves in my spirit. They must have been something that had kept spouting problems at every temptation that came down the road.

Mentally, I could picture what the angel was doing. He must have located some deep roots of sin and God had asked him to pull them out. My roots of sin were like a dandelion root that you are sure you pulled out long ago, but to your surprise, it crops up again and again. Having my sin roots pulled out didn't hurt. Instead it felt wonderful to have them removed and the relief that I would not have to deal with this weakness ever again was a beautiful gift.

Then a mental picture flooded my mind and I could see my soul as a flowering garden that the Lord had planted with an eye to beauty. I had allowed the sin/weeds to grow by not following the rules. In order to restore order and beauty, the Lord chose to send an angel to make sure that only the most beautiful, fragrant flowers and fruits were growing, and to pull out any weeds in my spirit that might produce something ugly and nasty, like sin.

When I woke up the next morning, my mind remembered the passages in the gospels where Jesus talks about the chaff and the wheat, and how the weeds would be thrown out into unquenchable fire.

> *"The four frees to which the Gospel calls us: First is the freedom from deliberate sin. Second is the freedom from the roots of sin, which are called, in spiritual theology, the capital sins. Third is the freedom that comes from friendship with Christ, and, still more, from bridal mysticism and conscious union with Christ—the experience of being loved by*

God and by loving God in return. And, finally, there is simply freedom: freedom to be with God in the present moment, whether that involves offering some tiny service."

— THOMAS KEATING

"For this Divine purgation is removing all the evil and vicious humours which the soul has never perceived because they have been so deeply rooted and grounded in it; it has never realized, in fact, that it has so much evil within itself."

— ST. JOHN OF THE CROSS

"These proficients have two kinds of imperfection: the one kind is habitual; the other actual. The habitual imperfections are the imperfect habits and affections which have remained all the time in the spirit, and are like roots, to which the purgation of sense has been unable to penetrate."

— ST. JOHN OF THE CROSS

"Put your hand to work and your hearts to God," said Mother Ann and again, (Shaker, Pleasant Hill) "Clean your room well, for good spirits will not live where there is dirt. There is no dirt in heaven."

— THOMAS MERTON

In the early morning of December 3, 2003, at about 4:00 a.m. to 5:30 a.m, as I lay in bed I felt a happy spiritual swirling. There was an angel dancing just above my head. I didn't have a clue why the angel was performing pirouettes and glissades around and through the headboard of my bed until I received a call from my brother, Mark. His son, Fletcher, had just been born at 4:47 a.m.

How interesting. The angel had come to awaken me with joy with the good news that I had a new nephew. Didn't that just remind me of the Christmas Story of the newborn king, Jesus? Maybe all births are announced this way, but one has to be awakened to understand that God rejoices over all new life. After the call I remembered that I had had a dream last night that my friend, Diana, had a baby boy. I found this very interesting coupled with the fact that I now had a new nephew.

(Family, babies, creation—ever ongoing and ever changing, and ever new. How we love our own children is a tiny reflection of the immense love God has for His children—every human totally unique. Be awed by nature and the beauty and wonder of it all, and its amazing diversity, intricacy, balance, complexity, and order.)

> *"Let the children come to me and do not prevent them; for the kingdom of God belongs to such as these. Amen, I say to you, whoever does not accept the kingdom of God like a child will not enter it."*
>
> – LUKE 18:16–17

I have had many dreams of angels, but one from September 2004 was memorable as well as breathtaking. It was of a whole troop of angels who looked like acrobats. Before they arrived on the train that was part of my dream, I had been having an awful nightmare where innumerable insects swirled all around my hands, stinging them. Then the scene changed with the arrival of the train, and the angels came running off the train over to me. The stinging insects immediately disappeared.

One of the angels stood right beside me and then sang a beautifully familiar church song to me. The music sounded distant at first, then it became clearer and nearer. The song was one of the regular church songs that we always sing. I remember his voice as he sang the words: "My yoke is easy and my burden is light." What was kind of amazing was that I could recognize that he was not human by his voice just as you can tell when a person from a foreign country is speaking English. You know that it is not his native language. His voice had a unique quality to it that was hard to pin down. It was not really a lilt, accent, or guttural sounds. Perhaps it was the way he formed the words, but I just knew that his primary language was angelic. Someday, I know that I will enjoy hearing him and all the other angels talk in their own language.

On Halloween night in the early evening, I saw the most beautiful angel cloud. The head and wings were extra large and it seemed to be looking directly at me. The next night, all Saints Day, a beautiful halo circled the moon.

Here is another story about a guardian angel, not mine this time, but my son Patrick's. I may need to ask his forgiveness for including it here, but it is

352

too good of an example of a child's guardian angel and the child's mother to leave it out. Mothers, please don't feel that you are ever alone in the work that you do for God.

On October 9, 2004, a Sunday night, we had the third drinking/marijuana problem with our son, Patrick. Christina was at a friend's house at a sleepover, and Sam was staying with friends in Maryland. It was just Patrick and I alone in the house. My son had lately been experimenting with alcohol and marijuana. He had been caught each of the previous two weekends. The first weekend he had been with his friend drinking straight shots of vodka until he threw up. On the second weekend, one of his other friends had brought marijuana over to my house, and I caught them both in the act.

This weekend I had been uneasy all weekend long, wondering what Patrick was going to try next. I was exhausted and needed to catch up on sleep, so I prayed to his guardian angel to keep him safe, and I went to bed around 10:30. When I retreated to my bedroom Patrick was still up, for I could hear him in our rec room downstairs.

I had been sleeping fitfully, when an overwhelming feeling of heat and also of pressure on my chest awakened me. It was a spiritual sensation, not a physical one. It felt like a spirit was pounding on my stomach and chest, and when I woke up, I felt nauseous. I prayed through the feeling when I heard sounds coming from downstairs in the rec room. Then I heard the outside door of the rec room opening to the backyard. Afraid of what Patrick might be doing, I went downstairs to find the rec room locked. I banged on the door to be let in. When he finally did open the door, I could smell the beer on his breath. He wouldn't admit it then, but he later confessed that he had taken four beers from the night of Christina's thirteenth birthday party, which we had given a couple of weeks ago, and had hidden them away. Tonight, he decided that he was going to get rid of the evidence by drinking all four a once. He had only drunk two by the time I came down. The sound of the door opening was Patrick tossing out the empty beer bottles and the two remaining full ones into the bushes in the neighbor's yard.

His guardian angel had awakened me alerting me to the fact that my son needed me to stop him from drinking any more. Thank goodness that his angel knew enough to come and wake me up.

> *"Faith sharpens the inner eye, opening the mind to discover in the flux of events the workings of Providence."*
>
> — JOHN PAUL II

Speaking of beer drinkers, perhaps you will remember Jacques, my fictional executioner who chased me into the words and stabbed me repeatedly in the Lenten Chapter section from *Pandora's Story*. I would like to circle back to him now for two reasons: One, to explain why God wanted me to write my own death scene and two, to let you know that even a killer like Jacques can be saved in the end with a little help from an angel.

You see, in order for God to allow me into the heaven scene to experience a taste of heaven, I did have to die—spiritually speaking—not physically, although the scene is written as if a physical death occurred. Interestingly, though, even though I get killed and buried, the scene holds a twist to show that even when all looks lost, there is always a way to arise from death. God instructed me to write the book this way. I admit to you that I was extremely uncomfortable inventing and writing about the mindset of my killer whom I call Jacques in the book. After all, it is pretty hard to imagine why anyone would want to kill you.

Yet there's a reason God wanted me to meditate on why one person kills another, and that was to see if I could find any compassion in my heart for my "killer." God definitely wanted to know if I would write up a way to get this man into heaven. For that is every saint's job—to get others into heaven. If I wanted to be a saint, I had better be able to understand Jacques and have compassion. Also, we must remember that Jesus forgave His enemies—his killers—before He died on the cross.

Mystic Julian of Norwich has a saying that if you trust in Jesus, "All will be well, and all will be well, and all will be well."

Here is an insert from the heaven chapter in *Pandora's Story* and what God had to say about Jacques:

"Yes, his name is Jacques Fournier. He has lately been very troubled. But his soul is salvageable. He has shown great remorse over your death. If a person can show remorse, can feel that what they did was wrong, and admit to me that they were wrong, and finally ask for forgiveness; then I will find a way to relieve their burden. Feeling sorry and asking for forgiveness, as well as true belief, are the keys. Jacques is receiving help. He, as well as all mankind, is in my hands.

"Jacques has been my instrument, and through him you are now being transformed. Through him you will see my infinite empathy of mankind's plight—my mercy, forgiveness, kindness, and divine intervention."

"The angels of God said to him, 'Take the meat and unleavened cakes and lay them on this rock; and pour out the broth over them.' When he had done so, the angel of the Lord stretched out the tip of the staff he held, and touched the meat and unleavened cakes. Thereupon a fire came up from the rock which consumed the meat and unleavened cakes, and the angel of the Lord disappeared from sight. Gideon, now aware that it had been the angel of the Lord, said, 'Alas, Lord, God, that I have seen the angel of the Lord face to face!' The Lord answered him, 'Be calm, do not fear. You shall not die.'" – Judges 6:20–23

꧁꧂

Jacques opens his third beer. After the note is finished, he lies back down on the bed and flips on the Channel 6 news. No new news only the same bad news. Soon there will be more. Jacques is so exhausted that he falls asleep before he can carry out his suicide plan. His dreams are haunted with his crime. Over and over the scene plays on:

꧁꧂

Jacques screams at her to stop. He feels his anger overwhelm him. Seeing the woman through a red haze—his vision bleary and indistinct—his hand brushes his pant leg, and then he remembers that he has his fishing knife in his pocket. On impulse he reaches in and pulls it out. He must stop her screams. They are echoing through the forest, and the very air seems to vibrate with them. Everything bad in his life suddenly materializes as a huge presence, and it takes over. The woman is struggling violently furiously beating his already pounding head. He takes the knife and drives it into her side. Again, and again, he thrusts. The woman sags against him.

As soon as the screaming stops, the presence leaves. He rolls off the woman. The full realization that he has just knifed this stranger to death sinks in. He is overwhelmed with remorse. He sits on the ground with his head between his hands and cries piteously for twenty minutes. His life is over—to hell he goes with a vengeance.

Oddly enough, the thought of hell makes him realize that he doesn't want to go there. As his anger leaves, his head clears. For the first time in a very long time he sees all the events that have led him to this place in time—the death of his father at a young age, dealing with his alcoholic mother during his teenage years, and the rough peer group he fell into. Before his dad had died, his family had been happy. He remembers attending Mass with his family every week and going to Sunday school. In his childhood heart, he believed in God. But life had proved too difficult, the trials too hard. Sometimes he blamed God for all his troubles.

Now he realizes that he had made some bad choices. He remembers trying to put himself through college, for a year, but finding the studying too hard, decided to work a job instead. Finding the job at the car dealership had been great, until the dealership had been bought out, and the management replaced. His new boss looked down on him because he hadn't finished his de-

gree. He had been lucky to find a great girl to marry, but lately his depression had changed the marriage. All his life the good things had turned to bad. And now it was too late to change. Now his life was irreplaceably broken. And now he is sorry because, suddenly he realizes that he would like another chance. "Oh God, I am sorry. All my life I have been a nothing. Good for nothing. I am not fit to live."

As rains pelts down on his face, it finally dawns on Jacques that he must do something with the woman. He looks around at the peaceful forest, and the stillness and quietness that surround him. The decent thing to do he thinks is to bury her. He looks down at his shirt and sees that he is covered in blood. He wipes his hands on the surrounding ground, then takes off his pants and sweatshirt, reverses them, then puts them back on. Walking back to his campsite watching for other people, he sees no one. Changing his clothing, washing his hands and face, and then grabbing a shovel from the back of his pick-up truck, he returns and digs a shallow grave. He tenderly places the woman in and covers her with dirt. He looks around for a suitable grave marker. He finds a small boulder and places it over the mound. Seeing some late wildflowers, he grabs a bunch, and neatly arranges the flowers in front.

Returning to his campsite, he quickly packs up his gear, gets into his truck and drives away contemplating what he needs to do. Heading to Rt.53, toward the north, he exits onto Route 3. There is no traffic, but Jacques decides that he will steer away from Boston and turns left at the merge onto Rt. 128. He has no real direction, only making turns on impulse. He follows 128 until it hits 93 North, and then decides to take that road. When he hits the New Hampshire border, he gets off the highway and instead travels the back roads. The beautiful country streets are lost on Jacques who is too deep in thought to notice.

Finally, after driving five hours, Jacques decides that he can't drive any further. He stops at a Motel 9 in Camford, NH, heads into the parking lot, and checks in. Across the street there is a chain drug store and a package store. After he checks in, he goes first to the drug store and buys three packages of over-the-counter sleeping pills. Then in the package store, he buys a six-pack of Miller High Life and two bottles of Scotch. He is not hungry so he does not bother with food.

Once back in the motel room, he lies down on the cheap, sagging mattress and flips the TV on. He reaches over for a beer from the six-pack sitting on the side table. Jacques has been contemplating suicide all day, in his mind he has been working up his courage. He has finally decided that taking three boxes of sleeping pills and chasing that down with as much Scotch as possible ought to do the trick.

He has accepted that he must die for his crime. He didn't bother covering up his tracks in the State Park, and he knows that it won't take long for the police to find him. The woman's body, laid in a shallow grave, the forest floor stained with her blood, and possibly even her car parked in one of the lots will soon be discovered. He feels very sad, remorseful. He will never see his wife or daughter again. The woman will never see her family, if she had one, again either. He gets up to write a long, tender suicide note to his wife on the two sheets of writing paper in the top drawer of the side table.

⚜

Around 2:00 a.m., Jacques, having fallen into an intoxicated sleep, has a very vivid dream. In it there is a very beautiful angel-girl. She is glowing white, with long strawberry blond hair, freckles across her snub nose, and sparkling green eyes. She is looking at him with a sad smile. The angel says: "Jacques, all is not what it seems. God is aware of your unhappiness. All is not lost. Have faith. Do not take the action you are thinking of. Pray instead, and wait. Be patient, your course will be clear."

Jacques awakens suddenly—the dream child-angel still so vivid in his mind that he can almost still hear the echo of her words as the sound dies. Jacques thinks for a moment then decides that he has nothing to lose. He will take the angel's advice at least for a day or two. He gets out of bed and onto his knees for a long, heartfelt prayer to God. In his prayer he tells God how troubling life has been, how he has despaired, and of course, how his anger led him to commit an act about which he is deeply sorry.

At 12:00 p.m., he realizes he is hungry and decides to get up, take a shower, and find something to eat. The vivid dream has had a calming effect. The angel said to wait for the time being and watch for a sign, and that is what he intends to do.

Two days later at 6:00 p.m., Jacques turns on the TV and tunes into Channel 6 news. The handsome newscaster, with his periwinkle blue eyes and perfect nut-brown cap of hair, takes a deep breath, turns toward the camera, and smiles. "We have tonight for you one of the most amazing stories that I can ever recall hearing. 42-year-old Irene Manian of Hingham was found alive today after having been buried for three days in Luddum Ford State Park in Pembroke. Ms. Manian is listed in stable condition at South Shore Hospital. The victim sustained multiple stab wounds to her abdomen. Apparently after she was stabbed, her attacker buried her. She remained alive because, by a stroke of luck, her face landed on top of a woodchuck hole. In case you viewers did not know this, woodchucks always dig an entrance and exit hole. Apparently she was able to breathe because the other hole was open and unobstructed. Hats off to the woodchuck. Her attacker is unknown and still at large. The park has been closed while the police launch a full investigation."

The newscaster chuckles under his breath and turns toward his co-anchor.

357

"Gee, I grew up thinking that woodchucks were a major garden pest. I re-member my grandfather getting very upset when one got into his garden since it would eat everything to the roots. He would take out his .22 and wait for the animal to reappear, then shoot it. I guess there is always some good in everything."

Back in the motel room, Jacques lets out a great shout of joy, then gets down on his knees and says a heartfelt prayer of thanks to God. He packs up his things, pays his bill, then heads back south to give himself up.

> "We can only get to Heaven by dying for other people on the cross. And one does not die on a cross by his own unaided efforts. He needs the help of an executioner."
>
> —THOMAS MERTON

✥

November 1st (All Saints Day) Channel 6 Newscast - "Today the Manian case took another bizarre turn, for last night a man named Jacques Fournier turned himself into the Pembroke police claiming full responsibility for Irene Manian's attack. Fournier is being held in custody until the case comes to trial, and refused to comment to our reporters." *The newscaster glances at his co-an-chor and says:* "I don't know about you, Jack, but I definitely think that God has worked a miracle here."

"Today, for a very pleasant change, I am very happy to report that all the news is good. In our other leading story, a number of local charities report that they are being simply deluged by people calling in to pledge money. Also, many people are simply begging to be allowed to volunteer in the various organiza-tions." *The newscaster again looks at Jack and mentions, almost as an aside,* "Its funny, but it's almost as if the Manian woman's miraculous survival has something to do with all the record-breaking charity numbers."

Jack looks back and responds: "No, can't be. Can it? Now on to sports with Bill Lyons."

✥

I hope you can all tell from this story of my fictional murder that God loves all no matter what they do. God is never going to give up on you, ever. Angels are only one of His tools. The spiritual gifts are another, but there are many more. In fact, in the next section, although the devil will never admit this, demons are another tool that must submit to the hands of God. These tools work by changing a person's direction. By the way, that is the true meaning of the word "repentance."

Angels Among Us
by the Daughters of St. Paul

I believe there are angels among us.
Sent down to us from somewhere up above.
They come to you and me in our darkest hour.
To show us how to give, to teach us how to live,
To guide us with the light of love.

When life held troubled times that had me down on my knees.
There's always been someone to come along and comfort me.
A kind word from a stranger
To lend a helping hand.
A phone call from a friend just to say I understand.
Ain't it kinda funny at the dark end of the room
Someone lights the way with just a single ray of hope.

I believe there are angels among us.
Sent down to us from somewhere up above.
They come to you and me in our darkest hour.
To show us how to give, to teach us how to live,
To guide us with the light of love.

They wear so many faces.
Show up in the strangest places.
They grace us with their mercy in our time of need.

19

DEMONS AND DESOLATIONS

Eerie Touch
Specter's Watching
Unfortunate Creature Of The Wrong Choice
Sad Thoughts Spring From
Evil We Create By Turning Away From God
A Reason For Every Demon
Ghosts, Ghosts, Ghosts

"As an artist, God makes use even of the devil."

— ST. AUGUSTINE

"It would, however, be a complete error on the nature of this victory if one did not see in it the end of a long struggle, with the intervention—through the means of human powers opposed to the Lord Jesus of Satan and his angels, as distinct from one another as from their human agents. It is in effect the Book of Revelation, which by revealing the enigma of the different names and symbols of Satan in Scripture definitively unmasks his identity. He is active in all the centuries of human history, under the eye of God." – Christian Faith and Demonology, Pauline Books and Media

"Do not suppose, then, that when God brings a soul to such a point He lets it go so quickly out of His hand that the devil can recapture it without much labour. His Majesty is so anxious for it not to be lost that He gives it a thousand interior warnings of many kinds, and thus it cannot fail to perceive the danger."

— ST. TERESA OF AVILA

"Terrible are the crafts and wiles which the devil uses to prevent souls from learning to know themselves and understanding his ways."
— ST. TERESA OF AVILA

Traveling back in time to when I was about twenty-two, I would like to share two stories that involve the devil. One is the conclusion of what happened after that fateful ESP Christmas Eve party, and the other—a terrifying experience that I was lucky to live through.

It was early January 1982, and I was alone in my usually bustling family home. With nine people living in one house, I rarely found alone time. Having two sisters and four brothers makes for a very hectic home life, but we were all close and basically got along well. In the past, before my Christmas Eve spirit encounter, I might have really enjoyed having the house to myself, but now I was uneasy.

As the last person closed the door behind them, I quickly gathered together all the materials for the project I had planning to keep me busy for the next few hours. It was a perfect winter's evening, and it would be good to keep my mind occupied. My winter coat's lining had became shredded, so rather than buying a new coat, which I didn't have the money for, I had decided to reline it. I started the project by picking up the dark green satin material I had chosen and placing it on the sea foam green rug of our family room. Our family room was just off the cozy wood paneled kitchen. I moved aside a couple of chairs and a cocktail table to make room on the floor. The sliding glass doors were darkened at the time, but in the daylight they revealed a view of a deck leading to a tiny lawn and then an oak and scrub pine tree forest. After I had laid the lining flat, next I methodically removed the lining from my old coat and ripped the seams, which held all the pieces together. I took each piece and pinned it to the new green satin. When everything was pinned in place, I cut out all the pieces and gathered the new lining pieces into a pile. While on my hands and knees, I grabbed all the small scraps and laid them in a pile to be thrown away later.

While I was working, I noticed that the room had grown steadily colder. This didn't immediately strike me as ominous. I just assumed that my dad must have turned down the thermostat automatically as he left the house without remembering that I would still be home. Getting up from the floor, I walked over to the thermostat and looked at the temperature that was registered there. It read 70 degrees. *Odd*, I thought, *it feels much colder that 70 degrees in here.*

With my sewing project foremost in my mind, I absentmindedly went to my bedroom to dig out a sweater from my bureau drawer and then returned to my project. When I returned I noticed that one large scrap was left over and decided to keep it for another project. So I took the piece and jerked it open prior to refolding it in a neater way, much like you would take a sheet and snap it open before remaking a bed. As the opened material of the scrap drifted and landed on the floor, I noticed something oddly sinister about it. I could clearly see a head with horns and outstretched, upraised arms in the material. *That outline looks like a line drawing of a devil*, I thought in amazement. Just as I had that thought, I became aware of what I had been trying to avoid noticing all evening—his negative, evil presence was with me in the room. So strong and pervasive did it hit me then that there was no way I could tell myself that he was a figure of my imagination. And once I became aware of him, he gained the ability to influence my perception.

I felt all the hair on the back of my neck rise, and the air in the room become putrid—I could clearly smell the sickeningly corrupt smell of newly burned bodies. It seemed to lift from the floorboards and mix with the oxygen of the room. Their decayed smell was utterly nauseating. He was very close—ready to spring into my mind, seep into my soul.

My sixth sense told me he was right behind my back, breathing down it, his pitchfork aimed directly between my shoulder blades, and he wanted me to know it. Obviously, he had taken advantage of my lonely evening for his own gain, to take something that I could sense he had been after ever since the Christmas ESP party. He wanted something that I was fond of and more than just a little attached to: my soul. He wanted what he always wants; it is why he comes, why he hangs around the earth, and his main priority—another soul for his side to fight against God at the end of time. All the better, no doubt, if the body can be entered easily, used easily like apparently mine could.

My soul quivered in fear, understandable given the fact that the greatest enemy loomed behind me. But from somewhere inside myself came the knowledge that I must not show fear in any way. He would use it to bend me to his will. My fear would make him much stronger and my soul weaker. So rather than freezing in fear or giving way to panic as he was probably sure I would do, I decided to take action. I used my adrenaline in a way that I hoped would show him that I was not easy prey. I quickly grabbed my scissors. Poised over the material, I grabbed the section that took the shape of his head and cut it off at the neck. I thought this would do the trick, but it didn't.

Cutting off the material at the neck didn't get rid of him. His hysterical, maniac-like laughter rang inside my head. I guess he thought my puny efforts were rather amusing. Forcing myself to picture the devil only in the material and not in spirit form behind me, I next hacked off his horns, then attacked the outstretched arms, and then finally the body. I took savage stabs at the material with my scissors until it lay shredded on my lap.

Full of false bravado, I screamed into the empty room and house: "You will never get me, do you hear?" My legs shook like quivering masses of Jell-O, but my surprisingly strong, loud voice, which was filled with revulsion, told the devil, "I will never surrender my soul to you. I choose God. Do you hear me? DO YOU HEAR ME? I choose God—NOT YOU. NEVER YOU!" The sounds of my shouts echoed through the empty house—dying a slow death.

On a spiritual level, his malevolent spirit breeze fluttered the papers on the oak side table. A current of evil air traveled from the family room and entered each room in secession—the kitchen, the guest bedroom, the master bedroom suite, the bathroom, and finally my bedroom. He was looking for a place to hide, another soul to attack. I could hear him actively searching for a place to descend into. Finally, after what seemed like an eternity, he circled around to the front door. An invisible force spiritually opened the door. Then just as quickly as it had opened it, it shammed it shut. The house shook with a vengeance. It was a small taste of the power of the dark side. Silence once again prevailed.

I grabbed the edge of the chair, knelt down, and prayed to God to come to me—to send me His light, love, and warmth to help me dispel the darkness. And then it came to me to sing a song—a song about a storm. Into to my mind came the perfect choice, one I had just recently learned during one of my voice lessons at the Cape Cod Conservatory in Barnstable. My voice instructor had thought this piece from the musical *Carousel* a good fit for my voice:

> When, you walk through a storm,
> Hold your head up high
> And don't be afraid of the dark
> At the end of the storm is a golden sky
> And the sweet silver song of a lark.
> Walk on through the wind,
> Walk on through the rain,
> Tho' your dreams be tossed and blown.
> Walk on, walk on, with hope in your heart,
> And you'll never walk alone,
> You'll never walk alone.

After finishing the chorus a second time, I heard the latch on the front door release. Thank you, God. It was my mom and dad and my younger brothers and sisters returning home from the school function they had been attending.

During the next few weeks, as if the encounter had somehow damaged my spirit, I began to see everyone with a negative cast and in a negative light. The confrontation had left me weak, frightened, and vulnerable to all possible demons and evil beings. I knew that I was in danger. I wanted to put some distance between myself and the other side of the veil, so to speak. The dark ones were invading. I knew I must shut them out. Find a way to return to the light and only the light. If I did not, I knew I faced madness ... or worse.

Over the course of the rest of the month, I prayed to God continually to help me to block the demons that bombarded my soul, and eventually I was able to regain inner peace. When Pat, my ESP teacher, called all group members to discuss plans to begin yet another "ESP class," I made a decision not to rejoin. I attributed to the ESP class some of what had happened that night when the devil had paid me a visit; for me, who was sensitive, it would a big mistake to continue. I felt bad about abandoning the group, because I had come to love all the members, but it was necessary to cut off my arm (so to speak) to save the rest of my body.

Battling the evil things that had been unleashed on that faithful night in December proved extremely difficult. I sensed I would travel back on the spiritual road to recovery when I cut my ties to the group and settled down to my own true religious path—the Catholic Church. Letting psychic wanderlust and ESP experimentation die in my heart was the right course for me.

When Pat had called she also mentioned something that really scared me. She wanted the group to have one of its next sessions at a sauna. We were all to go into the sauna together in towels, and then we would remove them. She felt that we would all get to know each other much better once we could not hide ourselves behind our clothes. True honesty. This idea scared me. I knew that I didn't want to be naked in the mixed group. What was she trying to turn the group into—a witches' coven? Were we all going to begin practicing magic "sky-clad"? That statement closed the final door on the class for me—my spirit rebelled at the mere thought of such a shocking possibility. I never saw any of the members of the ESP class ever again, but I never forgot them. I think of them still. They are in my memories, and in a way, through those memories, we remain bonded. I had opened Pandora's Box too soon, it seemed, before it was only filled with God.

⚜

My brother Peter's marriage in Washington, D.C., was the stage for an incident, which I hid away in my subconscious for a long time because it had been too painful to remember. I guess I still hadn't quite learned that the devil was still out there, ready to take advantage of any opportunity for attack. And during that happy time for our family, the first wedding of any of my brothers or sisters, I guess I thought I was immune to him. How very wrong I was. He can crop up in any number of disguises. In fact, where he did show up is a common, accepted setting. The event happened on our first night in town.

That first night was the night that I was raped.

It was a beautiful morning in early November 1982. All the members of my family were busy packing our personal belongings for our trip to Washington, D.C. in the two cars that we would take. Mom and Dad were both going to drive a car, and we kids were to be divided up between the two cars. By 6:00 a.m. we were ready to leave. My sisters Caroline, Anne, and I were really looking forward to the trip since we had never been out of New England, and we wanted to see some of our great country. Caroline was by my side in the car. We talked endlessly about the new sights—the rolling countryside of eastern Connecticut, our first glimpse of the New York City skyline, the ugliness of the part of New Jersey, which borders New York City, and finally our first glimpses of our nation's great capital.

When we arrived in Washington, D.C., it was around 4:30 p.m. Although we had planned to drive by some of the sights on the way to our hotel in Arlington, Virginia—the Washington Monument and the reflecting pool, the Lincoln Monument, the Jefferson Memorial, and the White House so grand sitting on its magnificent lawn behind the impressive wrought iron gates—by the time we got to our hotel, Dad was too tired after having left Cape Cod so early. Still it had been a wonderful day filled with new sights.

Caroline, Anne, and I all shared a room with our grandmother. We relaxed for a half hour, then met our brothers and parents for dinner in the hotel restaurant. After dinner, we girls were too excited to stay in our rooms for the night, so we called Peter's fiancée, Laura, to ask where the good nightspots were. Then we begged Dad for the keys to the VW Rabbit. He cautioned us to stay together but to have fun. Dad really knew how to have fun, so he understood our need to get out and see the town. By nine o'clock, after an hour of fighting for mirror space with my sisters, we were set to go. All three of us ready to knock the eyes out of those unsuspecting Washington, D.C. bachelors.

We drove to a trendy nightspot in Georgetown. It was so exciting—the exotic location (for us), the flashing lights of the noisy bar, the many men lined up against the bar on the prowl for women, and the feeling of being in such a famous city that we had always longed to see.

I state only the honest truth when I tell you that the sight of us three girls together was enough to make every man in the place stop talking and stare. The three fastest men got to us first. A conservative estimate was maybe five seconds. Anne is 5'11" with legs that go for miles and absolutely flawless, perfect facial features. Caroline is 5'7" with "Farrah Fawcett" hair, melting brown eyes, and perfect dimples that add a great deal of charm to her beautiful smile. She is so lively and witty that she soon had the men gathered around laughing uproariously at her many jokes. At 5'6" I was the oldest and the shortest of the three. My hair and eyes are near-black, and I am the quietest of the group.

Caroline and Anne were quickly surrounded, but a man whose face and hair were so unique that I have no trouble recalling them even now—over twenty years later—singled me out. I have forgotten his name, but he was tall, slender, with white-blond hair cut short but curled close to his head. His eyes were near colorless with only a touch of sky blue. They were the coldest eyes I had ever seen. Something about his eyes bothered me, but I didn't take the time to analyze what it was. I saw everything with a rosy glow that night—including his intentions. He was a just young guy out to meet women, and I accepted him as such.

He bought me a drink, and we talked for a bit at a tiny table hidden in a dark corner. He had a job on "The Hill" as a pageboy for a senator. His dad was a powerful lobbyist, and he was an aspiring politician-in-the-making. He had just finished his bachelor's degree and was applying to law schools for next fall.

"Are you here alone?" It was the first question he asked me.

"Why, no. Do you see that girl there and that one over there? Those are my two sisters. We just arrived today from Cape Cod in our family's squishy VW Rabbit to attend my brother's wedding, which, by the way, is the day after tomorrow. We were just dying to experience Washington at night," I answered him.

"Well, what do you say that I take you on a evening drive around town? All the monuments are beautifully lit up at night, and there's no traffic." I must say, he read me just right because this was exactly what I longed to do. I wanted to fill my eyes with the beauty that I had only briefly glimpsed today. Since I had just drunk my third drink, my naturally cautious personality was squelched, and I told him that sounded like a lovely idea.

"Let's go. I'll take you back to your hotel later. Tell your sisters you will see them back at the hotel."

I pushed my way into the crowd of men. "Caroline, Anne, we are going on a drive around D.C. to see the sights. I will met you back at the hotel room," I yelled to both my sisters over the surging crowd.

Anne gave me a look. "Irene, who are you with?" I pointed in his direction.

"Are you sure you want to leave the bar? Dad said to stay together," Anne asked with her perfect eyebrows up in the air.

"I know, I know, but I really want to go. I want to enjoy every minute of this trip. I'm a big girl and can take care of myself," I told her.

"Okay, if you're sure. See you later." One of the men at her side caught her attention, and she waved.

We walked out of the bar. When we were in the parking lot we passed our family's car. I pointed it out to him as we headed to his car. Then we set off and headed toward Capital Hill.

"Where are we going first? How about a walk under the monument?" I asked, thinking how wonderful that would be.

"Sure, okay. Mind if we stop by my apartment for a moment? I want to get something. Come with me, and I will show you where I live," he nonchalantly stated.

"Why not." I said, my mind obviously not focused or alert. We drove to his apartment building and parked the car on the street. He opened the door to the shared foyer with his key. Then we proceeded down the stairs to his "garden" apartment. He unlocked the door and held it open. I walked in and took a look around. It was an adorable studio apartment. There was a small galley kitchen on the left, next a bathroom, and then a large room that served as a living room and bedroom. There wasn't much furniture. Only a couple of chairs in front of a patio door, a table with a TV on top, a mattress on the floor, and books and other personal items in neat piles against the walls and in the corners. The place was barren, but it was clean. In fact, it looked just like an under-decorated bachelor's pad. I strolled to the far side of the apartment trying to see beyond the other side of the windows when I heard him twist the key that was in the door, locking us in.

I turned in time to see him pocket the key. "Why did you lock us in?" I asked, not particularly upset.

"You didn't really think we were going on a tour of Washington, D.C. by night, did you? After all, it's dark. What can you see?" He smiled the words, but his eyes became cold. I noticed something now that I had ignored before. His eyes were depthless; looking into them was like looking into a void. My eyes sought but did not encounter any presence of his soul. I knew from my own experiences in the ESP class that this was not a good sign because the eyes were always the windows of the soul.

"So you lied. Okay, what do you want?" I was still very fuzzy, because I had made the mistake of having too many drinks. In a way it was a good thing, because my adrenaline could not rush to flood my system, and I didn't panic. Oddly enough, I wasn't petrified. It was only him against me.

"I want you to take off all your cloths and lay down on the mattress." Boy, he sure wasn't wasting any time on the niceties, was he?

"Look, I don't know you, and I don't want to. Technically, what you are asking is rape. You do know that, don't you?" I asked in what I hoped came across as a bitchy, cross, patronizing voice.

He didn't answer me at first, but then he told me he disagreed. That what he was asking for was only what he was entitled to, what I had agreed to when I left the bar with him. He didn't look me in the eyes. Instead, he took a seat in one of the two chairs in the apartment. He seemed to be thinking and waiting. I proceeded to talk to him as I would have a small child telling him why what he was asking was wrong, and why I was objecting. I must have tried to talk him out of what he wanted for a full hour. By this time, I was quite sober. He had said very little during all the time I had talked. Finally, his patience wore out. He walked out of the room and into the galley kitchen. I heard him open one of the drawers. The rattle of the steel objects in the drawer was loud in the silent apartment.

I heard an urgent voice in my head say: "Go confront him, now. The best defense is a strong offence. Confront him. GO TO THE KITCHEN AND CONFRONT HIM, NOW," said the voice deep inside my soul.

I got up from the chair and rushed into the kitchen. He was just reaching for a large kitchen knife. "What is that you are holding? A knife? So you mean to use a knife to get your way? Fine, fine. You win. Put the knife down. I am going to take my clothes off and lay down on the mattress. I certainly hope you have a condom somewhere around here." He nodded his assent. "I want you to put it on." He followed me into the room and watched me without expression.

With sickening dread, I quickly removed all my clothes and got under the covers on the mattress. When I was done, he slowly undressed and lay down under the covers beside me. There were no preliminaries, no kissing, no fore-play, and no affection. He seemed only to want to put his engorged man-hood inside me. He couldn't bear to touch any other part of me. His face was turned away from mine, and his body was rigidly held as far away from me as possible. Only the critical parts touched. It was over very fast—in less than one minute. (Reflecting on this incident much later gained me the insight that whatever had possessed him had only one thing in mind: dominance.)

He rolled off. I lay still for a moment or two. I think I was in shock. Finally, I sat up and pulled on my clothes as fast as I could. I needed to find a way back to the hotel. Oddly enough, he became almost friendly then. He told me that he would take me back to my hotel. I readily agreed since it would mean that I could get out of the building. I would have to judge whether or not to believe him when we got out of the building and approached the car.

When we got to the car, I decided to go with the assumption that he really was going to take me back. After all, I was in a strange place and didn't have any idea of my location. Also, he had already gotten what he so obviously wanted. I prayed that as we began to drive, the road going back would begin to look familiar and that we would pass by some open stores in case I needed to exit the car quickly.

For some reason, he decided to take me back to the hotel. With a huge sigh of relief, we entered the lobby. He followed me up the elevator and insisted on walking me up to my room. The last thing he said was, "Maybe we can see each other again during your stay." I found this last statement profoundly shocking. He was asking me out again just like we had been on a first date at some fancy restaurant and had really hit it off.

I was so floored by his offer that I didn't say anything. I knocked on the door of the room, and my grandmother opened the door. I closed the door as quickly as I could, leaning against the closed door as if I could hold back the evil I had just encountered. She took one look at me and berated me on my late night. "It's 3:00 a.m. Where have you been? Don't you know that we were worried about you? Your sisters returned hours ago."

"Yes, Meme. I know it's late. Let's not wake everyone else up. I'm going right to bed." I agreed with her and knew I had made a huge judgment error but, thankfully, was going to live through the night.

For the next few days I was quiet and introspective. I was deeply ashamed of my foolish action of going with him. I walked through the Smithsonian with my family and, quite by accident, I became separated from them. My dad had told us all that in case we got separated to meet at a designated spot at 3:30 p.m. So no one worried about me until I failed to meet them back at the appropriate spot and time. I walked hours through the many rooms in a near trance-like state. When my family finally located me, I realized that I missed the time to meet back with the group by two hours. I had been lost in my own little world with my own terrorizing thoughts.

But in the cocoon of my close family, I eventually recovered and repressed the memory of that night. It was over ten years later when I found the courage to finally tell my mother about the incident. She related that something had always puzzled her about that trip. Apparently, the next morning she and dad had gone to the car to get something in the trunk. On the windshield written in soap was the message: "You get what you deserve." They had not known what to make of this message since it didn't seem to make any sense. But I knew exactly what the message meant. He had gone into the parking garage and located the car I had pointed out that night. He had left me this message because he wanted me to know that I had gotten what he thought I deserved.

I continued to wonder about that night for years. Should I have turned him in? It hadn't seemed to be the right thing to do since I would have ruined Peter's wedding, and I wanted to forget the whole thing ever happened. But his going through the bother of locating the car and writing the message, along with going into the kitchen and picking up a knife, signaled that he was truly mentally disturbed. If I had not pointed out my sisters, and if he had believed that I was alone and that no one could identify him, would he have killed me? I believe now that he would have. Did I leave a sexual predator out on the loose? Did he ever try it again, this time with a woman who was not with a group? My conscience has bothered me ever since.

BRIDGE OVER TROUBLED WATERS
by Simon and Garfunkel

When you're weary, feeling small.
When tears are in your eyes, I will dry them all.
I'm on your side oh when times get rough and friends just can't be found
Like a bridge over troubled water I will lay me down.
Like a bridge over troubled water, I will lay me down.
When you're down and out.
When you're on the street.
When evening falls so hard, I will comfort you.
I'll take your part, Oh when darkness comes,
And pain is all around like a bridge over troubled water, I will lay me down.
Like a bridge over troubled water, I will lay me down.
Sail on silver girl, sail on bye.
Your time has come to shine.
All your dreams will all come true.
See how they shine.
Oh if you need a friend. And sailing can be fine like a bridge over troubled water.
I will ease your mind.
Like a bridge over troubled water, I will ease your mind.

For the next twenty years I remained only on the physical surface, allowing my soul to totally heal. In general, God allowed me to become normal and like everyone else. I married and raised my children and did all the normal family type things. But my life would end up far from "normal."

After the awakening 2002

Thursday, February 21, 2002.

I felt a strong urge to attend morning Mass. Unavoidably I had missed Mass last Sunday due to the family ski vacation, and now I was very much aware of how my soul depended on the graces given there. After Mass I went to Nantasket Beach in Hull and took a long walk. It was a beautiful, balmy day for a February in New England. The feel of sand beneath my feet and the crash of waves against the shore offered strong medicine for me. My soul, deeply troubled, felt the need to get out and release some of my tension. It was craving the feeling of God's strong presence through the rhythmic ocean waves, the tranquil sky, the friendly clouds overhead, and the many animals who lived at the beach. The ocean was near calm with only one-foot waves breaking to the soothing whisper of the wind.

As I walked I felt the familiar numbing sensation in my left shoulder, which had come so often as I wrote *Pandora's Story*. From out of the thin cool air,

I felt every hair on the back of my head actually rise about an inch from my skin and my pleasure in my leisurely walk evaporated. There was something very angry and negative walking behind me, and I could feel stabbing pitchfork thrusts as I tried valiantly to turn my mind to God and happy thoughts. In sudden inspiration I thought of the holy water I had just blessed myself with earlier at Mass. In order to ward off the spirit, who was so strong that even broad daylight did not deter him, I dipped my hand in the seawater, recited a prayer, and flung the drops over my shoulder to the place where I could feel its presence. I did this half a dozen times before whatever it was gave up, and I was able to regain my peace.

> "Purgation, which is the remaking of character in conformity with perceived reality, consists in these two essential acts: The cleansing of which is to remain, the stripping of that which is to be done away. 1. The Negative aspect, the stripping or purging away of those superfluous, unreal, and harmful things which dissipate the precious energies of the self. This is the business of Poverty, or Detachment. 2. The Positive aspect: A raising to their highest term their purest state, of all that remains—the permanent elements of character. This is brought about by Mortification, the gymnastic of the soul: a deliberate recourse to painful experiences and difficult tasks."
>
> – EVELYN UNDERHILL

"Spiritual desolation means the feeling of abandonment by God, and of the absence of His grace. This feeling of estrangement may arise from various causes. It may be the result of natural disposition or temperament, or of external circumstances; or it may come from the attacks of the devil; or from God Himself when for our greater good He withdraws from us spiritual consolation." – From the Online Catholic Encyclopedia, New Advent Web site, State or Way (Purgative, Illuminative, Unitive)

"The spirit has an impregnable tower which no danger can disturb as long as the tower is guarded by the invisible Protector who acts unconsciously, and whose actions go astray when they become deliberate, reflexive, and intentional. The unconsciousness and the entire sincerity of Tao are disturbed by any effort at self-conscious demonstration. All such demonstrations are lies. When one displays himself in this ambiguous way the world outside storms in and imprisons him. He is no longer protected by the sincerity of Tao. Each new act is a new failure. If his acts are done in public, in broad daylight, he will be punished by men, if they are done in private and in secret, they will be punished by spirits." – The Way of Chaung Tao, The Tower of the Spirit

After Lent 2002 there was a bit of a spiritual break, which lasted through to June 2002, but then the most intense, difficult part of the purging would begin. That period took place from July 2002 through August 2002.

Over the Fourth of July weekend of 2002, seemingly in retaliation and response to the Father's "sun" and "ocean" Meditations and the Holy Spirit's first night of purification on July 2nd, the spirit of evil came for a visit. On the night of July 3rd, I felt his awful presence. He had come again in his guise of "demon lover." His stinging spiritual aura surged between my legs and tried to penetrate into my body spirit—a hideous invasion of privacy. The night before I had an incredibly beautiful experience of God, and so I had been hopeful that He was returning as His Holy Spirit or perhaps sending an angel.

However, it wouldn't be so.

Tonight, instead, the experience was frightening and upsetting because it came from the other end of the spiritual spectrum. There was no peace, no beautiful feeling. I prayed through the entire encounter hoping that my prayers would make it obvious to God that I was not sending out invitations to the devil. My heart was in great turmoil. Now I knew that it was possible for the other side to try and trick you into believing for a while that the experience was of God. From the book *Interior Castles*, St. Teresa confirms "in order to trick souls, the devil can send souls into fits of sexual delight." This retaliation seemed to confirm her counsel.

The spirit that had provided me with so many of my problems of the past through temptation, and actual sin was again trying to haunt me. The demon of lust, which had often come to visit and had such luck in the past of making me obey his will and chaining me to him, was back with full vengeance. I had been a slave to his insatiable passionate nature, driven by him into all sort of traps. He had lived through me, had come into the world often through me. It was time to put my foot down and overcome him, freeing myself from his bondage. Because my awakening was teaching me spiritual discernment, I became vividly aware of my past weakness. Now I would not be such an easy target. I endured his presence, which produced immense bodily pleasure, because I had no choice. Unhappy thoughts were chasing themselves around and around inside my heart.

The next night at Fire Island, the negative spirits were as numerous as the mosquitoes and deer ticks that were out in droves. Like a nest of angry yellow jackets, the demons surrounded me in a large cloud. As I lay on the hard twin bed, enduring the loud rock music floating over the Island from one of the two nightclubs call the In and the Out, my mind tried to distract itself from the barrage of the otherworldly army. Thoughts of all the drunken people in the bars at this very moment floated in and out of my awareness. Unfortunately, they were allowing the demons to have their fun in unseen ways. (I couldn't make any connections that night, but eventually upon reading one of the letters from St. Paul, where he mentions "party spirit" as an evil of society, I would remember these nights at the island and realize that that was exactly what they were—party spirit demons.)

> *"Trappists believe that everything that costs them is God's will. Anything that makes you suffer is God's will."*
>
> – THOMAS MERTON

Then I had an inspiration. I took the stones collected during my beach walk with the Father and held them in my hands. Then as if in a daze I pulled back the thin sheet from my twin bed and laid them all in a line so that as I lay back down upon them they were under my spine.

The stones lulled me to sleep. They seemed to have the ocean's vibrations and a peaceful cleansing sound in them—restful and perfect for sleep, purified and rounded in the great, powerful Atlantic Ocean. Somehow they seemed to neutralize the evil energy around me. Drifting in and out of sleep, I was aware of being caressed in three sessions of divine union, which felt like immersion in a bath of warm fire.

(Smokey quartz is useful in removing blockages to physical energy in relation to fear and its foundation. If these are of a sexual nature, putting them as close to your base Chakra is the most helpful—the base Chakra being under your tailbone or right as the base of your body begins. This crystal is useful in helping dissolve negative energy produced by the mind. The yellowish-brown stone of Citrine will not allow one to hold onto negative energy—it dispels anger—and helps one look forward to new beginnings. The rose quartz stone gives a beautiful calming effect to remove negative energy and reinstate soft loving and gentle energies. The frosted quartz was soothing and helped restore my balance.)

Because I needed to return to work on Monday morning, I headed home in the early afternoon. Sam and the children stayed on the island. Because he was retired, he and the children could stay and enjoy an extended weekend. His spirit was never troubled while he was there for some reason, but mine was never happy, so I always planned the shortest trip I could. The children seemed to also be protected from being disturbed.

Knowing that I needed to be home by the time the night arrived because the nights were lately so difficult spiritually, I planned an early start. I didn't know how well I would do driving home in the late evening. I never knew what to expect, because the experiences ranged the gamut from perfectly heavenly to absolutely hellish.

I packed my bags, walked over to the ferry dock with my suitcase, kissed the children good-bye, and reminded Sam not to let them out of his sight. As the ferry cruised in, I slowly boarded and proceeded up the stairs to find a seat on its open deck. As it pulled away, I waved good-bye to Patrick, Christina, and Sam, hoping that they would have a wonderful couple of days before they returned home. Then I shifted my thoughts back to my plan to outsmart the "Big D."

After the Fire Island Ferry landed in Bay Shore, I walked to the parked van, started the engine, and drove to the highway. I enjoyed the peace and quiet of that hour and a half drive alone. I thought of some of the wonderful gifts that God had just given me; they were wonderful food for thought. My mood was joyful as I passed corn and potato fields on upper, easterly Long Island. At a peach tree farm about ten miles from Orient Point, I stopped the car and purchased early corn, raspberries, and leaf lettuce. Just before the Orient Point car ferry dock, I turned right to go to the Orient State Park for a long walk along the shoreline as a way of relaxing. *So far, so good,* I thought.

Walking along at a rapid pace, enjoying the peace and quiet, my thoughts were centered on the beauty of nature and God. I felt safe and happy. Then I rounded a bend on the beach and as I lost sight of all people, cars, and buildings, a feeling of utter loneliness and desolation came upon me. The day shifted from bright sunshine-filled thoughts to dark, sinister, ominous ones as fast as I could snap my fingers. As soon as the sun sunk close to the horizon, he had seen his chance.

As if the sudden spiritual shift needed an exclamation point on it, just then my back felt a painful stab just in between my shoulder blades. Quickly, I turned around looking for a bee or wasp, which I hoped had caused the sting. Disappointingly, there was nothing there. I looked over at a deserted beach house in the distance further along the beach, and the thought crossed my mind that maybe there was a ghost living there who had decided to attack.

Walking fast to get that thought out of my head, and trying to quell the rising fear, I felt another painful jab in the same spot. Realizing that another powerful spiritual desolation was happening, I immediately cut short my walk and turned back toward the parking lot—all my peace at an end. Extreme negative energy caused all every hair on my head to stand up, and waves of horror threatened to drown me. Sickening dread and extreme nauseating fear arose at once, and I fell into a pit of panic.

As a little girl, in spite of my mother's disapproval, I had regularly watched the soap opera *Dark Shadows* every afternoon after school at a friend's house. The show was based in a Newport Mansion and was about ghosts and vampires. Barnabas was the name of the star vampire, and I have never been able to totally eliminate the fear that he placed in my young heart during those hour-long episodes. This spirit seemed to recall my childhood fears and bring them to the surface. I was now as terrified as I had ever been upon seeing Barnabas lift his coffin lid with a squeaky creek, slowly open his bloodshot eyes, and sit up. Then ready to emerge for his evening meal, he would carefully lift his legs over the edge of the billowy white satin coffin bed. In my mind, I could see myself trying to hide behind a tree or a door, praying that he couldn't see me. Now it was as if he had found my hiding spot, his eyes lit with a maniacal glow, his mouth opening with fangs bared and blood dripping. My childhood terrors and irrational fears seemed to rise from deep inside my soul.

My impulse was to run, but because I knew that I was not facing a physical danger, I forced myself to walk—albeit very, very fast. As I rounded the bend in the beach and caught sight of other people, a man fishing with his son, families with small children at the shore, I felt the tension and fear loosen from the binds of my rising panic attack, and I felt able to breath as I walked into the central beach area.

Letting myself into the van, I drove away from the parking lot sad that that outing had turned into a nightmare and now worried that I would be further harassed all evening. I drove into the crowded ferry parking lot hoping to keep the presence at bay. To surround myself in the lineup of other cars waiting for the late afternoon ferry seemed a good idea. There were lots of other people milling around, enjoying ice cream cones and watching their children, who were running off all their abundant energy. I tried very hard not to think of the long drive home alone and sleeping in the empty house.

The negativity generated by the spirit was strong even as I boarded the boat and throughout the peaceful evening boat ride. The sun set against a still ocean as we cruised into New London, and a more peaceful outer scene I could not imagine. As I got into my car and drove out of the ferry and onto the highway, I tried to distract myself with loud music. That didn't help any. I had found that loud rock and roll sound was making my spirit even more agitated, so I turned it off and begin praying hundreds of Our Fathers, Hail Marys, and Glory Bes to stay focused over the remainder of the drive. It proved to be an uncomfortable, scary experience. Just as I would begin to relax, another sensation or prick would assault me, keeping my terror constantly rising to the surface. My relief at making it home without a car accident was short-lived and quickly gave way to dread as I opened the door to my home.

> "At other times, when the spiritual communication is not made in any great measure to the spirit, but the senses have a part therein, the devil more easily succeeds in disturbing the spirit and raising a tumult within it, by means of the senses, with these terrors. Great are the torment and the affliction, which are then caused in the spirit; at times they exceed all that can be expressed."
>
> — ST. JOHN OF THE CROSS

> "We must observe, therefore, that it is for this reason that, in proportion as God is guiding the soul and communing with it, He gives the devil leave to act with it after this manner."
>
> — ST. JOHN OF THE CROSS

"At other times the devil prevails and encompasses the soul with a perturbation and horror which is a greater affliction to it than any torment in this life could be. For, as this horrible communication passes direct from spirit to spirit, in something like nakedness and clearly distinguished from all that is corporeal, it is grievous beyond what every sense can feel; and this lasts in the spirit for some time, yet not for long, for otherwise the spirit would be driven forth from the flesh by the vehement communication of the other spirit. Afterwards there remains to it the memory thereof, which is sufficient to cause it great affliction."

— ST. JOHN OF THE CROSS

Shutting the door behind me, I turned on all the lights and walked from room to room searching for any signs of anything amiss—nothing seemed disturbed, all seemed well. Since it was early evening, and I knew that my spirit might be further disturbed by a TV sitcom, or even music, I decided instead to gather all my stones, prayer books, cross, and blankets around me and spend the rest of the night quietly reading the Bible. I placed my angel overhead in a spot where it dangled from the lamp over the living room sofa. So agitated was my soul that I couldn't imagine getting a wink of sleep. I read for a time fighting massive spiritual anxiety. As evening grew darker, I heard a soothing voice in my head. "Get up and take one of your Xanaxes." My doctor had prescribed Xanax for anxiety just after my awakening. Obeying the voice, I got up from my makeshift bed on the sofa, went into the kitchen for a glass, filled it with water, and swallowed a tablet. After the medication took effect, I was rewarded with a full night's sleep. I hadn't had a sleeping stretch like that since early February.

The next night I again sensed the devil very acutely. I was up every hour with his stings. His presence stayed strong until the night of July 9, 2002. On that day I had decided to take a drive to my sister Caroline's house in Sandwich on Cape Cod with my children, Patrick and Christina, who had returned from Fire Island just a couple of days prior.

The visit was fun; the drive home was anything but. After we crossed the Sagamore bridge heading north on Route 3A, the devil decided to pay me another visit—his presence was nearly tangible this time. He put his hands around my head. I could feel the tips of his sharp dagger fingertips digging into my skull. He was squeezing my head with his negative energy until I felt as if I would pass out from the pressure being exerted. Something must have stopped him from the eternal side, though, because after a minute he released my head. But then as if he had decided to change tactics, I felt the same set of fingers move to my pant's leg, and I watched, as I tried to remain focused on the road, the material rise four inches up my leg from his invisible touch.

Since the children were also with me in the car, I had the thought that I should pray to the children's guardian angels to help me fight him, since this was my battle and had nothing to do with my children, and I needed to get them home. God must have decided to allow a reprieve because, after the prayer, the sensations passed. Later that night I slept well.

I am beginning to realize that a good night's sleep is always a great consolation.

> *"His Majesty will see that it is the gainer, and if He sometimes allows the devil to attack it, his efforts will be brought to confusion."*
> — ST. TERESA OF AVILA

> *"Do not suppose that the trials suffered by those to whom the Lord grants these favours are light ones. No, they are very heavy, and of many kinds."*
> — ST. TERESA OF AVILA

> *"Mara the Tempter, the embodiment of all the evil that plagues the mind, was terrified. He knew that if Siddharta successfully gained enlightenment, the power that delusion holds over the world would be threatened. Traditional texts use very dramatic imagery to depict the events that follow. As Siddhartha sat in meditation, the sons and daughters of Mara—the whole host of demonic interferences—began their attack, trying to disturb his concentration."*
> — JONATHAN LANDAW AND STEPHAN BODIAN

All through July I was to get few other reprieves; dreadful spirits almost never left me alone. They were always close. By late July 2002 there was an added spiritual issue. In the early dawn hours, I would wake up after having vivid nightmares. The nightmares were always accompanied with horrible thoughts.

Once I shied at the thought of having the Lord Jesus inside me spiritually, for Satan produced a vivid nightmare that pierced my mind with a strange image—having Jesus' spirit inside me was going to be like having a space alien living inside me. The dream was horrifying, and the dreadful thought stayed with me throughout the day, until I was able to identify that it came from a demon. A number of prayers allowed me to finally release the appalling concept. Later, St. John of the Cross's referred-to spirit of blasphemy would come to mind to describe this attacker.

During the coming weeks, I was assaulted right and left with filthy thoughts, many regarding my Savior Jesus, whom I thought of constantly. Often, after awaking in the morning I could still feel the arrows that the negative thoughts seemed to produce as they entered into my spirit. My soul was lacerated by their dreadful, sharp ideas. I noticed more and more a direct correlation between the sharp spiritual stings and the scary or blasphemous thoughts produced by the demons.

> *"At other times another abominable spirit, which Isaias calls Spiritus vertiginis is allowed to molest them, not in order that they may fall, but that it may try them. This spirit darkens their senses in such a way that it fills them with numerous scruples and perplexities. So confusing that, as they judge, they can never, by any means, be satisfied concerning them, neither can they find any help for their judgment in counsel or thought. This is one of the severest goads and horrors of this night."*
>
> — ST. JOHN OF THE CROSS

> *"At other times in this night there is added to these things the spirit of blasphemy, which roams abroad, setting in the path of all the conceptions and thoughts of the soul intolerable blasphemies."*
>
> — ST. JOHN OF THE CROSS

"The beast was given a mouth uttering proud boasts and blasphemies, and it was given authority to act for forty-two months. It opened its mouth to utter blasphemies against God, blaspheming his name and his dwelling and those who dwell in heaven." – Revelations 13:5–6

"As a rule these storms and trials are sent by God in this night and purgation of sense to those whom afterwards He purposes to lead into the other night."

> *"Let no one say this: You belong to your father the devil and you willingly carry out your father's desires. He was a murderer from the beginning and does not stand in truth, because there is not truth in him. When he tells a lie, he speaks in character, because he is a liar and the father of lies."*
>
> — JOHN 8:44

"Holy souls sometimes undergo great inward trial, and they know darkness." – Mother Theresa

One beautiful sunshiny morning, I sat in an open grass-filled pasture surrounded by a white post fence, watching my daughter's horseback-riding lesson. She was steering her palomino mount over a course of jumps. Thrilled
when she completed a round, her face was radiant with happiness. I was living in those perfect soaring moments with her. Then from out of nowhere,
because nothing in the scene had changed, nor was there any wind, a hor-
rific, putrid, rotten odor encircled the spot where I was sitting on my lawn
chair—the smell of death, burned flesh, decaying bodies heaped on top of a
mountainous mound of summer-ripened garbage. I couldn't bear to breath. I
wanted to pinch my nostrils shut, although I knew that my physical nose was
not inhaling the obnoxious odor, but my spiritual one. It was the smell of sin,
corruption, and hell itself. In addition to all its other woes, the smell in hell is
horrendous. And there will be no nice perfumes or blooming roses to mask
it. Luckily the desolation lasted only for a couple of moments, then the sweet
smell of the pasture returned. The scent could only have come from one being: the devil. I wondered if he had decided that since I liked the other recent
spiritual fragrances from heaven so much—especially the rose fragrance of
the Blessed Mother, the delicate smell of Easter Lilies from the Holy Spirit,
and the intoxicating aroma of Chrism—that I should experience one from his
hellish domain.

> "Man needs reckless courage to descend into the abyss of himself. In
> actual fact, these demons do not account for the entire subconscious.
> The primal energy of our souls holds a wonderful warmth and welcome
> for us. One of the reasons we were sent onto the earth was to make this
> connection with ourselves, this inner friendship. The demons will haunt
> us, if we remain afraid. All the classical mythical adventures external-
> ize the demons. In battle with them, the hero always grows, ascending
> to new levels of creativity and poise. Each inner demon holds a precious
> blessing that will heal and free you. To receive this gift, you have to lay
> aside your fear and take the risk of loss and change that every inner
> encounter offers."
>
> – JOHN O'DONOHUE

> "Remember that in few of the mansions of this castle are we free from
> struggles with devils."
>
> – ST. TERESA OF AVILA

> "Lewis noted that "when a man is getting better, he understands more
> and more clearly the evil that is still left in him. When a man is get-
> ting worse, he understands his own badness less and less. The more we
> struggle with our bad impulses, the better we know them. The more we

give in to them, the less we understand them. He writes, 'Virtue—even
attempted virtue—brings light, indulgence brings fog.'"

– DR. ARMAND M. NICHOLI, JR

"It is much easier to conquer a country than to conquer ourselves. Every
act of disobedience weakens the spiritual life. It is like a wound letting
out every drop of one's blood."

– MOTHER THERESA

In August 2002, I noticed yet another one of St. John's line-up of ghostly specters. In the coming weeks I was to live through the trials of the dark spirit of perfectionism, a close kin cousin of the spirit of blasphemy and nit-picking. Making me feel I should do more than my strength could handle, and then infusing tremendous guilt into my spirit, if I couldn't finish or perfect a task. And I would feel absolute horror over any signs that I was being even slightly impatient with others. For instance, although I was fasting on bread and water twice a week, dark thoughts came through to begin fasting three days. If I had given in and began fasting for three days, it would then have inspired four.

In my head I listed the demons I had now encountered—the party-spirit demons, the anxiety demon, the blasphemy demon, the nit-picking demon, the perfectionism demon, and last and most awful, the fornicator demon. How many more could there be? Probably seven. There seems to be seven of everything. It didn't take long to find out.

While praying over my rosary beads one night, the demons descended with another rather dreadful desolation. Something felt like it had pulled open the back of my shirt and dropped things onto the skin of my neck. I craned my neck around to make sure that there wasn't anything physically there. There was nothing that I could see. Almost immediately, though, I felt a sensation of multiple legs, larger than bugs, crawling all over my back. Soon they were traveling all over my body. And then some began stinging. A scorpion sting came to mind, because it felt like a needle/stinger went into my spirit and injected it with something like venom.

The demons were trying to distract me from saying my rosary. Perhaps their intention was to have me give up saying rosaries altogether. Fat chance. In fact, they inspired me to never, ever stop saying them.

"Locusts came out of the smoke onto the land, and they were given the same power as scorpions of the earth...There were not allowed to kill them but only to torment them for five months; the torment they inflicted was like that of a scorpion when it stings a person."
Revelations 9:3-6

"If he endures trials for God's sake, His Majesty will give him grace to bear them patiently, and sometimes even to desire them, because he also cherishes a great desire to do something for God."

— ST. TERESA OF AVILA

"Violent storms of hatred arose, but beneath the Bodhi tree, all remained calm. The demonic forces unleashed a barrage of weapons, but they turned into flower petals." – Jonathan Landaw and Stephan Bodian

On an evening in late September 2002, after I had settled into my bed to sleep, I felt a spirit hover and move all around me. I prayed, but the spirit persisted. Somehow, I could tell it was one of the bad ones. I thought back to what had happened earlier that day, remembering that I had worked the lunch shift at Rosie's Place. I wondered if I had picked up another spiritual hitchhiker or if it was possible to take someone else's demons home, like you could catch a cold or a virus from someone else.

Since I kept praying in the dark, and the spiritual energy did not stop, I could tell that this spirit could not read my mind, as some of the good ones seemed to be able to do. Then I had another thought that night, one that resonated for the entire evening. My daughter and my husband had exploded into a running verbal battle earlier. I found myself wondering if I had picked up someone's anger demon at Rosie's and if that dark spirit was playing havoc with Sam and Christina's spirits and darkening their moods. Was an angry demon influencing them?

I had a flashback to February, and how it had seemed that the children had been easily influenced by the evil that I had been battling during my own awakening. In my own mind, I began to really see a connection of how dark spirits can really cause havoc in everyone's lives, especially, it seemed, those who had no formed or living faith in Jesus. In fact, it really seemed like the devil, having lost some of his power over me, was taking great delight in disturbing me by using those closest to me. I became very aware of this particular upsetting trick of his, but there was little I could do about it, since each soul must individually choose to cast him out.

The spirit swirled around, and even though the evening was not particularly cold, my soul felt a great spiritual coldness, and I began to violently, physically shiver like a slab of thick ice rested against the backside of my soul. Finally I gave up trying to sleep. I looked at Sam, who was peacefully snoring, and decided to put on my bedside light and read my Bible. I read two letters from Peter and one from John. I noticed that as soon as I turned on the light and began reading the Word of God, the spirit weakened and left.

At my next spiritual direction session with Sister Margretta, I related the incident to her, and she told me that I should never give it my attention. Its sole aim was to pull my thoughts from God, and it liked it that I was spending time trying to figure it out.

⚜

Almost all the trials of the summer demons had passed by the end of September, and my spirit/soul was healthier than ever before. I had learned that if you could find out their name, you were almost halfway to defeating them. Somehow, since the name accurately described them, you could eliminate the negative elements they brought with them much easier. Rapturous joy ruled my mind and my heart for the next three months until after Christmas 2002—with the exception of a few stray demons that were waiting patiently for their turns.

> "Briefly, in this tempest, there is no help for it but to wait upon the mercy of God, Who suddenly, as the most unlooked-for hour, with a single word, or on some chance occasion, lifts the whole of this burden from the soul, so that it seems as if it has never been clouded over, but is full of sunshine and far happier than it was before."
>
> — ST. TERESA OF AVILA

It was almost the end of October 2002, and I was finishing up Joel's thirty-page pamphlet *Through Death's Gate: A Guide to Selfless Dying*. Thus far you have read many references from this pamphlet because a spiritual journey is similar to the final journey in death. Perhaps, though, my timing of reading it just before Halloween was poor. All the morbid Halloween decorations (which I used to love, by the way) of ghosts, witches, and my personal most scary—vampires—were really affecting my spirit in new and frightening ways. I couldn't wait for November 1st (All Saints Day) to take them all down.

On the night of October 30th, I experienced a difficult spiritual desolation. A spirit descended and began to wrap me up in some horrible spiritual material, something akin to strips. I could feel him moving in a circular motion above me and then below me, around and around, wrapping and covering my spirit. *A mummy*, I thought. *He is trying to bind my spirit in bindings signaling my death.* I couldn't have been more frightened than if I had gotten a deep unblinking stare from the Grim Reaper himself. "Stop," I told him. "Oh, stop." I battled him all night long.

On Halloween morning, I woke up still very sad and overwhelmed. After my early morning meditation of fire, love, and the rush feeling sent from God as a grace, I began to feel happier. Another grace received from God that

morning was the understanding that instead of thinking of last night's demon as trying to make my soul into a mummy, think instead that he had been
sent to preserve it just as the ancients had done with the human remains of
the Egyptians, or even the Lord as they wrapped his body with seventy-five
pounds of special burial preparations after his crucifixion. I wished I would
have thought of that the night before.

On the way to work, as I was driving down our neighborhood street, I
looked up and saw the most magnificent cloud formation. It looked exactly
like a big arrow. As I drove a little further, I saw the tip of the cloud arrow.
When I looked up for the third time, the arrow tip had grown a beautiful
rainbow, which was extending out from it. There had lately been so many
stings and difficult trials that God wanted to send the message that all trials
(symbolized by the arrow cloud) eventually end in beautiful rainbows.

As I sat in a bit of traffic along 3A, I continuously admired the beautiful
handiwork of God the Father. As I looked at the other drivers, I noticed that
no one seemed to be staring at the sky. So unfortunate, because they totally
missed this wonderful gift from the Creator. I knew that the arrow and rainbow were signs of God's love, and my body vibrated in unity with God as I
praised Him for the beautiful sign. God had been sending me some incredible rainbows to signal the end of some of my spiritual storms, just as He sent
Noah that same sign when the flood came to an end. I had passed another
portion of the purging on my spiritual journey—I fervently hoped that at
least some of the dark night of my soul was over.

When I later meditated about Mary and her saying "yes" to God, I realized that in a way the spiritual journey and eventual union with God can only
come after we say "yes." What she physically did, we can do spiritually, mentally, and emotionally, so that God can come into our souls and make us holy.
We can all become like Mary.

> "One day my Lord said to me: 'Believe me, my daughter, trials are the
> heaviest for those my father loves the best.' Trials are God's measure of
> love. How could I better demonstrate my love for you than by desiring
> for you what I desired for myself.'"
>
> — ST. TERESA OF AVILA

> "It is not oppressed for example, by the fear of hell, though it desires
> more than ever not to offend God (of Whom, however, it has lost all
> servile fear), it has firm confidence that it is destined to have fruition
> of Him."
>
> — ST. TERESA OF AVILA

"As for me, given a choice I would always choose the way of suffering, not just because it allows me to imitate the way of Jesus, but because it brings many other blessings with it. We cannot understand how suffering can be a grace and how great a blessing it is until we have left all things for the sake of Jesus."

— ST. TERESA OF AVILA

A chilly evening in November 2002 offered a sudden dawning that would change my mental state. I often wondered why from time to time I had become depressed. Upon further scrutiny, I realized that these were the times when I had stepped away from God. The reason for my self-isolation varied with each situation. Sin or pride or anger had caused me to separate myself from a close relationship with Him in shame, and I realized now that my soul had been very unset about being separated from God. My choices had overridden what my soul knew and had caused me to do things that were incompatible with God's law.

Now as God drew nearer and nearer, I recognized the intense joy, peace, and happiness that was totally the opposite of those other times. It came to me that unless your soul is happy, then your body and mind can only be "happy" momentarily, and then you will again feel that deep hunger for happiness. When you feel that hunger finally beginning to ease, it feels like heaven on earth.

After my desolations returned in 2003, I noticed that they were of a totally different nature than before. Whereas in 2002 they were all about changing me, straightening me out, and perfecting my spirit, in 2003 all the demons I sensed emerged from others and places around me. As if the devil, sensing that my soul was too strong for him because of my alliance to the Lord, decided to act through others in such a way as to really hurt me. Instead of his usual way, he needed to take a different tactic. The worst part—the other people are never aware that the devil was using them. This continues on to the present time.

Actually, this ability to discern others' demons, as well as my own, is a charismatic spiritual gift called, oddly enough, discernment of spirits. God decided to throw it into the mix. I know that God knows that I would really rather have preferred the gift of healing. Oh, to be able to walk into a children's hospital and cure every little boy and girl of their illnesses. Now that is a GIFT! But, alas, God has given me this one instead.

Toward the end of this section are my experiences of the ghosts that I have encountered. It was really a toss-up as to which were worst—the demons or the ghosts. Is it any wonder that I remain in prayer almost continually, with all the evil spirits I encountered on a daily basis, or that I have begged my family and friends to go back to church and to begin to follow God and His law more closely? What would you do if you were me?

"St. John of the Cross tells us that the purification of the spirit usually takes place after the purification of the senses. The night of the senses being over, the soul for some time enjoys, according to this eminent authority the sweet delights of contemplation; then, perhaps, when least expected the second night comes, far darker and far more miserable than the first, and this is called by him the purification of the spirit, which means the purification of the interior faculties, the intellect and the will. The temptations which assail the soul in this state are similar in their nature to those which afflict souls in the illuminative way, only more aggravated, because felt more keenly; and the withdrawal of the consolations of the spirit which they have already experienced in their greatest affliction." – Online Catholic Encyclopedia; New Advent Web site; State or Way (Purgative, Illuminative, Unitive)

One evening in January, as I was getting ready to leave the office, while in the ladies room I felt the strong pull sensation signaling a switch to an alternative consciousness (just like someone had flipped a light switch on or off in my brain). The feeling was so strong that I thought I was going to pass out. I could barely stay focused in the physical dimension, and I felt like I was being drawn away from it. When I fought back and refocused my attention back to our regular physical world, the center of my forehead throbbed, and I was left feeling weak, slightly nauseous, and afraid to drive home lest I get drawn back into that different consciousness again. The general feeling was really awful, so I could not imagine that it came from God.

So uncomfortable was it that I couldn't help but think of the devil pulling me away from the here and now. Perhaps he was angry that today was the night I was to present my ideas for the Easter craft fair to the other CCD teachers and my students. I had drawn up all sorts of plans and was feeling so excited about how we could get everyone energized about the Lord with a craft fair and a mystical prayer maze based on St. Teresa of Avila's *Interior Castle.* Surely the Lord would want me to present my ideas to the students and parents.

By the time 7:00 p.m. had rolled around and I was at St. Paul's surrounded by my fellow teachers and all the students, the feeling had passed, and I was again filled with joy and enthusiasm. I pitched the idea in high spirits and the night ended on a high with all of the positive feedback.

But this positive aura would only be temporary, for the Lord would allow me to experience more before this was over.

> *"The gates of hell will not prevail, as the Lord has said. But that doesn't mean we are exempt from the trials from and battles against the evil one."*
>
> — POPE JOHN PAUL II

Wednesday, February 5, 2003.

After an evening spent listening and taking notes in my MBA Microeconomics class, I drove home. The classroom had been full, with all thirty-six of us evening MBA students dutifully taking notes on the supply and demand curves of individual companies. Our desks rose up in four rows and curved around the lector stand, table, and overhead screen where the professor was lecturing. As I drove back home on Route 128 at 65 mph, I put on my Godspell CD, turned the volume up high, and sang along in an effort to stay awake. Upon pulling into the driveway, exhaustion hit me hard, so I headed straight to bed. Unfortunately, as soon as I had myself comfortably settled in bed ready to enter dreamland, I had the very strong feeling of an evil spirit. The spirit was with me for quite a while before my prayers dissolved its presence.

The next morning I awoke feeling totally despondent, like nothing I ever do will ever make any difference to anyone. All day long my thoughts lingered on the spirit as I tried to figure out the cause behind its visit. Until, that is, my inner vision showed me a picture of my economics professor, and then I began to wonder if the demon had been pursuing or bothering him, and for some reason had decided to hitchhike home with me instead. That's exactly what it felt like had happened after catching the professor's negative vibes. For the Professor had appeared very agitated and troubled. As he was working through the homework problems on the chalkboard, he interjected stories of how miserable he was and that maybe he should just commit suicide. His tone was teasing, but I for one did not buy into his lightness. Why even joke about suicide in front of a classroom of strangers? He related that he had recently been divorced, and that the divorce had been particularly nasty. He mentioned his loneliness more than a couple of times and how difficult it was to find a date. Jokingly, he pointed to the bald spot on the top of his head and asked the class if this was why.

Whatever I took home from class last night seemed to produce this awful, unhappy next day. His demon must have been one of despair/depression/hopelessness. My poor professor, I will send him my prayers.

"For example, one spirit revealed itself to be 'misery,' and that it entered the lady's life when she was raped as a teenager. There is usually some event that allows spirits legal entry into a person's life, such as drugs, alcohol, wrongful sexual activity, Occultist or satanic involvement, witchcraft, new age, false religions, and acts of abuse of violence committed against the person." – In the Manual For Conducting Truth Encounters; on the Demon Possession Web site

Sunday, February 9, 2003.

Close family friends joined us one evening for a leisurely dinner at Saporitos in Hull, MA. Saporitos was a tiny, fashionable restaurant serving mainly Northern Italian food about a ¼ mile from Nantasket Beach. Sam and I had dined there several times and had always enjoyed our meals. That evening over dinner and wine, we discussed a lot of topics, including religion. At one point I remember relating that I was reading a wonderful book called *In Search of Divine Reality*. When my friend asked me how I happened to come across such a book, I related parts of my awakening and spiritual journey. The dinner was lovely, but as was lately the case, my friend drank too much. At least my friend's spouse did not match her drink for drink, thank goodness, since he needed to drive them both home that night.

When my friend drinks she gets very giddy, and I couldn't help feeling sad that it takes a quantity of wine to make her feel good. She seemed overall well and happy, but her drinking has lately become upsetting. I had two glasses myself (one too many), so I didn't feel really well when I went to bed.

After a brief sleep, I was awakened and something drew my eyes to the velveteen beige flowered couch in the corner of my bedroom. There was a large, pulsating black shape sitting on the sofa. Then I remembered with relief that the shape was just my maroon bathrobe. Still, for some reason the image remained very disturbing. For one thing, it was much, much larger than my bathrobe should have been and it was growing larger all the time. Inflating before my very eyes, it almost seemed like the bathrobe was stuffed with balloons that someone was inflating, blowing more and more air into them. I kept closing my eyes and starting to drift off only to open them again on this image. I must have done this twenty times and thought every time that I should just go and hang up the bathrobe in the closet, but I couldn't bring myself to go near it. Finally, I fell back asleep around 4:00 a.m. When

I opened my eyes two hours later and looked again at the sofa, the bathrobe was still there and had returned to its normal size, and I could clearly see the sofa around it this time. The bathrobe was no longer making the sofa seem black.

That morning, I awoke with a subtle sadness, not my usual bubbly self. I remembered the black area on the sofa. I knew then that it had been a demon—my friend's—and because I had had a little too much to drink myself, God had allowed it to spend the night on my sofa as an ominous presence. I vowed that I would never have more than one drink again. Inhabiting people who use too much alcohol, it blinds them to its very negative impacts on their lives and the others around them.

> "Enter through the narrow gate; for the gate is wide and the road broad that leads to destruction, and those who enter through it are many. How narrow the gate and constricted the road that leads to life. And those who find it are few."
>
> – MATTHEW 7:13–14

Very early one Friday morning in May, as I lay on my side of our queen-sized bed, I felt a spirit hovering over my right side. The spirit seemed to be moving back and forth in a rocking fashion. Along with the energy movement, I went in and out of intensely overwhelming heat periods. My fear rose to terror level. I jumped out of bed and started the morning upset and trying to get past the fear. Several days later I remembered I had boasted in my mind earlier that night that Satan was not that hard to defeat. This visit seemed to be a chastisement or a humbling—a way to stop me from getting cocky. It was as if God was waving His finger at me back and forth as if to point out not to get too overconfident, for only Jesus can defeat our demons or the devil; we are powerless on our own.

After Mass one Sunday in May I went up to the lectionary at the altar of St. Paul's to do a trial reading. I was planning on joining the reading ministry in honor of St. Irene (as I had mentioned in the pre-awakening chapters), and a trial reading was a necessary part of the process. There I saw Eileen and Tim Lawsome. Eileen invited me to come to a faith sharing after Mass for her baptismal group and to help a cancer victim. Since both children had gone home with Sam, and I had no plans after Mass, I was happy to go.

We all walked up to the parish house where the baptismal meeting was being held. The parish house sits on a hill with magnificent statues of the Virgin Mother and the Risen Lord in the backyard. Once the home of a convent of nuns, sadly, since it had been unoccupied for so long, it had fallen into a state of disrepair. Lately, though, as more and more St. Paul parish functions began to take place there, it had slowly, little by little, been repaired and brightened. The baptismal group settled into the four main front rooms and the kitchen, which were furnished with comfortable, gently used furniture that had been donated by parishioners.

At the session I heard Art Boyle speak on his Medjugorje healing experience. Art had been miraculously healed from cancer after his trip to Medjugorje. Art was almost a celebrity, having been on numerous talk shows relating his amazing healing. It was wonderful to finally meet the Boyles after hearing so much about their story. After Art's talk ended, Eileen introduced me to Katy, who had been battling breast cancer. Judy Boyle was giving advice to Katy from her heart after having shared Art's experience. I listened, as I did not want to interrupt until Judy was finished, and then I added a few comments to Katy. It was obvious she was very depressed over her cancer and searching for ways to mentally cope with the illness as she searched for stronger faith. She seemed so lost. As I was getting ready to leave, I asked her if she knew how to pray the rosary. She said she did, but then I asked her if she had ever heard of the first Saturday Devotions to the Blessed Mother. She admitted she hadn't.

On inspiration, I quickly drove home to get my rosary booklet showing the first Saturday Devotion to the Blessed Mother to give to her. I knew that if she completed the devotion she would be under the Blessed Mother's protection should she die from cancer. As I scooped up my booklet from my top dresser drawer, my eyes fell on my own rosary beads. Pope John Paul II had blessed them from his balcony in Vatican City during Sam and my honeymoon trip to Europe. Sam and I had been to nine countries in sixteen days, and Rome, Italy, had been the last destination. It was a very special set of rosary beads that I treasured and had used to pray the rosary over the past couple of years.

I shed a tear because I was very attached to the set of beads, but I grabbed them anyway and quickly drove back to the parish house. I handed them to Katy along with the pamphlet on the first Saturday Devotion to the Blessed Mother. I just knew that this special devotion would really help her. The rosary beads were something I loved so it made a connection between us, and I promised to pray for her.

On Monday night/early Tuesday morning, May 27th, at 4:40 a.m. I awoke to a feeling of nausea. Peeling my eyes open, I found the room spinning. Negative energy swirled all around me trying to get into my spirit. I had a very strong feeling that the energy had to do with Katy, and I prayed fervently throughout the spiritual attack. The nausea and vertigo must be side effects of the many cancer treatments Katy was undergoing. Another uncomfortable thought occurred to me. I remembered there was a scene from the *Exorcist* where the room had spun. Someone had once told me that; I had never had the courage to see the movie myself. I prayed and eventually after three-quarters of an hour later, the feeling dissipated and left.

The next day during morning meditation, and another intense negative spiritual night where I prayed for hours and drifted in and out of sleep, I woke up thinking again of Katy, and I wondered if God had sent her to me to heal. Not in a physical way, perhaps, but in a spiritual way. Because I have become spiritually strong, I was able to take on her oppressive spirits to ease her burden, since right now she was weak and needed help. I began to feel like her spiritual warrior.

Perhaps God was giving me another charisma—healing souls through prayer. I told the Lord I was open to receiving it. After all, if I couldn't have the charisma of miraculous healing, then this one was the next best thing. A sudden inspiration lit my mind; when someone is awakened, then it becomes that person's job to support, love, and fight for all people so that all might feel God's love through the awakened soul.

> "For, as I said a little way back, perfect souls are in no way repelled by trials, but rather desire them and pray for them and love them. They are like soldiers: the more wars there are, the better they are pleased, because they hope to emerge from them with the greater riches. If there are no wars, they serve for their pay, but they know they will not get very far on that."
>
> — ST. TERESA OF AVILA

> "A great wrong, or a great trial, may cause them some momentary distress, but they will hardly have felt it when reason will intervene, and will seem to raise its standard aloft, and drive away their distress by giving them the joy of seeing how God has entrusted them with the opportunity of gaining, in a single day, more lasting favours and graces in His Majesty's sight than they could gain in ten years by means of trials which they sought on their own account. This, as I understand (and I have talked about it with many contemplatives), is quite usual, and I know for a fact that it happens. Just as other people prize gold and jewels, so these persons prize and desire trials, for they know quite well that trials will make them rich."
>
> — ST. TERESA OF AVILA

Sam and I drove to Mohegan Sun Casino in Connecticut in January 2004. Sam, who has always loved to occasionally play a game of blackjack, had talked me into going with him. It was a special treat that I was doing just for him. When we arrived at the casino, Sam headed straight to the blackjack tables to try his luck. I am not an avid gambler. I can barely stand the thought of losing any money that could be put to better use, but I allowed myself $25 to play the slots. I looked around at the massive, noisy, crowded room—the lights flashing and the backs of all the people intently staring at the mesmerizing twirl of the spinning wheels. It was not at all my kind of place, but marriage causes us to compromise what we would really like to make our spouses happy—at least occasionally.

For a while I wandered through the aisles of machines, hoping that one would draw me. Eventually, I found one that seemed like a good choice to start. I inserted my quarter and started playing a game of video poker. Very soon after I started, I drew a hand of an almost perfect straight flush. I was missing only one card. Then from behind my back, I felt a spiritual stab urging me to spin the wheels again. Something was giving me a heads up that this machine would be lucky for me and so I should just give it a try. So I pulled the handle down and the right card popped into place and I won. The spirit behind my back knew what was coming up next.

I collected my coins and turned them in. That had felt too much like cheating. And I didn't want to owe some anonymous gambler demon even the price of a cup of coffee. Later in bed at home, as soon as I lay down, I felt the strong feeling of a spirit at my back. It hovered around my legs and face while I lay on my back. I prayed myself to sleep.

❦

Upon awaking in the wee hours of the next morning, I noticed a spiritual presence laying heavily on me. As it touched my spirit, it warmed me and I went numb, similar to that of my meditations. I thought it amazing that the spirit's presence could feel so heavy but not disturb anything, just the blankets. This was the first time that I can ever remember that I was totally unafraid. This spirit was not at all frightening, whereas before I was always afraid, bordering on terrified. But I know now he must have been sent to Sam instead of me. I drifted off to sleep. Later that morning, Sam mentioned that he was taking the kids to Fire Island in the next week and would probably miss my birthday. Since this was the third time in four years that he had decided to take the children to Fire Island while I stayed home and worked over my birthday, I grew upset. For the last three years I had accepted that I would be alone on my birthday, but this birthday I got angry and had such a crying bout that I had to redo my makeup three times before I could leave to go to the office. I guess the situation just made me feel totally unloved and unimportant, not so much because of the presents and cake, but because I would be alone. I felt bad for even caring about my birthday; after all, what is the big deal anyway? Just think of all the kids who never even have a birthday at all. It was probably just another part of myself that needed to die—the child in me that still enjoyed birthdays.

Also, I recognized that some of the anger was due to the fact that I felt Sam owed me something nice for having cared for him as well as everyone else for two months during his back injury of the past spring, and I wouldn't dream of missing any of their birthdays.

After I left for the office, I wondered about the spirit again. I had just experienced a very difficult, upsetting morning, and I knew enough to connect the spirit to the experience. It hit me sometime later, and I knew exactly what demon it was—insensitivity and selfishness. I had felt it but had not been threatened by it since it never before had any power over me. It must have targeted Sam. I was sorry that I had given the demon the satisfaction of upsetting me. Next year, I would remember that he might crop up again and work out arrangements in June so that he would not be able to spoil another birthday.

Sam and the children did depart for Fire Island and were gone on my birthday, but in order to make the best of it, I decided to take a friend to dinner (somewhat of a birthday present to myself). I picked a friend that I knew could use a pick-me-up. She was lately so down on her life that I thought she might enjoy getting out. She was a single mother of two teenaged daughters whose husband had been abusive, but who had also passed away about eight years ago, leaving her a single mother.

I am afraid that our dinner, unfortunately, was not a success. I tried to bring up all the things that she normally liked to talk about, but she wasn't biting. I knew that she had had several profound spiritual experiences, and I thought that it might be fun to compare notes. However, I quickly realized, as she bluntly told me so, that for some reason she really, really did not want to talk about them. I found that odd, since it had always been my experience that you want to tell everyone how wonderful God is and how full of joy you are since finding Him. Cutting me short, she basically said that the experience was private and that she didn't want to share it—in essence that it was none of my business.

Later I found myself questioning whether she had found God or something else because something did not ring true—there was no joy or evident love in her voice when we spoke of the subject. I worried about her. In fact, at one point she got angry at me after she finished her meal, and as I was paying the bill, and stormed out of the restaurant without waiting for me. I had to run after her since we had taken her car, which struck me as very rude.

That night, as I was trying to put the disturbing evening behind me, I laid in my bed hoping to relax. The spirit that came that night had a very strong presence. I speculated that the spirit had something to do with my friend's sadness and anger that had somehow been displaced toward me that evening. Perhaps it was her dead husband hanging around. Something had obviously been bothering her.

So I spent the time praying for her. The spirit felt very oppressive.

> *"Ha! What have you to do with us, Jesus of Nazareth? Have you come to destroy us? I know who you are—the Holy One of God!" Jesus rebuked him and said, "Be quiet! Come out of him!"*
>
> — LUKE 4:34–35

The next day one of my office co-workers talked me into giving a party for the office saying that since I had just put on a new addition to the house, I should want to show it off. I had an uneasy feeling about the party, but I ignored it. I have always had a very hard time saying N-O. But I now know that the smartest thing I could have done with that suggestion was to say no. The day started out gloomy, with drizzle and periods of rain throughout the morning; I shrugged my shoulders at the weather. *Oh well,* I thought. I already made a decision and I knew that I wouldn't change my mind.

Earlier that morning on my way into work, I noticed that the cross over St. Jerome's Church in Weymouth looked unique—it resembled a sword. For the first time I noticed a bar below the cross, and the bar and the long pole were fully illuminated, but the cross high above blended into the sky. I noticed this but did not place any special significance to it. But the sword was clearly a sign to me, I would realize later. I was to be handed a sword, which I was going to feel compelled to use later the next week. Never would I have guessed how things would turn out from such an innocent event as an informal barbeque office party.

Luckily the weather miraculously cleared by party time, an answer to prayer. After I turned the corner onto Kilby Street, I saw a beautiful mini-rainbow. It was a sure sign that God was going to be present at the party, and that He was going to help in some way.

The main part of the party was a great success. I had laid out the crochet set and challenged the earliest co-workers to a match. Then Kevin, a co-worker who I am particularly fond of, started the grill, and we cooked hamburgers, hot dogs, and barbequed chicken. The twenty people who had come all had great fun and so did I ... until we neared the late evening. Only one time at the beginning of the party did I have an uneasy feeling. That had been when one co-worker came to the door carrying two quarts of vodka; however, I dismissed the thought. I shouldn't have done that, because he along with one of the women—two people I know least well—got drunk.

At 11:00 p.m. there were only two others besides them left. Drunk and amorous, although the man is married, the two locked themselves in our recreation room. The first two times this happened, I just knocked on the door with an excuse to come clean up the room, but by the third time I grew uneasy and uncomfortable and decided that it was time for them to leave. When I confronted the man, saying that it was getting late and we all have to work tomorrow, he replied saying that I could feel free to go upstairs to bed, and he would lock up.

His statement horrified me. Fat chance. Afraid that I would not be able to get them to leave, I enlisted the other couple to persuade them to stay for one final game of pool and then guide them out the door.

Interestingly enough, David and Sandi, the nice couple, were not even supposed to come. Sandi and I had instantly hit it off as soon as we met. I could recognize God's presence in her. I believe God had sent them along to keep me safe because He knew what Hal and Etta had been planning all along. I breathed a massive sigh of relief as I leaned against the door.

Even after they had left, through, the night was by no means over. As I went around the house picking up plastic cups, washing the floor, and cleaning up from the party, I noticed a car parked in my front yard then, almost simultaneously, noises echoing from the back of the house. I thought I had checked the street for cars after everyone had left, but I either missed it or else they had come back. That really frightened me, and thinking that maybe it was Hal and Etta trying to get back into the house, I didn't hesitate calling the police. When the police arrived and noticed that the car was sticking out on a blind corner, they decided to tow it.

Meanwhile, at 2:30 a.m., Etta and Hal, having gone off to a bar or a motel, came back to look for the car. I talked to them from an open window on the second story in answer to their pounding on my front door. No way was I going to let them in. I mentioned that they might look for their car at the police station. Thankfully, after that they left.

The next morning Etta came back alone looking for her wallet. She had left it in the recreation room and after everyone left I had found it. I noticed that she was all banged up on her legs with several large cuts. She said she had fallen on the rocks of one of the beach jetties. She left, and I got ready to go into work. All day that Friday I was in a state of semi-shock, really upset and wondering how I was going to ever work with those two again. I got through the weekend okay.

But by Monday I was so tense in the office that I thought I would explode. I asked my friend Greg to take a walk with me at lunch so that I could talk it out. His advice was to let it all blow over. But my conscience would not grant me that. I knew that I should do the hard, right thing to try and help Hal face his problems.

By Tuesday afternoon, still very upset and tense, I decided to go downstairs to see someone from HR. I told the whole story to one of the management staff, and they launched an investigation. Due to the fact that Hal was my boss's boss and Etta was a co-worker, and their actions had sexual overtones, the company knew that it was possible I could file a suit. Of course, I had no intentions of doing so. After talking to the HR vice president, I felt relieved, almost light-hearted. On Wednesday, my boss also got involved. I mentioned to him that I was working through something and was trying my best to re-solve it and to please trust me. He told me that he absolutely did trust me and that he would help in any way that he could.

All the rest of that week internal tension mounted within me. But I trusted in God that the problem had been given to me to solve for a reason, and that someday something good would come of it. This was my prayer as I went on vacation with my family to Busch Gardens, Charleston, SC, the Outer Banks, NC., and Chineteque Is., Virginia. I left the whole problem in God's very ca-pable hands, knowing that HR would finish the investigation and have some feedback for me. I was not looking forward to coming back, but I knew that I must, that I was needed there.

Ten days later on a Tuesday morning I went back to the office. I talked to the HR vice president early in the day to get an update. She had finished the investigation and had interviewed four people. She talked to Hal for four hours on Friday afternoon (the day I left for vacation). At first he wanted to lie to her, and he ended up storming out. But when he came back he was ready to tell the truth, and their talk really blew his mind. The next week both Hal's boss and the HR staff member sat with him again to give him a checklist of items he would need to stick to. Hal really had a hard time accepting any-thing they said. It was obviously a very painful experience for him. I thought about all this and wondered why. Something ominous occurred to me—pos-session. His very blindness and non-acceptance were clues. It was like he had a giant blind spot about himself. He really had no idea when he got drunk, and the spirit took him over, what came over him. He had no memory. I fervently hoped that somehow he would overcome his spiritual problem, that the whole incident would remove the blinders from his eyes so that he could see himself clearly. I think that what he eventually saw was hard for him to accept. I finally understood why God had wanted to be at the party and what He had hoped to accomplish through it. He was guiding me to help this one man overcome his enormous spiritual issue.

I too learned from the incident. I learned that all Christians are asked to carry crosses. I had been asked to carry the cross of Hal to help him get back on the right road. It struck me forcibly that God really loves Hal that he is one of God's children also, but he was traveling the wrong way. My job was to steer him back.

> *"We can only help a person transform his or her negative seeds if we are patient and kind."*
>
> —THICH NHAT HANH

Ghosts, disembodied human souls, who become attached to places are the final spirit type to cover. In the gospels, Jesus says to Thomas when He appears to His apostles after His resurrection that He is not a ghost. "Come and put your hands in my hand and your fingers into my wounds." With his statement He confirms that ghosts do indeed exist. I can positively confirm this is true. From my own experiences ghosts inhabit most old structures and many not so old ones. The question is not "if" but "why."

I believe there are several reasons for the "why" of ghosts. Were their souls so laden with sin that they were like balloons without helium, or just so deflated that they could not rise above this present day life? Were they lost in a limbo after death, but recognized their old earthy home, and not knowing what else to do stayed? Perhaps they were so attached to their homes or places of work that they simply refused to go. Were their hearts only in love with possessions such as homes or their own earthly achievement, leaving little room in their hearts for God? Whatever the reason, ghosts are stuck and frustrated spirits, lost and sometimes very angry.

Since my awakening, I have many times felt them in hotels or motels where I am staying overnight, or old mansions where I might be touring, and even places associated with famous people who have died. I am always so sad for them. They need my help and yours. On a Christmas tour of three Newport mansions on a cold, raw day in December one year, amidst the bright festive decorations, the ghosts seemed to lurk everywhere. I could feel them through my skin, touching me, wanting to communicate with me. I could only pray for them, while my imagination conjured up their vivid images. Who they were is anyone's guess. Was one a Vanderbilt daughter forced into an unhappy marriage for money? Or an Astor son who died young in one of the wars? Or one of the original brilliant businessmen of the family, trying to keep his arms around the money he had earned in this life? How futile.

When visiting the JFK Library in Boston to see a show featuring Jackie O's wedding dress, her engagement ring, and her wedding photos, I noticed a strong presence near the wedding dress on the ground floor level. While examining the exhibits and pictorial displays in their glass cases, I wandered around enjoying myself. I noticed the spiritual presence and said a prayer for it, but then just kept walking. It followed me around; every once and a while, it poked me in the back to tell me it was still with me. Since I gave up the possibility of ever trying to contact the spirits of the dead when I had made my choice after the ESP class, I did not even try. But who could it be but either JFK himself or Jackie O? What other ghost would be chained to this particular museum to wander the halls looking at past glories of the Kennedy earthly life? If it was him, I wanted to remind him to look toward the light, to call on Jesus, as he should very well know since he was Roman Catholic. After about an hour, finished with viewing the displays, I exited the museum and walked back to my car in the bright sunshine, a little sadder.

One February our family was again on a ski vacation—this time to Lake Placid, NY. On the last night of the trip, we were all seated at a round table in the middle of a crowded, family-style restaurant. The children were happily reading menus deciding among the appetizer and meal choices, and Sam was reminding them that they had better order only what they could eat.

As I was looking at my own menu, I became increasingly uncomfortable because from under our table I was getting bombarded with dozens of sharp spiritual stabs to my lower legs. I desperately wanted to excuse myself, go back to the hotel room, and forget about dinner. But I knew that such a possibility was out of the question, since everyone was starving and I could give no good explanation as to why I needed to leave. So I endured it realizing all the while that some demon was below trying with all his might to make me unhappy, uncomfortable, and if possible to get me to leave my family and the restaurant.

Eventually, the ghost left us alone after realizing that I was not going to budge no matter how much he stabbed me. Such encounters always left me to wonder if some unfortunate deceased soul was somehow trapped, in this case in a restaurant, and was begging me to help release him or her. This would be another version of hell, I thought. It occurred to me later to wonder if this person had been a glutton in his or her life—eating everything in sight, and possibly even depriving others at the same time. Imagine spending eternity trapped in a restaurant watching other people enjoy scrumptious dinners. "Must have been a big problem," I said to myself, "for them to end up in such a sad afterlife state." There was nothing I could do but pray, so I did. I prayed continuous rosaries all the way through dinner asking if God wouldn't help this unhappy spirit in whatever way might be necessary.

Later, back at the hotel room, as I lay on the hard firm mattress of the hotel bed, I could feel what I believed was the same ghost touching, stabbing, and causing discomfort not just to my legs but also all over my body. Again, I prayed through the experience. Then it did an even more disturbing thing; it reached over to my daughter and touched her. In her half-sleeping state, she asked me if I had just put my hand on her shoulder. I said no, that it was just her imagination—only, of course, I knew it wasn't. I left the double bed that I shared with Sam and persuaded Patrick to move in next to his dad. Next I grabbed my crucifix and Bible and slide under the covers next to Christina. I arranged the crucifix and Bible on the mattress between us and prayed to the Virgin Mother to send Christina's guardian angel back to work.

The rest of our vacation went rather seamlessly, but after I returned home I had a few more difficult nights of evil spirits/negative spiritual energy, then another break. I wondered if the negative side had become strong because I was unable to go to church during our vacation. Not because I didn't want to go, but on Sunday, our first day of vacation, Sam was dying to get on the slopes. Since we only had one car, I had to accept that church wasn't possible that Sunday.

During a family vacation week in Maine in the middle of summer 2003, I was laying in a rather hard bed in one of the two bedrooms of our rented cottage in Belfast, ME. The week offered us a wonderful exploration of the Maine countryside, swimming in the resort pool, and eating lobsters on weathered harbor piers. However, the nights were a different story. Every night I felt a ghost come and descend. In fact, there must have been more than one, because I could feel them all around me. But the Holy Spirit was also there, and He filled my soul with His fire. Several times during the week I awoke to feel a spirit trying to enter my spirit, so I placed my Bible and crucifix on my chest and prayed the Jesus prayer over and over. The ghosts were frightened off by Jesus' name. I could feel them traveling away from me—leaving my chest area and going down my legs and then nothing.

Two nights the ghosts brought several dreams. Some scary. Others beautiful, like an angel made up for it by providing a beautiful compensation dream.

One night the evil spirit sent a horrible dream about vampires. Any dream about vampires scares me to death. Somehow I am sure the demons know this weakness. .

In the other nightmare, there were snakes upon snakes slithering over my skin, in my hair, in my clothing. Although I rather like real snakes, especially the harmless New England garden snakes, and have had many as pets in the summers over the course of my childhood, these particular serpents had the ability to crawl into my skin. My skin was transparent, so I could see the snakes were crawling underneath it, weaving around my legs, stomach, and arms. It was rather gruesome.

⁂

On our first night in Charleston, during a family vacation to the Outer Banks and Chincoteague Island the following summer (shortly after that office party fiasco), I noticed spiritual presences as I went to bed. The Charleston spirit felt like a man who was in an aroused (sexually) state. Supposedly this particular hotel was inhabited by the ghost of General Grant. Gross, I thought, as the spirit made a real pest of himself as soon as I got into bed. "Don't you know that you have been dead for hundreds of years?" I told him. "Get away from me." I sure knew what had been his favorite sinful pastime in life.

The Outer Bank's spirit was the least scary of the three, though I don't remember any specifics. The Chincoteague Island ghost was by far the worst. Earlier that night, God had sent a beautiful rainbow right over the wild ponies of the island—along with an incredibly striking sunset. It was like He didn't want me to miss seeing the ponies. I had asked Him to let us at least spot them for Christina. I thought that she would be sad if she didn't see at least one. The entire evening had been especially wonderful, finding a beautiful place to stay for the night, driving through the park, seeing the scenery, ponies, the rainbow, mini-golf (I even won a free ice cream cone), and a tasty dinner. We were even able to get Christina a souvenir. It had been a perfect final evening to vacation.

Until, of course, I was woken up by the ghost of the inn where we were staying. The feeling he or she invoked was overwhelmingly oppressive and unhappy. I woke up around 4:00 a.m., and the ghost was with me. Instantly I became nauseous. Pulling myself back into a conscious state, I could feel it crawling all over me. The bad dream it had delivered hovered in my mind. I felt my head swim and feared that whoever it was tried very hard to shift me back into sleep. I thought I would pass out.

Clutching my rosary beads, I started praying the Divine Mercy chaplet and then the rosary. Like magic, after I finished the rosary, I felt blessed peace and was able to go back to sleep.

> *"But oh, when we come to interior sufferings! If these could be described, they would make all physical sufferings seem very slight, but it is impossible to describe interior sufferings and how they happen."*
>
> — ST. TERESA OF AVILA

Now I am very happy to say we are leaving the demons, evil spirits, and the ghosts behind. We are ready to move on to the final destination, the end of the spiritual journey—the gift of the sight of God in all three Persons, given to all who remain on course.

20

THE TRIUNE GOD

Vision Beyond All Visions
Hope Of All Christians Realized
Joy Unbounded
Sight Of The Eternal Kingdom

"Men have not become Trappists merely out of a hope for peace in the next world; something has told them, with unshakable conviction, that the next world begins in this world and that heaven can be theirs now, very truly, even though imperfectly."

— THOMAS MERTON

"The aim of spiritual life is to "die before you die" and like Muhammad, to ascent to the intimacy with God which he has withheld from angels and yet granted to his servants and lovers." – Quote from the thirteenth-century Sufi poet, Jalaluddin Rumi

"Those who have their minds chiefly fixed on God and their attention turned, either always or very frequently, to Him. It is the union with God by love and the actual experience and exercise of that love. It is called the 'unitive' way because it is by love that the soul is united to God. 'He who is joined to the Lord, is one spirit.' In every circumstance of their lives the supernatural motive which ought to guide their actions is ever present to their mind, and the actions are performed under its inspiration with a force of will which makes their accomplishment easy and even delightful." – New Advent Web site; Online Catholic Encyclopedia

Pope Leo XIII – "Besides, by grace God abides in the just soul as in a temple, in a most intimate and singular manner. From this follows that the bond of charity by which the soul adheres most closely to God, more than it could adhere to the most loving and beloved friend, and enjoys God in all fullness and sweetness. Now this wonderful union, which I properly called the indwelling and differs only by reason of our condition or state from that in which God embraces and beatifies the citizens of heaven, is most certainly produced by the divine presence of the whole Trinity: 'We will come to him and make our abode in him." (Jn 14:23)

Overpowering and bringing my body near to the point of death are good adjectives to describe the strenuous, Mount Everest-type "dead of night" spiritual trials I experienced in July and August 2003. The Holy Spirit, in order to make the final preparations to my soul for the greatest gift given to a Christian—the possession of the soul by the Beloved—was working every night on my soul. St. Teresa of Avila says it best: "It is God who does all," She emphasized that He "remakes me." He had been at His job of "remaking" my soul for the past year and a half, sending numerous trials, spirits, and specters of all types, along with beauty beyond my wildest imagination. Now only the final difficult finishing touches needed to be added.

One night He descended and lay atop me, allowing His weight to become a blanket on top of me—His spiritual weight much heavier than the air. On the next night, instead of just the weight, I also experienced an all body pressure on the spiritual level, especially around my head that evoked a sense of claustrophobia, as if my spirit was enclosed in a small box or force field. Both nights my soul felt warmed with intense heat. I prayed until I fell asleep. The next morning I read a section from one of Michael Yoseph's pamphlets, which describes how the Lord will subject a soul to intense pressure to transform it into a diamond. How extremely appropriate reading, I thought. Intense pressure had been just what I had felt. I remembered that God had also mentioned that I would be transformed into a diamond in *Pandora's Story*.

"The spirit has been greatly refined by the preceding horror of the evil spirit, in order that it may be able to receive this blessing; for these spiritual visions belong to the next life rather than to this, and when one of them is seen this is a preparation for the next." – St. John of the Cross

A week later, I felt an intense spiritual heat starting at my feet, working its way up my body ending at my breastbone. It felt as if another spirit had moved into my soul and was fitting himself into my spirit. There was a stretching and tugging and shaping of my spirit to the exact formation of this other spirit, like my soul had become a flat leather glove, and now the hand that had always been meant to fit inside was now putting me on. I fought the feeling for a while, but then my head started to swim. I prayed, but the feeling of pressure caused me to panic. The spiritual power of the feeling was so strong that

I feared that I would be totally overcome. Even though the feeling felt utterly spiritual, I wondered, even though I had no risk factors, if I was having a heart attack. There was an overpowering feeling of losing consciousness, heating, and pressure; it was so overwhelming that I didn't think I could possibility last even five minutes.

> "*The soul remains in this state only for a short time (three or four hours at most, I should say); for if the pain lasted long, it would be impossible, save by a miracle, for natural weakness to suffer it. On one occasion it lasted only for a quarter of an hour and yet produced complete prostration. She cannot hide her anguish so all who are present realize the great peril in which she lies, even though they cannot witness what is going on within her. This is a distressing thing, but it produces the most wonderful effects and the soul at once loses its fear of any trials, which may befall it; for by comparison with the feelings of deep anguish which its spirit has experienced these seem nothing.*"
>
> – ST. TERESA OF AVILA

After debating with myself for a few more minutes, I leaned over and woke up Sam. I stood up and waves of dizziness broke; I felt close to collapsing as I stumbled forward. Not really knowing what to do, but wondering if somehow the feeling was physical, and if I shouldn't try and get some help, I talked Sam into driving me to the South Shore Hospital. All the while I felt very foolish. What could the doctors possibly do? Of course, when we got there they ran a battery of tests and found nothing, but by then in the bright, white hospital setting, the final stages of my spiritual journey were completed. Amidst blinding overhead lights, in the tiny emergency room cubicle, under a thin blanket and hooked up to the EKG machine, the Holy Spirit completed His task, and my head cleared and I came back to myself. The Lord of all the heavens had moved into my soul to stay, never to leave again.

St. John of the Cross explains this nightmarish part of the spiritual journey best. It is like death. Keep in mind, though, that there always is a beautiful resurrection.

"When this Divine contemplation assails the soul with a certain force, in order to strengthen it and subdue it, it suffers such pain in its weakness that it nearly swoons away."

"Because the soul is purified in this furnace like gold in a crucible, as says the Wise Man, it is conscious of this complete undoing of itself in its very substance."

"God being in himself pure good can dwell nowhere except in the pure soul. He overflows into her."

— MEISTER ECKHART

As I wrote this passage, I was suddenly struck with the memory of a hospital scene from *Pandora's Story*. In fact, it was after I was taken from the grave, after the transformation process. How very odd given the fact that I had gone to the hospital the very night the Lord moved into my soul. Another prophesy from that book come true ...

Total awareness comes slowly. I hear the sound of people talking, and become aware that I am lying down on something soft. Dull pain radiates from my lower left abdomen. Slowly, I open my eyes. They take a moment to adjust to the bright lights. I turn my head, and try and make sense of my surroundings. I am in a bed in a beige hospital room. There is an IV line attached at my right hand, and I have a hospital johnny on. When I feel my stomach, there is tightness there. Reaching under the thin cotton fabric, I feel the stiff surgical tape and gauze of a large dressing. Out of the corner of my eye, I can see hurrying shadows as they rush past my door. I look around for a button to call a nurse, find one, and press it.

Almost immediately a nurse comes in. A large smile has lit up her plain face. Dressed in a light blue top with matching pants, her badge, pinned to her top, reads: Janet Topen.

"So you're awake. How are you feeling?" she asks.

"I'm in some pain, right here." I place my hand on top of my stomach.

"Yes, I imagine you are. We will get you something for that in just a minute. First, let's take your temperature and blood pressure." She inserts a thermometer into my mouth, and wraps a blood pressure cuff around my arm then listens to my heartbeat. "Temp is 98, blood pressure is 100 over 65. Normal. Unbelievable, but normal. You are just amazing. Do you know that? God was really watching over you. You are the talk of the hospital, and you have only been here about an hour." She leaves the room and returns in a minute with a syringe. "The doctor prescribed this for the pain. Turn on your side, you will feel a pinch, try to relax." She injects it into my buttocks. Ouch, but who is complaining?

"Where am I?" I ask her.

"You are at the South Shore Hospital in Weymouth. Do you remember what happened to you?"

"Yes, I remember. What day is it?" Of course, I remember vividly every minute detail.

"It is Wednesday, November 1st—3:00 p.m.," Janet responds.

I realize that I have been dead, gone, out-of-it since three days ago. The memory of the man chasing me in the woods returns in vivid detail. God said his name was Jacques Fournier, and he said that he was salvageable. I remember that I left Christina at her stable over 3 days ago. Sam must have been called to come get her when I didn't return. I began to worry about my kids. Are they all right? Has the hospital called Sam? I would have thought that he would be here.

"That's good, because there are police detectives who have been waiting to talk to you. I have orders to inform them immediately as soon as you wake up. And I must tell you that the press is also here. They want your story."

"Are my kids and husband here?"

"They were notified when you were brought in an hour ago. They should be coming in shortly. You will probably see them soon," Janet assured me. I reach up to scratch my head and find encrusted dirt on my scalp, and realize that I am filthy. I don't want to meet the police and possibly the press like this. "The children will be shocked when they see their mother like this," I think. "Vain, I know. I ought to be thinking on a higher plain, but I am back in mortal form, and I can't stand the thought of looking filthy." But just as I think this thought, music begins to play in my head. It is a song our group has sung during lent. The song is entitled Come to the Water *by John Foley. God is sending me a message that it is OK to go to the water. It is good to want to be clean.*

Come To The Water
By John B. Foley, New Dawn Music

O let all who thirst, let them come to the water
And let all who have nothing, let them come to the Lord.
Without money, without price.
Why should you pay price, except for the Lord?

And let all who seek, let them come to the water.
And let all who have nothing, let them come to the Lord.
Without money, without strife.
Why should you spend your life, except for the Lord?

And let all who toil, let them come to the water.
And let all who have nothing, let them come to the Lord.

Without labor, without rest.
How can your soul find rest, except for the lord?

And let all the poor, let them come to the water.
Bring the ones who are laden, bring them all to the Lord.
Bring the children without might.
Easy the load and light. Come to the Lord.

"Look before you tell the officers I'm awake, could you help me to get to a shower?" I ask her—my voice pleading. I feel almost normal—much better than I should, the pain killer is working. Swinging my legs over the side of the bed, I lower them to the beige ceramic tiles. The tiles are freezing cold below my feet. I stand up effortlessly. "Look, I can stand. Now will you take me?"

"Well, I guess we could try to wrap your dressings. Let me see what I can find. I will be right back." Janet leaves the room, looking for a plastic wrap to cover my stomach with. She returns with a plastic bag and a fresh johnny, and I lean heavily on her to get out of bed. I try and put on a good show. Although except for a little pain, I feel all right. God must have given me a healing to speed the process.

We walk to the shower room. Janet turns the shower knob, adjusts the temperature, and places a chair under the stream of water so that I can sit down. I drop the johnny to the floor, and both of us work on placing the plastic bag around the dressing. I sit down. The water pouring over my eyes and through my hair feels wonderful, so good. Janet pours shampoo on my head, and I work my nails in my hair to remove as much dirt as possible. Yuck. The rest is easy compared to that. Finally, I am satisfied. Janet and I towel me off, take the plastic bag off, and I slip a fresh johnny on. I feel I can now face the rest—the police and the news reporters. Worrying about my children, I vow to call home as soon as I get back to the room.

> "Create in me a clean heart, O God, and put a new and right spirit within me. Cast me not away from your presence, and take not your Holy Spirit from me. Restore to me the joy of your salvation, and uphold me with a willing spirit."
>
> — PSALM 51

⚜

The next day, a Sunday, I felt weak and fragile. All the work of the Spirit had been completed, but I still needed to regain my physical strength. Knowing that Mass would really help, I dragged myself out of bed, dressed, and headed to St. Paul's. Christina, Pat, and I sat in the middle of the church. Soaking up all the congregations' prayers and songs, my soul began to solidify again. I had no strength to sing, so for once I sat back and listened to their voices as they washed over me like a soothing balm. By the time I received Holy Communion, I was feeling much better, and my spirit returned to elation.

Several weeks earlier I had frequented a coffee shop in North Quincy. And as I often do while I wait for my coffee to be fixed, I read the horoscopes that are taped onto the countertop. Mine read: "Love has been the source of growth in your soul and now you are ready to welcome in a new intimate relationship." I wrote it down because it had been so beautiful. I was hoping that it would soon be true, not with a physical man, but with the Lord Himself.

On the early morning hours on July 26, 2003, in an intellectual vision, which flowed out of a dream, God gave me the crown of all my spiritual journeying, delight of my heart and its greatest desire. From the deep recesses of my mind after the nights of struggle toward dawn's first shimmering rays, I was given a sight I shall never forget—an intellectual vision most holy and profound.

The vision began with me suspended in midair. I looked all around, but the only sight was a cloud above me. That is, until I looked below. With crystal clear perfect vision I beheld an immense, terrifying, threatening monster of a tornado. Flames of orange-red flickered and jumped from its wide-open mouth, like they were being squeezed by the swirling action of the tornado. I thanked my lucky stars that I hovered high above it and its aftermath. Instead I was able to look upon it with no fear, because I realized with dawning realization that I had just passed through that frightening, black, fire-filled twister. It was symbolic of my past spiritual journey, and it had removed all the impurity, ugliness, and darkness in my soul.

From high above the ground I could see a desolate spiritual landscape. The baked dirt, boulders, and a black tar-like substance covered most of the sand-like terrain, where the sins and imperfections of my soul were clearly visible. The tornado must have ripped up everything that was wrong with my soul and left only this tar-like substance as a reminder of the massive amount of filth that had been hidden there. The tornado had been for me the cleansing fire of purgatory. It had scooped me into its turbulent, violent, swirling embrace and burned off all my sin. The sinful ashes that remained represented the heaviness that had so weighed down my soul, its chains melted and scarred beyond recognition. Now I was above it, lighter than air, rising still.

"The internal experience for the dying person is of a great wind sweeping away the whole world ... an incredible maelstrom of wind, consuming the entire universe." Joel, Through Death's Gate: A Guide to Selfless Dying

> *"This is not an intellectual, but an imaginary vision, which is seen with the eyes of the soul very much more clearly than we can ordinarily see things with the eyes of the body."*
>
> — ST. TERESA OF AVILA

> *"The word Spirit comes from the Hebrew ruah, which means breath, air, wind. The Spirit is God's breath, filling us with divine life, purifying our souls, sustaining our immortality until we love what God loves, do what God wants of us until this earthly part of us glows with divine fire."*
>
> — ALFRED MCBRIDIE

From the Web site near-death.com/experiences - Dr. Rene Turner's Near Death Experience: "I was moving head first through a dark maelstrom of what looked like black boiling clouds, feeling that I was being beckoned to the sides, which frightened me."

Continually rising, I found myself miles above the tornado and so high above the earth that I could no longer make out any features. I entered a fluffy white cloudbank and lifted my arms up to part the clouds with a swimming motion. The motion seemed to help, and like curtains opening on the final act of a play, the clouds parted, and I was bathed in brilliant white light. After my eyes adjusted, I noticed through the light the silhouetted top of a massive white stone building and just at that moment, my feet touched down on the top of one of the torrents of solid marble. My soul had always known the way home and now I was back—in the City of Peace—the Heavenly Jerusalem. My only problem now was that I was poised on the edge and needed to fly down to the street far below. Never having liked heights, I hesitated because the building was several stories high.

> *"Longing for the Lord and his temple – Like a deer that longs for springs of water, so my soul longs for you, O God. My soul thirsts for God, the living God: when shall I come and stand before the face of God?"*
>
> — PSALM 42

Then a reassuring voice spoke after reading my thoughts. "You have received wings and are now able to fly." Oddly, enough, I did not look back, but then I didn't have to because I knew it was the voice of my guardian angel who had never left my side. I am sorry now that I didn't turn around, since I am sure that I would have been able to see him face to face. What a magnificent sight he is, I am sure.

The angel read my thoughts and answered, "Don't worry about flying down, you will not experience a sudden belly-drop feeling." He mentioned this because this thought was running through my mind, and he was able to read it. I have always hated the feeling of flying down a roller coaster. He addressed my inquiry: "In heaven flying drops do not feel like that," he explained. So I spread my wings and with joy at the airless feather feeling, floated to the street below. In that moment I felt the air dance between a feather and the wind. Yet the feeling had significance, flying down is symbolic of penetrating down into the deepest, most inner part of my own soul.

Then I saw the vision that I had so longed to see: the Blessed Trinity. The Father, the Son, and the Holy Spirit. I called out to them. The words ripped from my soul-throat with utter joy and rightness: "Father, Jesus, Holy Spirit." How can you ever describe such a vision? It is said that to every soul, God looks different but right. The Heavenly Father gave me a vision of Himself that rather resembled an incredibly wise and handsome American Indian. His hair was salt and pepper. His eyes—deepest, heart-melting pools of chocolate brown that oozed kindness and love—met my own yearning eyes. He leaned over and gently touched my face with the back of His hand. So gently and loving was His touch that I felt as if I were a small butterfly and He was stroking my wings. I loved the Father more than words can ever express, and in my vision of Him, He returned my love. He is the epitome, the pinnacle, of a gentle, wise, all-knowing Father.

After one look at the immense smile beaming from my brother, Jesus, without any hesitation I threw myself into His loving embrace. He wrapped strong arms around me and hugged me right back. My spirit melted into His Spirit, and we were one. I felt as though I had walked a million miles for the sight of home, and in that split second I was able to return. I might have been lost before, but now I had definitely been found.

Jesus resembled a composite of all my various prayer cards. He is so beautiful. Long brown hair flowed freely over His shoulders. His eyes mimic the very same loving brown eyes as the Father. His smile was perfection; His features even, not specific to any one nationality. The feeling of being truly, wonderfully home in His arms was so strong. I burst into tears of joy, and the love in my heart was so powerful that it felt like it would explode (good thing the Holy Spirit had enlarged it). I wished I could hug Him forever, but even in the beauty of the moment, I knew that this would not be possible since I was certain I would return to regular physical existence. But forever I would be left with the absolute feeling of homecoming that I felt in His arms. I would often return to that joyful moment, which I am sure will remain with me for the rest of my earthly life.

> *"For this is the will of my Father, that everyone who sees the Son and believes in him may have eternal life, and I shall raise him (on) the last day."*
>
> — JOHN 6:40

> *"Jesus answered, 'My kingdom does not belong to this world, my attendants (would) be fighting to keep me from being handed over to the Jews. But as it is, my kingdom is not here.'"*
>
> — JOHN 18:36

"Then I saw a new heaven and a new earth. The former heaven and the former earth had passed away, and the sea was no more. I also saw the holy city, a new Jerusalem, coming down out of heaven from God, prepared as a bride adorned for her husband. I heard a loud voice from the throne saying, 'Behold, God's dwelling is with the human race. He will dwell with them and they will be his people and God himself will always be with them (as their God). He will wipe every tear from their eyes, and there shall be no more death or mourning, wailing, or pain, (for) the old order has passed away.'" – Revelations 21:1–4

> *"This instantaneous communication of God to the soul is so great a secret and so sublime a favour, and such delight is felt by the soul, that I do not know with what to compare it, beyond saying that the Lord is pleased to manifest to the soul at that moment the glory that is in Heaven, in a sublimer manner than is possible through any vision or spiritual consolation."*
>
> — ST. TERESA OF AVILA

Then I glanced over at the Holy Spirit and received my biggest surprise. He was in the form of a small boy, impish and totally adorable like an elf. He was shorter than I with light sand-brown hair and coffee-colored brown eyes—fathomless pools of wisdom that were out of character for a little boy of only about nine or ten. His eyes simply glowed with love, fun, and joy. They contained, if one could read them accurately, all the secrets of the eternal kingdom. I loved it that He would appear thus. He was so beautiful too. Then in a rush I understood, before my eyes, were all three generations of God. The Eternal Father who begot the Son and the Love that proceeds from them both—the Holy Spirit.

The vision ended abruptly at that point, sadly, instead of going on forever in an eternal present. I awoke, however, with a lovely feeling of God's special fire love—His electric blanket of warmth. Protective and loving. No words needed to be verbally spoken by God, but the understanding of being one with God was unmistakable. Each had welcomed me in a special way. Love beyond all measure had been bestowed. I was blessed beyond all my expectations. The vision would be a permanent memory, the purest of gifts, for the rest of my natural life. And it bestowed an eternal, for-all-time promise just as a lover might give a kiss to his beloved.

In the future, I was often to hear that people have their doubts about faith and don't believe in the Lord. I never fail to think when I hear their questions and doubts: "That's because they haven't been to heaven and seen His faces."

⚜

And now as confirmation for you that the gift of the sight of the Triune God is a beautiful, truly realizable part of the Christian mystic tradition, here are some references. I have also included several on Spiritual Marriage, which often accompanies this wondrous gift. Here are words from the experts:

> *"We must not think of souls like theirs as mean and insignificant; for each is an interior world, wherein are the many and beauteous Mansions that you have seen; it is reasonable that this should be so, since within each soul there is a mansion for God. Now, when His Majesty is pleased to grant the soul the aforementioned favour of this Divine Marriage, He first of all brings it into His own Mansion."*
>
> — ST. TERESA OF AVILA

"It is brought into this Mansion by means of an intellectual vision, in which, by a representation of the truth in a particular way, the Most Holy Trinity reveals itself, in all three Persons. First of all the spirit becomes enkindled and is illumined, as it were, by a cloud of greatest brightness. It sees these three Persons, individually, and yet, by a wonder kind of knowledge which is given to it, the soul realizes that most certainly and truly all these three Persons are one Substance and one Power and one Knowledge and one God alone."

— ST. TERESA OF AVILA

"Here all three Persons communicate Themselves to the soul and speak to the soul and explain to it those words which the Gospel attributes to the Lord—namely, that He and the Father and the Holy Spirit will come to dwell with the soul which loves Him and keeps His commandments."

— ST. TERESA OF AVILA

"The supernatural act of the created intellect by which the beatified angels and souls are united to God in a direct, intuitive and clear knowledge of the Triune God as He is in Himself. This direct, intuitive, intellectual vision of God with the perfection of charity necessarily accompanying it, is the consummation of the divine indwelling in the sanctified spirit or soul, for by this vision the blessed are brought to fruition in such a union with God in knowledge and love that they share forever in God's own happiness." – Pius XII in his Encyclical Letter on the Mystical Body of Christ refers to this passage from Leo XIII.

"Every man has an innate desire for perfect beatitude. Experience proves this. The sight of the imperfect goods of earth naturally leads us to form the conception of happiness so perfect as to satisfy all the desires of our heart. We cannot conceive such a state without desiring it. Therefore, we are destined for a happiness that is perfect and, for that very reason, eternal." – Catholic Online Encyclopedia, New Advent, Heaven

"In heaven the just will see God by direct intuition, clearly and distinctly. And because this vision is immediate and direct, it is also exceedingly clear and distinct. Consequently, the second and essentially higher way of seeing God by intuitive vision can but be a gratuitous gift of Divine goodness." – Catholic Online Encyclopedia, New Advent, Heaven

"To enable it to see God, the intellect of the blessed is supernaturally perfected by the lift of glory. For the beatific vision transcends the natural powers of the intellect; therefore, to see God the intellect stands in need of some supernatural strength, not merely transient, but permanent as the vision itself. This permanent invigoration is called the "light of glory." According to the view commonly and perhaps most reasonably held, the light of glory is a quality. Divinely infused into the soul and similar to sanctifying grace, the virtue of faith, and other supernatural virtues in the souls of the just." – Catholic Online Encyclopedia, New Advent, Heaven

"Beatrijs—Her vision culminates in the experience of the mystery of the Trinity as well as participation in the love and knowledge of the blessed spirits. In one vision she sees God as the source of a river from which flow different streams and rivulets. The river is for her the Son of God, the streams his stigmata, and the rivulets are the gifts of the Holy Spirit." – Ursula King

SPIRITUAL MARRIAGE

"The metaphysical mystic, for whom the Absolute is impersonal and transcendent, describes his final attainment of that Absolute as deification, or the utter transmutation of the self in God." – St. John of the Cross

"The mystic for whom intimate and personal communion has been the mode under which he best apprehended Reality, speaks of the consummation of this communion, its perfect and permanent form, as the Spiritual Marriage of his soul with God." – St. John of the Cross

"This is the end and aim of prayer, my daughters; this is the object of that spiritual marriage whose children are always good works. Works are the best proof that the favours which we receive have come from God." - St. Teresa of Avila

Perhaps when St. Paul says: "He who is joined to God becomes one spirit with Him," he is referring to this sovereign marriage. - St. Teresa of Avila

"His telling the glorious Magdalen to go in peace; for the words of the Lord are like acts wrought in us, and so they must have produced some effect in those who were already prepared to put away from them everything corporeal and to leave the soul in a state of pure spirituality, so that it might be joined with Uncreated Spirit in this celestial union." - St. Teresa of Avila

"He asked that they might become one with the Father and with Him even as Jesus Christ our Lord is in the Father and the Father is in Him. I do not know what greater love there can be than this." - St. Teresa of Avila

> "I cannot, however, promise you security from many frights, beatings, and other ill-usages and temptations of all kinds, yet if you only have courage and patience enough to suffer them without quarreling, or resisting, or troubling yourself about them, but pass on quietly, having this only in your mind, and sometimes on your tongue. 'I have naught, I am naught, I desire naught but to be in Jerusalem,' my life for yours, in due time you will get there in safety."
>
> — HENRY SUSO

Take All Of Me
Words and Music by Tom, Tyler, and Erick Coomes

Take all of me
Take all of me
In a world that's lost help me count the cost
Take all of me.
Oh my God, be my symphony,
Take all you can, take all you will, take all of me.

Let my spirit sing,

Do a brand new thing,
Take all of me.

"I am quite dazed myself when I observe that, on reaching this state, the soul has no more raptures (accompanied, that is to say, by the suspension of the senses,) save very occasionally." – St. Teresa of Avila

When you reach the pinnacle, and become a mature Christian and Jesus lives inside you, the special effects do diminish. But God sends occasional reminders of His love and special messages from heaven. And you simply never know what form they will take. But just like all the gifts, graces, and blessings, they are sure to be awe-inspiring.

The following divine experience is from my spiritual journal of September 8, 2005. There was an enormous message in this passage from God to me. To carry this huge revelation, He sent one of his finest and smallest messengers.

The messenger was lying flat, upside down, and in the middle of my office parking lot in the middle of a hot summer afternoon. In my rush out to lunch, I skittered to my car parked at the far corner of the lot, bordered by a swampy marsh-like grass as tall as a basketball player. I spied the insect against the steamy, black-tarred pavement, his yellow-green wings opened and his legs in the air. He was absolutely motionless. I stopped and leaned down over him and came to the conclusion that he must be dead. But just to confirm, I ventured to touch one of his tiny spindly stick legs. To my surprise, it moved. A smile lit my face. "So you are alive after all?" I asked him. "Maybe you were just stunned? Did you hit one of the cars in the parking lot as you came zooming in for a meal?"

As yet I had no idea that he had really been sent to teach me and to give me a message.

I talked to him a bit—soothing him, telling him that I did not want him to get crushed so I was moving him to another spot somewhere safe. "Oh you poor thing. Don't you know that parking lots are like vast deserts to you and are very hazardous to your health? Let me move you to a better spot away from any passing cars. You would do best to find a lovely, grassy meadow out in the country, you know." I took a napkin from my lunch bag and brought it down to where his legs could fasten on to it, and when I had noticed that he had a good hold, I gingerly carried him across the parking lot to the edge where there was a stand of overgrown lawn—the blades gently curved in a semi-circular arch—and laid him down gently. Then I turned him over so that he was right side up. I watched as he walked to a piece of grass and climbed up it. The grass swayed with his weight like a tiny teeter-totter that a child had just jumped off to run to another activity. Finally, as he settled himself, and kept his hold on the blade, I was satisfied that he would be okay. Then I told him: "Mr. Praying Mantis, you should stay out of parking lots. There are so many cars, and you are extremely fortunate to not be crushed. Please stay away from the cars and have a marvelous life."

I rushed back to my car and drove off to Wollaston Beach for my sandwich and daily lunchtime walk with God. My mind switched now to thoughts of peace.

The next mid-morning, as I was sitting at my desk on the eighth floor working on my computer, but still facing the windows, I saw an astonishing sight. A praying mantis landed right in the middle of the window not more than five feet in front of my desk. The mantis had flown all the way up eight stories. I walked around the walls of my beige cubicle and placed my hand over the window glass on the spot where he had landed on the outside of the window. For one split second we were one, the connection so strong that I could feel it through the glass. Certainty that this praying mantis was the very same one I had saved only yesterday flooded me. Awe arose in my heart at the beauty of the moment. The praying mantis stayed only a moment or two and then took flight again. "God must have sent him up to thank me for saving him," I said to myself. "My, my. What amazing manners he has." Then I wondered if there was a deeper message and significance to his visit.

Turning back to my computer, I looked up the words "praying mantis" on the Internet. The Insecta-Inspecta Web site popped up, and I read up a bit on my insect friend. Camouflage is very important for the praying mantis's survival. Because they have so many enemies, such as birds, they must blend in with their habitat to avoid being eaten. *What a risk he/she took to fly up to the eighth floor to find me. We have many birds flying by all the time.*

There was information on the ultrasound ears on their metathorax. Apparently, the mantis in flight will drastically change its flight pattern when the mantis hears certain frequencies of sound. This made me wonder if he could hear my voice in the office through the glass and was somehow drawn to the sound. What an incredible feat. I was filled with delight at this wonderful gift from God—whose love in connecting us all can be felt in every living creature, even the smallest ones. I could hear the whisper of the Lord's voice in my heart saying, "No kindness that you ever do will go unnoticed."

I read on to find the meaning behind his name. The word mantis means "prophet" or "soothsayer." How amazing; so his name is totally symbolic of God. He is a praying prophet. Why, how biblical. I spent the rest of the day pondering the meaning of his name. I knew that a prophet was simply God's messenger sent to the people to deliver a message. Then I knew with certainty and it all become clear that I was to be one of God's prophets and my book was my message. Only God could think of such a creative way to confirm to me my mission.

This was the third prophetic message that the Lord had sent regarding my book. First, the Father sent the giant whale cloud symbolizing the book of the prophet Jonah. Next, the Lord had whispered into my heart that I should wish to be a prophet not a priest. Now here the Father revealed yet another message of "prophet." As I reflected on my calling, I knew I had better get writing. Who knows what might happen during a future visit to the ocean.

> *"No one can come to me unless the Father who sent me draw him, and I will raise him on the last day. It is written in the prophets: 'They shall all be taught by God.'"*
>
> – JOHN 6:44–45

"It will come to pass in the last days," God says, "that I will pour out a portion of my spirit upon all flesh. Your sons and your daughters shall prophesy." – Acts 2

"One who prophesies does speak to human beings, for their building up, encouragement, and solace. Whoever prophesies builds up the church." – 1 Corinthians 13:3–4

"Prophecy is not for unbelievers but for those who believe." – 1 Corinthians 3:22

"And if I have the gift of prophecy, and comprehend all mysteries and all knowledge; if I have all faith so as to move mountains, but do not have love, I am nothing." – 1 Corinthians 13:21

Later that night:

"Dear Father, I thank You for the gift of this beautiful day. So I am to be a prophet for Your Kingdom. What joy there is in my heart of this revelation. I pray to You, dear Lord, for the words that I should use and the inspiration that will cause people to seek the wonderful spiritual gifts of Your Kingdom—to believe, and to open their hearts up to allow Your grace to work in new ways, and to allow the world to soar to new spiritual heights. May they see, feel, and hear the amazing spiritual gifts that You send all around them, which are born of faith.

"I know that my message is contained in this book and that it is to be sent to all the churches and all faiths. The message is in my name, and it is the reason You have bestowed 'Pandora' on me, which means 'all gifts.' Your calling to me is to 'open the box of my inner journey' and share all the gifts I have received with the world. I am also to remind all people of Your spiritual gifts of three types—gifts, blessings, and vocations or charismas. The spiritual gifts of faith, selfless love, charity, empathy, trust, patience, and perseverance; the blessings which are mystical experiences and are born from the original gifts; and the spiritual gifts called vocations or charismas. I pray that the seeds of these gifts, already placed in all souls, are born and sprout in all hearts that wish to receive them. May they grow into a beautiful spiritual garden that You can look upon and walk amongst with delight.

"Or if their hearts desire to give the world other gifts, such as: strength, courage, kindness, gentleness, chastity, humor, and clear-sightedness, for example. Or any seven other gifts that they may feel especially called to bring forth to the world, may they understand that they must humbly approach You, dear Father, and ask. With a heart full of sincerity, and true desire to bring about goodness in the world with these gifts, You will listen to their requests. They should listen to the words 'Be Not Afraid' because Jesus goes always before them. With trust in the Savior, they will be released from all that would hinder or interfere with receiving or giving their gifts to the world. They should knock and the door shall be opened, and seek and they shall find.

"I pray that my joy in you will be their joy, also. Dearest Lord, I will do my best to bring this message to the world, and I know that my best will be what You want. I will remember St. Theresa of Avila, St. Augustine, and St. Paul's advice as I work to bring fresh hope to the world."

> *"More courage is required of those who set out on the road to perfection than of those who suddenly become a martyr, for perfection is not attained overnight. You are traveling by the royal and safe road along which our Lord, all the elect, and the saints have passed. Put aside the misgivings that the world would impose upon you. Take no notice of public opinion. This is no time to believe everything you hear. Be guided only by those who conform their lives to the will of God."*
>
> — ST. TERESA OF AVILA

> *"Give me what you have chosen for me and bring about in me what you desire for me."*
>
> — ST. AUGUSTINE

"We cannot, in fact, earn a single hour of the satisfaction, joy, and delight which God can bring to our soul. 'All the trials of the world,' says St. Paul, 'are not worthy to be compared with the glory for which we hope.'"

"Our deepest fear is not that we are inadequate. Our deepest fear is that we are powerful beyond measure. It is our Light, not our Darkness, that most frightens us. We ask ourselves, who am I to be brilliant, gorgeous, talented, fabulous? Actually, who are you not

to be? You are a child of God. Your playing small does not serve the world." – Marianne
Williamson

Song at the Empty Tomb
Based on Mark 16:1-8,Music by Marty Haugen, based on Victimae
Arranged by Kurt Kaiser

Now you leave us trembling and weak,
No more the sureness of death,
No more the world that I knew,
Life that is new with each breath.

Where now is the body you wore?
What is this dark empty hold?
Where is the one that I loved?
Where is the fire of my soul?

You who were the truth of my life,
You, now, my fear and my hope,
Who shatters death and the grave,
Who goes before me alone.
You who shake the earth and the stars,

Who opens tombs in my soul,
Who knows my weakness and pain,
You tear and rend and make whole.
Here beyond the shadow of death,
Here where the day breaks anew,

There is no future but faith,
There is no promise but you.
Here in the midst of death,
We shall see the birth of life;

Now in the darkest hour,
We shall know the face of God.
Here in the midst of life,
Here within each fearful heart;

Now in each human form,
You shall be the risen One.
Here in the midst of death,

We shall see the birth of life;

Now in the darkest hour,
We shall know the face of God.

Here in the midst of life,
Here within each fearful heart;
Now in each human form,
You shall be the risen One.

Grant to us this day of your life when all your people shall see,
When death itself shall have died,
When we your kingdom shall be.

In closing, I would like to leave you with a beautiful dream sequence from *Pandora's Story* that was actually the epilogue to that original book. It recounts my arrival into heaven, where I take my first stroll through the rooms of my very own mansion in heaven. Put yourself in my shoes, because I believe that there is a happy ending awaiting every loving soul.

St. Michael, the Archangel, had pointed his finger to this mansion, and so I now stood in front of a brass trimmed, solid oak door with an elaborate burnished knocker in the form of an angel. My hand reached for the knob, and with a slight push I found myself inside. Emerald-pearl marble tiles sparkling brilliantly as though alive, were the first thing to catch my eye. Then as my eyes traveled up to the walls, I immediately noticed the beautiful mural scenes on all the surfaces of the entryway. Why, there are Patrick and Christina, my toddler children, sledding with me on the back of our blue saucer sleds. We are on our way down one of the hills of the South Shore Country Club in a mid-winter day in the mid-1990s. Tearing my eyes from the joyful scene, I see another one of me holding my Babson MBA diploma. Next I see myself as I was at sixty holding my first baby grandchild against my own heart. The joyful moments of my earthly life are here for me to see and cherish for an eternity. How beautiful.

With a sweeping glance all around the landing, I see three doors opening to the rooms on the first floor and three doors opening from the top of a majestic, curving oak stairway. Tucked under the stairway is a stone fireplace with brass lions—all the stones are weathered beach quartz arranged in a multi-colored rainbow pattern. The fireplace is perfectly clean. I can see that no fire has ever been lit there. As I peek into one of the doors, a number of perfectly arranged sky-blue, overstuffed chairs and a large matching sofa meet my eyes, definitely a sitting room or living room, I realize. The chairs look regal against the beige

419

striped silk wallpaper, and atop a royal blue Persian rug. As I walk across, my bare feet feel as if they are on deep moss forest floor—heaven.

Curious, I walk out and try another door. A ten-foot long mahogany table has been set for two with fine bone cream and platinum china, framed with snow white napkins, and heavy silver utensils. The crystal wine and water glasses are as sparkly as diamonds. The ruby red wine casts rainbows on the walls as the glasses catch the light. I wonder what we will be eating.

A loud, booming knock suddenly sounds at the door. Then it swings open before I can reach it. "Hello, How is everything?" Even before he enters the foyer, I recognize the voice. I run as fast as I can and throw myself into his arms.

"Do not let your hearts be troubled. You have faith in God; have faith also in me. In my Father's house there are many dwelling places. If there were not, would I have told you that I am going to prepare a place for you, I will come back again and take you to myself, so that where I am you also may be. Where I am going you know the way." – John 14:1–4

"Oh, how I have missed you. I am so happy to be home," I tell God with all my heart.

"Having fun looking through your mansion?" He inquires

"It's utter perfection, but since you know me so well, I shouldn't be surprised," I tell Him.

"Come let us take a walk through together," the Lord says and so we do. Returning to the living room, the Lord and I look out the large bay window that I hadn't noticed before. Deep blue/teal ocean surf pounds the pink sand beach only about 100 yards away. There were beautiful rock formations to be seen on the beach. "You know, Lord, those formations look just like the ones on Bermuda on the south shore beaches."

"That is because they are, my dear."

We moved into a new room and find ourselves in a library. The walls are lined with shelves upon shelves of books. Every book you could possibly think of. "Wow, I could spend my eternity reading with total pleasure and enjoyment without any interruption whenever I wished." The books held my attention for a moment, but then I walk over to the window and look out. What magnificent vista will I find here, I wondered? "Oh Lord, would You just look at this view. If I didn't know better I'd say that we are at Half-Dome in Yosemite."'

"That is because you are, my dear," said the Lord.

"Why, this place is truly amazing, not only are the rooms perfectly furnished, but we seem to be surrounded by views on all sides of my favorite places on earth." Incredible, I think.

I suddenly can't wait to see if there is a bedroom. I know I will never have to sleep again, but it would be nice to have one just because. Up the stairway we glide, our snow-white robes brushing as we walk side by side. The bedroom is a truly sumptuous display. I catch my breath in the back of my throat. Pale gold wallpaper sparkles from the walls. Incredible, inspired artwork adorns the walls. I stare hard at the artwork. Two look like David's work. Another one is a rather plump, but adorable cupid that has to be, must be, by Rueben. Two more on the opposite wall are magnificent landscapes. I walk closer to them. Yes, I am right. In the left-hand corner, Cole's signature is unmistakable.

The room, filled with beautiful polished wood furniture, has a patina so strong every item looks as if an army of maids waxes them every day. Stately, and enormous, the bed dominates the room even though there are many other objects to catch the eye. "Look at this canopy; if I didn't know any better I'd say this material was made of clouds sewn together with silk thread. It's so finely made. Wow, I'll make sure that You always supervise the redecorating. Oh Lord, this is so beautiful. No place could ever be so wonderful. Do you think the children will come to visit?" I ask Him.

"I know they will when they are ready." He smiles his assurance.

So I stroll over to the bedroom window and pull the heavy silver silk draperies to the left, a wonderful view of rolling green mountains meets my eyes. "Those mountains are so gorgeous, but You know they somehow look familiar," I say to the Lord. As I stared harder, I recognize them. These are the very same mountains that you see when you are on the top of Mt. Washington in New Hampshire and look east.

"By the way, Pandora, there is a spot for you in the choir. I know that you will make a wonderful addition. All your parents and relatives have been looking forward to seeing you, whenever you are ready, just say the word and you will be there," the Lord says.

Theme Song
Dr. Zhivago

Somewhere, my love,
There will be songs to sing.
Although the snow covers the hope of spring.
Somewhere a hill blossoms in green and gold,
And there are dreams
All that your heart can hold.
Someday we'll meet again,
My love.
Someday whenever the spring breaks through.
You'll come to me out of the long ago,
Warm as the wind,
Soft as the kiss of snow.
Till then my sweet,

Think of me now and then.
God speed, my love,
'til you are mine again.

Do not say it is impossible to receive the divine Spirit.
Do not say that without him it is possible to be saved.
Do not say that one can possess the Spirit though unaware of it.
Do not say that God cannot be seen by human beings.
Do not say that it is not possible for humans to see the light of God.
My friends, it is never impossible.
It is more than possible for those who desire it.

Symeon the New Theologian

"Hence comes foreknowledge of the future, understanding of mysteries, apprehension of what is hidden, distribution of good gifts, the heavenly citizenship, a place in the chorus of angels, joy without end, abiding in God, the being made like to God, and highest of all, the being made God (this is, sharers in the divine nature)." – Novena to the Holy Spirit

Better is one day in your house
Sung by the Daughters of St. Paul

How lovely is your dwelling place, oh Lord Almighty
For my soul waits for you.
For hear my heart is satisfied within your presence.
I sink beneath the shadow of your wings.

Better is one day in your court.
Better is one day in your house
Better is one day in your court than thousands elsewhere.

One thing I ask, and I would see your beauty
To find you in the place your glory dwells.
Better is one day in your court. Better is one day in your house
Better is one day in your court than thousands elsewhere.

When I walked up to the altar to sing for the Lord that Palm Sunday in 2001, although I didn't know it then, I was destined to live out an amazing spiritual adventure. My entire journey began with a simple "Yes" to the Lord's request. So when you hear his voice, don't forget to listen and follow his directions. Trust him. You will be in for the greatest journey of your life—one that will lead to the eternal side of tomorrow and onward to forever.

APPENDIX

THE TRIAL OF ST. IRENE, ST. AGAPE, AND ST. CHIONIA

From the Web site of Saint Patrick's Church, here is the transcript that I mentioned from the Pre-awakening chapter—the recorded words from the trial of St. Irene and her sister saints. Every time I read her words, I am struck again at how brave and loyal she was. Though centuries have expired since her time on the earth, she feels as close as my own guardian angel.

In 303, Emperor Diocletian issued a decree making it an offense punishable by death to possess any portion of sacred Christian writings. Irene and her sisters, Agape and Chionia, daughters of pagan parents living in Salonika, owned several volumes of Holy Scriptures, which they hid. This made the girls very unhappy because they could not read them at all hours as was their wont.

The sisters were arrested on another charge—that of refusing to eat food that had been offered to the gods—and taken before the governor, Dulcetius (Dulcitius). He asked each in turn why they had refused and if they would still refuse. Agape answered: "I believe in the living God, and will not by an evil action lose all the merit of my past life." Some of the transcript follows:

Dulcetius: "Why didn't you obey the most pious command of our emperors and Caesars?"

Irene: "For fear of offending God."

Dulcetius: "Agape, what is your resolution? Will you do as we do, who are obedient and dutiful to the emperors?"

Agape: "It is not proper to obey Satan; my soul is not to be overcome by these discourses."

Dulcetius: "And you, Chionia, what is your final answer?"

Chionia: "Nothing can change me."

Dulcetius: "Have you not some books, papers, or other writings, relating to the religion of the impious Christians?"

Chionia: "We have none: the emperors now reigning have taken them all from us."

Dulcetius: "Who drew you into this persuasion?"

Chionia: "Almighty God."

Dulcetius: "Who induced you to embrace this folly?"

Chionia: "Almighty God, and his only son our Lord Jesus Christ."

Dulcetius: "You are all bound to obey our most puissant emperors and Caesars. But because you have so long obstinately despised their just commands, and so many edicts, admonitions, and threats, and have had the boldness and rashness to despise our orders, retaining the impious name of Christians; and since to this very time you have not obeyed the stationers and officers who solicited you to renounce Jesus Christ in writing, you shall receive the punishment you deserve.

"I condemn Agape and Chionia to be burnt alive, for having out of malice and obstinacy acted in contradiction to the divine edicts of our lords the emperors and Caesars, and who at present profess the rash and false religion of Christians, which all pious person abhor. As for the other four, let them be confined in close prison during my pleasure."

Thus, Chionia and Agape were condemned to be burned alive, but, because of her youth, Irene was to be imprisoned. After the execution of her old sisters, their house had been searched and the forbidden volumes discovered. Irene was examined again.

Dulcetius: "Your madness is plain, since you have kept to this day so many books, parchments, codicils, and papers of the scriptures of the impious Christians. You were forced to acknowledge them when they were produced before you, though you had before denied you had any. You will not take warning from the punishment of your sisters, neither have you the fear of death before your eyes. Your punishment, therefore, is unavoidable. In the mean time I do not refuse even now to make some condescension in your behalf. Notwithstanding your crime, you may find pardon and be freed from punishment, if you will yet worship the gods. What say you then? Will you obey the orders of the emperors? Are you ready to sacrifice to the gods, and eat of the victims?"

Irene: "By no means: for those that renounce Jesus Christ, the Son of God, are threatened with eternal fire."

Dulcetius: "Who persuaded you to conceal those books and papers so long?"

Irene: "Almighty God, who has commanded us to love Him even unto death; on which account we dare not betray Him, but rather choose to be burnt alive, or suffer anything whatsoever than disclose such writings."

Dulcetius: "Who knew that those writings were in the house?"

Irene: "Nobody but the Almighty, from Whom nothing is hid: for we concealed them even from our own domestics, lest they should accuse us."

During the questioning Irene told him that when the emperor's decree against Christians was published, she and others fled to the mountains without her father's knowledge. She avoided implicating those who had helped them, and declared that nobody but themselves knew they had the books.

Dulcetius: "Where did you hide yourselves last year, when the pious edict of our emperors was first published?"

Irene: "Where it pleased God, in the mountains."

Dulcetius: "With whom did you live?"

Irene: "We were in the open air, sometimes on one mountain, sometimes on another."

Dulcetius: "Who supplied you with bread?"

Irene: "God, Who gives food to all flesh."

Dulcetius: "Was you father privy to it?"

Irene: "No; he had not the least knowledge of it"

Dulcetius: "Which of your neighbors knew it?"

Irene: "Inquire in the neighborhood, and make your search."

Dulcetius: "After you returned from the mountains, as you say, did you read those books to anybody?"

Irene: "They were hid at our own house, and we dared not produce them; and we were in great trouble, because we could not read them night and day, as we had been accustomed to do."

Dulcetius: "Your sisters have already suffered the punishments to which they were condemned. As for you, Irene, though you were condemned to death before your flight for having hid these writings, I will not have you die so suddenly, but I order that you be exposed naked in a brothel, and be allowed one loaf a day, to be sent you from the palace; and the guards do not suffer you to stir out of it one moment, under pain of death to them."

Irene was sent to the soldiers' brothel, where she was stripped and chained. There she was miraculously protected from molestation. So, after again refusing a last chance to conform, she was sentenced to death. She died either by being forced to throw herself into flames or, more likely, by being shot in the throat with an arrow. The books, including the Sacred Scripture, were publicly burned.

The one expanded version of the story relates that Irene was taken to a rising ground, where she mounted a large, lighted pile. While singing psalms and celebrating the glory of the Lord, she threw herself on the pile and was consumed.

Agape and Chionia died on April 3: Irene on April 5, which is her actual feast day.

In art, this trio is represented generally as three maidens carrying pitchers, though they may be shown being burned at the stake. They are venerated in Salonika.

BIBLIOGRAPHY

The New American Bible, World Bible Publishers, Inc. 1987,

Old Testament: Nihil Obstat: Stephen J. Hardegen, O.F.M. S.S.L., Christian P. Ceroke, O Carm..., S.T.D. Imprimatur: Patrick Cardinal O'Boyle, D.D. Archbishop of Washington,Revised New Testament: Nihil Obstat: Stephen J. Hardegen, O.F.M. S.S.L., Censor Deputatus, Imprimatur: James A. Hickey, S.T.D., J.C.D. Archbishop of Washington, Revised Psalms: Imprimatur: Most Reverend Daniel E. Pilarczyk, President, National Conference of Catholic Bishops

I Delight In Your Will, Mary's Journey of Faith, The Word Among Us Press, 1999

a Kempis, Thomas, The imitation of Christ

Bauerschmidt, Frederick, Why Mystics Matter Now, Sorin Books, 2003

Bourne, Edmund J. Ph.D., The Anxiety and Phobia Workbook, New Harbinger Publications, Inc., Third Edition, 2000

Brother Lawrence, "The Practice of the Presence of God: The Best Rule of Holy Life

Chilson, Richard, 30 Days with a Great Spiritual Teacher – Julian of Norwich, All Will Be Well, July 1995

Connell, Janice T., The Visions of the Children–The Apparitions of the Blessed Mother at Medjugorje, St. Martin's Press, 1992

Cunneen , Sally, In Search of Mary – The Woman and the Symbol, Ballantine Books, 1996

Destefano, Anthony, A Travel Guide to Heaven, Doubleday, 2003

Dionysius the Areopagite, The Cloud of the Unknowing

Dubruiel, Michael, The Power of the Cross

Eckhart, Meister, From Whom God Hid Nothing, Sermons, Writings, and Sayings, Shambhala Publications, Inc., 1996

Enoch, Book of, Wesley Center for Applied Theology

Fanstone, Michael, Raising Kids Christian When Your Husband Doesn't Believe, Servant Publications, 1999

Ferguson, John, An Illustrated Encyclopeadia on Mysticism and the Mystery Religions

Hanh, Thich Nhat, Living Buddha, Living Christ, Riverhead Books, 1995

ICWA, Outreach Department,The Interpretation of the Glorious Quran

Keating, Thomas, Fruits and Gifts of the Spirit, Lantern Books, 2000

King, Ursula, Christian Mystics–Their Lives and Legacies Throughout the Ages, Hidden Spring, 2001

Kirvan, John, 30 days with a Great Spiritual Teacher Series – Let Nothing Disturb You – St. Teresa of Avila, Ave Maria Press, Notre Dame, Indiana 46556, 1996

Kirvan, John , Living in the Presence of God, The Everyday Spirituality of Brother Lawrence, 1997, Quest Associates

Kirvan, John, Simply Surrender– Sayings of St. Therese of Lisieux, Ave Maria Press, Notre Dame, Ind., 1996

Kirvan, John, Set Your Heart Free, The Practical Spirituality of Francis de Sales, Ave Maria Press, Notre Dame, Indiana, 1997

Landaw, Jonathan and Bodian, Stephan, Buddhism For Dummies, Wiley Publishing Co.. 2003

Lewis, C.S., Letters to Malcolm: Chiefly on Prayer, Estate of C.S. Lewis, First American Edition, 1963

Lewis, C.S., Miracles

Lewis, C.S., Surprised by Joy, an Autobiography, The Shape of My Early Life, Harvest/HBJ Book, 1956

Merton, Thomas, From Mornings with Thomas Merton, 1998 Servant Publications

Merton, Thomas, Mystics and Zen Masters, Farrar, Straus, and Giroux, Latest reprint, 1967

Merton, Thomas, New Seeds of Contemplation, New Directions Publisher, 1961

Merton, Thomas, The Seven Storey Mountian,, An Autobiography of Faith, Harcourt Brace & Company, 1948

Merton, Thomas, The Way of Chuang Tzu Penguin Books, Canada, Ltd., 1965

Mother Teresa, A Guide to Daily Livng, The Joy in Loving-Mother Teresa, compiled by Jaya Chalika and Edward Le Joly, Penguin Group, 1996

Mother Teresa, Blessings of Love, Servant Publications, 1996

Mother Teresa, No Greater Love, foreword by Thomas Moore, New World Library, 2001

Moynahan, Brian The Faith: A History of Christianity, Random House/Doubleday, 1941

Muller, Wayne, Sabbath, Finding Rest, Renewal, and Delight in our Busy Lives, Bantam Publishers, 1999

Nicholi, Armand M. Jr , Dr., The Question of God, Free Press, Simon & Schuster, Inc., 2002

O'Donohue, John, Anam Cara, A Book of Celtic Wisdom, 1997

Reilly, Patricia Lynn, A God Who Looks Like Me, Ballantine Books (a division of Random House), 1995

Schaef, Anne Wilson , Meditations for Women who Do Too Much, Revised and Updated by Harper Collins Publishers, 2004

Schafer, Professor, In Search of Divine Reality

Sister Miriam of Little St. Theresa , Three Addresses for the First Profession of Sister Miriam of Little St. Theresa, July 16, 1940

St. Augustine, The City of God

St. Bernard, The Mystical Doctrines

St. Ignatius of Loyola, The Spiritual Exercises of St. Ignatius of Loyola,Translated from the autograph by Father Elder Mullan, S.J.

St. John of the Cross, The Dark Night of the Soul, Translated and edited by (introduction by E. Allison Peers), and from the critical edition of P. Silverio De Santa Teresa, C.D.

St. John Paul II, Quotable John Paul II, Words of Wisdom, Faith, Solidarity, and Salvation by and about John Paul II, Mike Towle, TowleHouse, distributed by National Book Network, 2003

St. Teresa of Avila, The Interior Castle

St. Teresa of Avila, The Way of Perfection, translated and edited by E. Allison Peers – www.cheraglibrary.org/christian/teresa/way.html

St. Theresa of Lisieux, Little Book of Therese of Lisieux, Pauline Books and Media, 2002

Stein, Edith, The Hidden Life, III The Marriage of the Lamb, September 14, 1940

Stokes, Penelope L. Ph.D., The Complete Guide to Writing and Selling the Christian Novel

Suso, Henry, The Parable of the Pilgrim

Thomas, The Gospel of, The Gnostic Society Library – The Nag Hammadi Library, translated by Thomas O. Lambdin

Weible, Wayne, Medjugorje, The Message, Paraclete Press, 1989

Underhill, Evelyn, Mysticism – A Study in the Nature and Development of Spiritual Consciousness, Dover Publications, 1911 Young, Katherine, Her Voice, Her Faith, Westview Press, 2003

ARTICLES and PAMPHLETS

"Awakening the Mystic Within", Frank X. Tuoti, Impact Series, Renew International

"The Call to Contemplation", M. Basil Pennington, O.C.S.O

"The Catholic Answer Bible" , Our Sunday Visitor, Wed, Oct 2, 2002.

"Christian Faith and Demonology", Pauline Books and Media

"Collegeville Bible Commentary, The Book of Revelations" Pheme Perkins, 1983, 1991 by the Order of St. Benedict, Inc., Collegeville, Minnesota

"Coming Home: The Journey Within", Janet Malone

"Devotions to the Holy Spirit", Brian Moore, SJ, St. Paul Publication, 1976

"The Eucharist as a Presence", Pope Paul VI, Credo of the People of God, 26), (cf. Paul VI, Mysterium Fidei, 39)

"The Father Speaks to his Children", Pater Publications. The revelation given to Sister Eugenia Elisabetta Ravasio, recognized as valid by the Church.

"Feeling and Pain and Prayer", Margaret Bullitt-Jonas

"From Shame to Joy: Julian of Norwich, Companion on the Journey to Spiritual Wellness, Helen H. McConnell

"The Human Character of Conversion, Joanmarie Smith

"Holy Face Association", The Devotion as revealed to Sister Maria Pierina

"The Meaning of the Contemplative Life According to Thomas Merton", Fr. James Connor, OCSO, Abbey of Gethsemani

"Mystical Moments in Daily Life", Matthias Neuman, Father Harvey Egan, SJ

"Novena to the Sacred Heart of Jesus", St. Alphonsus Liguori, edited by Thomas M. Santa, C.SS. R., Liguori Publications, 1997

"The Number Seven" , H. P. Blavatsky

Our Daily Bread, 2002 RBC Ministries, April 1, Tuesday, March-April-May 2003, Mart De Haan, II

Our Sunday Visitor, May 2004, On-line magazine, Excerpt from Teen Guide to the Bible by Alfred

McBridie, O.Praem

Pope Paul VI, "Our Sunday Visitor", Wednesday, May 7, 2003

"The Pain of Life", Stephen Tumilty op, Spirituality

"Perseverance: Letting the Goodness Out", Melannie Svoboda SND

"Playing Pan", Donagh O'Shea, OP

"Prayer: Participation in Communion", Michael Downey:

"Purgatory", Marianne Lorraine Trouve, FSP, Daughers of St. Paul

"The Second S. Francis – Francesco (Padre Pio)", "The Angelus", August 2002, Volume XXV, Number 8, T. Francis Ryan M. Gerhold

"Silence in the Liturgy", Joseph Dougherty

"Solutions", Ursuline Press

"A Spirituality for the Second Half of Life", Joan Chittiser, OSB

"Taking the Psalms to Heart", Francis Dorff

"That They May Be One", Ecumenism—The Journey toward Unity, Fr. Patrick Granfield, O.S.B

"Joel: Through Death's Gate: A Guide to Selfless Dying, 1996 by The Center for Sacred Sciences, 1430 Williamette Street, #164, Eugene, OR 97401-4049.

"Whatever Happened to Asceticism? Does it have a place in Christian life in postmodern Western Society?" – Joseph MacMahon, OFM

"Windows of the Soul", Walter Ciszek

"Unceasing Prayer: Romancing the Divine",Jerry D. Keeney, September-October 1998

WEB SITES

Activella Website on Menopause, Hot Flashes, and Night Sweats

Angelfire website – Animal and bird totems

Website: biblewheel.com/topics,seven.

Bulfinch Mythology, Chapter 2 – www.greekmythology.com

The Institute of Carmelite Studies, on the work of Edith Stein, Copyright 2000, Website – cin. org/archives/cinlit

Catholic Forum Website on Patron Saints. St. Francis of Assisi

Catholic Encyclopedia – Exorcism – www.newadvent.org

Catholic Encyclopedia – New Advent Website – State or Way (Purgative, Illuminative, Unitive

Catholic Church website by Prof. Michael Lapierre – The Beatific Vision – Pope Leo XIII

Catholic Church website by Prof. Michael Lapierre – Pius XII in his Encyclical Letter on the Mystical Body of Christ

Centering Prayer website – Fr. Thomas Keating, Chapter 11

Chakra and Energy website – geocities.com/goddesslit/

Chakras – From the Website of the Brofman Foundation for the Advancement of Healing

Contrary, Heavenly, and Cardinal Virtues – from the Website – deadlysins.com/virtues.html

Crystal Healing – Metaphysical Properties of Quartz Crystals, www.kacha-stones.com/quartz_crystals_properties.htm

The Eckhart Society – Eckhart von Hochheim – Meister Eckhart - Website: members.aol.com/

heraklit/eckhart.htm

Internet Encyclopedia of Philosophy – www.utm.edu/research - Meister Eckhart (1260 - 1328)

Website of the Encyclical Epistle of the Church at SMYRNAM – www.coptic.net/boston/heros/irene

EveryStudent.com (explores questions about life and God)

Gemstone Therapy: The Healing Properties of Gemstones and Crystals (www.gems4friends.com) and The Wand Workshop websites (www.raven9.freeserve.co.uk)

Glastonbury Abbey Website, Fr. Timothy J. Joyce, OSB

Website – hematite– "What is Hematite?"

The Holy Martyrs Agapia, Chionia, and Irene (April 14th (April 1st Old Calendar) from the website – www.fatheralexander.org/booklets/english/saints

Holy Protection Russian Orthodox Church's website, Fatheralexander.org on the Holy Martyrs Agapia, Chionia, and Irene – April 14th

The Holy Spirit and Spiritual Gifts – From the Website – new-life.net/sprtgift

The Internet Encyclopedia of Philosophy – Meister Eckhart – www.utm.edu/research

Website – Janes76.freeserve.co.uk/Exorcism

The Last Supper and the Passover Haggadah Website – by Richard D. Kirkham

Manual For Conducting Truth Encounters – on the Demon Possession website

Website: .messagenet.com/myths/bios/promethe

Names of God – from the MustardSeed Website

Website: near-death.com/experiences

Website: near-death.com/forum

New Life website on Baptism and filling of the Holy Spirit

Website – The Novena of the Seven Gifts - ewtn.com/devotionals/Pentecost/seven

Website: www.cw.utk.edu/mclennan - On Roman Holidays which required sacrifices: A sampling of Roman Festivals in March and April

St. Irene Catholic Community of Faith Website: www.st-irene.org/patroness.html

Saint Patrick's Church: Saints of April 3: Saints O'the Day – April 3rd. From the website: users.erols.com/saintpat/ss/0403.htm

Website of St. Thomas the Apostle Roman Catholic Church – The story of Saints Agape, Chionia, and Irene – (Martyred A.D. 304) – www.stthomasirondequoit.com

Spiritual Gifts Profile sheet (www.cforc.com/sgifts.cgi)

The theozfiles.com/history website – Australian UFO History – Tales of "Feather Foot" and Phantom Pregnancies

MUSIC

Be Not Afraid

I love You Lord

See Me, from the musical "Tommy"

Rocky Mountain High, John Denver, Music by John Denver and Mike Taylor (Slightly Altered)

City of God, by Dan Schutte, New Dawn Music, 1981

Love is Still the Lord

Never, Never Land, from the musical Peter Pan, (altered)

You are Mine, Words and Music by David Haas, Arranged by Donald Neufeld

Un Lugar Celestial, sung by the Daughters of St. Paul

Born Free, sung by Andy Williams, words by Don Black and music by John Barry

Here I am, Lord, Dan Schutte, New Dawn Music, 1981

It's Our Confession, sung by the Daughters of St. Paul

Jesus, What a Beautiful Name, words and music by Tanya Riches, 1995

I Give You My Hear, Words and Music by Reuben Morgan

By My Side (Godspell), Lyrics by Jay Humburger and Music by Peggy Gordon

The House of the Great King, Simply Worship CD

Take My Life, Scott Underwood

Sweet Mercies, David Ruis

Come to the Water, John B. Foley, New Dawn Music, 1978

Come, Holy Ghost – attributed to Rabanus Maurus, tr. by Edard Caswall, 1814-1878, and Music by Louis Lambillotte, SJ, 1796-1855

Ave Maria

Hail Mary, Gentle Woman, Carey Landry, OCP Publications

The Greatest Love of All, sung by Whitney Houston

Not Too Far From Here, sung by the Daughters of St. Paul

When the Saints Come Marching

Angels Among Us, sung by the Daughters of St. Paul

When You Walk Through a Storm, from the musical Carousel

Bridge over Troubled Waters, Simon and Garfunkel

Come to the Water, John B. Foley, New Dawn Music, 1978

Take All Of Me, Words and Music by Tom, Tyler, and Erick Coomes

Song at the Empty Tomb, Based on Mark 16:1-8, Music by Marty Haugen, based on Victimae arranged by Kurt Kaiser

Somewhere My Love, from the movie "Dr. Zhivago"

Better is One Day In Your House, sung by the Daughters of St. Paul